A History (

Twillingate, New[...],
Fogo Island and Change Islands,
Newfoundland and Labrador
Revised edition

Newfoundland and Labrador is Canada's newest Province, but was known for centuries as "Britain's Oldest Colony." Europeans established a permanent presence there following John Cabot's voyage in 1497, yet the island of Newfoundland, and the "Big Land" of Labrador, were home to Native peoples for thousands of years before this.

In this work David Clarke zeroes in on the rich history of one part of this fascinating place. The former Provincial electoral district known as "The Isles of Notre Dame," encompasses historic towns such as Twillingate, Herring Neck, Moreton's Harbour, Change Islands, Fogo and Tilting. This portion of Newfoundland's Notre Dame Bay was settled by immigrants from England's West Country, and the east of Ireland, starting in the early eighteenth century. For generations they and their descendants eked out a living from the resources of the sea. Today they continue to do so in the face of declining fish stocks and the collapse of the traditional cod fishery.

In his opening chapters Dr. Clarke presents the reader with an overview history of all the Isles' modern communities, while subsequent chapters focus on specific aspects of regional history. These include, relations between the Beothuk and European settlers, the *Twillingate Sun* newspaper, local health care, communications, early trade unionism, the World Wars, and a number of local personalities. Together, these comprise a one volume introduction to the history of this region suitable for locals and visitors alike.

DAVID CLARKE is a graduate of Memorial University of Newfoundland's Doctoral programme in history. He has taught students at Memorial, and at the University of Liverpool. Dr. Clarke has worked on a number of historical projects on Fogo Island, and in Twillingate. An officer of the local Masonic Fraternity, he currently makes his home in Twillingate.

Cover Image: "Steaming Along." Off Fairbank, NWI. Author's photograph.

Author portrait: Ms. Brenda Shand.

A HISTORY OF THE ISLES

Twillingate, New World Island, Fogo Island and Change Islands, Newfoundland and Labrador

Revised edition

DAVID J. CLARKE

DJC

2016

For my Parents, John & Margaret Clarke, my Grandmother, Barbara Burton, and in memory of my Grandparents, Stewart Burton, and Leonard & Dulcie Clarke

By the Same Author

St. Peter's Anglican Church, Twillingate. From the Nineteenth to the Twenty-First Centuries (Prepared for the St. Peter's Anglican Church Women).

Sunspots – Best of the Twillingate Sun, 1880-1953. Vol I.

Sunspots – Best of the Twillingate Sun, 1880-1953. Vol. II.

An Historical Directory of the Isles – Twillingate, New World Island, Fogo Island and Change Islands.

The Isles Historical Dictionary – Featuring, Twillingate, New World Island, Fogo Island and Change Islands, Newfoundland & Labrador.

Stories From These Shores – Newfoundland & Labrador, and the Isles of Notre Dame.

All titles available at www.amazon.ca and www.amazon.com

Contents

Preface & Acknowledgements

This book is intended as an accessible compilation of the many historical traditions and literature concerning Twillingate, New World Island, Fogo Island and Change Islands – until 2015 officially known as "The Isles of Notre Dame" District (Collectively, "The Isles"). The work represents the end product of several years worth of research conducted in a number of institutions, including Memorial University of Newfoundland (MUN), the Provincial Archives of Newfoundland and Labrador (PANL), various local libraries, and historical collections like those of the Twillingate and Moreton's Harbour Museums. I have also collected some material from the internet, an increasingly valuable resource for researchers.

Tourists and locals alike may be interested in the varied and fascinating histories of the many communities that have sprung up on the islands since the early eighteenth century. A great deal has been lost from our early history. I hope that my humble contribution will generate some discussion of that history, while informing readers about the rich heritage of these islands clinging to Newfoundland's wind-swept northeast coast.

For readers who prefer the "short story" approach, each chapter can be enjoyed as a topic unto itself. Since my work draws on various primary material, plus the labours of many other researchers, I have tried wherever possible to acknowledge authors' ideas and theories in-text, as well as providing references for archival documents. Apart from a number of quotes, I present the sum of facts and opinions in a form of my own. The bibliography gives a full listing of sources, though most articles without an author's name are represented simply by the magazines or newspapers from which they were drawn.

The sources sometimes give conflicting accounts of events. For example, there are a number of theories as to Lady Pamela Fitzgerald's parentage, and some authors even discount Fogo Island as her birthplace. By the same token, the exact numbers of early settlers in places like Moreton's Harbour, and when they first arrived, are often unclear. Things get even more complicated when we remember that many traditions surrounding Notre Dame's historic isles are just that – traditions. These have sometimes been presented as established fact. Where alternate versions of events exist, or where a source is doubtful, I have tried to be transparent. One goal of this work is to entertain, but it is also meant to inform. I apologise in advance if I have accidentally passed along any inaccurate information.

One feature of this book might strike readers as they leaf through its pages; not all communities are given equal space. This is not because I undervalue any particular locale. My hometown Twillingate takes up the lion's share of the work. I first intended to write a stand-alone history of the town, but was later advised to broaden my outlook. For this reason my early research was carried out almost entirely on material relating to Twillingate. There appears to be more written and archival material available on Twillingate than on other nearby communities, except maybe Fogo. This is understandable, as Twillingate was one of the earliest European settlements in Notre Dame Bay. For many years it was the hub of the bay, and its largest settlement, earning Twillingate the nickname "Capital of the North."

The community of Fogo, now part of the amalgamated municipality of Fogo Island, is also prominent. At least as old as Twillingate, if not older, it is certainly one of the most historic settlements in the region. It was long considered the unofficial capital of the old Fogo District. A centre of the Slade family's mercantile enterprises, in the early twentieth century it was the base for a wireless relay station operated by the Canadian Marconi Company. Having worked for the Fogo council on a project connected with this station, plus other historical research from 2008 to early 2011, I compiled a great deal of local material for my employers. The data collected forms the bedrock of my account of the town of Fogo.

In the case of some other Isles towns, I was fortunate to find a good cache of materials to draw upon. This was certainly true of Moreton's Harbour. Their museum has a small but very useful set of writings on the community, allowing me to build a nice overview of the settlement's past. The towns of Cottlesville and Change Islands both have locally produced histories that were helpful. In cases where less was found the town histories are more threadbare. Still, I hope that residents of *all* the Isles communities will find out something new about their homes through this book.

I must thank a number of people who contributed to this history, actively or otherwise. First of all are the many authors from whose works the stories were reconstructed. Of particular help was Joseph R. Smallwood's *Encyclopedia of Newfoundland and Labrador* (ENL). These volumes give a tremendous insight into the peoples and places of our Province, while providing a springboard for more in-depth research. People still debate the political legacy of our late Premier, but I think most would agree that his unique encyclopedia must stand in the plus column. Smallwood and his successors are owed a vote of thanks for their contribution to this Province's rich heritage. Though out of print, the work can still be accessed through a CD-ROM version, and on-line.

A number of good general works on Newfoundland and Labrador history were also consulted. The man who might be called the Father of Newfoundland/Labrador history, Judge D. W. Prowse, has been followed by a number of worthy successors, including Kevin Major, Sean Cadigan and

Patrick O'Flaherty. On the local scene, writers like Gary Saunders, Amy Louise Peyton, Harvey Bulgin, Patrick Pickett, Don Downer, Cyril Chaulk and Eric Witcher have all made notable contributions to preserving our past.

Of course, not all authorship takes the form of books; a number of newspapers figure as important sources. The Isles' own local paper, the *Twillingate Sun*, is the best contemporary source for local events from the 1880s through to the 1950s. In more recent years the *Lewisporte Pilot* has filled the same role, often recounting valuable historical traditions and stories. Many newspaper reporters have commented on Isles history, but in the Twillingate context few have been such a font of information as my former high school English teacher, Howard Butt. Mr. Butt's articles have appeared in both the *Pilot* and a new version of the *Twillingate Sun*, launched in the 1990s for the area's Fish, Fun and Folk Festival. Benson Hewitt's column, "The View from Fogo Island," is another historical treasure trove from the *Pilot*.

One of the nicest sources for Newfoundland and Labrador community histories is in the now defunct *Decks Awash*. During the 1970s and 1980s the magazine published a series of profiles on communities like Twillingate and Change Islands, along with the towns of Fogo and New World Islands. One can do much worse than finding old copies of *Decks Awash* to gain insight into our vibrant local heritage. The articles also remind us of a time not so long ago when our future looked much brighter *vis a vis* the fishery.

Upholding the proud tradition of publications like *Decks Awash* is *Downhome* magazine, formerly the *Downhomer*. *Downhome* is a valuable source of information, containing a wide variety of material on communities, characters, culture and history from all over Newfoundland and Labrador. The magazine's affiliate, James Lane Publishing, has produced a number of notable books, including the *Dictionary of Newfoundland and Labrador*, and a work on Twillingate's Captain Peter Troake.

Today the printed word is supplemented by numerous internet resources. While not all are equally reliable, some good websites focus on Newfoundland and Labrador history; a number of these have been consulted for this work. Two excellent sites offering on-line genealogical and historical material are the *Newfoundland's Grand Banks* and *NL Gen Web* sites. The sites are searchable by region, and contain an extensive range of material. Everything from photographs, to church records, old journal articles, military records, and newspaper transcriptions (including the *Twillingate Sun*), are found here. Well worth a person's time!

An outstanding on-line educational resource – one of the best for general Provincial history – is the *Newfoundland and Labrador Heritage* website. The Heritage site is an award winner; once you check it out you will no doubt see why. Newfoundland and Labrador Heritage has an invaluable resource in its Co-ordinator Vince Walsh, whom I'd like to thank for his help and kindness over the years.

Another important internet resource is Memorial University of Newfoundland's Digital Archive Initiative (DAI). The efforts of MUN staff and faculty have resulted in a large and ever-growing collection of on-line resources relating to the Province of Newfoundland and Labrador. History, geography, culture and folklore all have a home here. The university's Centre for Newfoundland Studies, and its Maritime History Archive, have especially useful sets of materials available, including digitized maps, images, books and periodicals (mostly rare and out-of-print).

A number of municipalities maintain their own websites, and these can be a valuable window into particular communities. The old town of Fogo's website has a nice historical overview of the town, along with some interesting photographs. The same holds true for Twillingate's recently revamped website. In some other cases the local history is less detailed, but still provides a quick introduction to the community's past. A number of tourism websites, like the Kittiwake Coast, are also worth consulting (Internet addresses can be found in the bibliography).

Books, periodicals, and websites are only as good as the people behind them, and many persons have been helpful in preparing this work. As valuable as his magazine was, I owe *Downhome* founder Ron Young an even bigger thank-you. Ron evaluated an early version of this work. It was he who suggested that I expand it to include not only Twillingate, but also the surrounding area. Ron also shared advice on getting my manuscript published, or going the self-publishing route.

I am grateful to Mrs. Irene Pardy for sharing items from her informative collection of historical material, and for our discussions of Twillingate history. I must also thank Irene for her diligence in spotting an error in my first edition, which I have now been able to correct. Irene was also able to provide me with some extra tid bits of info in time for the second edition.

Like Irene, Jim Troke and Milt Anstey put their historical expertise to good use, enabling me to revise other minor errors in the first edition. Milt was kind enough to share some of his extensive genealogical research with me, while Jim did likewise with his material on Twillingate's Sons of Temperance branch. Many thanks to you both.

Mr. Harry White was good enough to provide me with some background on his relatives and their maritime connections, the Whites being one of Twillingate's most prominent seafaring families.

I would like to thank Twillingate Town Manager David Burton and the council office staff for allowing me to access some of the materials they have on local history, including a good run of *Decks Awash* and back issues of the new *Twillingate Sun*.

Kudos go to Twillingate's public librarian, Barbara Hamlyn, who introduced me to the many useful items in the library's Twillingate history collection, including its photographs. Librarian Deborah (Hayward) Chaulk, who filled in for Mrs. Hamlyn in 2008-9, was also very helpful.

Linda Blondin and her staff at the Twillingate Museum and Craft Shop were just as accommodating during my research, as were employees of the Summerford Public Library, the Moreton's Harbour Museum and the Fogo Island Public Library.

Most of my primary source material, apart from copies available on-line, was gathered in St. John's. I am grateful for the dedication and thoughtfulness of staff at PANL, based in the Rooms, who helped me locate many useful documents. Likewise, Head Archivist Heather Wareham and her colleagues at the Maritime History Archives, Memorial University of Newfoundland, have been very friendly and accommodating over the years. The same goes for all staff at MUN's Centre for Newfoundland Studies.

Heartfelt thanks go out to those individuals who gave of their time as readers and reviewers, including Ron Young, mentioned above. I appreciate their insights into my manuscript. In some cases errors had crept in, and were found through their diligence. Any that remain are entirely my responsibility! In other cases readers provided valuable new information.

Those sections relating to the town of Fogo, and Fogo Island generally, were ably evaluated by Andrew Shea. A long-time teacher, businessman, town councillor and, most recently, Mayor of Fogo Island, Andrew's love of local history is apparent to all who have had the pleasure of working with him. He is likewise noted for his dedication and thoroughness, traits he put to good use in giving my manuscript the once-over! Andrew has conducted extensive primary research on aspects of Fogo history, particularly its merchant houses; my interpretation of the town's past is much better for his contribution.

My material on the other communities of Fogo Island was reviewed by Benson Hewitt whose column, noted above, provided an informative source for the history of these towns. Many thanks for your suggestions Benson, and for your vote of confidence in the quality of my work! I am also grateful to Keith Ludlow, a direct descendant of Fogo's first policeman, for providing *his* evaluation of this material, particularly that on Joe Batt's Arm.

During my time at Fogo in 2006 Ms. Elaine Anton, Collections

Manager, Archaeology & Ethnology at The Rooms Provincial Museum was quite helpful in providing images and information. She was equally accommodating in reviewing my material on Native cultures, especially the Palaeo-Eskimos. Like Elaine, Ken Reynolds of the Provincial Archaeology Office provided me with some very useful suggestions, and an early nineteenth century newspaper reference to the Beothuk. Many thanks to you both.

I am indebted to Twillingate expatriate Donald Loveridge, who is greatly interested in the history of his hometown. Apart from evaluating my Twillingate material, and providing me with additional information, Don went beyond the call of duty in making available electronic copies of his Grandfather Stephen Loveridge's diaries for the years 1926-45, which he has transcribed. The journals contain many insights into life on the Isles a few generations ago. Don has my thanks for granting permission to use short quotes from the diaries in this book.

The history of outport Newfoundland cannot be fully understood without a knowledge of the merchant houses, and their role in the economy and society of pre Confederation Newfoundland. I am therefore indebted to Ms. Audrey Ashbourne for valuable insights into her family history, and for helping to correct some of my material on the Ashbourne business. Likewise, she provided me with information on her maternal ancestors, the Roberts, who tended the light at Long Point for several generations. Audrey also reviewed my material on Change Islands, a portion of the Isles with which she has ties. Thank you very much, Audrey!

Christopher Osmond, a retired educator formerly of Moreton's Harbour, examined my chapter on New World Island, and provided me with material on the shipbuilding industry in his hometown. Chris and I served together on the executive of a local heritage Committee for a number of years. He is a great colleague, and has my gratitude.

Frank Gogos, author of *The Royal Newfoundland Regiment in the Great War. A Guide to the Battlefields and Memorials of France, Belgium and Gallipoli*, has my sincere thanks for his willingness to plow through my material on the World Wars, especially that pertaining to the Great War of 1914-18. I appreciate Frank's kind assessment of these sections, and his well thought out suggestions for strengthening them. He also provided me with info on enlistment numbers, and background on a pair of schooners lost in 1917-18.

Kudos go out to my friend, Ms. Elizabeth Jenkins, a former Deputy Mayor of Twillingate. As both a registered nurse and a nurse practitioner, Elizabeth put her knowledge to good use in evaluating my chapter on local medical history. Ms. Jenkins has cared for patients at both the Change Islands' Clinic and the Notre Dame Bay Memorial Health Centre. She also serves in

Labrador, and along with her partner, Stephen Loveridge, operates a home care agency for seniors in the Isles region. Elizabeth's invaluable insights into health care, and her guidance on correct terminology, were very much appreciated. Among her many talents, Elizabeth has quite an artistic flair. For this revised edition she graciously permitted me to use her original oil painting depicting the Long Point Lighthouse.

I worked with the old Fogo Town Council on four occasions from 2006 until amalgamation in 2010. I owe them a big vote of thanks for allowing me to adapt my 2006 tour guide manual as a source for this book. I am particularly grateful that my work on this manuscript was incorporated into our 2009-10 historical project, as another means of preserving Fogo history. Former Town Manager Bruce Pomeroy, his successor Pat Donahue, Assistant Town Clerk Tracy Torraville, and Assistant Researcher Courtney Brown, were excellent colleagues. Mayor Shea and the entire Fogo Council, along with employee Norman Jones, and a number of Fogo Island residents, were very helpful and giving of their time. I particularly appreciate the continued friendship of Sidney and Bridget Leyte, with whom I stayed while at Fogo in 2006.

As you will see, this work is illustrated throughout. While most images are in the public domain, or from the author's own collections, some come from family albums or other private sources. I would like to thank all those who've granted me permission to use their photographs.

Many others have been a source of support and inspiration over the years, none more so than my Parents, Jack and Margaret Clarke. Thanks Mom and Dad! I owe you more than I can ever say.

The fond memory of my late Grandparents Leonard & Dulcie Clarke, and Stewart Burton, inspires me to be my best. I also cherish the continued love and encouragement of my Grandmother, Barbara Burton.

My girlfriend, Brenda Shand, has been a great supporter and promoter of my work practically since the day we met. She believes in me unconditionally, and is truly my Muse!

I would like to acknowledge my university graduate supervisor, Dr. Lewis R. "Skip" Fischer, for the many hours he patiently spent working with me over the years. If my output leaves anything to be desired it is my failing, not his.

My former colleagues of the Isles Wooden Boat Building Committee (On which I served from 2008-15) – Kay Boyd, Marion Chaffey, Herman Crewe, J. Sterling Elliott, Eric Facey, the late Michael Geiger, Mike Johnson, Alf Manuel, Chris Osmond, Eric Pardy, Amanda Pelley, Mark Racicot, Joan Sharpe and Jim Troke – are another source of inspiration; their dedication to preserving local history and culture is outstanding.

Likewise, my Brethren of Twillingate Masonic Lodge No. 7 (Too many to list individually, but good souls all), deserve much credit for their civic sprit and efforts to maintain the heritage building that is in our care.

A special thank you goes out to my Great Aunts, Joyce (Clarke) Skanes, with whom I stayed during a portion of my graduate studies, and Annie (Clarke) Linthhorne, who early on made a donation to help with my writing efforts.

In this revised edition I would like to thank all those who have supported my efforts by purchasing copies of the book's earlier versions. I am humbled by the many compliments and words of support I have received from my readers. I have had a long-standing passion for our history, and am glad that so many of you do as well.

I am blessed with many supportive relatives and friends. Though too many to list here, I send all of you my heartfelt thanks. You have made the journey worthwhile.[1]

1

In extending my thanks, I cannot forget the contribution of retired Senator, Hon. William Rompkey. An earlier version of this work contained an overview history of the Province. I am very grateful to Senator Rompkey for reviewing the section on Labrador. He provided many thoughtful insights on this material, which has now found a home as part of my work, *Stories from These Shores*. Senator Rompkey's long and distinguished connection to Labrador, as an educator, a politician, and a writer, made him a natural choice as a reviewer. I had the honour to work for the Senator as a researcher on a number of occasions, and found him a most kind employer.

Newfoundland, with "The Isles" (inset)

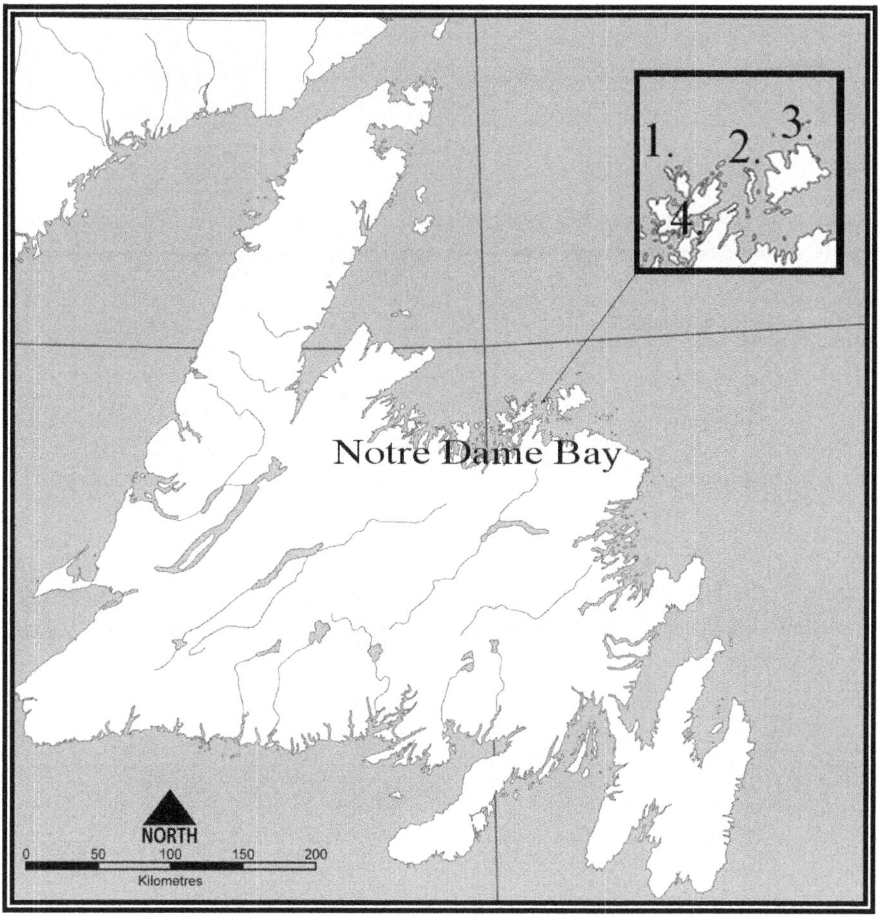

The Isles region consists of: 1. Twillingate;
2. Change Islands; 3. Fogo Island; 4. New World Island

1

The Isles

Notre Dame Bay & The Isles – Geography

The former Provincial electoral district called "The Isles of Notre Dame," encompassed Twillingate and New World Island, along with Fogo Island and Change Islands (As noted, I use the term "Isles" in referring to the area collectively).[1] The Isles make up a small part of the Canadian Province of Newfoundland and Labrador, itself comprised of two distinct regions. Its collective area is about 405,000 km^2, larger than both Japan and Britain, though its 2011 population stood at only 514,536. The Province's island portion – Newfoundland – is the fifteenth largest island on Earth. Newfoundland and Labrador was "discovered" in 1497 by explorer John Cabot (c.1450-c.1499), sailing under the patronage of England's King Henry VII (1457-1509), but was home to aboriginal peoples for thousands of years before. Around 1000 AD the Vikings briefly visited. For many years a British colony, Newfoundland and Labrador is Canada's newest Province, joining Confederation in 1949. Although initiatives like oil and gas, and tourism, are important to the Province's modern economy, its lifeblood has always been the cod fishery. It remains important even after a cod moratorium was imposed in 1992 due to declining stocks. As early as 1612 colonizer John Guy (d.1629) wrote that "...the Newfoundland [cod] fish, being so acceptable in France, Spain and Italy, may...yearly return great quantities of money."[2] This was true for nearly 500 years. Like most Newfoundland coastal communities, those on the Isles owe their existence to the sea's bounty.

The old Isles of Notre Dame District was located on Newfoundland's northeast coast in an area called Notre Dame Bay (NDB) – "Bay of our Lady". The bay is broad, and deeply indented, having the most irregular coastline and the most islands – about 350 – of Newfoundland's major bays. NDB is also the largest of all the Island's great bays. The outermost of the bay's islands, along with its headlands, are frequently exposed to remorseless North Atlantic winds, ice, and tides. Those areas lying inside the coast's many islands or within the inner depths of Notre Dame Bay, and called bays themselves, are better sheltered and home to thick stands of timber. The northwestern headland of Notre Dame Bay is Cape St. John, known simply as "Cape John" by locals. The bay's eastern terminus has never been agreed upon – it has been located as far west as Long Point, Twillingate, and as far east as Cape Freels at the eastern extremity of the Straight Shore. Author/politician Frederick W. Rowe considered Hamilton Sound, southwest of Fogo Island, the eastern entrance to Notre Dame Bay. The smaller Bays making up NDB are, from west to east:

Green Bay, Little Bay, Halls Bay, Badger Bay, Seal Bay, New Bay and the Bay of Exploits. "Green Bay" was once used in referring to that portion of NDB lying between Twillingate and Cape St. John, and the label often appeared on maps. Today, Green Bay refers only to a small indraft adjacent to the Baie Verte Peninsula. The Bay of Exploits is one of the largest bays making up greater NDB. It stretches far inland to the mouth of Newfoundland's longest river, the Exploits.

Once the whole of Notre Dame Bay was part of a French fishery preserve known as the French Shore. The French continued to hold fishing rights in Newfoundland into the twentieth century. At its greatest extent (1783-1904) their treaty area stretched from Cape St. John on the Island's northeast coast, to Cape Ray on Newfoundland's southwestern tip. Originally the French Shore started at Cape Bonavista, the northern boundary of English settlement, and extended to Pointe Riche on the western side of the Great Northern Peninsula. Although a few places like Twillingate and Fogo were inhabited by the English earlier, the growth of European settlement didn't take off until the French Shore boundary was moved westward in 1783. By 1857 Notre Dame Bay was home to over 7,000 permanent residents, the vast majority living east of Exploits. Almost all of these people were English West Country Protestants. The only large concentrations of Irish Roman Catholics in Notre Dame Bay settled at Tilting, on eastern Fogo Island, and at Fortune Harbour.

The portion of NDB we are concerned with are the islands stretching from Twillingate in the West to Fogo Island in the East. Twillingate and New World Island can be reached by turning off the Trans Canada Highway (TCH), and taking route 340 – the Road to the Isles – north from Notre Dame Junction near Lewisporte. Just one kilometre east of the route 340 exit is Notre Dame Provincial Park, which provides campgrounds and cabins, plus cross-country ski trails in Winter. Visitors can also exit farther west along the TCH at the town of Gander, home to the Isles' nearest airport, and take routes 330-1 north; these routes connect with route 340 southeast of the settlement of Boyd's Cove. For the first-time arrival, Visitor Information Centres located at the route 340 exit, and at Gander, provide travel information including attractions and ferry schedules.

The mainland portion of route 340 is still heavily forested, and the timber industry has been important to the area for most of its history. An attraction of the route are stands of hardwoods like maple and birch, whose leaves turn to brilliant reds, oranges and yellows in the Fall. From Notre Dame Junction and Lewisporte travellers head in a northeasterly direction along the coast of Notre Dame Bay, passing alongside Indian Arm and its Brook, site of the town of Campbellton. From there it is on to Loon Bay, passing through the community of the same name. These towns, and others like Michael's Harbour, Baytona, Birchy Bay, and Boyd's Cove lie in one of the most engaging areas of a beautiful Province, and have attracted humans since the stone age.

The alternate route, north from Gander (330-1), also makes for a charming drive. Travellers can avail themselves of the airport town's many attractions and services, including shopping malls and a fine aviation museum. The communities of Gander Bay, stretching along the Gander River, are natural jewels. Once we reach Boyd's Cove/Harbour, and the first of the causeways, it is on to the islands themselves.

The largest of the islands on this portion of the Road to the Isles is New World Island (NWI). It is approximately thirty-two kilometres by twelve kilometres at its widest point. A description given in ENL describes New World Island as being "shaped somewhat like a cupped hand, with the fingers towards the east and the thumb extended to the west."[3] Friday's Bay almost bisects NWI, which at its narrowest point between Virgin Arm and Dildo Run is only a kilometre wide. The centre and east of New World Island are generally low lying. The western portion of the island is higher and more rocky, with certain cliffs up to thirty metres high. New World Island, and its neighbour Chapel Island, generally have a much thicker forest cover than the Twillingate islands. In the past Twillingate was the economic heart of the area, with New World Island's more scattered communities being less developed, though a number of initiatives like the Rural Development Centre at Newville, and a multi-grade school between Virgin Arm and Summerford, have been undertaken. There are many small settlements on New World Island, often with very picturesque names. They include: Bridgeport; Chanceport; Cobb's Arm; Cottlesville; Herring Neck; Hillgrade; Indian Cove; Moreton's Harbour; Parkview (Originally Dark Hole); Pike's Arm; Summerford; Tizzard's Harbour; Too Good Arm; Valley Pond (Formerly Whale's Gulch), and Virgin Arm.

The southern portion of New World Island flanks Dildo Run. This strait is about sixteen kilometres long, and very narrow in places. The run is also full of small islands and shoals – said to number over 300 – making boat traffic treacherous. Navigating the Run without a knowledgeable pilot was never recommended, and a number of vessels have been lost on the rocks there. For this reason few communities, except Summerford on NWI's southwest corner, are found there. Despite the hazardous navigation, many small boats use Dildo Run in Winter and Spring to avoid the ice packs that accumulate to the north. The largest sailing vessel believed to have passed through the run was the schooner *Bessie Marie* out of Twillingate (See Chapter Two). The Run was once used by vessels transporting limestone from a quarry in Cobbs Arm to the town of Botwood and the Grand Falls paper mill. Before the causeways and roads were built Dildo Run was also a main artery of travel for passenger vessels and freight boats. Today, spanned by a bridge, the Run is inaccessible to vessels with masts of over fifteen metres tall.

Twillingate South Side c.1900

North of Dildo Run and NWI lies one of the most populous communities along the Road to the Isles, Twillingate. Near good headland fishing grounds, with abundant seals and seabirds, humans have called the area home since prehistoric times. Twillingate is spread across two islands. The islands are separated by a narrow passage named Shoal Tickle. The tickle used to dry up at low tide, but has been dredged to permit small boat traffic at all times of day. South Twillingate Island, or "South Side" as it is known to residents, is the larger at almost ten kilometres by six. North Twillingate Island (North Side) is smaller, six and a half by three and a half kilometres. North Side has less forest cover than its sister island, and was described as having "...high cliffs on the northern end... [and being] high, rounded, barren...rather like a turtle's back."[4] The two islands form a good harbour providing some shelter from the prevailing winds. Occasionally a north-northeast gale can blow straight into the harbour mouth. On rare occasions, like the years 1782 and 1907, the gales last several days, causing extensive damage to vessels and fishing equipment. At 1.5 km wide by four km long, and sandwiched between North and South Island, the harbour can accommodate most vessels, including cruise ships in recent years. A third large but barren island – Burnt Island – lies at the mouth of the harbour, giving extra protection from the stormy North Atlantic. Though it was not favoured by settlers, Burnt Island was once used as a burial ground for Smallpox victims. Since North Island experiences heavy seas during any high northeast wind, vessels have been known to retreat to the safer anchorage of Main Tickle, separating South Twillingate from New World Island. Safely navigating harbours like that of Twillingate has always been a concern for mariners. The following nautical guide to Twillingate (Toulinquet) harbour appeared in Edmund Blunt's *American Coast Pilot* of 1847:

> TOULINQUET HARBOUR.—This harbor is sheltered from all winds but those which blow from the north and north-east, when, in heavy gales, it becomes dangerous. In entering, either by the east or western channel, you must take the greatest care to avoid the White Ground, to clear which, you bring Messrs. Slade's dwelling-house open of Sim's Island, and keep it so, until French Head opens through the Eastern Passage. This is very commonly called Burnt Island Tickle, and should not be attempted without you are thoroughly acquainted with the navigation, or in cases of general emergence. The anchorage is mostly foul, but the best and most secure is about 5 or 6 fathoms, off Colburn's Stores. Both water and wood are scarce. If the mariner should be here either early or late in the year, Back Harbor, which lies off the western side of the table land, will be found a preferable place for shelter, and a few small vessels may ride there with much safety. You may proceed in on either side of Gull island, lying with the Western Head open of Batrix Island and the Bluff Head, or with the Eastern Stage on Batrix Island. The islands about the harbor of Toulinquet are moderately high, and bounded by dark-colored slate cliffs. It may be readily known by the Gull island or table land.[5]

Once, the main town of Twillingate was but one of several communities on the two islands, along with Bluff Head Cove, Gillard's Cove and Manuel's Cove (Bayview); Hart's Cove, Upper & Lower Jenkins' Cove, Gillesport and Blow-Me-Down (Durrell); and Crow Head. South Island is home to the unincorporated communities of Kettle Cove, Little Harbour and

Purcell's Harbour.[6] These three settlements are about the only communities on South Island's eastern end. Another settlement in the area was Codjack's Cove, which is now abandoned. Most of the incorporated towns became part of the larger town of Twillingate in January 1992, except Crow Head, which remains a separate municipality. In fact, in 1960 Crow Head became the *first* municipality on the Twillingate islands.

Twillingate North Side c.1900

For most of their history Twillingate and New World Island were separated from the rest of Newfoundland by the sea. Following extensive road construction during the 1950s, a series of causeways was built in 1962, running north, and forming the Road to the Isles. From the first community in the south, Lewisporte, through to the Twillingate islands, the Road to the Isles runs for about eighty-five kilometres. The first causeway, over Reach Run, connects Chapel Island to Boyd's Cove on the main island. From there travellers pass over the Curtis Causeway traversing Dildo Run and Northern Tickle. It is named for lawyer/politician Hon. Leslie Roy Curtis (1895-1980), a Twillingate native, and Liberal member for Twillingate District when the causeway network was built. The Curtis Causeway takes travellers as far north as New World Island.

In the first few years after causeways linked New World Island and the mainland, Twillingate still had to be reached by ferry. Originally the ferry *Ambrose Shea* served on the run, but it was burnt on 1 February 1965. The *Ambrose Shea* was replaced by the eighteen-car ferry *John Peyton*, named after a well-known former resident, whom we will meet later. In 1973 a final bridge, now called the Walter B. Elliott Causeway, was built across Main Tickle, completing the road network. This causeway was named in honour of a Crow Head resident who was active in local and provincial politics. Twillingate's north and south islands had been connected by a bridge decades earlier.

Twillingate ferry, MV John Peyton, *undergoing repairs on the ice*

Even today not all Isles communities are linked by causeways. Fogo Island and Change Islands are reached by turning off Route 331 at Gander Bay, near Boyd's Cove and the Twillingate/NWI causeways. A drive of about twenty kilometres separates this turn-off and Farewell, terminal for the Fogo Island/Change Islands' ferry service. The route is known as "The Islands Experience." Farewell is located on the tip of a small peninsula separating Dildo Run from Sir Charles Hamilton Sound. The ferry service bridges the distance from Farewell, across Hamilton Sound, to both Fogo Island and Change Islands. Fogo Island – farthest offshore, heading west – lies about sixteen kilometres from Farewell. For a number of years the run was serviced by the 2,100 ton MV *Captain Earl W. Windsor*. In 2015 the 200 passenger ferry, MV *Veteran*, named in honour of locals who served in conflicts from World War I through to Afghanistan, made its debut. The crossing takes around twenty minutes one way to Change Islands and about forty-five minutes to Fogo Island, where the ferry docks at Man o' War Cove. A warning to the traveller: Arctic ice flows sometimes create delays in the Winter and early

Spring.

At about 182 km^2 Fogo Island is the largest of all Newfoundland's offshore islands. It is comprised of volcanic and sedimentary rocks dating from the Precambrian to Paleozoic eras, with prominent granite formations and an overlying moraine of shallow stony soil. A great attraction for settlers over the centuries were the rich fishing grounds of the shallow Fogo Shelf. Its geography shaped by ancient glaciation, Fogo Island has many small ponds but little good agricultural soil; residents have always relied mainly on the sea for their living and survival. Although its northeastern half has few trees, except in isolated stands, to the southwest Fogo Island retains considerable forest cover. The island's rocky shoreline is heavily indented, with many coves, but ENL asserts that these offer little protection for ships, apart from fairly small craft. Blunt gives this description of certain anchorages on Fogo Island as they appeared in 1847:

> THE FOGO ISLANDS lie to the north-westward of the Wadham Islands. Great Fogo is a large island, 4 leagues long and 9 miles broad. Off its south-western point lie the Indian Islands; and N. E. By N. 4 miles from the body of Great Fogo are the Little Fogo islands. Numerous other rocks and small islands are scattered about.
>
> SHOAL BAY.—This harbor is very secure, with good anchorage in any part above the Harbor Rock; it has two tickles, so called in Newfoundland, and intended to describe narrow passages between islands and rocks; these may be entered with any wind except from the south to the S. W. which wind blows out of both. To enter the Eastern Tickle, you should borrow on Rag's Island, keeping the extreme of Fogo Island nearly open of Lane's Island, until Gappy's Island comes open of Simon's Island; you will then clear the shoals of Filly's Point. To avoid the Harbor Rock, bring Slade and Cox's Flagstaff on with the eastern chimney of their dwelling house; it will be necessary to get this mark on before Boatswain's Island closes Bullock's Point. In coming from the westward, it is advisable to make free with Fogo Island, in order that you may distinguish the small islands that form the tickle which, if passed with westerly winds, can never be regained, owing to the constant set there is to the eastward. Having passed Little Motion, keep the extreme point of the head over the Narrows Point, until you get past Bullock's Point, when the above directions will clear all the harbor's

dangers.

Coming from the eastward, and bound to Fogo Harbor, N. W. part of Fogo Island, you must be careful to avoid the Dean's Rock, which is a sunken rock, and lies between Joe Batt's Point and the harbor. Steer W. N. W. until Brimstone Hill, a remarkable round mountain, appears in the centre of the harbor; then steer for the East Tickle, which may be known by the lantern on the top of Sim's Island. Make the west side of the tickle. Give a good berth to the point on the starboard side, and run right up the harbor, keeping near the south side, and you will carry from 5 to 3 fathoms through. Immediately you get round the point, steer S. W. to avoid the harbour Rock, and follow the directions given above for anchoring. The middle tickle appears the widest, but it is fit only for boats. The other two must be adopted as best suits the wind.[7]

Fogo, North Side, c.1900

Like Twillingate and New World Island, Fogo Island's resources were first exploited by Natives, including the Maritime Archaic, Groswater-Phase Palaeo Eskimos, and the Beothuk. However, from the sixteenth century on, Fogo's rich fishing attracted the attention of Europeans. The toponym Fogo may originate from the Portuguese, though it was the English, along with some Irish, who settled Fogo Island. Apart from its oldest community, and namesake, Fogo Island is home to a number of settlements, including Barr'd Islands, Deep (Hare) Bay, Island Harbour, Joe Batt's Arm, Little Seldom,

Seldom-Come-By, Shoal Bay, Stag Harbour, and Tilting. There were twenty-one communities on Fogo Island as of the 1911 census, but this number had dropped to ten by 1951. In later years some of the older communities such as Barr'd Islands, Joe Batt's Arm and Shoal Bay were incorporated together as combined municipalities.[8] A number of small communities like Lion's Den and Eastern Tickle, established near the town of Fogo, were abandoned by the mid twentieth century.

Bishop Edward Feild

Although the descendants of Dorset mariners and Waterford fishers have long made their living on the island, Fogo's geography has not always charmed European visitors. In 1846, while performing pastoral duties there, Bishop Edward Feild (1801-76) gave a description of Fogo Island to his friend, Reverend E. Coleridge of Eton. Bishop Feild's assessment of Fogo's natural charms was not altogether flattering:

> The most barren and unpoetical imagination could hardly descend to a scene so bare and desolate as this island of Fogo – a mere rock of bluff heads and huge boulders, with occasional patches of green in the valleys, but not a tree or shrub of any kind. The houses are all of wood, and generally

> coloured red, and all stand, as do the churches and other buildings, on sticks or shores; and the fish-stages and flakes in like manner, supported from rock to rock, and running into the sea, present an appearance and scene which is so foreign and strange, that no description could...make you understand it...[9]

Fortunately, attitudes towards the natural charms of the region have changed considerably over the last 160 years. One of the areas increasingly recognized for its natural beauty is Change Islands. Like most communities in Notre Dame Bay, Change Islands was founded on the fishery, although in this case permanent European settlement post dated the readjustment of the French Shore boundary in 1783. The community rests upon two islands containing some of the oldest rocks on the North American continent. In the past Change Islanders settled on various parts of the two main islands, but the incorporated community is now centred around the shores of the narrow tickle separating the north and south islands. Of this pair the southern island, oriented in a north-south direction, is by far the larger. The south island has more boggy, marshy areas, and is more wooded than the north island, which tends to be more barren.

As we will see, in common with Tilting on Fogo Island, Change Islands has preserved a good deal of its historic infrastructure, especially its fishery stages and stores. As one of the more unspoiled locales in the Province, Change Islands may become a major tourist destination in future, a role its inhabitants have actively cultivated.

....

A History of Notre Dame Bay, Home of the Isles

The history of Notre Dame Bay is a microcosm of Newfoundland's past. Native peoples like the Maritime Archaic and Dorset called the bay home for hundreds of years. This was especially true of the Bay of Exploits. The Exploits River, taking them south to Red Indian Lake, was an essential Winter hunting territory for the Beothuk. The first European to sight NDB may have been Portuguese explorer Gaspar Corte Real (c.1450-c.1502), who is said to have coined the name *Baia Verde*, or Green Bay. In 1534 French navigator Jacques Cartier (c.1491-1557) is known to have traversed the bay, visiting Fogo Island *en route*. NDB was an early centre of the French fishery, and has a French name, but the region has fewer toponyms of French origin than any other stretch of Newfoundland's extensive coast; Twillingate (*Toulinguet*) is one of the only exceptions. Although the French were well aware of the abundant marine resources at Fogo and Twillingate, they made no concerted effort to explore the bay's inner reaches. NDB was officially part of the French Shore from the Treaty of Utrecht in 1713 to the Treaty of Versailles in 1783, but French rights there were not vigorously enforced. By 1783 the French fishery was concentrated to the north of Cape St. John, and NDB experienced English in-migration, especially at Twillingate. With official recognition of English settlement rights after 1783, new communities spread outward to New World Island, Exploits, Burnt Islands and west. The main "point men" of this settlement trend were fishers and fur trappers, whose role in settling the northeast coast has never been thoroughly examined. A negative by-product of this expansion was the decline of the Native Beothuk, and their supposed extinction in the late 1820s (See Chapter Six).

An important development for the region was the discovery of a vein of copper at Tilt Cove, fifteen kilometres to the southwest of Cape St. John. This discovery led to a brief copper boom in Notre Dame Bay, which spun off into mining ventures at places like Twillingate and Moreton's Harbour. These mines, profiled in Chapters Two and Three, had little significance to the economies of the two communities over the long run. The larger copper boom made more of an impact. A goal of the politicians and entrepreneurs who initiated a trans-Newfoundland Railway in the late 1800s was to link the Avalon Peninsula with the northern "copper belt." Though the copper boom was short lived, the mining tradition did not completely disappear, and 1928 saw the establishment of an important base metals mine at Buchans in the interior. There was also a revival of mining in Green Bay, but this died out in the 1970s.

An economic development which greatly impacted Notre Dame Bay was the growth of sawmilling in the region. By the turn of the twentieth century a number of communities like Campbellton had their own productive lumber mills. Some of those involved in the industry attempted to consolidate their holdings along the Exploits River and thus encourage a large-scale timber industry. The business took off after 1909 when the Anglo-Newfoundland Development Company (AND), part of the British Harmsworth interests, opened a pulp mill at Grand Falls. People from Notre Dame Bay travelled to the mill for work, or were employed in the interior by AND at its Winter lumber camps. Residents of Notre Dame Bay also helped found communities based around another pulp mill at Bishop's Falls, and Botwood, transshipment port for the region's paper products. After 1923 Baymen, with their reputation for woods work, were a major component of the work force at a new Corner Brook mill. Until mechanization of the industry in the 1960s, logging was the most important source of paid employment in NDB. This landward orientation was not only a result of growing opportunities there, but of problems with the traditional fishing industry.

Since the early 1700s fish merchants in Notre Dame Bay had by-passed the French Shore, travelling northward to fish the Labrador coast. The fishery was conducted from vessels called schooners, usually of around 100 tons or less and carrying fore-and-aft sails, normally on two masts. The Labrador fishery reached its height from the 1880s through the 1890s, when almost 2,000 bay residents were employed during the Summer months. After 1900 the fishery declined. In 1911 only about 800 people and 100 vessels were travelling to "the Labrador." By 1921 these numbers were halved, and the Labrador fishery was all but gone in the 1930s. An inshore lobster fishery and expansion into the French Shore provided some compensation, but the trend toward interior employment continued.

Pair of schooners in full sail, with dories

While such employment was fairly common, most goods and passengers in Notre Dame Bay travelled by sea via Newfoundland's coastal boat service. For much of its history the Island had poor overland transport services, a trend still visible to some degree in Labrador. The Newfoundland Railway did not connect communities in the Colony until the late 1800s, and the TCH only opened for automobile traffic in 1965. The first regular passenger air services didn't arrive until the second half of the twentieth century. Prior to the 1800s there were few government marine transportation services. Those that did exist were naturally reliant on sail, and at the mercy of variable winds and tides. As colonial settlement expanded, calls grew for improved living conditions, including the regular transport of mails, freight and passengers. The nineteenth century saw the first subsidized coastal boat services in Newfoundland and Labrador. Eventually, these became so important to the small outports that the government wharf became a community gathering place much like churches and shops.

The House of Assembly approved a grant for a Conception Bay steamer service in 1852. Soon there were steam services in a number of bays, although many people felt the service was not expanding quickly enough. Even so, slow but steady progress continued. A line of American and Canadian steamers added St. John's to its schedule. By the 1870s many settlements benefited from regular mail and transport steam services. One of the earliest providers of such services was the Liverpool/St. John's firm Bowring Brothers. In 1898 Reid Newfoundland Company was granted a monopoly over the coastal boat service and an annual subsidy of almost $100,000.00. To meet its obligations Reid built its famous "Alphabet Fleet."

Bay boat SS Clyde *at Twillingate, early 1900s*

By the twentieth century Notre Dame Bay communities were linked by coastal and bay boat services based at Lewisporte. Regular passenger and cargo stops were made at Twillingate, Fogo and smaller ports along the coast. The bay service was handled for many years by the 439 gross ton SS *Clyde*. Part of the Alphabet fleet, the *Clyde* was built by A. & J. Inglis of Glasgow, Scotland in 1900. Constructed at a cost of $100,000.00, the vessel was named for the Scottish river on whose banks most of the fleet's ships were produced. A 1910 sailing schedule for the *Clyde* notes the following:

> The s. s. *Clyde* leaves Lewisporte for the South side of the Bay every Monday (except in four winter months), calling at the following places : – Campbellton, Laurencetown, Botwoodville, Exploits, Moreton's Harbor, Tizzard's Harbor, Twillingate, Herring Neck, Little Beaver Cove and Beaverton (alternately), Dog Bay, Change Islands and Fogo.[10]

The *Clyde* was first captained by Job Knee. Hailing from Pools Island in Bonavista Bay, Knee had been both a sealer and a Labrador fisher in his youth. He received his first command, the Bowring vessel *Falcon*, in 1889. According to Alphabet Fleet biographer Maura Hanrahan, the name Job Knee was well nigh synonymous with that of the *Clyde*. Knee's final trip on the *Clyde* was made in 1923, the old skipper passing away a year later aged seventy-two.

Upon Knee's retirement the *Clyde*'s regular master was Twillingate native John "Jack" Butcher (or Boutcher). Captain Butcher remained at his post till virtually the day he died, making his last run in November 1941. On that trip he collapsed unconscious as the *Clyde* docked at Campbellton. After putting Butcher in his bunk the crew headed for the hospital at Twillingate, but were stopped by high seas and forced into Exploits. Captain Butcher arrived at the hospital four days after his collapse, only briefly regaining consciousness. He died on 3 December, ending an era in Notre Dame Bay navigation.

One of the *Clyde*'s most interesting adventures happened in December 1919, and involved another member of the Alphabet Fleet, the SS *Dundee*. A sister ship to the *Clyde*, the *Dundee* was also built by A. & J. Inglis in 1900, and was the same tonnage. Sailing from Herring Neck, birthplace of the Fisherman's Protective Union (FPU), the *Dundee* was bound for Port Union, the FPU's new base of operations. On Christmas day the vessel grounded on Grassy Island. Locals could see the distressed steamer signalling for assistance, but were unable to reach it due to slob ice around the island. The *Clyde* was despatched to aid the *Dundee* after word of the incident was relayed to St. John's. The story ended on a happy note, as all passengers and crew were rescued, although attempts to save some of the vessel's fittings were thwarted by heavy seas. Punctured in two places, the *Dundee* was never salvaged, its broken hull remaining on Grassy Island for years.

Another of the *Clyde*'s famous exploits occurred around the outbreak of World War II. As Hanranhan reports, the freighter *Christoph V Doornum* out of Emden, Germany was lying at anchor at Botwood waiting on a cargo of lead-zinc concentrate intended for Belgium. With war threatening the vessel was unable to leave port due to mechanical difficulties. The ship was seized by representatives of the vessel's London-based mortgage holders under an Admiralty writ. The Captain and crew, three of whom had tried to escape, were held under guard. Around mid September, with war officially declared, the ship was considered a prize of the Newfoundland government and its sailors prisoners of war. Previously, on 11 September, the *Clyde* had been used to tow the much larger vessel to moorings in Botwood Harbour. An existing photograph of the event shows the *Clyde* practically dwarfed by the German craft. The prisoners of war were interred for a time in Newfoundland until they were transferred to camps in mainland Canada. Sadly, two of the prisoners, who were apparently innocent of any espionage, died before making it home. According to one of Hanranhan's sources the others returned to Germany at war's end only to find that their relatives had all died.

Though she remained in service for much longer than her sister ship, the *Clyde*'s end was just as sad as that of the *Dundee*. The vessel remained on the bay service until 1948 when it was sold to Crosbie & Company. It was lost off Williamsport on 17 December 1951. The *Clyde* was replaced on the bay service by the SS *Springdale*, captained by Alfred Elliot of Twillingate.

The bay service had its problems with the ice that blocked Notre Dame Bay for up to six months each year. At times horse and dog sleds running over the ice were the only way to get passengers, mail and freight in and out of bay settlements. In his memoirs of life at Twillingate American doctor Robert Ecke recounted such an instance early in the Second World War. The *Clyde* under Captain Butcher, and the *Sagona* under Captain Knee, were behind schedule due to inclement weather. When the vessels arrived at Twillingate with Winter food supplies they found their way blocked by early ice flows. Butcher and Knee rammed their vessels as far as possible into the ice, then signalled to those ashore using their ships' whistles. All dogs and horses large enough to take a harness were employed to tow flour, molasses and other staples across the rough ice; all told hundreds of tons of foodstuffs made it into Twillingate that day. This kind of problem gave rise to the expression "the lean and hungry month of March." By March the ice had been inshore for two or three months, and Winter supplies were beginning to run thin. In April the ice had often broken up sufficiently for the steamers to get through.

The coastal boats which put into Notre Dame Bay were the *Prospero* and *Kyle*, the latter especially esteemed in Newfoundland folk memory. The *Prospero* was built by the firm of Murdoch & Murray, Glasgow in 1904. It was sold in 1937. The *Kyle* was built in 1913 by Swan Hunter of Newcastle. It was sold out of the coastal service in December 1959. The *Kyle* ran aground at Harbour Grace in 1967, where it remains. The vessel lay derelict for some years, but has been partially restored.

In 1923 the Newfoundland Government purchased Reid's

transportation holdings for $2,000,000.00. The Alphabet Fleet was gradually replaced, although the *Kyle* was retained, along with the *Glenco* and a few other boats. With Confederation Canadian National Railways (CNR) assumed control of the coastal service under the Terms of Union. Coastal vessels were the main link many Newfoundland communities had with the outside world through to the 1960s.

SS Kyle, *1913*

Reliance on the coastal boat service was not the only commonality of NDB communities. An interesting feature of Notre Dame Bay was its political homogeneity. For many years following the grant of colonial government the region frequently returned Conservative candidates. For example, Conservative Sir Frederick B. T. Carter (1819-1900) represented Twillingate and Fogo District, which then covered much of the bay, as a Member of the House of Assembly (MHA) during his second term as Prime Minister, from 1874-8. The attachment of Notre Dame Bay to Conservatism is not surprising in an era when the party was usually associated with Protestantism, the religion of most bay residents. In 1858 merchant agent Charles Edmonds, writing from Twillingate, noted that "...Mr. Bryan Robinson would be a person in whom every confidence could be placed [as a political candidate, and furthermore]...[w]e must return a Protestant and a Conservative." The late MHA William H. Ellis was, in Edmonds' opinion, "...an almost irreparable loss, he being a staunch Conservative and Champion of Briton's rights"[11]

Despite an inclination towards the Conservatives, party affiliations in the bay were not so entrenched as they later became.[12] One of Newfoundland's great political leaders was William Vallance Whiteway (1828-1908). For much of his career his supporters were known more for following Whiteway personally then any established party. He was first elected to Twillingate and Fogo District as a Conservative in 1859. Whiteway was re-elected as one of the district's MHAs in 1861 and 1865. He came out of retirement for the 6 November 1889 election, this time under the Liberal banner against incumbent Premier Sir Robert Thorburn (1836-1906) and his Reform Party. Whiteway won.

Newfoundland Prime Minister, and Twillingate District MHA, Sir Robert Bond

The now separate Twillingate District (still including most of central and western NDB) returned three Liberals. For many decades thereafter the district was solidly Liberal. In September 1895, after his appointment as Colonial Secretary by Whiteway, future Prime Minister Robert Bond (1857-1927) was elected to the Twillingate District by acclamation. Bond represented Twillingate District throughout his Premiership, and for the rest of his active political career. During the 1920s Twillingate and Green Bay Districts were a bedrock of support for the Liberal/Union Party, in part a creation of William Ford Coaker (1871-1938) and his Fisherman's Protective Union, which originated at Herring Neck (See Chapter Ten). One of the few Liberal defeats in Twillingate District during this era occurred in 1932 when Lady Helena

Squires (1879-1959) ran unsuccessfully following a previous by-election win in Lewisporte District.

The 1932 election was the beginning of the end for Newfoundland's system of "Responsible Government," established in 1855. In 1934 the British Dominion, beset by financial crises and corruption, relinquished democratic government to a panel of non-elected bureaucrats called Commissioners, Chaired by the Newfoundland Governor. This was the beginning of Commission of Government. Residents of the Colony did not go to the polls again until 1948 to vote on union with Canada. In the second Confederation referendum held that year more than seventy-five percent of voters in the districts of Twillingate and Fogo supported future Liberal Premier Joseph R. "Joey" Smallwood (1900-91) and the union. Here is how *Twillingate Sun* editor Ernest Clarke summed up the issue for electors in the Bay:

> ...For better or for worse the first day of April [1949] should see us the tenth Province [of Canada] with whatever benefits, responsibilities and changes in our way of life is therein entailed.
>
> Few if any of us swallowed all of the propaganda so lavishly distributed during the recent campaigns. For example we were told that never again would children in this country know hunger; that an era of prosperity for everyone was indisputably tied up with union. No government can guarantee that...[B]read is dependent on employment and employment is something which is not always available...
>
> In the past fifteen years we have had a form of government which in the main was conscientiously administered. Much good was done and the proof today is apparent. There is much more which it will not be possible to correctly assess for at least a generation...
>
> There is, however, one point which stands out. During the fifteen years of Commission Government, the people of this country were deprived of political activity. There were no elections, no campaigns, little if any interest in the Island's affairs. The electorate gradually developed an attitude of almost complete indifference, became content to allow a small and none too representative body of men to run things as they saw fit...
>
> That is the danger which we face today and in the years ahead, the inclination to "let the government do it." We have forgotten that we are the government. As citizens we

> have a responsibility and a right to make our will felt in each and everything which affects our lives and those of our countrymen. But that will must be an intelligent one if it is to be effective and have worthwhile results. It can only be so if the electorate are prepared to think, to discuss, to maintain interest and to act.[13]

In post Confederation politics the Twillingate, Fogo and Green Bay Districts, which have since been renamed and realigned, often gave Liberal candidates large majorities at both the Federal and Provincial levels. The Liberal stranglehold on the districts was finally broken in the election of 1972 that saw Joey fall from power. That same year future Premier A. Brian Peckford (b. 1942) won Green Bay for the Conservatives. Peckford was the first of several candidates to sunder the Liberal hold on Notre Dame Bay, but the area is still an important source of support for the party.[14]

Notre Dame Bay's greater political volatility since the 1970s might relate to the economic difficulties it has faced in common with the rest of the Island, and Labrador. As the Grand Falls paper mill aged, closing in 2009, and mechanization took hold, work in the logging sector declined. Green Bay's second mining boom had also ended. Today the major centres in NDB are not resource-based, but service centres such as Lewisporte. By the 1990s, following years of over-exploitation, the traditional fishery had taken a beating with the near-extinction of cod stocks. Some fishplants have closed down. Others, including the Twillingate plant, have switched to alternate species like shrimp, employing far fewer people than in the 1970s and 1980s. Still, Notre Dame Bay is peopled by a hardy stock who have faced down adversity in the past and will likely do so again.

2

Twillingate

The Native Heritage

Since we've taken a look at the Isles in general, we will now focus on one of the area's largest and oldest communities, Twillingate. The area around Twillingate has been inhabited for about 3,500 years. The first settlers lived on the islands from approximately 3500-3200 BP (Before Present). Their culture was spread throughout New England, Atlantic Canada and the Lower South Shore of the St. Lawrence River. We will never know what these early people called themselves. Their culture was first named the "Red Paint" tradition, from their extensive use of red ochre. More recently they have been referred to as the Maritime Archaic.

Most of their remains have been lost over time, but archaeologists have found many stone tools like spear points, knives and scrapers. A child's burial from L'Anse-Amour, Labrador is one of the oldest found in North America, dated at 7500 BP. Because most of this culture's sites have been found near the coast it is thought they relied heavily on marine resources such as seals, walrus, seabirds and fish, along with inland species like the caribou. The Maritime Archaic people spread out from southern Labrador about 6,000 years ago and then to Newfoundland a thousand years later. One of the most impressive Maritime Archaic sites on the Island is a cemetery at Port au Choix on the Great Northern Peninsula. The area contains the remains of at least 100 persons buried from about 4000 to 3500 BP. The numerous artifacts found with the skeletons include not only weapons and tools, but what are likely religious and magical objects. At Port au Choix the objects found weren't just made of stone, but from bone, ivory and antler as well. The use of marine creatures like whales, seals, fish and seabirds is clearly shown by remains found at the site. One of the most interesting Port au Choix objects is an effigy thought to represent a killer whale. We don't know exactly why it was carved, but perhaps it was used to harness the strength and power of the animal by magic. Although their numbers were probably never very large, the Maritime Archaic lived in Labrador and Newfoundland for thousands of years. Around 3,000 years ago, for reasons unknown, they either emigrated from, or became extinct on the Island, but may have survived longer in southern Labrador. There is some evidence that the Maritime Archaic Indians could be ancestors of both the Beothuk and Innu peoples.

A major find of Maritime Archaic artifacts occurred on 2 September 1966 at Back Harbour, Twillingate. Brothers Frank and Stanley Curtis were digging an outhouse pit when they came across an impressive array of items, a number of which were dug up with pick and shovel. The following year

Donald Macleod of the National Museum of Canada and archaeologists from McMaster University were called in, adding to the tally of artifacts. The site was located about seventy-six metres from the shore of a west-facing and protected cove. This was typical of the Maritime Archaic culture, whose sites were always located near the sea or navigable rivers. Over seventy-five items were recovered from the site including projectile points, gouges, adzes and crystals. Many artifacts were found in a bed of red ochre, and the whole appearance suggests a cemetery. One grave contained beach pebbles, and was likely shored up to a depth of one metre by a wall of rocks. Little organic material was found at the site, and no human remains. One item that did survive was a piece of charred leather, or bark, that might have been a burnt food offering or part of the grave's mortuary wrappings. With so much of their material culture decayed, many questions about the Maritime Archaic remain unanswered, but they have the honour of being Twillingate's first residents.

In more recent times the Maritime Archaic were supplanted at Twillingate by the Dorset Eskimos. Archaeologists consider the Dorset the "late" phase of what they call the Palaeo (old) Eskimo tradition (See Chapter Four). The Dorset first settled in northern Labrador around 2500 BP, and about 500 years later in Newfoundland. They are still remembered by the modern Inuit as the Tunit people, making them the earliest inhabitants of the Province for whom a contemporary name survives. The Dorset occupied many parts of the Province, and may have been the most widespread of all our prehistoric-peoples. The Dorset had a variety of tools and weapons similar in usage to their predecessors, although their form was quite different. Unlike some other Palaeo-Eskimos, the Dorset don't seem to have used bows and arrows, or domesticated dogs. Their hunting was more focussed on ice-edge species like seals and walrus. The Dorset were great artists, and their soapstone carvings representing animals and humans are still admired. The Dorset people inhabited Newfoundland for around 1,000 years and then were gone, although they lived on for several hundred years more in northern Labrador. Dorset artifacts were found at Twillingate about 180 metres from the Maritime Archaic grave site, and closer to the shoreline.

....

The French

French Breton fishermen were probably the first Europeans to sight the Twillingate islands in the 1500s; we may recall that Cartier crossed the bay around this time. The French method of fishing involved heavily salting catches, which did not require on-shore drying facilities. Except for wood cutting and finding drinking water the French seldom went ashore, establishing few settlements in Newfoundland. French fishers frequented Notre Dame Bay seasonally in the second half of the seventeenth century.

Perhaps as early as 1650 the French gave Twillingate its name, derived from the word Toulinguet. One old theory about the name's origin suggested that it derived from French words meaning "all tongued." This supposedly referred to the topography of the harbour, thought to have many points of land or "tongues" sticking out into the sea. Archbishop Michael Howley (1843-1914) felt that this was unlikely. He believed that the word was no more than a well-known Breton, or more properly Basque, proper family name such as Touloujin or Touculotte. Another possibility involves an island group off Brest on the Brittany coast that resembles Twillingate from the sea – it is named Toulinguet. Likewise, a defence work that once guarded the entrance to Brest Harbour was called Fort Toulinguet. Whatever its origins, the name was in use prior to the Treaty of Utrecht in 1713, and appeared on European maps by the 1720s.

In 1697 Abbé Jean Baudoin (c.1662-98) estimated that 150 men in fourteen vessels were using Twillingate and Fogo as seasonal fishing stations. The French maintained a presence off Twillingate for some time. As late as 1768 Governor Sir Hugh Palliser (1722/3-96) reported that a French vessel, the *Bon Ami*, was paid a bounty to fish off Twillingate. Its job was not just to fish, but also to irritate and hopefully drive away English settlers. The French supposedly abandoned their local fishery in response to early English incursions, retreating west to White Bay and the Northern Peninsula. This was not their only incentive to move on. The French fishers were also said to have feared the bay's Native people. These were no longer the Dorset, who disappeared from Newfoundland centuries earlier. By the historic period the main indigenous group on the Island were the people now known as Beothuk.

....

The English

The Beothuk enjoyed sole possession of the Twillingate area until the eighteenth century, when the first Englishmen arrived. Twillingate – vacated by the French – seemed like a good place for English settlers, escaping poor fishing and overcrowding in eastern Newfoundland, to relocate. There are two versions of who Twillingate's original "livyers" (live-heres, or permanent settlers) were.

In 1905 journalist/politician Alexander A. Parsons (1847-1932) produced a short article on Twillingate's early settlers and their relations with the Native Beothuk. During the course of his research Parsons communicated with Thomas D. Scanlon, a man associated with the New York, Newfoundland

and London Telegraph Company from 1854 to 1873. Scanlon was described by Parsons as "one of the best informed Newfoundlanders of his day," and he was an informant for Judge Prowse during the writing of his Newfoundland history.[1] Scanlon reported to Parsons that in the early 1870s he had found a tin cannister under the remains of a West Country-style fish flake located in Back Harbour. Inside the cannister was a very old "Diary of Events," recording some of the earliest history of Twillingate. In an interview given a few years before he died, Scanlon assured Parsons that some of the diary entries were made by members of Twillingate's prominent Peyton family. The major drawback with this tradition is in the nature of the evidence. In a student paper on the growth and development of Twillingate and Fogo, Cyril Chaulk notes that sources like the old Peyton diary "...have conveniently disappeared. They belong to folklore rather than history."[2]

Poole Harbour, Dorsetshire, 1830s. Many of Twillingate's early settlers came from this area.

Perhaps. But if we accept Scanlon's story – there seems no obvious reason for him to lie – the diary noted that four families, probably from the English Counties of Hampshire and Dorset, were Twillingate's first settlers. Arriving around 1700, each fished on their own account. Back Harbour was settled by a planter named Moore. South Island was settled by the Young family, while the Baths made Jenkin's Cove, Durrell their home. North Island became home to Lawrence Smith, after whom a hill – Smith's Lookout – is named. There is a tradition that Smith, or his Son, built a sort of fort atop the Lookout, though little hard evidence has been found. Mrs. John Lunnon, a twentieth century Twillingate resident who lived into her nineties, was said to have been the Great-Grand Daughter of Lawrence Smith's own Granddaughter.

Given that the Peytons first arrived at Twillingate in the late 1700s, they may have received their information directly from the children or grandchildren of the original settlers. In the earlier period the French still held treaty rights to the waters off Twillingate, and these first residents may have settled over such a wide area to avoid attracting the notice of fishing vessels. Whichever part of the Twillingate islands a ship might land on, its crew would find only a single family, hardly enough to warrant a complaint.

Most of the early settler surnames still exist in the town. The fact that many of these immigrants hailed from a fairly small area in England shapes Twillingate's character and culture to this day. As Dorsetshire native Roger Guttridge chronicled in *Downhome* magazine, virtually all of Twillingate's older family names can still be found in County Dorset. During a visit to Twillingate in 1993 Guttridge also noted similarities between the Twillingate and Dorset accents, including dropping the letter "H" at the beginning of words.

A more firmly authenticated tradition concerning Twillingate's first settler(s) comes from a letter written to cartographer/explorer James Cook (1728-79) by George Davis on 14 March1764. Davis was a merchant operating in Poole and Newfoundland. He wrote the letter from Poole while Cook was surveying the west coast of Newfoundland at the request of Governor Palliser. Aside from his work as hydrographer, Cook was collaborating with Lord Egmont to settle questions relating to the French Shore boundary. Evidently, Davis had just returned from Newfoundland. Cook had asked him to ascertain the length of time, and extent to which, English fishers had been using places like Twillingate, which technically fell within the French Shore.

Davis' letter alleges that the first Englishman who "ever drove a nail" (built a permanent dwelling) in Twillingate was Thomas Fizzard or Tizzard, originally from Bonavista, in 1732.[3] Tizzard's Wife was a native of Bonavista and her Uncle, John Walcome (Wakeham) died at age eighty, probably in the 1730s. He was said to have been the first English "manchild" born at Bonavista. Along with their children, the Tizzards sailed for two days before reaching Twillingate, where their descendants lived for many years. One of the Tizzards later moved his family to Salt Pans, now Hillgrade, on New World Island in 1876. Davis spoke to Thomas Tizzard in person, so the reference to his having arrived in 1732 is probably correct. Whether or not he was actually the first settler is another matter. Human nature being what it is, Tizzard might just have wanted credit for being the first Englishman on the islands. It is also quite possible that with very small numbers of settlers then inhabiting Twillingate, and few means of communication, Tizzard may have genuinely thought he was the first permanent inhabitant, whether or not that was really the case.

In his 1911 historical geography of the British colonies J. D. Rogers claimed that settlers were overwintering at Twillingate and Fogo by 1729, salmon and seal fisheries having been established there some seven years earlier. Whichever settlement tradition you believe, there is no doubt that English migratory fishermen were using Twillingate as a base by the time Tizzard claimed to have settled.

English fishers in Newfoundland c.1710. From Herman Moll's map

The Davis letter is not the earliest English record we have of Twillingate. Obviously, Cook's interest was sparked by prior accounts of English activity there. Twillingate was a well-known settlement by the year 1750, and had already acquired its modern name, an Anglicized version of the old French term. The first systematic, official record of Twillingate was made in 1738, more than a quarter century before Davis' visit. Six years earlier Newfoundland's Naval Governor had been instructed to include Twillingate and Fogo in his accounts of the English fishery. Bureaucracy being what it is, the survey wasn't conducted right away.

The Governor in 1738 was Royal Navy Captain Philip Vanbrugh (c.1681-1753), who visited Twillingate that year. As he reported to his superiors, 184 people, or sixteen families, were then living in Twillingate, at least in the Summer months. Their number included 114 servants from England – settlers might hire as many as twenty men and women to help with the fishing. These fishing servants signed on for a term of one to three years. Normally a settler would divide about a third of his catch equally among the servants. With their help Twillingate fishers caught and dried 8,000 barrels, or 12,000 quintals, of fish.[4] Twillingate residents also produced seal oil valued at £440, a goodly sum in those days. The fledgling town boasted two ships plus sixteen smaller craft. English fishing vessels were also active off the islands, and caught 4,000 barrels of cod in 1738. In the Fall three vessels returned to England with the Twillingate catch, and 152 residents stayed behind for the Winter.[5]

In those days sharemen in Twillingate's cod fishery were reportedly paid off by 20 September each year. With their newfound "wealth" settlers supposedly spent their time dancing, drinking and playing cards. This round took them from house to house in the community and often resulted in fights. This state of affairs seems to have ended by the early 1800s, once Twillingate residents became more settled and prosperous.

....

Growth

Despite tense relations with the Native Beothuk, Twillingate continued to grow. In the years immediately after 1732 Tizzard was followed by other settlers, from Bonavista and elsewhere. By this time Twillingate had replaced Bonavista as the most northerly English settlement in Newfoundland. In 1739 Twillingate's Winter population was reported as 386, a figure which seems rather large, given that around 150 residents were reported the previous Winter. Still, there is little doubt that Twillingate's permanent settler population was on the rise in these years.

Along with the fishery, the town's growth can be attributed to the settlement's expanding land-based seal hunt. Laying directly in the path of Arctic ice flows, Twillingate was ideally suited for sealing. In 1742 Twillingate and Fogo produced seal oil to the value of £2,550. Still, Twillingate's marine resources, while considerable, weren't always dependable. During Vanbrugh's visit the populations of Twillingate and Fogo were about the same. Then, in 1786, Twillingate suffered through a particularly bad fishery; its population that year fell to only a third of Fogo's.

....

Wars and Privateers

Such setbacks never permanently curtailed Twillingate's growth, any more than military troubles did. During the Revolutionary War (1775-83) the town was troubled by privately-outfitted American warships, or privateers, commissioned under a "letter of marque" to attack enemy shipping. According to Prowse, Twillingate planters suffered some of the Colony's most severe attacks at the Americans' hands. In the Spring of 1779, for example, a small privateer armed with only four guns raided the settlement. Had a warship been nearby the little vessel would probably not have dared to attack. Unfortunately there was no protection, and the Americans were able to capture a vessel owned by merchant John Slade (1719-92). A cargo of fish was taken and the privateers broke open Slade's stores, distributing the contents to the "poor inhabitants" of Twillingate.

American privateer, early nineteenth century

After their successful foray the rebels, as the British called their American opponents, headed to Labrador. There they once again attacked property belonging to Slade. Governor Richard Edwards (c.1715-95) made extensive preparations to ward off this kind of assault, but the Americans knew to confine their incursions to the early Spring and late Fall when British men-of-war were not on the Newfoundland station. For his part Slade did not take the attacks passively, outfitting several of his own vessels, including Captain Marmaduke Hart's twenty-four gun *Exeter*, as privateers. The raids on Twillingate must have made some impact on local military planning. When Britain and the United States went to war again in 1812 engineers suggested mounting cannon at Crow and Carter Points to guard the harbour entrance and protect the growing fishing community.

Neither the War of 1812 nor the Napoleonic Wars seriously disturbed the peace of Twillingate and the Isles. Nevertheless, letters written to English merchants John and William Fryer in 1809 suggest that there was some indirect suffering caused by the conflicts. On 4 June Walter Ogden of Twillingate wrote that he had sent the merchants a letter and a small bill by "Mr. Coabins schooner" the previous Fall, but that everything in the vessel was lost when she was captured by the French. In 1809 an Anglo-French conflict had been raging for the best part of twenty years; like their Cousins across the sea, Isles residents were suffering from war-weariness. A 10 June letter to the Fryers from William Newbury and J. Wagg of Fogo lamented that "...[w]e should be glad if you could send us the good news of Peace But God knows when the end of this War will be..."[6]

....

Continued Prosperity

When the American Revolution ended in 1783 the French Shore boundary was redrawn as part of the peace negotiations. The area south of Cape St. John was thereafter excluded from French influence. This increased Twillingate's importance as an English fishing settlement. A Labrador fishery had been started in the community in the 1760s. For the next two hundred years vessels would be outfitted each Spring for the journey to Labrador and the Summer fishery. Other resources like timber, seals and salmon also attracted settlers, most of whom originated from Dorsetshire. Despite the setback of 1786, Twillingate's resident population, including Durrell (Farmer's Arm), reached 400 in 1798. This number doubled by 1819, and increased to 1,315 in 1836. By 1857 the population stood at 2,348, including clergy, a doctor, mechanics, fishermen and merchants. With its good harbour and proximity to rich fishing grounds, Twillingate grew steadily over the next 100 years, becoming one of Newfoundland's great fishing ports. In 1857 Twillingate boasted some 400 fishing vessels with 793 nets and seines. About forty vessels were also engaged in the seal fishery. Twillingate residents owned around 1,000 farm animals, such as pigs, milk cows, sheep, goats and horses. A variety of crops were grown including 7,141 barrels of potatoes, 154 barrels of turnips, and non-food crops like hay; nearly 3,000 kilograms of butter were churned and nine boats built.

....

The Cholera Scare

Sadly, progress was only one side of Twillingate's story. The fishery failure of 1786, and the round of military conflicts weren't the last difficulties the community faced. In the nineteenth century few years could have been worse than 1832-3. The Summer of 1832 saw Twillingate attempting to deal with the threat of a cholera epidemic. In that year the disease was raging in Great Britain and British North America. The Newfoundland authorities imposed a quarantine on St. John's and the larger outports, while establishing local boards of health. As a centre for several fisheries, Twillingate was regarded as a potential entry point for the contagion. A contemporary noted "...that the disease may be brought [into Twillingate] from the French shore and Labrador by fishing or trading vessels..."[7]

The Provincial Archives hold microfilm copies of many letters written to the Colonial Office from Twillingate in 1832-3. These documents detail community leaders' plans to implement quarantine regulations. In June of 1832 Robert Tremblett (c.1794-1842), newly-appointed health officer for Twillingate, noted that a Committee had been formed "...for the purpose of examining schooners and vessels bound to this port to prevent as much as possible the Cholera...from being brought amongst the inhabitants."[8] Tremblett was one of nineteen men on the Committee, which included Rev. John Chapman, Andrew Pearce (1772-1841), Twillingate's first collector of customs, and his Son, Abraham Akerman Pearce (1806-81), a longtime Court Clerk in the community.

By September Tremblett and his colleagues had engaged a guard boat to watch the entrance to Twillingate harbour lest any infected vessels enter the port. John Moore was employed as pilot and quarantine officer, followed by Edward Burt. Moore and Burt were assisted by other residents, who took turns in rotation. A charge to Burt dated 29 October 1832, noted that he was expected "...to proceed to the Harbours[*sic*] mouth in the watch at Day light...and to remain on watch until half an hour after sunset unless a sail should be seen in the offing, and should that be the case not to come in till you have spoken to [the] vessel & brought her in safely..."[9] By late November, with no more foreign arrivals expected, the guard boat was discontinued and Burt discharged. Around this time the government despatched anti-cholera medicines to the district via John Peyton, these being entrusted to Tremblett at Twillingate, and to a Slade Company agent at Fogo.

The threat had not ended. Cholera plagued the UK and British North America again in 1833. A Quarantine Act was proclaimed by the fledgling Newfoundland Legislature, established only the year before.[10] In the Summer of 1833 the Twillingate Committee hired a new quarantine officer, James Rice, after some difficulty in filling the post. It seemed that everyone wanted "extravagant wages" to take on the responsibility. Rice agreed to a salary of ten shillings per vessel examined, a sum to be increased if his season's fish catch suffered as a result of his quarantine duties. Rice went on to inspect some sixteen craft from 2 June to 18 October, including the Brigantine *Otter* from Poole and Fogo, the schooner *Lord Wellington* from Cadiz, and the brig *Atlantic* out of Poole.

....

Starvation?

As authors Melvin Baker and Janet Miller Pitt observe, Newfoundland was spared the scourge of cholera through the 1830s, but even as the Colony celebrated its escape from the disease in 1832, another serious crisis was in the offing for Twillingate. The details of this new crisis can be found in letters from Tremblett, Pearce and Chapman to the St. John's authorities. On 28 September Chapman noted that the season's fishery had been very poor due to the "innumerable masses of ice on the fishing grounds up to a very late period, about to the end of the caplin season..." He also blamed the severe weather conditions for "...the great failure of the potatoe[*sic*] crop in this part..." and predicted that the coming Winter would be one "...of greater distress than ever happened before in this vicinity..."[11]

In November the failed potato harvest became even more serious when provisions expected from Poole failed to arrive. Chapman felt that unless the schooner *Elizabeth* made it safely to St. John's for bread, flour and other foodstuffs, the situation would be grim, placing "...numbers in this vicinity in such a state of distress as never was felt before in this part..."[12] Writing from St. John's, Thomas Bennett informed the Colonial Secretary that many fishers in the Twillingate area had returned home from the French Shore fishery without buying any Winter provisions, wrongly believing that they could purchase such goods from local dealers.

On 2 February 1833 a Committee was formed of merchants and leading citizens hoping to allay some of the distress, and provide supplies to those in absolute want. Chapman singled out a number of people for particular thanks, including Andrew Pearce Sr., John Colbourne, and two agents of the Slade firms. Chapman asked that the Governor send forty to fifty barrels of potatoes for seed, as there were none whatever in the neighbourhood. Though

Chapman blamed some residents as the authors of their own distress, the efforts of the missionary and Committee must still be applauded. Likewise, another relief Committee was formed at Herring Neck, under Messrs., Randle, Stucky and Warren, which received a gift of provisions from the generous inhabitants of Fogo, whose distress was obviously less severe.

Exactly what happened to any particular Twillingate residents is uncertain; perhaps some actually starved to death, or came very close. It *is* certain that the town overcame the difficulties of 1832-3, though this wasn't the last time of hardship townsfolk had to face.

....

Nineteenth Century Hardships

Records left by Stipendiary Magistrate John Peyton Jr. (See Chapter Six) provide another record of the suffering endured by Twillingate and Isles residents in the nineteenth century. The miserable Winter of 1832-3 was preceded by fishery failures in 1815 and 1822, the latter on the heels of a Winter of scarcity similar to that a decade later.

On the plus side, Peyton's correspondence makes clear that even in those days the Colony made some provision for persons who could not provide for themselves. In one instance an elderly man and his Wife residing at Herring Neck, "wholly destitute of any means for support," were provided with about £3/9/0 worth of provisions for a three month period. A widow resident at Twillingate received a similar amount. The system also helped those who were rendered unable to work. In one case this benefited a fisherman crippled during exposure to severe February weather. Peyton also sent his superiors in St. John's lists of persons unable to pay for "medicine or medical advice," suggesting that some provision was made for settlers' health – Twillingate had its own resident doctor, though no hospital, by this time.

Peyton's missives give some background into the hardships settlers routinely faced. In a letter of October 1853 Peyton informed the Commissioners of the Poor that the previous year's shore fishery had been a bad one for many settlements. The years 1848 to 1852 saw repeated fishery failures that left many bay residents in extreme poverty. This was compounded by another potato crop failure, this time due to disease. Most NDB settlers were English, but for recent Irish immigrants this must have brought back horrendous memories of the great potato famine in their homeland. Inland, Gander Bay experienced a poor salmon fishery, causing much misery there as well. For a few people road building provided some able-bodied relief, but Peyton felt the Gander Bay settlers were too far away for such projects to be of much use. Attached to Peyton's appeal on the residents' behalf was a list of fifteen names from Twillingate, Moreton's Harbour, Herring Neck and Tizzard's Harbour (among others) whom Peyton knew to be in need of relief all Winter long. This was a pattern repeated many times over in pre Confederation Newfoundland, and these poor souls were just some of many. In 1860 Peyton sent another report of misery due to fishery and potato crop failure, this time accompanied by a measles epidemic.

John Peyton Jr.

....

Twillingate's Historic Churches I – St. Peter's Anglican

Suffering can test one's faith, but luckily there was no shortage of religious fervour in nineteenth century Twillingate. Even so, the trappings of this faith took some time to appear. As we've seen, the town was settled in the early 1700s, but for many years there was little provision for organized religious worship. In its first decades the community did not have its own clergyman, much less any churches. This deficiency was finally rectified in the mid 1800s. The result was one of the most beautiful, and oldest, church buildings on the Isles – St. Peter's Anglican. Much of what we now know about the building's early history, and that of its predecessor, comes from the diary of Mr. Joseph Pearce.

No church can function without clergy. Twillingate's first resident clergyman was John Hillyard (Born c.1771), who arrived in 1799 and remained until 1802. Hillyard is thought to have been a Congregationalist, or even a Baptist. He was succeeded by Rutler (or Rutley) Morris, who only remained for about a year. Both men appear to have taught day school during their tenures. In the early 1800s residents petitioned the Anglican Society for the Propagation of the Gospel (SPG) to send a regular minister, whom they agreed to pay themselves. In response to their petition Rev. John Leigh (c.1789-1823) arrived in the community on 3 October 1816.

The climate at Twillingate was not conducive to the reverend's health, especially after he contracted scurvy. In 1819 he was sent to preach in the more developed settlement of Harbour Grace. Leigh had the distinction of being the only Anglican minister to serve as a Newfoundland Justice of the Peace, and it was while serving in this capacity at Harbour Grace that Leigh created a controversy by ordering a man flogged. It was not the type of punishment Leigh imposed that provoked comment, but the number of lashes administered – thirty-six. Still, Leigh was normally a compassionate man and strongly advocated the case of the indigenous Beothuk. While living at Twillingate the reverend compiled a list of 200 Beothuk words from a Native woman called Demasduit.

At the time of Leigh's arrival the first St. Peter's Anglican Church was built, although its construction was supposedly of poor quality. The church building was not consecrated until 1 July 1827, at which time ninety-three people were confirmed.[13] The community was made up of Wesleyans as well as Anglicans, and initially all Twillingate's population – excepting about thirty Roman Catholics – attended the Anglican church.

Rev. Leigh was succeeded by Reverend Thomas Greenshill Laugharne (or Laughorne. c.1794-1844). During his tenure the Anglican congregation in Twillingate stood at 550, with numbers on the rise. However, all was not well during Laugharne's incumbency. In 1823 a number of prominent Twillingate residents, including Robert Tremblett, Andrew Pearce Sr., Richard Newman and James Rice, sent a letter of complaint to the Governor for transmission to the Bishop of London. The letter complained that Laugharne lacked "good morals," and that many persons had stopped attending divine services. As a result Laugharne was removed from the Parish and sent off to visit "outharbours" around St. John's, where he could be closely monitored.

Laugharne was replaced by the third Rector, John C. Chapman (See above), who stayed on at Twillingate for twenty years.

By Chapman's day St. Peter's had become too small for its growing congregation. A meeting was held at the original church in May 1838 to discuss construction of a replacement, and work began on the new building six months later. The original church continued in use as a parish hall, Sunday school and day school until 1870, when another parish hall was built. The new church's cornerstone was laid by Collector of Customs Pearce in 1839. The first service was held at St. Peter's on 11 December 1842, although it was another two years before the building was completed. The spire on the church's tower was finished by William J. Murphy on 14 September 1844. In 1845 the new St. Peter's was consecrated by Bishop Feild, and its first minister was Rev. Thomas Boone. Seating in St. Peter's was provided for almost 900 people, a number later increased to 1,000. The total construction cost for St. Peter's was about £1,000. £100 was donated by a pair of English religious societies, while £10 came from the Newfoundland church. The remainder of the money was all raised from the local congregation. This fine building was modelled on St. James' Church in Poole, the ancestral home of many early Twillingate settlers.

St. Peter's chandeliers were from St. James'. They were purchased after the Poole church switched to gaslight in 1844, and were one of several gifts donated by John Slade Jr. The chandeliers were first lighted on 24 August 1845, just four days after their arrival. These were but one of many donations given to the church by Twillingate's merchant community over the years. The chancel was extended in 1884 as a memorial to Edwin Duder, along with a memorial plaque, both given through the generosity of Duder's Son. The work was carried out by the Father and Son team of Titus and Alfred Manuel, who between them put in over 2,000 hours of work. Titus received fourteen cents an hour, his Son, ten.

In the early twentieth century St. Peter's suffered a major setback when, on 27 January 1915 the congregation lost its rectory to fire. As the *Twillingate Sun* reported:

> Wednesday morning...the cry of fire went round...Many men rushed to the scene, but quick as they were the fire was quicker, and even the first comers could not reach the head of the stairs against the reeking smoke which filled everything, and was already pouring out under the eves...[A]s no fire fighting apparatus was available, and water was scarce little progress was made...Within an hour after the first alarm the building was in ashes...

> It is not definitely known how the fire started, but it began in the south east bed room in a clothes closet next [to] the chimney (which must have been defective, as it collapsed very early in the fire)...
>
> The building is a comparatively new one having been completed only a few years ago, and cost about 1700 exclusive of the material taken from the old parsonage. It was completely free of debt, and the tax on St. Peter's and St. Andrew's congregations will be heavy...[14]

Parishioners met their hardship with resilience. A new residence for the minister was begun on the foundations of the old parsonage, under Mr. R. Hinds as voluntary foreman. By mid March the roof was up and shingling due to begin. In June the contract for finishing the interior was awarded to builder John Roberts, his very first contract. The new rectory was originally three storeyed, with the top floor meant to accommodate guests such as visiting clergy. In later years, as the town became less isolated, and long stop-overs unnecessary, the third floor was removed. This rectory remained in use until the early 1970s when a new one was built next door. Incumbent minister Reverend John Spencer then approached his congregation with the idea of turning the old structure into a museum. The idea was approved, and the Twillingate Museum and Craft Shop is still housed in the old church rectory.

Construction of a new parsonage was not the only change for St. Peter's. A pipe organ was installed in 1897 to coincide with Queen Victoria's Diamond Jubilee. For over 100 years the church used traditional lighting methods. In 1949 it was decided to switch both the church and its parish hall (See below) to electric lights. In those days there was no general electrical provider to most Newfoundland communities, so the church needed to buy its own generator. To raise the money the congregation put off plays and held other fund-raisers. An order was then placed with Lloyd Hann of Wesleyville for a 5,000 watt generating plant to illuminate the premises. The old chandeliers were kept, but converted to electric lighting. Almost fifty years later the church was given a new distinction. On 18 April 1998 St. Peter's was designated a heritage structure by the Heritage Foundation of Newfoundland and Labrador.

In 1914 the congregation received a new parish hall, replacing the structure built in 1870. The ground floor of the new hall was used as a day school through to the 1960s. The building's second story was used not only as a Sunday school, but also for church socials and meetings. Like St. Peter's, the parish hall is still used today.

St. Peter's Church (right), with the parish hall and former rectory (left)

A second Anglican church on the Twillingate Islands was St. Andrew's on South Island. The original opened on 7 December 1879, and was then the only church located at Durrell. This structure was torn down in 1960 and replaced with a more modern house of worship. The new St. Andrew's cost around $7,000.00 to build, excluding some $3,000.00 worth of free labour. The church officially opened on 2 July 1961 under incumbent minister Reverend Raymond Brett (1931-2015). With its building debts quickly repaid, St. Andrew's was consecrated by Bishop J. A. Meadon on 27 August. When the church opened the congregation stood at some seventeen families. By 2008 parishioners numbered a mere ten persons, many of whom were seniors. It was decided to close the church. The last service was held at St. Andrew's on 6 July 2008, and the building was officially deconsecrated. The ceremony was presided over by Bishop David Torraville, a former parish priest at Twillingate, and by rector Rev. Daphne Parsons. Rev. Brett, there for the opening of the church nearly fifty years earlier, was also in attendance.

....

Twillingate's Historic Churches II – Methodist/United

The second St. Andrew's had a fairly short life, but three other Twillingate churches had longer histories. Like St. Peter's, they are survivors from the nineteenth century, though one is greatly-altered; neither is still in use as a church. All were built to serve Twillingate's largest denomination, now part of the United Church of Canada. This congregation, first known as Methodist, has roots at Twillingate nearly as long as the Anglican. A history of the faith's development at Twillingate and Notre Dame Bay – printed by the *Twillingate Sun* – was written in 1931 by W. Edgar Mercer, a reverend and Chair of the Twillingate Presbytery of the United Church.

When missionaries first expressed interest in tending to the flock in Newfoundland permission was given more readily to members of the official English church. In time dissenting Protestant faiths, and eventually Roman Catholics, were allowed in to perform missionary work and set up community churches. One of the most important of the early Protestant sects was the Wesleyan or Methodist. The Methodist/Wesleyan faith grew out of the established Church of England, and more specifically from the ideas of the Reverend John Wesley (1703-91). By the mid 1700s the movement was established on the Island of Newfoundland.

One of the first Methodist ministers to reach Notre Dame Bay was Rev. George Smith, who in 1794 extended his missionary work north from Carbonear as far as Green Bay. In the early 1800s Smith was recorded as holding services at Twillingate in the home of one Marian Whellor. Early accounts of Methodism in Twillingate tell of friction between their congregation and that of the established Church of England. In the settlement's first years relations were apparently amicable, and the two groups shared a common meeting house. Due to a lack of clergy, the meeting house fell into disuse by 1815. The Wesleyans hoped to use the old meeting house for their own services, but were attacked by a mob armed with sticks and other weapons. The violence was almost certainly not spontaneous, as the attackers were supported by certain local officials and a Church of England lay reader. One of the Wesleyan leaders, Mr. Newman, was dragged outside and the door padlocked. The matter was finally settled when the Methodist congregation agreed to pay £70 to the Anglicans, who gave up their claim to the meeting house.

By the year 1831 a number of Wesleyans were meeting at the homes of Brother Moores, Back Harbour; Brother Roberts, Bluff Head Cove; Brother S. Wheeler, Twillingate Harbour, and Brother Dowland at Little Harbour. The "New Society" as they were called, held cottage or class meetings. The Methodist adherents had no Minister of their own, but Rev. John S. Addey, a founder of Green Bay Methodism, may have visited Twillingate in these years. The congregation grew to such an extent that it was decided a chapel should be built. In 1842 Twillingate and district received its first official Methodist minister.

Reverend William Marshall (1811-46) was Twillingate's first resident

Methodist missionary, and his ministries took in all of Green Bay as well. Until the first Chapel was completed in 1843, Marshall continued the tradition of meeting in private homes.[15] Rev. Addey is thought to have played a significant role in securing Marshall's appointment, and Addey was revered by local Methodists for many years afterwards. Marshall's duties meant extensive travels to perform services like baptisms and marriages. His first marriage was solemnized at Change Islands on 9 October 1842. The first baptism took place at Exploits Harbour on 30 June 1842. Marshall's first baptism and marriage at Twillingate took place that same year. Reverend Marshall died at the age of only thirty-four. At the time of his death church membership stood at 131, with seventy-six children attending Sunday School. Reverend Marshall is buried on the grounds of Twillingate's South Side United Church. A Sunday school, built in 1880, was named in his honour. The Marshall Hall still stands, but has been converted into apartments.

Twillingate's old South Side United Church, now the Northeast Church Museum (centre). The former Marshall Hall can be seen to the right of the church

Marshall was succeeded by Rev. John S. Peach, who ministered to the district for four years. He was particularly noted for his work with the Sunday School. Peach was then followed by Rev. John Brewster. Brewster arrived in

Newfoundland during 1845, and was stationed at Twillingate from 1850-3. During his pastorate Twillingate's parsonage was renovated and finished. Brewster also organized the first Trustee Board in the town. Reverend Thomas Fox was the next Minister, remaining for three years. Fox was succeeded by Paul Prestwood (1856-9), then Thomas Harris (1859-62), and later (1862-3) Charles Comben. Harris became the first clergyman responsible for the new circuit of Twillingate and Moreton's Harbour. As of 1863 Comben had gone, and the circuit's new minister was Rev. James A. Duke. Duke remained for three years, but was not in the best of health, and found the district responsibilities difficult. During his first year Moreton's Harbour and surrounding area were separated from Twillingate. By the end of 1865 Methodist numbers at Twillingate stood at 162. The next year John Goodison arrived to take charge of the church in Twillingate.

A major setback occurred during Goodison's tenure when on Thursday morning, 13 February1868, both the chapel and parsonage on South Side burned down. Goodison discovered the fire and raised the alarm, but the blaze couldn't be stopped during the bitter, cold day. A strong Northerly breeze only fanned the conflagration. Funds were raised to replace both structures, and the new church was finished during the tenure of Rev. Henry Laird Cranford, who took over in 1869. At the time it was built South Side Methodist Church was one of the largest churches in Newfoundland. Including the galleries that ran all around its interior, it could seat about 1,000 persons. The pews were constructed according to an old pattern with straight backs, and the pulpit was noted for its height. When first constructed the church had a pair of low spires, created by Jacob Wheeler, and fashioned almost like a hand "with the index finger pointing to the skies," as Mercer put it.

The church built by Reverends Goodison and Cranford stands proudly on South Island. Although no longer used for services, it survives as the North-East Church Museum. The building was taken over by the North East Church Heritage Association Inc. in 1987 after the church was deconsecrated. This beautiful building has been used to stage events like plays and concerts, and the grounds are still home to a church cemetery, although no new plots are being added. Several of the Parish's former incumbents are buried here, including its first, William Marshall. Among the church's features is its 1903 Bevington pipe organ (See Chapter Fourteen). From the end of Cranford's incumbency through to 1929 the South Side Methodist Church was served by about twenty more pastors, and a number of important developments occurred in this period.

Twillingate's old North Side United Church, c.1900

A second Methodist church was built at North Side in 1881 during Rev. Thomas W. Atkinson's tenure (1879 to 1882). Often called "the Church on the Hill," by its old-time parishioners, the North Side United Church was built at the top of Church Hill, named for St. Peter's, located at its base. A meeting was first held to discuss the need for a new church in May 1881, and a Committee was formed headed by Reverend Atkinson to put the plans into effect. The piece of land used to build the Church was supplied by William Waterman & Company; Josiah Roberts and Samuel Manual were given the building job, along with Andrew Linfield as contractor. When completed the church measured about twenty by ten metres. It had three galleries, plus a choir gallery that held a magnificent pipe organ. Smaller than its counterpart on South Side, the North Side church's auditorium and galleries could still seat around 500 parishioners. At the time it was built the church's placement atop a hill gave its tower the highest altitude of any structure in Twillingate. The church's pews were described as comfortable, but designed with the old straight backs, like those in the South Side church. The pulpit was also noted for its elegance. The church had a history of more than a century. It opened for worshippers on 1 September 1881. Rev. Webb Percival, Chair of the St. John's District, travelled from St. John's for the opening and dedication. Rev. F. R. Duffill was named the first Junior Minister for the church (under Atkinson), and was succeeded by W. T. D. Dunn. The first sexton was Samuel Manuel.

The building still stands, but has been converted into efficiency units, and its tower is gone.

A venerable building associated with the North Side United Church was its old Sunday school, Fraser Hall. The hall was built sometime after 1902 in memory of Reverend George C. Fraser, who died that year. Fraser was only forty-seven when he passed away, having served the Twillingate Methodist parish for about a year. Despite his short tenure, Fraser was much respected by his parishioners, as the construction of Fraser Hall testifies. For more than fifty years the hall played host to Methodist/United children as they learned their Sunday lessons. In June 1959 the parish built a new Fraser Hall across the street, nearer to the church. The old hall was then taken over by the Provincial Department of Highways, and its most recent use was as the town of Twillingate garage. The historic building was earmarked for renovation, but was found to be structurally unsound and demolished in June 2008. The second Fraser Hall remains, but it has been put to other uses, including the Twillingate Golden Age Club's meeting place; it is now a nightclub.

The Church on the Hill and the South Side church weren't the only places at which local Methodists worshipped. The small settlement of Little Harbour, on South Island, had its own church which opened for worshippers on 10 May 1885. Its inaugural service was presided over by Rev. H. Hatcher from Moreton's Harbour. Its first organ was installed in 1914, and a bell was added in 1924. The Little Harbour church closed in 1987. Still standing, the building is now privately owned.

When the Notre Dame Bay Memorial Hospital was built at Twillingate following the First World War new duties were added to local pastoral work. United Church ministers were now responsible for tending to patients, some of whom must have been suffering greatly. In 1931, on the heels of the hospital opening, the Church decided to erect its own memorial to the servicemen of the Great War. A belfry was constructed on the hill behind the South Side church, using free labour supervised by Frederick Phillips and Edward Smith. It was fitted with a bell made by Messrs. Mears and Stainbanks, Church Bell Foundry, England. The bell was inscribed with the words, "Twillingate Circuit Memorial Bell, erected 1931." In addition to commemorating local veterans, the bell would ring in tribute to Methodism's hundredth anniversary at Twillingate, and for the North Side Church's golden jubilee. A brass plaque made by Maile & Son of London, England was fitted to the belfry. It read in part: "To the glory of God and in grateful memory of the men of this Church who fell in the Great War, 1914-1918...Also to commemorate the Centenary of Twillingate Methodism, 1831-1931, and the jubilee of the North Side Church, 1881-1931..."[16] The belfry on the hill was used until the 1950s when a new bell tower was built onto the church itself. The plaque was then mounted to the side of the church where it remains.

The Memorial Belfry was overseen by Reverend Mercer, who assumed charge of the Circuit in 1929. In his book Mercer made note of the growing strength of his church in Twillingate. By the late 1800s Methodists outnumbered Anglicans in Twillingate – in 1884 the town had 2,477 Methodists to only 1,109 Anglicans. Even today Methodism's successor, the United Church, still has the largest congregation in Twillingate. In May 1987 a new United church was opened on South Side, a project for which the local United Church Women helped raise $240,000.00.

....

The Long Point Lighthouse

The building of parish churches reflected Twillingate's coming of age as a community. Its growing importance was reflected in other ways. The settlement was a customs port for foreign trade, and a focal point for northeast coast shipping. Increased shipping traffic prompted the building of Long Point Lighthouse, Crow Head, as part of a network of thirty-three lighthouses stretching from Twillingate to Port aux Basques. Funding for the structure was provided by an 1874 Act of the General Assembly of Newfoundland, which set aside twelve thousand dollars for the purpose. The area's first light house, the Long Point light was constructed mainly to aid passage around a shallow underwater feature named Old House Shoal (Possibly the same feature now known as "Old Harry"). This shoal claimed many vessels until the lighthouse was built. Since then wrecks there have been practically nil. A contract for the light's construction was signed between the contractors Messrs Coleman and Kelly, and Board of Works Chairman Charles Duder. Coleman and Kelly were to receive the sum of $5,700.00, with the expectation that work on the light tower and associated buildings would be finished before 1 October 1875. The builders were paid in three installments, with the final payment due when Superintendent of Lighthouses John T. Nevill, or another surveyor, officially certified the quality of the work. The facility opened in 1876.

Standing at about eighty-five metres above sea level, the lighthouse was built of brick, an unusual construction material at the time, iron being preferred for most important lighthouses. The decision to use brick was probably questioned when the tower developed a large crack in 1885 – this damage was caused by the tower's own weight. The crack was soon repaired, but another formed in 1929. This resulted from a powerful undersea earthquake off the Grand Banks, the same seismic event that triggered a tsunami (tidal wave) on the Burin Peninsula. After this second event the Long Point tower was reinforced with an extra foot of concrete and iron rods. Most of the original material for the lighthouse likely came from England, and was dragged up over Long Point's cliffs. Remains of the old landing area survived into recent times. Originally the light was turned by revolving gear powered by a system of weights hanging down the tower, a system that lasted until the 1950s. Long Point's revolving light is now powered by electricity.

The Long Point light tower, oil on canvas, by Elizabeth Jenkins

The lighthouse's first assistant keeper was James Henry Preston of Devon, an expert on lighthouse mechanisms. Preston worked under Samuel Roberts of Bluff Head Cove. Roberts remained on the job for sixteen years, until 1892. He was then succeeded by his Son, Robert Samuel "Bob Sam" Roberts. For nearly a century the job of principal light keeper at Long Point was a family affair. Bob Sam was succeeded by his Son, John Thurston "Jack" Roberts in 1927. Jack Roberts served no less than forty-two years at the facility, his tenure ending in 1969.

Long Point is now one of Newfoundland's few manned lighthouses, although the keepers no longer live there. In February 2005 the Federal Department of Fisheries and Oceans transferred ownership of most of the lighthouse property to the town of Crow Head; the light tower and an office used by the keepers were retained under government control. At the transfer ceremony the lighthouse was designated a Federal heritage building, recognising its historic and cultural importance to the area. On the weekend of 1-3 September 2006 the Long Point Lighthouse celebrated its 130th anniversary, with commemorative events organized by the Twillingate Islands

Tourism Association (TITA), which operates the lighthouse as a tourist facility on behalf of Crow Head.

With its long history it comes as no surprise that the lighthouse (reportedly) has a ghost or two. As paranormal researcher Dale Jarvis recounts, one spirit is credited with saving a life. An old story alleges that in the early 1900s one of the light keepers fell twelve metres from the top of the lighthouse shaft. This keeper may have been trying to free the revolving gear's cables and weights, which sometimes tangled. The fall onto a hard brick floor should have killed or gravely injured the man. At the time there were no supports for the light keeper to grab onto. Just before he hit the unforgiving floor our keeper fell into the arms of a woman dressed in white, saving him from disaster. Normally, no one could safely catch a grown man falling twelve metres, and when the light keeper came to his senses the lady in white had vanished – to this day no one knows who the woman was.

Other strange events at Long Point revolve around an old tar mop that has been located at the tower's base for many years. Never used for its intended purpose, the tar mop has been kept around since it seems to have a life of its own. According to legend, the mop repeatedly changes position when no one is around. Like the woman in white, the story of the tar mop was passed down through the generations of light keepers, but no one knows its origins.

....

Judicial Infrastructure

From an early date Twillingate was a judicial centre in the Colony of Newfoundland. In 1824 the British Parliament passed "An Act for the Better Administration of Justice in Newfoundland..." This Act established the framework of the Colony's justice system, creating a supreme court and repealing the authority of the "fishing admirals," who had previously been charged with law enforcement in Newfoundland. Another result of the Act was the creation of three court districts. Twillingate was part of the Northern District, along with Harbour Grace, Trinity, Bonavista, Greenspond and Fogo.

Less than twenty years after passage of the Act geologist Joseph Beete Jukes (1811-69) visited Twillingate. In 1839 he was appointed geological surveyor for Newfoundland, spending about sixteen months completing his work. Apart from his invaluable geological records, Jukes' greatest contribution to posterity was his written account of life along the coast. During a stop-over at Twillingate contrary winds prevented Jukes from making a quick departure, and he was forced to stay in the town longer than he'd intended.

His stay produced a short but informative description of the criminal justice system in mid nineteenth century Twillingate. By this date the community had its own court house, built around 1836. This structure must have been the community's second court building, as there are records of a meeting held at Twillingate's court house in 1827. The second court house was a wooden building two storeys high, with a central tower of three storeys. Judicial proceedings were conducted in one large room, with lodgings for the jailer and one or two cells below. The judge's seat was a simple arrangement, consisting of a chair set upon a platform of boards with a table in front. A few extra chairs placed alongside the "dias" served for the sheriff and lawyers. Each side of the room was occupied by benches, one for the grand jury, the other for common juries. To consult on verdicts the common juries were taken outside by a constable and assembled on a large rock until a decision was reached. Jukes doesn't say so, but this probably led to speedy verdicts in cases tried on inclement days! A court house remained in use at Twillingate until fairly recently. The last one burned to the ground on 19 February 1968, a fate that claimed its predecessor in February 1883.

Court House (left), May 1935. Decorated for King George V's silver jubilee. Preston's Shop is at right

Besides presiding over the Twillingate Court House, district judges in Jukes' day travelled through the region dispensing justice in a hired merchant brig. The vessel was specially fitted with accommodations for everyone from the judge to the solicitor-general, clerks and constable. Jukes wondered what English judges would think about spending a month or two every year sailing over rough seas to perform their jobs.

Jukes' description mentions a constable, sheriff and jailer. In this era at least two of the three jobs were held by James Rice (1790-1872). Rice was born at Cullompton, Devonshire and was married to Ann Mary May of

Somerset. In his position as constable Rice was considered a minor court official with the power to serve writs and make arrests. Since he was also the town jailer Rice and his family lived in the court house. Documents held by the Provincial Archives make reference to Rice's role as Twillingate's constable. It was noted that he was paid fifteen pounds sterling out of a licence fund for the period from October 1832 to October 1833. In 1837 Constable Rice was recorded as earning £12/10/0 on a half-yearly basis.[17] Described as a "small, short man," Rice may also have been the sheriff, or *deputy* sheriff, Jukes mentioned. His Son, Richard Pigeon Rice, later campaigned to have the court house repaired while running for election as a MHA. The work was obviously needed. That same year (1882) a correspondent to the Sun newspaper, perhaps the younger Rice himself, described the Court House as "the pig's sty."

....

Education

Nineteenth century Twillingate saw new educational as well as judicial infrastructure. The islands' first day school was opened in October 1829. At the time education in Newfoundland was carried on by the Newfoundland School Society, a body organized by merchant Samuel Codner. William Walker was the Twillingate school's first teacher/principal, and it boasted a student enrollment of sixty. There was also an adult school operating under Walker's auspices, with an enrollment of fifty. Thirty years after Walker founded his school, a tea meeting was convened at Twillingate to discuss the prospects of education in the community. Held at merchant Edwin Duder's establishment, the meeting was attended by all prominent Twillingate residents. Although the level of education provided to the islands was "deplored," several years passed before further action was taken.

Significant innovations came from the Methodist church. In 1875 Reverend John Reay was granted permission to convene a board of education for the Twillingate-area. The board's first meeting was held at Twillingate's Wesleyan parsonage on 29 July. Reay was elected Chairman and secretary, with one pound allocated for the year's postage, stationary, and other supplies. A Sunday school at South Side and a chapel at Little Harbour were used for students until new schools were built. William Thomas Roberts and Jasper Dowland were appointed teachers for the two schools, at the rates of £40 and £25, respectively.

The Wesleyan board of education planned a school to serve Durrell's Arm, Jenkin's Cove and part of South Side. Other schools were anticipated for Ragged Point, Bluff Head Cove, Little Harbour and Purcell's Harbour. With the board's support, workmen completed the school houses, giving every second day in free labour. In 1896 a superior or high school was built at South Island, with A. Hoskins as Principal, succeeded by I .S. (later Dr.) LeDrew, in 1897. One of the driving forces behind the superior school was J. P. Thompson, founder and former owner of the *Twillingate Sun* newspaper. Thompson was a member of the Wesleyan board of education, and for several years its recording steward. Thompson's successor as Sun editor, George Roberts, also succeeded him on the education board.

Durrell Academy School. 1908

Like the Wesleyans, the Anglicans had their own school at Twillingate, St. Peter's, on North Side. John Peyton's correspondence makes reference to a school house begun at Back Harbour on 27 December 1866. An Anglican board school also operated at Durrell's Arm from the early 1870s. This facility was originally founded by schoolmistress Mrs. Hardiner twenty years earlier. As of 1872 enrollment was reported at thirty-nine.

During the 1800s there was even a Congregational School on South Side near where the modern high school now stands. By the early 1900s Congregationalist numbers had dwindled and their church was closed, the small parish having no minister. The property was sold to Dr. Woods. The old school house still stands, and is now used as a shed. In 1907 Twillingate boasted eight schools, two of them superior schools. The number of schools later increased to thirteen, three of these for older students. In later years the Salvation Army founded its own schools at Twillingate.

....

Bridges, Roads & More

As Twillingate's population grew, it was felt the town needed a bridge connecting the North and South Islands. In 1844 Magistrate Peyton sent a petition to the colonial Governor explaining the need for such a structure. In the petition he explained how residents of Twillingate had "...suffered great loss and inconvenience in consequence of not having a bridge across the...Tickle..." The Newfoundland Legislature approved £250 "to be appropriated in deepening the Tickle at Twillingate and in erecting a bridge across the same...,"[18] providing an equal amount of money was raised locally. With this provision met, Magistrate Peyton, along with John Slade, Abraham A. Pearce, and Samuel Prowse were appointed as a board of commissioners to see the work completed. Engineer William Thomas Wells was brought in from Nova Scotia to oversee the construction, at a rate of ten shillings per diem. Wells travelled to Twillingate on the vessel *Caledonia*, and the Slade merchant house paid £2/17/9 toward tools he would have difficulty purchasing locally.

The project got off to a good start, but it was not long before trouble arose. The commissioners accused Wells of not conducting himself "...with that sobriety and attention which we had a right to expect from you..." The engineer was further reprimanded for "gross negligence" and being absent from his duties. Wells was later fired, the Commissioners telling him that "..from and after this date [25 July 1844] we cannot recognise you as our servant and that you are at perfect liberty to seek any other service or employment you may think proper."[19] Following Wells' departure both Pearce and Prowse resigned from the Board.

Troubles aside, the bridge *was* eventually completed, and the board of commissioners remained active. In November 1853 new appointments to the board included Peyton, along with William Stirling, Charles Edmonds, John Meadus and John Colbourne. Shoal Tickle Bridge was repaired or replaced a number of times over the years, including 1907 and 1927. The latter project is mentioned in the published journal of John Froude, a local master mariner who worked on the concrete structure from July to August of that year. During construction a telephone line was put out of service, leading the local telephone company (See below) to bill the Highroads Commission for the cost of labour in putting the line back in service.

The old Tickle Bridge, c.1950

The bridge was just one part of the town's road network, something that few smaller outports would have had in the 1800s. Twillingate's old carriage roads were generally considered excellent, no mean feat in colonial Newfoundland! Its roads were described as clean, and made of whitish-brown gravel and limestone. This mixture baked to the hardness of concrete and was considered superb for cyclists. By 1906 the Twillingate islands had about sixty-four kilometres of roads.

Although good by the standards of the day, Twillingate's thoroughfares had their problems. In 1911 a *Twilllingate Sun* reader complained that Tickle Bridge was too narrow for carriage traffic; riders frequently had the paint scraped off their vehicles' wheels or risked losing them altogether. This reader felt that the local road board should widen the structure, but it seems this was not done at the time. By the 1930s new problems arose. The old roads weren't as well maintained as they had been twenty years earlier, and were never intended for automobile traffic.

Although its nineteenth century roads linked settlements on the Twillingate islands, they remained isolated from the outside world, despite the coastal boat service. This isolation was reduced in 1885 when Twillingate was first joined by telegraph to the New York, Newfoundland and London system. The line to Twillingate was installed under the auspices of engineer Alexander M. Mackay (1834-1905), formerly Superintendent of the Nova Scotia Telegraph. This branch line took Mackay through 547 kilometres of wilderness, and cost $45,000.00. The local telegraph office, which sent and received its first messages on 5 October 1885, was located in Twillingate's court building; the telegraph operator had an apartment there as well.

Seal of the Twillingate Telephone & Electric Company, Ltd.

By the early twentieth century the town could boast of its own Twillingate Telephone and Electric Company – Mackay had installed Newfoundland's first telephone at St. John's General Post Office in 1878. The Twillingate company originated in 1913 with *Twillingate Sun* editor William B. Temple and J. A. Templeton of the Bank of Nova Scotia as its promoters. The business was incorporated the following year. The company Directors originally intended to connect only prominent businesses, but expanded the system in response to public demand. While the company had no telephones in operation during 1914, by 1915 the Twillingate area was served by some thirty telephones, a number that had risen to forty in 1924. The telephone company was not meant to turn a large profit. As Temple explained, the business was "...just a mutual affair to give us a phone service around the town...and the amount of stock allowed any [share]holder is limited to $50.00 paid up..."[20] In the company's early days the importance of its service was not appreciated by all residents. In 1920 company secretary Arthur Manuel, through the pages of the *Twillingate Sun*, warned people hauling houses not to cut company lines without permission to gain clearance, thereby disrupting local telephone services! The company provided phone service to Twillingate until 1951, when its operations were taken over by Canadian National Telecommunications (CNT), which installed a dial exchange.

....

Merchants I – The Slades

Twillingate's activity and growth were stimulated by, and attracted, a number of merchant houses. English businessmen were lured by Twillingate's fine fishing grounds, and fitted out vessels to send to the islands for cod. During the community's early years merchant representatives conducted business through their ships. These arrived in Newfoundland each Spring, and in the Fall departed to Spain and Portugal where the fish was sold. The merchants often remained in England, and it was these West Country merchants who set the tone of the Newfoundland fishery for well over a century. In time the migratory fishery died out. Thereafter resident fishers were supplied by merchants, or their agents, who also lived in the community. The merchants imported food, fishing supplies and salt which they provided in return for Twillingate's salt fish. This marked the beginning of a barter system which lasted into the mid twentieth century. Under the "truck system," as it was known, many fishermen never received cash for their labour. This system was not unique to Twillingate, but was widespread throughout Newfoundland. Local merchants like those at Twillingate were in turn supplied by the Colony's largest merchant houses, based at St. John's.

It is reported that Twillingate's first resident merchants were the Nobles, who operated in the community until 1848. In the year 1790 the Noble family's fishing operation brought in £1,000, a substantial sum in the eighteenth century. As early as 1760 the Nobles bought nets, lines and cordage to sell to local fishers, and in turn purchased their catches. Nobles' main suppliers were the Slades of Poole, Dorsetshire.

The Slade mercantile business was founded by John Slade. Information uncovered by researcher Milt Anstey suggests that John was born in a village outside Poole, the Son of John Slade and his Wife, Mary (Hodder). Slade was baptised on 10 June 1718 at Winfrith Newburgh, Dorset. Slade biographer W. Gordon Handcock believes that the youth received some education, including an apprenticeship as a mariner. This was not surprising, given that the Slades hailed from the hinterland of Poole, a city that author Daniel Defoe (1660-1731) pronounced one of southern England's greatest seaports. In Defoe's era Poole carried on a considerable trade with Newfoundland, a connection that grew even more important in Slade's day.[21]

John Slade's earliest known sea voyages were made in the 1740s when he commanded a number of vessels from his home port to locales like Ireland and the Mediterranean. He travelled to Newfoundland in 1748 as master of the trader *Molly*, in the employ of Quaker merchant Joseph White. In 1751 Slade assumed command of the *Dolphin*, 100 tons, owned by William Kittier. Slade captained the *Dolphin* for two years, voyaging between Newfoundland, Poole and the Mediterranean, the last destination an important market for Newfoundland salt cod. By 1753 Slade had bought his own ship, the ninety ton *Little John*, and was trading on his own account.

Slade's career was also aided by an advantageous marriage to Martha, Daughter of influential Poole merchant John Hayter. Handcock feels that her inheritance and social standing greatly aided Slade's rise to prominence. From this union Slade's only legitimate Son, John Hayter (Haitor) Slade, was born.

Slade was one of a number of entrepreneurs who capitalized on French distractions during the Seven Year's War with England (1756-63), pushing north to White Bay and Labrador. Most of Slade's rivals withdrew after the Treaty of Paris was signed in 1763. He persevered, and ten years later opened a major branch of his business at Battle Harbour, Labrador. Interested in salmon and furs, the Slade firm's agents were active farther south in the Bay of Exploits, and on a smaller scale in Halls Bay. In the period 1764-70 Slade operated three to four ships – averaging sixty tons each – per annum in the Newfoundland trade.

Battle Harbour, Labrador, 1857. An early centre of the Slade business

His fishing crews worked out of Twillingate, Fogo and Tilting. With the support of his Poole neighbour, merchant Isaac Lester, Slade was made naval officer for Twillingate in 1774, being reappointed the next year. Unconcerned with a political career, this was the only official position John Slade ever sought or received. By the start of the American Revolution Slade was firmly ensconced in Twillingate, his main Newfoundland base of operations. Although these years were troubled ones for Slade, who suffered from natural disasters and raids by American vessels, his fleet grew to some fifteen to twenty craft, averaging almost 100 tons apiece. In 1782 the firm's fortunes were bolstered by the bankruptcy of rival Jeremiah Coughlan (*fl.* 1760-82). Unlike Coughlan, who was based at Fogo, the elder Slade ultimately did quite well out of the Newfoundland fishery. At his death in 1792 he left a fortune of around £70,000, an enormous sum in those days.

Slade had returned to Poole in 1777, leaving his Newfoundland and Labrador operations in the care of his Nephews John, Robert, Thomas and David, along with a Nephew by marriage, George N. Allen (The merchant had been grooming Son John Hayter Slade to take the company's reins, but this plan came to nothing following the younger Slade's death from smallpox). Sometimes referred to as the "Northern Slades," this new generation were pioneers of shipbuilding and salmon fishing in western Notre Dame Bay.

The family business tradition continued into another generation. A document held at the Provincial Archives records the Deed of Gift through which John Slade transferred his interest in the Twillingate branch of the business to Robert Slade, and John Slade Jr., Sons of his Brother, Reverend David Slade of Lytchell, Dorset. The document, dated 6 April 1815, states that, "...in consideration of five shillings...[Slade transferred]...all those Fishing Rooms or Plantations situate...at or near Twillingate...called Slade's Rooms...," the transaction including dwelling houses, storehouses, wharfs, stages, flakes, schooners, traps, etc.[22]

By the 1840s another John Slade Jr. was Newfoundland manager for Slade's at Twillingate. This John Slade died in 1847, before his twenty-ninth birthday. Arriving at Poole from Newfoundland aboard the schooner *Jessy* on 19 December 1846, he passed away at Thames Street on 9 January. John Slade Jr.'s short life was packed with activity. He became Fogo District's member of the Colonial House of Assembly in 1842, and promoted civic improvements at Twillingate. A monument to John Slade Jr. can be found at St. Andrews Anglican Church Cemetery in Fogo, where the family had a thriving branch.[23]

After John Jr's death his successor, Robert Slade, cut back on John Slade & Company's role in supplying fishers. By the Spring of 1852 Slades discontinued their practice of giving credit to dealers, operating only through cash or barter. That Fall Robert Slade offered all his local debtors a one-half rebate if the other half of their outstanding accounts were paid up right away. By 1870 the Slades had sold off all of their Fogo and Twillingate interests and ceased to trade in Newfoundland.

Another Poole firm connected to Slades was William Cox & Company, formerly Slade & Cox (See Chapter Four). The Cox firm did business in Twillingate, Fogo and Greenspond, handling a good deal of these towns' fish products. By the end of the 1860s Cox & Company was also gone, closing their Twillingate operations in 1868.

....

Merchants II – Slade Successors

Hodges. Many of Slade's successors (or *their* successors) are still remembered in Twillingate. Like the West Country English merchants, Twillingate's resident houses bought from inshore fishermen, outfitted schooners for the Labrador fishery, and sold large quantities of salt cod to foreign markets.

Hodge's Cove, Twillingate, Winter, 1957.
Hodge family home and business premises at left

At one time the islands were home to more than a dozen fish merchants, including the Hodges at Path End, North Side. The founder of Hodge's Twillingate enterprise was Richard Dorman Hodge. Born at Crewkerne, Somerset in 1845, Hodge started in business with Cox & Company. During the 1860s both Richard and his Brother, Thomas, were mentioned in connection with the business by the firm's Fogo agent, Charles Edmonds. It is clear from Edmonds' letters that the Hodges worked closely with another Cox Company stalwart, William Waterman (*fl.* 1867-90), to whom they were related. When Waterman founded his own company in 1867 the Hodges were in on the ground floor, becoming partners in the enterprise.

Richard arrived at Twillingate in 1871, along with his Wife, Grace Helen (Purkis). Richard, and Brother Thomas, acquired Twillingate premises formerly owned by the Slades, which they operated along with members of the Waterman family as William Waterman & Co. By the 1880s the Waterman business was in decline, and Richard later ran the Twillingate branch mainly on his own account (Thomas having moved to St. John's). It was reported that by 1895 Richard had become insolvent, perhaps as a result of a major bank crash the previous year (See below). His Brother, John Wheedon Hodge (c.1851-1936), took control of the business, though Richard continued to be actively involved.

Richard Hodge died on 3 April 1908 and his Sons, Arthur H. (1881-1963) and Cyril L. ("Bertie." 1887-1963), operated the firm's Twillingate branch under John Wheedon's direction. When John Hodge retired to Toronto in 1918 the business, thenceforth called Hodge Brothers, was run exclusively by the two siblings. Arthur managed the business office and acted as the firm's express agent, while his Brother was shop boss. On 22 September 1916 their Brother, Harvey Lionel Hodge, enlisted in London with the Honourable Artillery Company. He was killed fighting in France the following year, aged thirty-four.

Bertie Hodge remained a bachelor all his life, but in 1927 Arthur, one of the local hospital's original Directors, married Elsie B. Wood. Born in Massachusetts, and a registered nurse, Elsie was a Niece of Twillingate doctor Albert J. Wood. Elsie had worked with Dr. Wilfred Grenfell (1865-1940), who later performed the Hodges' marriage ceremony. She was serving as a volunteer at the local hospital when she met her future Husband. The Mother of two girls, Mrs. Hodge was closely involved with the Girl Guide movement, and was a devoted supporter of St. Peter's Anglican Church. She also helped establish the hospital's Well Baby Clinic, and was a founder of the Twillingate Hustler's Club theatrical group. In 1943 Mrs. Hodge became an original member of the Twillingate Library Board, serving as its secretary for many years. She was also an advocate for municipal government and improved roads; in the late 1950s Mrs. Hodge wrote a poem titled "Who Seconds the Motion?" to promote these dual causes.

Known for entertaining foreign visitors like Portugese fishermen, the Hodges remained in business at Twillingate until the early 1960s. Arthur and Bertie Hodge both died in 1963, and their business closed its doors for good. Following Arthur's death Elsie returned to live in the United States, passing away in 1994. A memorial service was held in her honour at St. Peter's Church. A reception followed, hosted by Elsie Hodge's former Brownies and Girl Guides.

One of the Hodge buildings still stands. Information provided by Kevin Anstey suggests that this building was built in 1914 by Benjamin and Thomas Roberts of Wild Cove to replace an older store used by both Hodges and Watermans. The Roberts men were known as top-notch carpenters who built a number of schooners. They may also have constructed Twillingate's Orange Lodge, a tribute to their craftsmanship. The Hodge family residence once stood on the site now occupied by the Anchor Inn Hotel and Restaurant.

Linfield's retail store, early 1950s

Other North Side Merchants. Just "up the road" from Hodges was Joseph B. Tobin and Company, then taken over by W. J. Scott, and finally by the Linfield family. The latter business was founded by draper (dry goods dealer) Frederick Linfield. In 1886 he purchased fishing rooms and premises on North Side from a planter named James Manuel Senior. The Linfield establishment was originally located between premises owned by William Roberts and John Moss. Frederick Linfield opened for business on 15 July 1888. On the firm's seventieth anniversary (1958) a commemorative book was issued. In its pages were recounted the names of some of Linfield's customers, along with their purchases, during the store's first week of operation. We are told that Ms. Lousia Lunnen bought one pound of velvet for thirty-five cents, the Methodist Board of Education spent a full fifty-two cents on a pair of carpet brooms, while Newfoundland Constabulary Sergeant Nathaniel Patten took home two white aprons and some sweets, costing him thirty-five cents in all. Later run by descendants named Loveridge, Linfields continued as a grocery and drygoods concern for almost a century, closing out in 1981. In its later years the business was known as E. J. Linfield's, after Frederick's Son Edward J. Linfield, its proprietor from 1924-51.

Manuel's shop (Left), with Bank of Nova Scotia, 1920s.
Business founder Arthur Manuel is at right

Rounding out Slade's successors on the Northside were the Manuels. Opening in 1898, the Manuel business operated for over 100 years, only closing out in the Fall of 2006. The business was founded by Arthur Manuel, and passed down through three generations of his family, its final owner being Arthur's Grandson, Ernest. Born in 1872, Arthur Manuel was the Son of Titus W. Manuel, and gained his first business experience in the communities of Tilt Cove, Round Harbour and Nipper's Harbour. Soon after opening his Twillingate store Manuel bought premises once owned by Slade and Cox, and expanded further by constructing another shop. The business was first concerned exclusively with the salt fish trade, but the Manuel firm eventually focussed on retailing. Originally married to Georgina Maidment, after her death Arthur wed Margaret Mitchard. As a leading citizen of Twillingate, Arthur Manuel was involved in many local voluntary organizations. A master of the Masons and Society of United Fishermen, Manuel was also a warden of St. Peter's Anglican Church. He even served as Twillingate's hospital association secretary. Manuel was secretary of the Twillingate Telephone and Electric Company for the best part of a decade, from 1916-25. By the time

Arthur Manuel died in 1942 the family business was being run by his Son, John.

John Maidment Manuel was born in 1911 to Arthur and his first Wife Georgina. Educated in his hometown, and at Toronto's Dominion Business College, Manuel married Daisy Anstey. Aside from taking over the family business, John Manuel was Twillingate's first Mayor when the town was incorporated in 1965, a position he retained until 1974. As ENL notes, the Manuel business expanded under John's control, installing an artificial fish drying unit in 1956. Manuel passed away 21 July 1977, at which time Son Ernest assumed the reigns. The old Manuel establishment was once home not only to their business, but also the local Bank of Nova Scotia, now located near Tickle Bridge.

Duders. In its heyday the business founded by Edwin Duder Sr. was one of the most important on the Isles. Duder was a native of the English West Country town of St. Mary Church, Devonshire. His parents, Thomas and Ann Congdon Duder, immigrated to St. John's in 1833 when John was eleven. Twenty years on Duder was one of the most prominent merchants in Newfoundland's capital, owning premises all the way north to Twillingate. His firm also had branches in Herring Neck, Change Islands, Barr'd Islands, Joe Batt's Arm and Fogo. In his collection of Newfoundland biographies politician/journalist Henry Youmans Mott (1855-1946) described Duder as "a gentleman universally known and respected throughout the island for his business capabilities, and integrity."[24] In 1848 Duder married Mary Ann Edgar of Greenspond, and after her premature death wed Mary Elizabeth Blackler. Like many prominent businessmen of his era, Duder was involved with various organizations and charities, including the Church of England Asylum for Widows and Orphans. He was also President of the Terra Nova Cricket Club, and a Director of both the Newfoundland Commercial Bank and the Union Marine Insurance Club.

For a number of years Duder worked in partnership with his Brother-in-law Robert Livingstone Muir, who married Duder's Sister Emma in 1847. Their company was known as Muir & Duder until Muir's death in 1865. Like other merchants, Duder and his successors supplied fishers in return for their catches of cod. In the years 1840 to 1889 his family business ran a fleet averaging around 4,500 tons, trading to the West Indies, South America and Europe. Buying a portion of Slade's former Twillingate assets in the 1870s, Duder further added to his prominence in the area. By the time he died in 1881 Duder was head of one of the Colony's most successful merchant houses.

Starting in the 1850s Muir & Duder's operations in Notre Dame Bay were managed by Edwin's Brother, John Congdon Duder (1817-94).

According to author Cyril Chaulk, John spent more time in the area than any other member of the Duder family. In 1861 he married Lavinia Ann Pearce at Twillingate, and records uncovered by Chaulk indicate that the couple had at least three children. Around 1880, with the opening of a copper mine at Betts Cove, Duder moved there to take up the position of customs officer, though Chaulk contends that he and Wife Lavinia always considered Twillingate home.

Another member of the Duder family with close connections to the Isles was Charles Duder (1818-79). After working for a number of years in St. John's, Charles and Wife Katherine (McLachlan) moved to Twillingate in the early 1860s. In 1869 Charles ran for election in the two member district of Twillingate-Fogo, along with Smith McKay. This was not long after Canadian confederation – Duder and McKay ran on a platform opposed to joining the new nation. Their pro-confederate opponents included future Prime Minister Whiteway. In the end Duder and McKay won a decisive victory. Charles Duder was reelected in 1873, and from then until 1878 served as Chairman of the Board of Works under Sir Frederick Carter.

After Edwin Sr.'s death the family firm was divided between his two Sons, Edwin John and Arthur George (b. 1859). Edwin John became a partner in the 1860s, and when Arthur came on board in the early 1870s the company was renamed Edwin Duder and Sons. Arthur George died soon after his Father, and Edwin Jr. became sole head of the company. Born in 1853, Edwin Jr. was educated both in his hometown, St. John's, and London, England. Married to Margaret E. Stead, Duder maintained a country residence – Carpasian – noted for its herds of livestock and dairy cows. Although not active in politics, Duder's prominent business position earned him an entry in Mott's work, which profiled notable colonial personalities.[25] Like his Father, Edwin John was a Director of the Commercial Bank, and helped found the Newfoundland Electric Light Company in 1885. Mott felt that Duder may have been the largest shipowner in the world, as measured by the number (rather than tonnage) of vessels he owned. In 1888 the Twillingate Mutual Insurance Company insured 134 craft owned by the Duder concern; all their other clients accounted for only forty-nine vessels.

Mott's short biography praised Duder for his success in maintaining an enterprise on such a scale. Unfortunately for Duder and his family, this glowing praise was premature – the business didn't outlive its founder by many years. The company's first difficulties arose during Edwin Sr.'s tenure. In the 1860s the elder Duder invested heavily in sail vessels and in supplying the Labrador fishery. Steamers were introduced for the seal fishery in 1863, shifting the hunt's focus away from Twillingate. Over the next few years steam vessels also penetrated the Labrador fishery, causing more problems for the business. Arthur had predeceased his Mother, and upon her death complications arose over her will. Though intended to inherit the Duder business in its entirety, Edwin John had been obliged to pay his Sister-in-law half the company's worth in cash. Chaulk contends that this left Duder with inadequate capital. Along with its other troubles, this severely weakened the Duder firm.

Edwin John Duder

Chaulk notes that, as a Director of the Newfoundland Commercial Bank, Duder could easily secure credit from the institution; paying this back was another matter. By 1889 Duder was seriously indebted to the Commercial Bank. The evidence suggests that he had been since shortly after his Father's death. As a result, all of the Duder properties and infrastructure at Twillingate and Fogo were mortgaged to the bank, with Duder expected to make twice yearly payments at six per cent interest. Failing this, the Commercial Bank could "...sell and absolutely dispose of...the said lands easements and premises aforesaid...by private sale or public auction..."[26] The arrangement worked for a while, but in December 1894 the Commercial Bank called in amounts due it by various merchant houses after coming under pressure from English banks. With the merchants unable to pay, the Commercial Bank closed its doors, the Union Bank soon following suit. Duders didn't survive the financial collapse.

"Black Monday," as it was called, had a severe impact on Twillingate and the Colony in general. The collapse of E. J. Duder, along with Thorburn & Tessier, and John Munn and Company, affected about 19,000 employees. In an 1897 speech Prime Minister Whiteway even cited the Duder firm's collapse as an example of the economic distress caused by the bank failure.

Though its loss was a great blow, not everything connected with the Duders at Twillingate was swept away in the 1890s. St. Peter's Anglican Church preserves a memorial plaque to Duder, erected by Edwin John upon his Father's death in 1881. Although a touching tribute from one generation to another, this plaque is not the most impressive reminder of Duder's place in Twillingate history.

The Ashbourne Longhouse

A house with connections to the Duder family still stands on South Side. It is most likely the oldest building in Twillingate. This large dwelling is now called the Ashbourne Longhouse. Built in the Georgian style, the residence may have been constructed as early as 1780, and certainly no later than 1820. In a 2008 interview with *Lewisporte Pilot* reporter Howard Butt, Ms. Audrey Ashbourne stated that the house was constructed in stages. With pine ceilings and floors reportedly all cut at Twillingate – no pine stands remain on the islands today – the Ashbourne Longhouse once had a full veranda. Its first owner was William Menchinton. Menchinton was a planter and trader who hailed from Somerset, England. Like the Slades, he and a business partner named Harris maintained a branch at Twillingate. Although not built by Edwin Duder, the Longhouse was owned by his family for over forty years, purchased by Duder and Muir on 29 May 1852. It was then used as a residence by members of the Duder family, their agents, and sundry guests. After Edwin Sr. died Edwin John inherited the house, which was sold to William Ashbourne (See below) on 7 January 1897. It is still owned by the Ashbourne family. Restoration work was carried out on the house by contractor George Whitehorne, and in May 1991 the Ashbourne Longhouse was designated a Registered Heritage Structure.

Ashbournes. Slade's pair of "big rooms" on South Island were purchased by their former clerks, Owen & Earle (See Chapter Four). In 1893 John Woodhouse Owen (c.1831-1902) and Henry John Earle (1841-1934) dissolved their partnership, with Owen retiring. For nearly a quarter century Henry Earle and his family operated a branch business at Twillingate. The decision to close this location in 1915 benefited business rival William Ashbourne.

As we have seen, Ashbourne bought out some of Edwin J. Duder's assets in 1897, and operated from the central part of South Island. Ashbourne purchased Earle's Twillingate assets for the sum of $22,000.00. For his outlay Ashbourne received:

> ...all that and those land and mercantile premises consisting of dwelling house out houses shop stage store and wharves situate on the South Side of Twillingate Harbour Newfoundland which said piece of land contains by admeasurement 12 acres 2 roods 25 perches or thereabouts and is bounded on the North by the waters of the Harbour on the West by land of one Hayward and the Main Road to Little Harbour and on the East by a Branch road to the South Side connecting with the said Main road and also by land of Phillips...[27]

As part of the deal Ashbourne was assigned all debts due to Earle Sons & Company at Twillingate and Durrell's Arm, along with "...that portion of the island known as Harbour Rock Island containing 32 perches more or less...,"[28] granted to Henry Earle by the Crown in 1904. As vendor, Earle also acted on behalf of his former partner's Widow, Louisa Owen. A large piece of land on South Side, originally granted to Owen in 1869 and still owned by Louisa, was included in the transaction. Located near where Twillingate's fish plant now stands, these "new" premises became known as Ashbourne's "Upper Trade." The Upper Trade opened for business on 21 March 1915, with George Nott as bookkeeper and Stewart Roberts in charge of the store. Not everyone was content with the changeover. A. Colbourne set up his own, smaller operation on South Side, along with several other former Earle employees.[29]

Only two years after buying out Earles' local assets – 27 January 1917 – the Ashbournes suffered a major blow when portions of their South Side (central) premises were heavily damaged by fire. The *Twillingate Sun* noted that,

> ...on Saturday afternoon, at about quarter after five...[o]ne of the large patent mantle lamps which was used for lighting the store exploded, blowing burning kerosene all over the place [and] several people were hit. In a moment a sheet of flame flew around the shop catching dry goods piled on the shelves...With great presence of mind Mr. Arthur Young closed the main entrance doors, and prevented the inrush of wind to fan the flames. A couple of extinguishers were got to work, and with the assistance of some buckets of water the fire was quickly put out, but not before considerable damage was done...It is impossible to estimate the damage. Half the ceiling of the shop is charred and the paint raised in great blisters...while all over the shop things are scorched and seared...[30]

The Ashbourne business rebuilt, and upon William's death in 1922 its principal owner was Thomas Gordon William Ashbourne, who became Managing Director of the business.[31] Born 4 December 1894 to William and his Wife Lucy G. (Linfield) Ashbourne, Thomas inherited a major stake in the business from his Father. After graduating from the University of Toronto with a Bachelor of Arts, young Thomas enlisted with the Canadian Army during the Great War. Anxious to get to the front lines, he transferred to the Royal Garrison Artillery, and served with the rank of Lieutenant. The local paper followed Ashbourne's officer career:

> Lieut. Tom was observation officer for a battery of 6 inch howitzers whose work was the destruction of enemy wire entanglements...[H]is duty took him into the front line trenches where he had to note effect of his battery's fire and instruct by telephone.
>
> He had a dugout, close to the front line and very

> shortly after getting in both he and his orderly were gassed, and were sent out for three days rest...
>
> After he returned to the line again he was in his dugout one night and awoke with a sense of everything going to pieces. When he looked up he could see the stars through the roof of the dugout and knew it had been blown out...[W]hen he secured help and his electric torch he found the dugout in ruins and the orderly lying with a dreadful gash on his forehead. He was removed to the hospital and died the next day.
>
> Tom also had the misfortune...to cut his foot with a piece of barbed wire, and that began to swell and fester. Added to this the effect of the first gassing began to show on his heart and he was ordered to hospital, his foot being so bad that he became a stretcher case.
>
> In the explosion of the shell which blew up the dugout he escaped death by a matter of two inches only...[32]

Returning from the Western Front, Thomas Ashbourne not only played an important role in the family business, but also entered into a successful political career. From 1924 to 1928 Ashbourne served as Twillingate District's member of the House of Assembly. He also served with the National Convention on Confederation, travelling to Ottawa as part of a convention delegation in 1947. Following the union with Canada in 1949, Ashbourne was elected to represent the Federal district of Grand Falls-White Bay-Labrador, being re-elected on two occasions. Thomas passed away in 1984.

On 16 June 1925 Thomas had married Annie Bernice Roberts (1905-2005), with their Sons eventually assuming control of the business. Howard Butt states that, like many of its competitors, the Ashbourne business operated primarily as salt fish exporters, and did not make the switch to fresh fish production, closing its doors for good in 1981.

Thomas Ashbourne (left), with light keeper Jack Roberts at Long Point

Ashbourne Vessels. As fish merchants, the Ashbournes owned or chartered many schooners which were outfitted for the Labrador fishery. They also shipped freight for the business and brought in coal from Sydney, Nova Scotia. A Twillingate diarist writing in 1907 noted that one of these coal vessels, the *Edward Arthur*, grounded at Bridgeport Point on its return from Sydney that year but was refloated an hour later.

Another Ashbourne vessel, the *Bessie Marie*, was the last three-masted schooner built in Newfoundland. It was constructed by Eleazer K. Mills of Burlington, Green Bay, on order from Ashbournes, and was launched on 14 June 1929. An account of the building process was given by Mills' Grandson, Gus Rideout, in a 1992 *Decks Awash* article. At 208 tons the tern-rigged craft was the largest ever built at the Mills Cove dockyard. Used by the Ashbourne firm from 1929 to the early 1960s, the schooner was captained for fourteen years by Billy Roberts. Among her other skippers were Cecil Stockley and Jim Gillett. For most of its career the schooner's chief engineer was George Burton, who installed the vessel's original engines. Like the *Edward Arthur*, the *Bessie Marie* served in the Sydney trade, returning to Twillingate with cargoes of retail goods along with coal. The schooner was noted for its success in the seal fishery, with the products being refined at Ashbourne's premises.

In 1942 the *Bessie Marie* had its bowsprit removed and was converted to a two-master. As she got older the proud vessel became inefficient to repair. The *Bessie Marie* was anchored at Purcell's Harbour in 1962, where she remained for a number of years. In 1971 the vessel was towed to Black Island in the Twillingate-New World Island Main Tickle and left to decay. Today the Durrell Museum preserves the *Bessie Marie*'s wheel.

The schooner Bessie Marie *in the ice off Twillingate*

Ashbournes briefly owned the schooner *Sydney* (or *Sidney) Smith*, built in 1895. A three-masted Welsh topsail schooner out of Portmadoc, the vessel was constructed for the Newfoundland fish trade. At almost 177 tons, the *Sydney Smith* was one of the largest vessels constructed at Portmadoc in the era. For more than a decade the schooner travelled as far afield as Labrador, Malaga and St. Petersburg. In 1912 the *Sydney Smith* grounded and wrecked at Twillingate. Five years later, with World War One raging and tonnage in short supply, the old vessel was salvaged, with Ashbournes as its new owner. Officially certified as seaworthy, the ship departed Twillingate for Gibralter with a cargo of cod on 5 December 1917. The *Sydney Smith* was commanded by Augustus "Gus" Taylor of Carbonear. A long-time mariner, Taylor lost a vessel to a German submarine in the Mediterranean earlier that year. Captain Taylor was uneasy about the weather the day the *Sydney Smith* set sail, and it appears the schooner soon encountered a gale. The full details of the vessel's fate will never be known, as the *Sydney Smith* and her crew vanished without a trace.

Only a month after the *Sydney Smith* disappeared another Ashbourne vessel met an identical fate. The *Ada D. Bishop* was a ninety-three (net) ton schooner that sailed from Twillingate to Gibralter in early 1918. Captained by Arthur Holwell, the *Ada D. Bishop* departed Twillingate with a cargo of codfish on 10 January, and was never heard from again. Although it was wartime, no German submarine commander ever took credit for sinking the *Ada D. Bishop*.[33]

Though neither vessel was confirmed lost to enemy action, the crews on both the *Sydney Smith* and the *Ada D. Bishop* are commemorated on memorial plaques at Beaumont-Hamel and St. John's to those men of the armed services in the Great War who have no known grave. They are: *Sydney Smith* – Captain Gus Taylor, Carbonear; Eli Hawkins, Change Islands; Hubert Hull, Twillingate; Stewart Hull, Twillingate; Henry Porter, Change Islands; Hubert Wells, Twillingate. *Ada D. Bishop* – Captain Arthur Holwell, Herring Neck; Arthur Atkinson, Herring Neck; George Atkinson, Herring Neck; Earle Burgess, Twillingate; Mark Burton, Twillingate; Frederick Lambert, Twillingate; Arthur Licence, Stoke, Ipswich, England.

Most of the Ashbourne firm's maritime history did not involve such tragic losses, though there were a few close calls. In his work *Newfoundland Ships and Men*, Andrew Horwood recalls that in December 1899 the forty-three ton schooner *Myra*, outfitted by Ashbournes, was making its way home loaded with Christmas supplies ordered by William Ashbourne. A sudden wind squall off Gander Bay dismasted the little vessel, leaving it adrift. A nearby schooner, the *Spectator*, offered to take off all the crew. The *Myra*'s owner, Captain John Hillier, felt he could save the distressed vessel and its cargo. He asked for volunteers to stay aboard but no one came forward. Hillier was still determined to stay with his craft and save it, alone if necessary. With only his Newfoundland dog for companionship, the mariner jury-rigged masts on which to set small sails. Amazingly, Hillier and his dog made it safely to port after three days. The captain wired Mr. Ashbourne saying that the vessel and its cargo were all safe, although its Christmas treats would be late in arriving. The Hillier family were overjoyed to learn of the Captain's safe landing, but as Horwood tells it, Twillingate's young children could not understand why Father Christmas was off schedule that year.

Howletts. The Ashbournes weren't the only local merchants with an interesting history. Of all the mercantile firms on the Twillingate islands one of the most unusual, at least for its location, was situated on Howlett's Island, Durrell. Today, looking at the small rocky outcrop, connected to the mainland at low tide, one would never think a commercial establishment could have been operated there. Yet in the 1800s William Byrne, Son of an immigrant from Callan, County Killkenny, Ireland opened the first merchant house on the little island. Byrne was in business at Durrell by 1864 as a "dealer and chapman," continuing on as a merchant and general dealer until 1895, when his namesake Son assumed control of the firm.

Around the turn of the twentieth century the enterprise came under the direction of Harry (or Henry) J. Howlett. Howlett was a Grandson of William Byrne Sr. through his Daughter Mary. An early reference to Howlett at Durrell's Arm comes from McAlpine's 1898 Directory, where he was listed as a clerk, most likely working for his Uncle, William Byrne Jr. McAlpine's 1904 Directory lists Harry Howlett as a general dealer in Durrell's Arm, so he must have taken the reigns sometime between 1898-1904. In the beginning Harry was in partnership with his Brother William M. Howlett, who left around 1913 to take up cabinet making in St. John's.

Like many merchants, Howlett's community involvement ranged beyond business affairs. The *Twillingate Sun* reported that on 26 November 1910 an Agricultural Society was formed at the Twillingate Court House. Harry Howlett represented Durrell on its seven member executive, with Leonard Earle as President. In 1915 Howlett was among the members of a General Committee supporting prohibition.

The Howlett premises, Durrell, early 1900s

In its heyday Howlett's Island was home to a grocery and hardware store, storage sheds, a cellar, wharf and stages. The island was connected to the mainland by a 150 metre long bridge. As there was no water supply on the island a pair of 386 litre barrels of fresh water were delivered every two or three days by Harry Hicks of Durrell. Although it seems an unlikely place to operate a business, Howlett's Island was quite suitable, having fairly deep water on its far side. Schooners could safely dock there, even at low tide.

This came in handy, since the Howletts owned schooners that were outfitted annually for the Labrador fishery. The firm also bought catches taken by other vessels. On 13 August 1910, for example, the Sun reported the arrival of the schooners *Gozzard* (Capt. Boyd) and *Gleaner*, landing a total of 260 barrels of fish for Howletts from the "Treaty Shore." Apart from its schooners, the business kept another vessel used for ferrying freight and passengers between Twillingate and Lewisporte.

In January 1913 Howlett entered into an arrangement with the Earle family, transferring the goodwill of his business, along with fishing gear and boats, to them. A Provincial Archives source notes that Howlett agreed to stay on as manager of the business for nine years at a rate of $1,000.00 per annum.[34] Howlett retained his Durrell properties, which he rented to Earles for $400.00 a year. It is not known if Harry Howlett had the same arrangement with the Ashbournes when they bought out Earle's Twillingate branch in 1915. By 1920 Howlett was advertizing the sale of his properties at Durrell in the Sun newspaper, making the offer again in November 1922. The Howlett business closed soon afterwards, and Harry took his family to live in St. John's.

Howlett's retail store was eventually bought by Ashbourne's Limited. Stephen Loveridge's diary records that it was hauled away from Howlett's Island on 14 March 1926. Afterwards the workers were treated to a dinner at the Lad's Brigade Armoury (See below). The retail store was moved to Farmer's Arm, and this branch of their business was familiarly known as "Ashbourne's Lower Trade." The Farmer's Arm shop was moved to a third location, a short distance away, in 1951. The Lower Trade remained in business until the 1970s, and the old shop was later purchased by the Bath family. In 2011 it was relocated to North Island by the Isles Wooden Boat Building Committee, with the intention of preserving the historic structure.

The Howlett family home was sold for use as a hotel, intended to serve patrons of Twillingate's new hospital (See Chapter Thirteen). Doctors Parsons and Wood, along with hospital Director George Blandford, were all involved in the venture. Too large to move in one piece, the house was sawed in two under the direction of William Earle and George Saunders. Led by Captain Tom White and his Son Joseph, a large group of people then hauled the structure overland, the first stage of the move taking place on 17 February 1927. This portion of the house was hauled from Hart's Cove over the harbour ice, and was landed around four o'clock in the afternoon near George Blandford's. The second portion of the house was brought ashore by the

Blandford property on the twenty-first. Standing on the former site of a home owned by John Hudson, the house was operated for a number of years on behalf of the original buyers, as the Harbour View Hotel, by Mrs. William Penn of Exploits. It was later sold to Captain Saul White, who ran the hotel until the 1960s. It was demolished in 1971 to make way for Twillingate's new Town Hall/Fire Department building, which is still located there.

The Merchants and Community Life. Newfoundland's old merchants are sometimes seen in a bad light. The truck system often left fisher-families in long-term debt. Still, towns like Twillingate would probably never have survived without the activities of their merchants. Without men like Harry Howlett and their vessels, Twillingate fishers would have had no way to get their fish to the markets in Portugal and Spain. These ships also carried most of the early settlers to Newfoundland and gave them work when they arrived. As in all Newfoundland communities, Twillingate's merchants were at the top of the social ladder, and often filled important appointments like Justice of the Peace. They also tended to be prime movers in improvement initiatives like road and educational boards. Likewise, merchant families actively contributed to the town's spiritual life. They were sometimes helpful in other ways. In 1891, long before the advent of a coast guard, Richard Hodge put a schooner at the disposal of the community to help rescue stranded sealers:

> Thursday morning [9 April 1891] the wind and weather proving favourable, a large number of our people went off on the ice to endeavour to procure a haul of seals. It was considered by those on shore that the chances were entirely in favour of such a result. During the day, however, the ice slacked off, the wind shifted, a heavy sea arose, and as we learn from the men, lakes of water [were] made and separated them greatly. Towards night great alarm and excitement was occasioned on shore by the non-appearance of the breadwinners, and wives were anxiously looking for the return of husbands and Sons. Unable to bear the pressure of suspense, many hurried to Long Point to seek intelligence of the missing ones. We are, however, pleased and grateful to know that all have returned and [are] restored to their homes, but in many cases after most miraculous escapes.
>
> We cannot withhold a high need of praise to R. D. Hodge, Esq., who at once placed the schooner *Firefly* in the hands of rescuers, and fitted her out with the necessary supplies to proceed in search of the men, but happily her

services were not needed, as all hands got ashore as stated above. Still this detracts nothing from the generosity of Mr. Hodge who richly deserves the thanks of a grateful community. Many of the men of the harbour whose names are most worthy of record, worked all night with the most praiseworthy activity in fitting out the schooner and getting boats ready for the rescue, and though their voluntary services were not required, still they no less deserve the thanks of our townsmen, which, no doubt, will be fully accorded them, such neighbourly efforts on their part being fully recognized and appreciated by a grateful people.[35]

....

The Great Gale of 1907

The seal harvest, and more especially the cod fishery, provided a (generally) reliable livelihood for Twillingate residents. By the turn of the twentieth century the town was one of the most important settlements in the Colony of Newfoundland. Schooners departed with fish and arrived with goods from all over the globe. Many of these vessels were protected by the town's Mutual Insurance Company. The value of this protection was evident during the great gale of 18 September 1907, remembered locally as the "Liner Breeze." Stipendiary Magistrate J. B. Blandford cabled the Governor, reporting that, "on the eighteenth instant Twillingate experienced the heaviest gale of wind north north east that has occurred within my time of fifty eight years fortunately for owners of craft there was no ground sea otherwise the loss would have been fourfold...we estimate approximate loss...at thirty thousand dollars"[36]

Twenty-eight schooners were at anchor in Twillingate harbour waiting to discharge their cargoes of fish, and some were already in the midst of doing so, when the storm blew up. All of the schooners except the *Mayflower* and *Zinnia* were blown ashore, either dragging or breaking free from their moorings. One schooner, the *Swallow*, even drove its mast through Hodge's store window as workers watched! Another schooner, the *Victoria*, was driven into the side of a business, causing extensive damage to the building. The government wharf and several private wharves were also severely damaged. The Newfoundland *Year Book and Almanac* for 1908 reported on the damage caused to the government wharf and its navigation light. The light, first lit in 1885, "...was destroyed by sea, which carried away the wharf in Sept. '07." The Almanac informed readers that "notice will be given when it [the light] is re-established."[37] Though the wharf and its light were casualties, only two vessels were destroyed, and no one was hurt, at least not in Twillingate.

Schooners driven ashore at Twillingate after the great gale of 1907

A first-hand description of the great gale was written on 23 September 1907 by Leonard Earle, representative of the family merchant business at Twillingate. As Earle recounted to his Brother William:

> Dear Will
> I can't commence to describe the scene here...26 craft many houses halls fences stages flakes fish & nearly everything seems gone. Around our premises is a fearful sight & craft are piled in. The Ariel is the worst we have & I don't know her damage. The Bloomer is a total loss on the breakwater with Young's. we are landing fish from the wrecks & everything is in a litter & no one can estimate the loss & this on top of a very bad fishery...our men have nothing & the fish we saved will have to make on the premises as nobody can handle it.[38]

The effects of the 1907 gale were wide-ranging. Magistrate Blandford noted that telegraph lines were down from Twillingate to Fogo, and had not been repaired as of 23 September; most messages reporting on the gale were received by the Department of Marine and Fisheries via the SS *Portia*. The *Leslie L*, owned by Ashbournes, was driven ashore at Change Islands while making its way homeward. Captain Snow and his men managed to make it to the rocks but spent a miserable twenty-four hours there without food or shelter.

The sixteen-man crew of the *Effie M* was not as fortunate as those from the *Leslie L* – all went down with their schooner at Great Brook near Old Perlican. In all about ninety vessels were wrecked in places like Fogo, Eastern Tickle, Harbour Grace, LaScie and Musgrave Harbour. From Bonavista Magistrate John Roper reported that the storm had been "...one of [the] most destructive on record..."[39] Seven vessels were wrecked at Bonavista, including a Norwegian sloop, which had two of its crew drowned. One of the most unusual victims of the '07 gale was Carbonear's United Towns Electric Company, whose wires were heavily damaged by the event. A new facility, it was built to serve its hometown, along with Harbour Grace and Hearts Content.

Such harsh weather was nothing new on Newfoundland's northeast coast – many Twillingate residents could remember another destructive gale of 19-20 November 1894. Still, the liner breeze was significant enough to catch the attention of Government officials in London. Newfoundland's Governor was sent the following telegram by Colonial Secretary Lord Elgin (1849-1917): "...I much regret to hear in the newspapers of a severe storm in Newfoundland. I earnestly trust that disasters to fishing fleet are not so widespread as was first reported. I shall be glad to hear particulars."[40]

....

Community Organizations & Meeting Halls

Setbacks like the 1907 gale had little effect on Twillingate's general prosperity; mass out-migrations like 1786 were not repeated until the modern fishery crisis (A smaller proportion of residents have left since 1992 than departed after 1786). As one of the largest settlements in Notre Dame Bay Twillingate became known as the "Capital of the North." With an active community life, the town had a number of fraternal societies including the Society of United Fishermen (SUF), the Loyal Orange Association (LOA), and the Masonic Order. All three of the societies, or lodges, had their own halls which are still standing.

The Masons were first established at Twillingate on 9 February 1889 at a meeting held in the town court house. Among those in attendance was *Twillingate Sun* founder Jabez Thompson, and for the next seven months Saturday night meetings were held. On 17 September the District Lodge sent the Twillingate chapter their official warrant as a constituted lodge, number 2,364. The Masonic had a smaller membership than Twillingate's other Lodges, and was mainly composed of the town's elites, especially businessmen and professionals. The Masons were impacted by the 1894 bank crash, losing all their savings, but not their drive to continue the chapter. In December 1898, still meeting at the court house, members first proposed construction of their own lodge building. The project came to naught until 1905, when a house and land belonging to the late Thomas Every was bought for $250.00. At first the Masons hoped to convert Every's large home into their lodge. In the end a completely new structure – the present lodge – was agreed upon. Though only twenty-five members strong, the Masons duly began construction of their "Temple," as Masonic Lodge buildings are sometimes called. Work started in 1906, with Josiah Roberts (who received $1.50 a day) in charge of the project. Total expenditure amounted to just over $3,100.00, including the cost of materials, labour, and the initial land purchase. The dedication ceremony had originally been planned for October 1906, but weather and transportation problems delayed the event until July 1907. On the fifteenth of that month delegates, including Hon. J. A. Clift, the Lodge's acting Deputy Grand Master, arrived on the *Clyde* to help celebrate the occasion. A holiday was proclaimed the next day, and the building's cornerstone, including a time capsule, was laid at noon. A morning luncheon was followed by a social and a ball at the court house that went on until midnight.

More than a century later, the Masons remain active in Twillingate, and their temple is a true jewel of local architecture – it became a Registered Heritage Structure in April 1998. Like many Masonic Lodges in the Province, its exterior is elaborately detailed with the Masonic emblems and pilasters. The topmost windows are crowned with curved arches, while those on the bottom floor have triangular pediments. The lodge has an offset tower, giving it almost the look of a church, though an egg-shaped dome atop the tower lessens this impression. On 3 November 2007 the Twillingate Masonic Lodge celebrated the building's 100th anniversary, with a banquet attended by dignitaries including Most Worshipful Bro. Maxwell Squires from the provincial Grand Lodge in St. John's.

Twillingate's Masonic Temple, opened 1907

The LOA met in the Alexandra (or "Alexandria") Hall. Completed in 1907, the hall was likely named for Alexandra of Denmark (1844-1925), Queen consort of the reigning sovereign, Edward VII (1841-1910). The cornerstone of the building was laid down by the order's Grand Master, Donald Morrison, on 12 July, less than a week before the Masonic Lodge was dedicated. Morrison and his Wife arrived from St. John's on the *Clyde* at 7 pm, laying the cornerstone a half-hour later. The LOA celebrated their dedication less grandly than the Masons, but no less enthusiastically. A cricket match was played between the Orangemen and the "Outsiders," which the Outsiders won by more than thirty runs! The game was followed by a picnic "on the green." The Orangemen's fine new lodge was heavily damaged by the great gale two months later, but this was soon repaired.

Although 1907 was an eventful year for Twillingate's Orangemen, the local chapter already had a fairly long history. The first LOA member initiated at Twillingate was George Hodder, on 26 September 1871. The Royal Scarlett Chapter of the LOA, later known as The Edward the Seventh No. 3, was instituted at Twillingate on 30 October 1880. At the first meeting eight "Sir Knights" were welcomed, and the minutes were recorded by one Titus Linfield. By the 1930s the Orange Lodge had nearly 400 members. During the Confederation debates of the 1940s the Alexandra Hall was used for political meetings, and housed patients during a hospital fire in 1943. Today the hall has been given the name "Touton House" and is used for musical performances during the Summer months. Until 1909 the LOA held a share in the SUF Hall, of which they were co-tenants until moving into their own quarters.

<u>Society of United Fishermen</u>. Just across the street from the Alexandra Hall, the SUF is the oldest of Twillingate's surviving lodge buildings. In his history of Twillingate Methodism Reverend Mercer says the hall was built in 1873 by the LOA and Sons of Temperance, while information collected by researcher Jim Troke reinforces this tradition. Prior to this date another structure stood on the spot. It appears that this building was used as a storeroom by William Waterman and Company (Waterman assumed the reigns of the former Cox and Company c.1867). The storeroom and surrounding land were purchased from Watermans for the sum of £45, some time around 1869-70, by the North Star Division, Sons of Temperance. The Sons of Temperance was an anti-alcohol organization which initially met in a Commercial School building on South Side. At their first meeting on 2 August 1864 a motion was adopted that any Brother or Sister of the Division would be fined ten shillings if caught smoking or chewing tobacco. In 1872 the Sons of Temperance and LOA decided to began construction of a new building to replace the old Waterman store, which both organizations were then using for meetings. The contract was awarded to Samuel Roberts, and the Division held their first meeting in the new hall on 10 July 1873. The building was initially known as the Victoria Hall, in honour of the reigning monarch, but the Sons of Temperance's tenancy gave rise to another name, the Temperance Hall. In 1917 the Temperance Society sold out their share in the hall. After some wrangling the sum of $150.00 was agreed upon for the sale. The Sons of Temperance's last meeting at the hall was in September 1917. With their departure the hall's sole tenant was the Society of United Fishermen, who had been co-tenants since 1875.

The SUF was founded by Anglican Minister George Gardiner as the Heart's Content Fisherman's Society in 1861. The society grew rapidly, and on 1 January 1873 it was re-organized as the Society of United Fishermen. They adopted as their symbol a triangle representing the triangular shape of Newfoundland with its points Cape Bauld, Cape Race and Cape Ray. In the triangle's centre stood a Maltese cross whose eight points symbolized the eight beatitudes. Also included was the society's motto, "Love, Purity, Fidelity." In the first ten years of the SUF's existence forty-two lodges were formed in Newfoundland. By 1922 one branch was even operating in Nova Scotia. The Twillingate chapter – St. Peter's Lodge – received its charter as the twelfth SUF branch in June 1875. Eight days after the charter was signed Brother Philip Freeman joined the lodge; his is one of the earliest known Membership Certificates originating from Twillingate.

Twillingate SUF members parade in celebration of the branch's fiftieth anniversary. The LOA's Alexandra Hall, now the Touton House, is at left

In 1926 Stephen Loveridge recorded details of the society's preparations for their fiftieth anniversary celebrations. On the fifth of April SUF members erected a bough-covered arch near the Victoria Hall, and the following day members paraded under it to St. Peter's Church, where Reverend H. Gilbert preached a sermon from the Book of John, "Peter said I go a-fishing – go with thee." Members of Loveridge's family not only participated in the parade and a celebratory dinner, but entertained SUF members and photographed the event for posterity (See above).

The SUF had reason to celebrate their achievements. Over the years the local Society of United Fishermen contributed greatly to charitable causes. They helped start a successful drive for a community hospital, donated money for the maintenance of hospital beds in World War I, and were active contributors to Dr. Wilfred Grenfell's Deep Sea Mission at St. Anthony. The Twillingate branch also had a connection to the 1914 *Newfoundland* sealing disaster (Chapter Eleven). Although none of their branch were lost, a number of the dead were SUF brethren. The lodge immediately sent a cash donation to aid victims' families. During the 1940s the SUF, supported by the Masons and LOA, petitioned the Commission of Government to construct a canal across New World Island for small boat traffic. Although the lodges got thousands of signatures, the idea was shelved when Confederation with Canada focussed priorities on road building.

The SUF sold the lodge in 2003, and the structure received a municipal heritage designation on 5 November 2007. It is now privately owned.

Arm Lads Brigade. The membership of most lodges was only open to adult males, although dances, youth events, and concerts were held in their halls, entertaining a wider circle. The communities on Twillingate Island also had organizations for women and children, especially after 1900. One of the oldest was based on the well-known Church Lad's Brigades. The [Durrell's] Arm Lads Brigade (ALB) was started in 1908 by a veteran of the Boer War. Hailing from Jersey in the Channel Islands, this veteran, whose name is now forgotten, spent a month living at Durrell. While there he drilled interested youths in a military style, meeting three nights a week at the Howlett merchant establishment. When the old soldier left his place was filled by locals who continued the boys' training. In 1910 a twelve by eighteen metre drill hall or Armoury was built atop a Durrell hill called the "Old Maid." Free labour was supplied by members, who also provided materials. Surplus Boer War rifles were purchased for drills, and a military-style uniform was adopted. One of their uniform patterns (replaced in the 1950s) consisted of white pants with a vertical red stripe. Blue dress shirts were emblazoned with the red letters ALB on the breast pocket, and the whole was topped with a navy blue tam. The ALB had a brass band sporting their own distinctive jackets. The Brigade's first Captain was William J. Minty, assisted by naval veteran George Rogers. Members were accepted from the ages of ten onward with an entry fee set according to age, plus a monthly ten cent charge. ALB rules and regulations were to be strictly adhered to. Drill was based on the British military's 1902 manual *Infantry Training (Provisional).*

When war erupted in 1914 thirty-two ALB members volunteered for service. The value of their regimen was proven when the young men were sent overseas without the need for further drill training. In 1917 one former ALB member, Private Augustus Bulgin of the Newfoundland Regiment, was awarded the Military Medal for bravery in the field (See Chapter Twelve). About twenty years later another eight ALB members enlisted for the Second World War. Like their Fathers, they were well advanced over most recruits.

Enrollment in the ALB remained steady through the 1960s, but dropped off quite a bit in later years. Finally, the Arm Lads Brigade was wound down. In an effort to preserve the Brigade's memory the hall was donated for use as the Durrell Museum. The Durrell Museum Association was formed at a public meeting held at Durrell Academy (now the Auk Island Winery) on 17 September 1973. At the meeting a Board of Directors was elected for the coming year, and $12,000.00 was raised to renovate the building. The institution opened in June of 1978, celebrating both the ALB and

Durrell history. Though the original organization is just a memory, the impact the ALB made on several generations of Durrell youths is not forgotten. On 18 July 2008 the museum was host to official ceremonies marking the 100th anniversary of the ALB's foundation, followed by a celebration banquet at the local Lion's Den the following evening. Nearly 100 former ALB members attended the event, including the oldest living member, Mr. Bert Waterman, then aged ninety-five.

The former Arm Lad's Brigade Armoury, atop the "Old Maid"

More Youth Groups. Another group for boys in Twillingate was the Scouts, originally founded in Britain by General Lord Robert Baden-Powell (1857-1941). The 1st Twillingate Boy Scout Troop was organized by United Church Minister W. Edgar Mercer, who came to Twillingate in 1929 (1930, according to some sources). In that era the Scouts met at the Masonic Hall. The work of Scouting was appreciated within the community. In 1932 former opera star and Twillingate native Georgina Stirling (see Chapter Nine) made an address to the local troop, presenting them with sixty dollars raised through production of a stage play. About the same time the Scout's Sister organization, the Girl Guides, was established at Twillingate. The 1st Twillingate Company Girl Guides originated in the 1930s with Mrs. W. E. C. Hollands as their first captain. As we have seen, Elsie B. Hodge was closely involved with Twillingate Guiding, both as a founder and leader. The Twillingate company was duly registered at headquarters on 13 December 1933. In more recent times, boys and girls at Twillingate could join a variety of youth organizations, including the Cubs, Brownies and Sea Cadets (RCSCC 83 Briton).

RCSCC Briton met at the Masonic Temple from 1953 to 1980, and later at the J. M. Olds Collegiate gymnasium. This branch of the Sea Cadets had its origins in the Fall of 1952 when Arthur Butcher hired a local youth, fifteen year-old Jim Young, to attend a movie wearing a Cadet uniform. Butcher's intention was to interest other Twillingate youths in forming a Sea Cadet corps. His efforts were a success, and 83 Briton was launched under its first Commanding Officer, Wilson A. Manuel, who served until 1959. Other Commanding officers include Harry A. Young, James S. Young (who wore the cadet uniform at Butcher's behest in 1952), Howard Butt, Garry Elliott, Calvin Boyde, Bruce Greenham, Melvina Hull (first female Commanding Officer) and Rick Dalley. RCSCC Briton takes its name from the Royal Navy ship HMS *Briton*, formerly HMS *Calypso*. Used as a training vessel for the Newfoundland Royal Naval Reserve, it was later moored in Lewisporte harbour.

The Women's Institute. Another organization, intended for women, but serving the public generally, also has a fairly long history in the community. The Women's Institute was first organized in Ontario in 1897. In Newfoundland it had its roots in the Service League. This organization was founded by Lady Anderson, Wife of Newfoundland Governor Admiral Sir David Anderson (1874-1936), following the disastrous tsunami that hit Newfoundland's south coast in 1929. In 1935 the Service League changed its name to the "Jubilee Guild" to commemorate the Silver Jubilee of King George V (1865-1936). In 1945 the Jubilee Guilds became constituent members of the international body of Women's Institutes. In 1951 they joined the Canadian branch, called the Federated Women's Institutes of Canada. Their first Convention was held at Springdale in July 1954 with the Institute's World and Canadian Presidents in attendance. The Institute's motto is "Confidence, Courage, Unity." By 1968 the Women's Institute had expanded its focus to urban as well as rural settings. In 1991 the Newfoundland and Labrador Women's Institute earned the Canadian Citation for Citizenship. Today the Institute has more than fifty-five branches in the Province with over 1,000 members.

An unofficial branch of the Institute was started at Durrell in 1946 (another source says this was in the late 1930s). In 1968, after a letter by local members to the Institute's Provincial board, the branch was made official. At the time the branch had about eighteen to twenty members.

A prime mover in the process was Twillingate resident Lorna Stuckless, formerly of Eastport. Following in the footsteps of her Mother, a President of Eastport's Jubilee Guild, Mrs. Stuckless' career with the Women's Institute has seen her take on numerous positions of responsibility, including President of the Twillingate branch, District Representative, and

Provincial Convenor of the Home Economics Area.

At Twillingate the Institute's logo is a ship's wheel encompassing the words "Newfoundland and Labrador Women's Institute," with Newfoundland's Provincial flower, the pitcher plant, inside. The wheel reflects Twillingate's close association with the sea, especially the fishing industry which the Institute supports. The Twillingate Women's Institute has been involved in many worthy activities over the years, including the promotion of local crafts, pap smear clinics, scholarships, and global awareness programs like UNICEF. They also play a role in the Twillingate/NWI Fish, Fun and Folk Festival, which Mrs. Stuckless helped found in 1981, and the local high school's Safe Grad program. In the late 1960s the Women's Institute expanded to New World Island, and for twenty-five years ran a craft shop at Summerford (This building was constructed of round logs and built with free labour). Today the Twillingate Women's Institute branch meets in the historic building that once housed Twillingate's customs office.

The Women's Institute Building. Like the lodge halls, the old customs house is a fascinating study in itself. Located near St. Peter's Anglican Church, it was constructed as a public building in the late nineteenth century. The ground floor was used as a local post office. It was nicknamed the "Tory Post Office," since the Conservative ("Tory") Party was then in office under James Spearman Winter (1845-1911). The first Post Master was John White, who served until his death in 1922. The post office was moved to the court house in 1945, and finally to its current location in April of 1958. The building's top floor was intended for use as a town hall, but was taken over by the Customs Service in 1920 when the section was divided into three rooms. Customs services were discontinued in 1949 when all public buildings came under Ottawa's jurisdiction. Customs duties were transferred to Gander, and during the process the deeds to the building were lost. The building was without an official owner. About the same time Twillingate's Girl Guides found themselves without a meeting place. Their Commissioner asked permission to use the old customs house, so in 1951 local MHA and Attorney-General Leslie Curtis granted the Guides a ninety-nine year lease on the building. The Girl Guides met regularly at the hall, and the bottom floor was used as a public library. The Guides were joined by the Lion's Club, which renovated the building, five years after the local Lion's chapter was founded in 1953. By 1977 the building was showing signs of disrepair. A Winter Works Grant was received to renovate the building's interior and exterior, while retaining much of its original form. The library had moved to Twillingate's high school building so the Women's Institute moved into the ground floor. Their occupancy of the old Custom's House continues to this day.

Outside the Women's Institute building is a World War I mortar, possibly of French or German origin. If German, it was most likely a war prize. According to an old diary, on 24 May 1921the mortar was moved to its present location from the government wharf, where it had arrived by steamer. Magistrate Isaac J. Mifflin (1865-1942) was in charge of the operation, assisted by Great War veterans and the general public. Though no plaque is associated with it, the gun was mounted as a tribute honouring the memory of fallen comrades of those vets who helped place it.

The Women's Institute building, Twillingate's old customs office

....

Home-Grown Industry – The Sleepy Cove Copper Mine

By the time the old mortar was erected outside its customs house Twillingate was already one of the most important centres on Newfoundland's northeast coast. A vital aspect of Twillingate's community life during the pre Confederation era was its relative self-sufficiency. While the town was reliant on shipping from the Spring through to late Autumn to bring in many necessary items, it was important that the area be able to meet as many of its citizens' needs as possible.

With their community built on islands, accessible only by sea, or over the ice in Winter, residents depended on a plethora of local services and small craft industries. For more than seventy years the town was served by its own local newspaper (See Chapter Eight). As late as the 1940s Twillingate had three coopers (barrel makers), including the Verge family, who operated at Upper Jenkins' Cove, Durrell. According to Peggy Linfield, the Verges were some of the Cove's earliest settlers. In addition to making casks for firms like Ashbournes, they also fashioned coffins, and even operated a kind of pharmacy where they treated "water whelps," a form of boil or sore common among fishers. In this era Twillingate had a trio of blacksmiths, one of whom was Ned Young, whose forge was located on South Island, near where the local Riff's department store now stands. There was also a tin shop, along with a furniture factory owned by the Colbourne family.

James Oakley's boot store, North Side, probably late 1800s.
One of Twillingate's many local services before 1949

While very important to Twillingate, these service industries were only supplements to the cod fishery, which remained the bedrock of its economy. As the fishery failures of 1786, 1832, 1848-52 and 1860 demonstrate, relying on a single industry was risky. To combat this problem, attempts were made to diversify the local economy. On the Twillingate islands the largest, and best known, industry of this kind was based at Sleepy Cove in what is now the municipality of Crow Head.

In the 1860s a copper mine opened at Tilt Cove in western Notre Dame Bay. The mine's early success encouraged prospectors and entrepreneurs to descend on the Bay and stake out claims. All were hoping to reap the rewards of an expected copper bonanza. The process was spurred even further when Prime Minister Charles Fox Bennett (1793-1883), himself an owner at Tilt Cove, abolished mining royalties in the Colony. From the 1880s until the Great War more than two dozen copper mines opened in Notre Dame Bay, and Newfoundland was briefly the world's sixth-largest copper producer. A *Twillingate Sun* article reflected optimism at the prospects for mining in Twillingate:

> ...we remember [a Twillingate resident] saying: "Never you mind the bay; there is plenty of mineral in the bowels of Twillingate North Island. Yes, sufficient to give every man, woman and child on the island a fortune."...Recent discoveries have changed the opinions of former pessimists, who regarded this a very unlikely locality. The vein of splendid copper lately discovered at Long Point has positively convinced experienced miners, who have spent years prospecting, that there is a big lode of that mineral somewhere in the neighbourhood...
>
> The splendid find of good copper by Messrs James Hodder & Co., at Long Point this past fall has awakened the possibility that Twillingate North Island will yet be a busy mining centre...We congratulate Messrs James Hodder and Company on their grand find, and trust they will dispose of it to good advantage; and speed the time when the place where the fishermen hang their nets will resound with the echo of the miner's hammer.[41]

There is more than one version of how the Sleepy Cove Mine originated. Both of these stories involve Obediah Hodder, a Pennsylvanian born at Crow Head. According to a contemporary newspaper report, Hodder was visiting his hometown in 1905 when he rediscovered a copper vein he had first noticed as a child. The other story alleges that Hodder's Father James discovered the copper deposit (See above). It seems that James Hodder and his Son Edgar, along with a number of associates, laid claim to the Sleepy Cove deposit around 1902, selling their stake to Obediah for $5,000.00 in 1906. As part of the deal James and Edgar were to receive a royalty of twenty cents per ton of ore. Hodder incorporated the Great Northern Copper Company, based in North Dakota, which took control of the claim. Obediah assumed the dual role of General Manager and Treasurer of the company. Hodder ignored the fact that Sleepy Cove's deposit was not very large, having a limited (though high quality) copper content. He thought this could be offset by using the latest sophisticated mining equipment, investing $225,000.00 on American-built machinery. These included a 150 hp power boiler, a jaw rock crusher, a belt conveyor (about 150 metres long), and a ball mill, just to name a few. The equipment arrived at Twillingate by steamer in the Fall of 1908. Men from the community helped haul it in pieces for ten kilometres over the snow on horses and carts to the mine site. As surviving images reveal, the mine was impressive in its heyday, with a large loading wharf and shed for ore storage. A wood-burning steam engine was used to carry ore up the shaft to the mine entrance, while another took cable cars along a tramway between the mine shaft and the rock crusher. Ore was centrifuged from the rock on a turntable, while another steam tramway carried ore to the pier.

The Sleepy Cove copper mine, with founder Obediah Hodder (inset)

For all its sophistication, Hodder's mining machinery didn't translate into success. Only three vessels ever arrived to export the ore. One load of 560 tons of ore was shipped out in 1910, but the destination is now forgotten. A second attempt at loading was aborted when high winds drove the steamer onto the rocks. The third shipment was sent to New York, but went unclaimed for months before it was bought by the American Smelting and Refining Company around 1915 or 1916. Obediah Hodder got out of the mining business in 1917, starting a cooperage at Twillingate before returning to Pennsylvania. The same year Hodder abandoned his mining venture it was reported that the "St. John's papers contain the notice of a Sheriff's sale at which were to be sold...the land, mining rights, stores property &c. of the Great Northern Development Co. Messrs. George Roberts and Ob. Hodder are the plaintiffs. So ends the Sleepy Cove mine apparently."[42] The mine closed for good about 1920.

Today, little remains of the original mine structures, but visitors can still see pieces of the mine equipment and its site in the former Sea Breeze Park (Now privately-owned). Contemporary pictures of the mine are on display at the Twillingate Museum, and the Twillingate Public Library has its own interesting collection of mine images. The Town Hall at Crow Head has an impressive painting of the old mine, with an inset of Obediah Hodder, by the late Melvin Sharpe.

Miners working at Sleepy Cove

....

The Twentieth Century & Beyond

The failure of the Sleepy Cove copper mine, while a setback, was no disaster for Twillingate – life continued much as always. This despite the wartime service of certain residents and the deaths this entailed – about two hundred of Notre Dame Bay's young men perished in World War I (See Chapter Twelve). Despite their undoubted patriotism and courage, Bay residents did not go along with all their government's wartime plans. By 1917 the slaughter on the Western Front slowed recruitment considerably, and Prime Minister Edward P. – Later Lord – Morris (1859-1935) proposed conscription. According to Patrick O' Flaherty, in certain outports a backlash arose against military recruitment. In May locals tore the Union Jack from its staff at Twillingate's recruiting station. A year later Twillingate's Fisherman's Protective Union Council suggested that a referendum be held to decide on enacting conscription. With FPU founder William Coaker now allied to the government, little came of the Twillingate proposal. Coaker did try to alleviate concerns, stating that conscription would not interfere with the Labrador fishery, and that only young, unmarried men would be drafted. In fact, he said, conscription might never be needed at all! Ironically, the Twillingate FPU proposal actually spurred on the government's conscription plan. As O'Flaherty notes, the government also hoped to bring in a bill extending its term of office, tying this to the need to enact conscription. Despite opposition, conscription became a fact in May 1918, but no Newfoundland draftees arrived in time to fight in Europe. The Colony's manpower requirements had been met by volunteers, like those two hundred NDB men who sacrificed their lives in the conflict.

The conscription crisis was largely forgotten in the post war economic downturn Twillingate faced along with the rest of Newfoundland and Labrador. Despite economic hardships, the town's fishery continued throughout the "Dirty Thirties," and men set off for Winter woods work as they had done for decades. In 1939 another World War erupted. A second generation of young Twillingate men volunteered for service in the armed forces, foresters and merchant marine. Apart from the absence of these men, Twillingate was directly affected by the War in a number of ways. The local Hospital's staff was severely reduced and, more positively, a number of our American allies arrived. During the war the United States Coast Guard maintained a station at Twillingate to aid in shipping and air navigation. Located near Hospital Pond on South Island, the once secret installation was home to fifteen servicemen at any given time through to 1945. Only three years after the war ended Twillingate joined the remainder of Notre Dame Bay in voting for Confederation.

The Wars, and new initiatives spurred by the Canadian union, gave Twillingate life the appearance of a "golden age." In reality the town was past its peak, at least as the hub of Notre Dame Bay. A railway built in the late 1800s to link eastern and western Newfoundland was much closer to the community of Lewisporte than Twillingate. By the twentieth century more and more goods were being shipped by rail, and Lewisporte replaced Twillingate as the Bay's main *entrepôt* for goods and services. Lewisporte's position was further strengthened when a paper mill opened in Grand Falls. Men from Twillingate then headed for Lewisporte to board trains for their Winter lumber camps. The population of Twillingate, including Durrell and Bayview (as they are now called), peaked at 3,694 in 1884, but fell to around 3,000 by 1924. It rose again through to the early 1990s, but then fell once more. The recent decline of the town's traditional industry, the fishery, has seen many young families leave, never to permanently return. Formerly the heart of the Bay, the Capital of the North became just one of many out of the way communities on the northeast coast.

Still, Twillingate's story is really a positive one. In the Summer of 1960 a fresh-frozen fish plant opened, costing about one million dollars to build. When the plant was first launched by Fishery Products it employed over 100 men and women. During its first week of operations the plant processed about 6,800 kilograms of fish. At its peak of operations more than 300 employees worked for the Twillingate fish plant. Originally power was provided by diesel generators, but this was later switched to hydro power. The plant's emphasis has changed (along with several owners) from cod to shrimp, but it still operates on South Island near the former site of Ashbourne's Upper Trade.[43]

Twillingate fishers landing their catches at the new fresh fish plant, 1963

The late twentieth century also marked the end of Twillingate's physical isolation from the rest of Newfoundland. For many years the only link Twillingate had to the Island was by boat or over frozen harbours and channels in Winter. Since 1973, however, the community has been linked to the mainland by a modern causeway and the Road to the Isles. The fishery is in decline, but Twillingate has become one of the Province's great tourist attractions. The community has received Tourist Choice Awards as the number one town to visit in central Newfoundland, not to mention winning a Provincial Tidy Towns competition in 2002. Some of its old buildings, like St. Peter's Church, Hodge's premises and the Ashbourne Longhouse, remain. The Twillingate and Durrell Museums continue their mission to preserve local history. Despite its eventful past, the town's primary attraction is probably its natural beauty. Hundreds of people each year come to see beautiful sunsets, great crystalline icebergs from the Arctic, and playful pods of orcas and humpback whales.

....

Crow Head

Most of the old settlements on the Twillingate islands, like Durrell and Bayview, are incorporated into the municipality of Twillingate.[44] With so much of the islands' history encapsulated under one jurisdiction, we have examined Twillingate as a whole, unlike Fogo Island, Change Islands and New World Island, which we'll look at on a community by community basis.[45] There is one other town on the Twillingate islands that still forms a separate, incorporated municipality. For this reason we would be remiss if we left the area without taking a brief look at the town of Crow Head.

View of Crow Head, with salt fish drying on flakes, c.1950

Few tourists visiting Twillingate miss Crow Head. Found on the northwest portion of North Island, the community is home to one of the area's most famous historic landmarks, the Long Point Lighthouse, and is popular with visitors as the home of the Twillingate Dinner Theatre. Crow Head is also the site of Seabreeze Municipal Park, where Obediah Hodder's copper mine once operated. Like Twillingate, Crow Head has a history of European settlement stretching back three centuries. Although the settlement was first mentioned as a separate community in census records only in 1911, when it had 205 residents, Crow Head likely dates back into the eighteenth century. There are surviving land grants from the 1880s, and Crow Head was home to a Church of England school as early as 1876.

The 1911 census preserves a record of a prosperous fishing community which harvested salmon and herring alongside the main catch species, cod. Crow Head residents were also employed in Newfoundland's mainland lumber industry and in mining. A Methodist school served Crow Head in 1911, and in this era most residents were Methodists. As of 1928 nine surnames were reported in the community: Andrews, Bath, Dove, Elliot, Hamlyn, May, Mugford (Mutford), Stockley and Sharpe, most of which are found at Crow Head today.

Town of Crow Head, 2011

In the post Confederation era fishing remained the primary economic activity at Crow Head. As ENL reports, Crow Head was considered one of North Twillingate Island's most productive fishing centres in 1951. At this time most of Crow Head's catch was salted and sold to local fish merchants or via a co-operative established in 1960, the same year the town was incorporated. The previous year a community stage was constructed, and by then most fishers were selling to the local frozen fish-plant. By the 1980s Crow Head was home to about a dozen fishers who were by now harvesting a diverse range of marine species apart from cod. Some employment was also generated through service industries in other parts of the Twillingate islands.

By the early 1990s the future seemed fairly bright for Crow Head, whose population had risen through the thirties and forties, and remained generally stable thereafter. At this point, however, the cod moratorium hit. The town's 1991 population stood at 280, but by 2011 this was down to only 203, slightly less than it had been a century before. The future presents many challenges for the town of Crow Head, but residents are ready to meet these head on. With the popular lighthouse located in the community, a number of small tourist ventures have been launched in recent years.

3

New World Island

Although Twillingate is the largest settlement on the Isles (by population), it is only one of many. Bigger than the Twillingate islands, New World Island has an especially large number of communities. Although most have never been very populous, these settlements have an interesting past all their own. Like Twillingate, New World Island was only accessible by sea for most of its history. This finally changed after Confederation when the Road to the Isles was built in the late 1950s, and the causeways in the early 1960s. A road to Summerford was begun in 1952, soon making its way through the communities of Moreton's Harbour, Tizzard's Harbour and Bridgeport. In 1954 work started on a stretch of road linking the community of Virgin Arm to Herring Neck, and running north to the Twillingate ferry at Indian Cove. A full road link with mainland Newfoundland became a reality in the Summer of 1964 when the causeway network was completed. Although most of the roads weren't immediately paved, they were a godsend to the people of New World Island. Below is a historical look at some of the NWI communities that were linked by the new road/causeway network.

......

Bridgeport

Located on New World Island's southwestern side, this community's harbour is deep and resembles a small fiord. When the first settlers arrived the locale's rocky landscape and sparse soil led them to gravitate toward fishing. Bridgeport was first named Big Chance Cove, and was originally a Wintering station for Moreton's Harbour fishermen who used it to cut wood and built boats. Despite its lack of fertile soil, the area was home to excellent timber stands. Bridgeport was first settled permanently in the 1880s by one Josiah Noel of Harbour Grace. He was soon joined by Jeremy Colbourne out of Carbonear, and James Jones of Western Harbour. In 1884 the settlement boasted a population of thirty three, the number growing to ninety in 1901, 225 in 1940, and 292 in 1966. Ten years later numbers dropped as youths left home in search of work.

The town's first school and church were built in 1908, and it acquired its modern name in 1915. This name was chosen by Adam Chaulk who had just returned home from Bridgeport, Nova Scotia. That same year the community's first post office opened. In 1920 Bridgeport was home to the first telephone on New World Island. Bridgeport's economy has historically been based on the fishery, this activity including a lobster cannery in the early 1900s. There was also some saw milling, and in 1915 copper prospecting.

....

Carter's Cove

Carter's Cove is located in western New World Island between Virgin Arm and Chanceport. For much of its history the unincorporated settlement has been a fishing community, built on inshore herring, cod and lobster. It was originally settled around 1850 by two fishermen from nearby Tizzard's Harbour, George and Thomas Burt. The pair were attracted to Carter's Cove by the rich herring grounds and an abundant supply of timber.

Unlike many nineteenth century settlements, Carter's Cove had a school from practically the time it was settled. There was later a chapel and a church built. Like many communities on New World Island, Carter's Cove had a lobster factory at the turn of the twentieth century. This one seems to have been larger than most, employing eight men. By 1940 Carter's Cove even had its own post office.

....

Chanceport

A small fishing community on the western side of NWI. Like Bridgeport, Chanceport's geography is generally rugged and hilly. Chanceport is found in an east-facing inlet with its entrance west of Virgin Arm. The harbour is known as a good boat anchorage. Until 1921 the settlement was called Chance Harbour. It was originally located about 1.6 km to the north of modern Chanceport. Its first settlers were likely from Twillingate, and arrived in the mid 1800s. Family names like Young, Dove, Wheeler and Scott are common to both communities. Apart from being hilly, Chanceport shares another feature with Bridgeport – abundant stands of good timber. This resource was certainly attractive to early residents. In the census of 1884 Chance Harbour was listed as having thirty-three residents. All were members of the Methodist faith, as most residents still were in 1921, and the breadwinners listed themselves as fishermen. By 1911 the population had risen to seventy-nine, or sixteen families. That same year the community's fishers brought in over 10,000 kilograms of fish, one of the largest hauls on New World Island! Chance Harbour had its own canning factory. Its two employees tinned salmon, lobster and herring. Although its original fishery was inshore, a Labrador fishery was based out of the settlement by 1901, and continued until 1945. A Salvation Army school, doubling as a chapel, was opened in 1909, and this was joined by a Methodist school in 1911. This school was probably used by several denominations and remained in use until 1968.

Throughout its history the fishery has been the community's main occupation, but there was a considerable woods industry during the Winter months from the 1920s on. In 1957 Chanceport was moved to its present site by residents without the aid of government funding. A road built nearby in 1952 could not reach the town due to its hilly terrain. Taking matters into their own hands, the people of Chanceport were connected to the outside world by land for the first time.

....

Cobb's Arm

Cobb's Arm is found on New World Island's northeast side. Located at the western entrance to Dildo Run, it is nestled on the shores of a deep arm of the sea which then splits into a pair of inlets. Before the terminal was moved to the town of Farewell, Cobb's Arm was also the departure point for ferry traffic to Change Islands.

The Baxter Fudge Memorial Hall, Cobb's Arm.
Formerly a school house and United Church

As of the 1911 census the residents of Cobb's Arm, all Methodist fishers, numbered seventy-seven. Ten years later the population increased to ninety-seven. The Cobb's Arm fishery was mainly based on cod and herring. There was also a lobster factory. In that year the community had its own

Methodist church and school.

A notable geological feature of Cobb's Arm is a forty-six metre thick bed of medium to coarse limestone. Around 1870 one Thomas Burridge of St. John's started a limestone quarry in the community, selling the property to George Davey and James R. Chalker in 1912 for $800.00. Three limestone products were produced at the quarry, including "agstone," agricultural lime used in soil. Quicklime was produced, mainly for use at a mine in Buchans to neutralize acidic tailings. The majority of the product was taken in raw form by schooner to Botwood and then to the Grand Falls Mill where it was employed in paper making. The Corner Brook paper mill was also a Cobb's Arm limestone buyer into the 1940s. Cobb's Arm's most productive years as a limestone producer, at least in terms of employment, were from 1930-60. As of the early 1950s the quarries had an annual output of around 5,000 tons. By the 1960s the quarrying was carried out by the Newfoundland Lime Manufacturing Company Limited. Although many reserves still remain, the old quarries ceased production in 1966.

....

Cottlesville

Located on the southwest portion of New World Island, Cottlesville is comprised of the settlements of Cottle's Island and Luke's Arm. The community occupies three coves in a small peninsula bounded by Luke's Arm, Puzzle Bay (to the north), and by Cottle's Bay and Cottle's Island to the west. Off the tip of Cottle's Island lies a smaller landmass known as Storehouse Island. According to ENL, both islands may have served as Summer stations for New World Island fishers who eventually settled Cottle's Island and Luke's Arm year-round. A local history – *Cottlesville, Cottles Island. Memories of Yesterday* – contends that the area's first European inhabitants lived on Cottle's Island, later moving to the main island. To distinguish between the two places settlers used the names Cottle's Cove and Cottle's Village. Information provided by Milt Anstey suggests that the first permanent settlers were Stephen Cooper and Joseph Anstey, who arrived in 1873.

The official name "Cottlesville" is fairly recent. It was decided on after a town referendum in 1980 in which eighty per-cent of residents voted in favour. The local history says that this was the first time the area had an official name, with many variations appearing on maps over the years.[1] Like many Isles towns, Cottlesville's toponym is mysterious, the exact meaning of "Cottle" being unknown; it may originate in an old surname like Cotel or Coutelle. The other portion of Cottlesville, Luke's Arm, was recorded as a separate community in the 1911 through 1945 censuses, but has been included with Cottle's Island since 1951.

Cottle's Island was first recorded in the 1884 census, at which time it was home to twenty-five persons of the Methodist faith, who likely came from Twillingate. A number of the early family names found at Cottlesville – Anstey, Cooper, Moors, Rideout and Watkins – are associated with Twillingate to this day. As of 1891 the population stood at forty-seven, the number growing to seventy-six in 1911. At this time Luke's Arm was originally recorded, with a population of sixty. By 1921 Cottle's Island was home to ninety-three inhabitants, and Luke's Arm sixty-seven, numbers that rose steadily though to the Confederation era. By 1966 the population of the combined community of Cottle's Island-Luke's Arm rose to over 400, as residents of nearby island communities moved there under the Smallwood Government's resettlement programmes. Population numbers in the town remained over the 400 mark until the 1990s.

The early settlers earned their living from the inshore and Labrador cod fisheries, along with a lobster harvest. Like some other communities on New World Island and Fogo Island, Cottlesville was home to lobster factories in the early twentieth century. Anywhere from three to seven of these family-owned operations were based at Cottlesville from 1901 to 1921. Lobster became even more important to the local economy following the failure of the Labrador fishery in the early 1900s. Other marine species like cod, salmon, herring and mackerel were also caught, but mostly for local consumption.

In tandem with its fishing ventures, Cottlesville had its own small shipbuilding industry. Samuel Rideout, settled in the community by 1902, was noted as a schooner builder. He was said to have constructed his first vessel before the age of eighteen. In 1907 Rideout built a schooner named *Snowbird* at the location where Clarence Rideout later opened a garage. This vessel has a special place in local lore. The community history reports that while Rideout was in the process of building it a great storm, remembered as the "April Batch," blew up, burying the unfinished schooner. When finally completed the vessel took its name from this unusual event. In 1910 Rideout built the forty-five ton *Halley's Comet*, his largest vessel. According to author Calvin D. Evans, Rideout built his last vessel in 1926, though another source contends that he was killed in action during the Great War.

While the vessels built by Rideout and others helped provide locals with a livelihood, it was their faith that really sustained them. As we have seen, the earliest settlers were Methodists, and the first church was built around 1876 under the jurisdiction of Herring Neck. According to the local history, the Methodist minister did not visit the community on a regular basis and church enrollment declined. By 1903 the Salvation Army had established a barracks (or church) in the community under the direction of one Captain Wiltshire. A new facility was soon constructed which served until 1966. The third Salvation Army barracks lasted less than twenty years, being destroyed by fire on 2 March 1983. In 1930 Cottlesville's third major denomination arrived when Pentecostal Pastor E. R. Pelley held the first services in the Methodist church. Two years later the town's first assigned pastor, Maude Evans, arrived and construction of the first Pentecostal church was begun.

Each of the three denominations operated schools at Cottlesville, the first opened by the Salvation Army in 1911. Ten years later a Methodist school was in operation, serving local children until it closed in 1944. The Pentecostal denomination conducted classes in their church until 1949, at which time a school was built under the auspices of Pastor Callahan. This school remained in operation until 1970 when educational facilities were consolidated and Cottlesville pupils were bussed to other locations on New World Island.

Longliners at the Cottlesville crab plant, prior to a fire in 2015

The second half of the twentieth century brought change to Cottlesville. Starting in the 1950s income from forestry work at Grand Falls and Bishop's Falls became an important pillar of the local economy. With the Road to the Isles linking New World Island to the mainland, commuting to forestry jobs became common. This tradition is continued by the Cottle's Island Lumber Company, Ltd. Originating in the 1960s with a small, family-owned sawmill on nearby Chapel Island, the business grew under owner/operator Rex Philpott into one of the largest employers in the Cottlesville area. Along with forestry, fishing has remained an integral foundation of Cottlesville's economy. One local concern, Breakwater Fisheries, was especially viable, even as problems in the northern fishery led it away from a traditional reliance on cod into the processing of caplin and crab (Sadly, the Breakwater crab plant was destroyed by fire on 22 March 2015, and as of this writing its future is uncertain).

Over the past decades Cottlesville – now incorporated – has seen its residents make tremendous efforts to improve their town. In 1969 a Committee was formed to deal with a water shortage and other problems besetting the community. Through the 1970s and 80s the Committee, forerunner of a Local Improvement District, made great strides in partnership with the Provincial Government. This era saw improved roads, electric power, and a full water and sewer system. Efforts were also made to establish an industrial park and to build a municipal park.

Even so, all has not been smooth sailing for Cottlesville. In 1991, before the cod moratorium, the population stood at 375, a number which has since fallen steadily. By 2011 only 272 residents remained, more than a quarter of the population having gone to seek greener pastures.

....

Fairbank

Found on the shore of Friday's Bay, the community of Fairbank was originally called Boyd's Cove. Boyd's Cove was first noted in the census of 1901, and was probably included under the general heading of Friday's Bay before then. In 1901 the residents, all Methodists and born in Newfoundland, numbered thirty. The fishery was the settlement's primary occupation. Lobster and herring were both important species, and there was one lobster factory reported in 1901.

As of 1911 the population had increased to forty-three, and local children studied at a one-room Methodist school. Nine persons gave their religion as Church of England. The name Fairbank was first used in the 1935 census, and the population had risen to sixty-two. The main occupation continued to be fishing, along with some subsistence agriculture.

As of 1951 the population increased to 141, but this dropped to only sixty-seven ten years later. By 1981 the population had risen again, standing at 322. In that decade most of Fairbank's labour force was employed lumbering and fishing. The Salvation Army was by then the most important faith, and a new citadel was built in 1956. By now there was no community school, and youths were bussed to other parts of New World Island.

....

Green Cove

This small community lies at the northeast end of New World Island, situated between Pike's Arm and Too Good Arm. Along with these two communities, and Cobb's Arm, it was originally counted as part of Herring Neck in censes. First recorded separately in 1901, the little settlement had a population of sixty-six. Though its economy was primarily based on inshore fishing, Green Cove also sent one schooner to the Labrador fishery in 1901. The population held steady until the Great Depression. There were ten families in 1935 but by 1971 Green Cove had only a single family.

Although it has always been a small community Green Cove was home to a number of religious denominations in 1901, with thirty-eight Methodists, twenty-two Anglicans and six Roman Catholics. Later there was also a Salvation Army presence. In 1901 the settlement was home to its own Methodist and Anglican churches, plus an Anglican school.

....

Herring Neck

View of Herring Neck, c.1900, with Goshen's, or Goldson's, Arm extending into the distance

For a rich history few Isles communities can top Herring Neck. It is located at the extreme northeast of New World Island. Herring Neck is made up of a number of smaller settlements. Exactly which settlements are included as part of Herring Neck has changed over the years, but since 1981 they have been Sunnyside, Merritt's Harbour, Salt Harbour and Ship Island. Cobb's Arm and Too Good Arm are also officially included, but they are dealt with here as separate communities. Like many settlements on NWI, Herring Neck could only be reached by boat until the first highway in the 1950s. The community was first called Goshen's Arm; Herring Neck then referred to today's Pike's Arm and Green Cove. The economy has always been based largely on fishing, an activity aided by a sheltered harbour. With its hilly terrain – in some places rising to forty-six metres – and exposed bedrock, large-scale farming was never an option. There is a plentiful supply of coniferous trees nearby, and in 1940 three sawmills were operating in the area.

Herring Neck was one of the first places on New World Island visited by Europeans. It is likely that French and Portuguese fishers were active in the area in the 1500s-1600s. English vessels might have been fishing the grounds off Herring Neck then as well. The name Herring Neck probably derived from the early fishers' practice of carrying loads of herring across Pike's Arm's narrow neck. Herring were plentiful, but were hauled overland to avoid the Arm's treacherous headwaters. Reportedly, Natives also used the area. These were probably Beothuk, but may have been Mi'Kmaq.

Herring Neck's first European settler is believed to be one Jimmy Chant in the 1760s. By the 1790s he was joined by a family named Walsh. As of the 1857 census the population of the area then called Herring Neck was 610. There were eighty-eight families residing in eighty-one dwellings. Twenty years later Herring Neck's planters included Daniel and Edward Blandford, Samuel and William Card, Charles Cullen, Thomas Daily, Joseph Kearly, Henry Mills, William Mursell, John Warren, and T. Woodford. The population peaked at about 1,000 persons in the 1880s, remaining steady until the 1930s-40s when a decline set in.

In its early days Herring Neck was mainly an inshore fishery centre, but the Labrador fishery became more important by the late nineteenth century. Around 1900 Herring Neck sent ten schooners to Labrador, the hnumber rising to twenty-five before declining in the Depression years. By the end of World War II Herring Neck's traditional Labrador fishery was all but gone.

Like Twillingate, Herring Neck was a fish merchanting centre. In 1871 the community had four merchant houses – Thomas Ashman, Henry Daily, Charles Mursell and William Tracey. E. J. Duder maintained a branch there until the firm's bankruptcy. Their premises were taken over by George Carter and other successors until they too went out of business in the 1960s. In the early twentieth century the Carter business was known for getting early cargoes of inshore fish catches off to the European markets. In 1908 the *Twillingate Sun* reported that on 22 July the three-masted English schooner *Geisha*, commanded by Captain Euon, loaded 2,700 quintals of shore fish at Carter's, sailing for Europe the very next day. An even larger load – 2,800 quintals – was loaded on another English schooner, *Little Mystery*, on 4 August. As the Sun noted, "her genial commander Capt. Greet, looked smiling on getting such a fine quantity over her charter."[2] Merchant firms like Carters weren't the only businesses in the community. Herring Neck's first general store was Mundys, which later became Howells & Sons, and finally Herring Neck General Store.

Herring Neck, c.1900, with Parson's Point at Centre.
The Carter Merchant premises can be seen at left

The merchants may have done a good trade, but it wasn't all smooth sailing. In 1949 the *Twillingate Sun* reported on a major fire suffered by one of Herring Neck's merchants (a firm we'll hear more about in connection with Fogo), less than nine months after Confederation with Canada:

> One of the most serious fires to occur on the Northeast coast for many years was experienced at Herring Neck on Saturday past when the premises of Earle Sons & Company were almost completely destroyed. The value of the buildings and their contents lost to the flames is estimated at around seventy five thousand dollars. Some insurance was carried but the company has sustained a very heavy blow as the greater part of their winter supplies had been received and stored before the disaster.
>
> The premises, which were under the management of Mr. Claude Howell, consisted of shop, fish store, provision store, salt and coal sheds, and an oil store situated on the wharf. Only the oil store escaped complete destruction.

Nearby houses would have gone as well but for the fact that wind at the time was quite moderate.

Cause of the fire has not been definitely established, we understand, but it originated in a room immediately over the office section of the shop where goods were opened. Funnelling from the office stove entered the chimney in this room and it is thought that the elbow may have become accidentally unjointed from the piping.

The first sign of fire was noted by men on the wharf a few minutes after nine in the morning, when flames were seen through the window of the storage room. The alarm was raised immediately and an effort made to fight the blaze at the point of origin, but flames forced them outside where a ladder was raised to the window but nothing could be done there as a few seconds later flame burst through. Levi Smart and Geo[rge] Miles then mounted the roof and chopped holes through which they poured water passed to them by a bucket brigade. For a few minutes it appeared that the fire could be controlled by this means but such was not the case. The fire had gained so much headway before discovery that the interior of [the] building was soon a mass of flames. With the aid of a small pumping engine from the firm of G J Carter and the bucket brigade men worked furiously to save the nearby buildings but the fire could not be got under control until practically the whole premises had been destroyed.

Casks of oil, barrels of beef, pork and molasses were thrown over the wharf into the water and later salvaged. A quantity of flour, butter and other provisions was also saved. But the amount snatched from the flames was insignificant compared to that lost, among which are included four hundred quintals of fish, some thirty-five tons of coal, and nearly all the contents of the various buildings.

Mr. Howell saved all office records and we understand the firm is making provisions to supply its dealers through the winter by building and stocking a small supply store to serve until rebuilding of the premises can be undertaken next year.[3]

While merchants like the Earles and Carters were important pillars of the community, Herring Neck also saw the beginning of a movement opposed to merchant interests. The town is famous as the birthplace of the FPU. A one hundred year old building in the community played a central role in this event. Herring Neck's Loyal Orange Lodge, number 116, was built in 1904 by Thomas Blandford. Strangely for an Orange Lodge, it was patterned after the capital city's Roman Catholic St. John the Baptist Basilica. Local lodge members provided free labour during construction. In 1931 a pair of spires on the sides of the entrance were shortened since they often cracked during very high winds. This caused leaks which damaged the floor. Like most rural Orange Lodges, the structure didn't just serve the Orangemen, but the community in general. It was used for dances, concerts, wedding receptions, and even served as a kind of town hall. In its role as a community meeting place it launched Coaker's FPU in November 1908 (More on this event in Chapter Ten). The Herring Neck LOL was designated a Registered Heritage Structure by the Heritage Foundation of Newfoundland and Labrador in 1998.

Even more important to early outport dwellers than societal halls were their churches. Like the first residents of Twillingate, Herring Neck's original settlers had no regular clergy. The first Anglican church, St. Mary's, was built in the 1830s. It continued in use until 1870, when it was destroyed by fire. In 1875 a new St. Mary's was completed to replace the original. Around the same time a Methodist congregation was established. In 1910 the Methodists built a church, thought to have been their second local place of worship, on Ship Island. The builder is believed to have been carpenter George Blandford. This church was abandoned, along with Ship Island, in the 1960s. By the 1891 census 246 of 942 residents of Herring Neck were Methodist. As of 1910 there were about 100 members of the Salvation Army, and a new citadel was built for their worship, although Salvationist numbers declined in later years.

There was no formal school at Herring Neck prior to the 1840s, and the first opened either in 1846 or 1848, depending on the source. Its master was John Moss who, although well-qualified as a teacher, ran afoul of the locals, and a new school was set up in competition with his. Despite having two schools in the 1850s, there was still no official school building. Pupils studying at Salt Harbour did so in a private residence, while the others met in a small store. A new school house was erected by 1880, and others were added as the population grew. A number of these schools remained in use until a new integrated school was opened at Newville in the 1970s.

Before 1949 no community on New World Island predominated as a service centre like the towns of Twillingate or Fogo. To some extent, however, Herring Neck *did* fill the same role on NWI. Around the turn of the twentieth century, for instance, several private-practice doctors made Herring Neck their home (See Chapter Thirteen). Like Twillingate and Fogo, Herring Neck was a centre for the administration of justice. Provincial Archive documents indicate that by the early twentieth century the town had its own court house, though it seems this facility was no longer in use by the mid 1930s.[5] While in operation the Herring Neck court house would have heard cases presided over by the Twillingate Magistrate, although it does not appear that Supreme Court cases were adjudicated there. In October 1918, for instance, the *Twillingate Sun* noted that Magistrate Roberts and Constable Tulk had just travelled to Herring Neck to hear cases involving the theft of pit props.

By 1918 both the Magistrate and nearest police Constables were based at Twillingate, but Herring Neck had a one-man Constabulary detachment for a brief period in the late 1800s. The community probably had no law enforcement of its own up to the early 1880s; most likely Herring Neck came under Twillingate's jurisdiction. In 1887 Constable Michael Sullivan arrived, remaining until around 1890, when he was succeeded by Benjamin Day. Day remained on duty at Herring Neck until sometime before 1896. *The Year Book and Almanac of Newfoundland* for that year listed no Constable at the Herring Neck detachment, which soon disappeared from the records altogether. Their stay was brief, but to date Sullivan and Day appear to have been the only full-time police officers based on New World Island.

New developments occurred in the post Confederation period. For many years Herring Neck had its own fresh-fish plant. The plant was opened in 1972, and constructed as a project of the Twillingate Island/New World Island Development Association. The plant had a number of owners over the years, processing species such as cod, capelin, herring, turbot and mackerel, all of which were fresh frozen. Unfortunately, Herring Neck's fish plant was downsized in 1991 and ceased operations in 2004. Given such economic setbacks, many youths have left the community in search of better opportunities. Herring Neck is still home to about 200 people, many of whom continue to make their living in various fisheries.

A community spirit is very much in evidence at Herring Neck, and in recent years the area around a nearby pond has been turned into a day park. The pond has its own boardwalk with facilities for swimmers and picnickers A walking trail extends around the pond and up to a nearby lookout. Atop the lookout is a spectacular view extending from southern Change Islands to Friday's Bay.[4]

Tranquil walking trail near Herring Neck

....

Hillgrade

Hillgrade consists of the two communities of Seal Cove and Salt Ponds. Around 1950 Seal Cove, or "Swile Cove," as it was known to locals, was renamed Hillgrade by Alex Sanson. The name referred to a steep hill located at one end of the community. Salt Ponds, also called Saltons and Salt Pans, became part of Hillgrade later.

Local traditions hold that the first settler in Seal Cove was a Sanson (Samson or Sampson). This Sanson was a cooper who was originally brought to Twillingate by an English firm. The settlement was first enumerated in the 1911 census, and had a population of twenty-six. All Methodists, the residents were active in Newfoundland's shore fishery and cultivated small plots of land. Salt Pans originally appeared in the 1891 census with twenty-seven settlers who were also Methodists. By 1901 the population had risen to 136, but the numbers dropped to fifty-nine a decade later. By the outbreak of World War II numbers had dropped again to only twenty-nine. By in large, however, population levels in both Seal Cove and Salt Pans stayed about the same.

At the turn of the century the community had its own post office, Methodist church and school, plus a LOA Hall. The Orange Hall dated from just before World War I, and followed the founding of a Loyal Orange Association at Salt Pans in 1907. Originally the building faced southeast and its steps were practically on the roadside. In the 1940s this was changed, and the building shifted to the southwest. Meetings were usually held on Tuesday evenings, except in Summer. The lodge was also the site of community social gatherings, known locally as "times." Such activities were typical of communities along the northeast coast, as was the presence of the LOA in the largely Protestant region.

As was always the case in outport Newfoundland, earning a living trumped social activities, and there were three sawmills in operation by 1940. In the late twentieth century the major economic activity in Hillgrade was fishing, with catches mainly sold to the fish plant at Twillingate.

Old lodge hall at Hillgrade

....

Indian Cove

Indian Cove is located on the west side of New World Island, near the causeway connecting NWI to South Twillingate Island. A small fishing village, it had thirty-four residents in 1901. Fifteen were Church of England, sixteen Methodists, and three Salvation Army. Mainly involved in the inshore fishery, inhabitants of Indian Cove caught a number of species including salmon, lobster and herring. There was also some pastoral activity raising cows, sheep and poultry. To haul winter supplies of wood settlers also kept sled dogs. Over the following decades Indian Cove's population was fairly constant. In the years 1911-61 resident numbers varied from thirty-one to fifty-two. At the turn of the twentieth century fishing was still a major activity in Indian Cove. Until

1973 the main Road to the Isles passed through Indian Cove, and the ferry terminus from Twillingate docked at the community's northern end. Today, the road and causeway bypass Indian Cove, making the town that much quieter these days.

....

Moreton's Harbour

Like all other Isles communities, Moreton's Harbour's traditional economy was based on the fishery. Hugging the northwestern most portion of New World Island, the community is made up of three principal parts. The main settlement is situated at the bottom of the harbour and connected to "Taylor's Side" and "Small's Side"(also known as "Sligo Shore") to the east and west, respectively. The exact origin of the community's name is not certain, but it could have been named for an early settler named Moreton. On the other hand, it was referred to as "Morden's Harbour" in the 1836 census. There is a locale in Dorsetshire, England called Morden. When we Consider that many settlers in the area came from Dorset, this might account for the name. The spelling could have been changed to Moreton in tribute to a pair of early missionaries, the Brothers John and Julian Moreton. An early Methodist minister is also credited as a possible source of the name.

Moreton's Harbour, c.1900

Wherever its name came from, Moreton's Harbour was one of the first settled areas of Notre Dame Bay. The early residents were no doubt attracted by the excellent harbour, close by fishing grounds and goods stands of timber. There are at least two traditions about who Moreton's Harbour's first settlers were. One version of the story holds that the area was settled in the late 1700s by a family named Horwood from Carbonear, while another account alleges that the Small family were the original inhabitants, arriving in the early 1800s. The earliest person said to have had a fishing room listed at Moreton's Harbour was a Robert Horwood in 1807, while a man named Thomas Knight was noted around 1810. Shortly afterwards a family of Taylors arrived, and the population increased rapidly.

As early as 1828 there were 100 settlers, a number which doubled ten years later; by 1891 this rose to 500 residents. Settler numbers declined in the early 1900s along with the local fishery. The biggest decrease was in the years 1911-21, through emigration to the US and Toronto. As of 1877 family names found at Moreton's Harbour were: Britt (or Brett), Covill, Deer, Dowill (Dowell), Hann, Knight, Miles, Osmond, Rideout, Russel, Taylor, Wall and Wolfrey. One of the earliest surviving land grants at Moreton's Harbour was made to Mr. Robert Woolfrey, followed by Anglican school teacher Justinian Dowell (1836-1911). Hailing from Dorsetshire, Mr. Dowell taught school on Small's Side in an area still called Dowell's Ground. Dowell lived in the community in the 1860s and 1870s before moving on (briefly) to Wild Cove, Twillingate, and then to Change Islands. Most of the town's early residents arrived from other parts of Newfoundland, especially Conception and Trinity Bays. Some, like Dowell, came directly from England, and possibly Ireland – an Irish presence may have given rise to the name Sligo Shore. In the 1857 census eight people gave England as their place of birth.

Although it has a 200 year history of European occupation, Moreton's Harbour has little close connection with Newfoundland's aboriginal peoples, but at least three visits by Native individuals are recorded in community history. It is reported that in 1819 a Beothuk woman named Demasduit or Mary March (See Chapter Six) stayed at Joseph Taylor's home after her capture by European settlers. In recent years Ms. Amelia Taylor donated a basket, reportedly made for her ancestor by Demasduit, to a Grand Falls museum. In 1822, just three years after Mary March's stay, a man thought to have been Mi'Kmaq visited Moreton's Harbour. This created great excitement among residents, most of whom had never encountered a Native, except possibly Demasduit. The man reportedly visited the residence of Henry Knight. Reverend Thomas Laugharne of Twillingate also arrived to meet the Native visitor. The incident was later recorded in court documents. After Knight alleged that Laugharne was just as much an Indian as his other visitor, the Reverend became angered and a fight ensued. Laugharne then took Knight to court over the incident. It is interesting to note that, as we've seen in the last chapter, Langarne's general conduct resulted in his removal from the Twillingate parish not long after this incident. About twenty years later another Mi'Kmaq stopped at Moreton's Harbour while acting as guide for the Slade firm's agent, Mr. Salmon, who was making a journey to St. John's.

Osmond Brothers' general store. Built by Mark Osmond in the late 1800s

Visits by Native persons were outside the pale of everyday life in Moreton's Harbour. Most time was spent simply in making a living. Although it had its ups and downs, the fishery was always the economic bedrock of Moreton's Harbour. Cod was fished locally, along with herring and some salmon and lobster. With its robust fishery the community became a commercial centre, and six merchants operated out of the area by 1921, including the Osmonds and Bretts. As early as 1787 six families living at Western Head, near Moreton's Harbour, were supplied by the Slade concern, which established a storehouse at Moreton's Harbour around 1830. Local historical tradition says that the community's first merchant was Thomas Colbourne of Dorsetshire. John Bartlett, acting as agent for John Colbourne of Poole, set up shop about 1832. Located at the bottom of Bartlett's Cove, the company's premises were taken over by Joseph Bain Osmond in the 1890s. Bartlett's old home still stands in the community. Osmond's business was located at Osmond's Side, near Riverhead. Joe Bain managed the firm along with Sons Dave and Lou. Having its own large wharves, storehouses and a cooperage, the business was later run by Fred Osmond, Hedley Brett, Charles Hoffe, Hardy Small and finally, Bud Osmond. Joseph Knight started a merchant house at Moreton's Harbour around 1900 which was located at Knight's Side, Riverhead.

By the late 1800s the settlement had become a centre of the Labrador fishery, sending nine schooners to Labrador in 1874. The need for larger vessels encouraged a local shipbuilding industry which started around 1850. Hamilton May reports that all of the vessels built at Moreton's Harbour were two masted, single decked craft ranging from twenty to seventy tons. From 1865-80 one or more schooners were built at Moreton's Harbour per year. In the period from 1883-8 sixteen vessels were built at Moreton's Harbour, a number of these under the aegis of builder/merchant, Mark Osmond. The French and Taylor families were also shipbuilders. One of Thomas French's creations, the eighty-nine ton schooner *Champion*, is featured in Roberts and Nowlan's work on Newfoundland sail vessels. Although a fine painting of the little vessel exists, not much is known about its history. French constructed the craft in 1888 for Moses Monroe of St. John's, and it was used for fishing and coastal trading. The *Champion*'s registry was closed in 1933, the schooner apparently being lost at sea years earlier. In 1900 French built the *Nellie M.*, a three-masted schooner of 261 tons, at Burnt Bay. By 1890 the local shipbuilding industry was in decline as nearby sources of good timber were used up. The last schooner constructed at Moreton's Harbour was the thirty-five ton *Fisherette*, built by George Taylor at Taylor's Room in 1926. Even with the local building industry losing ground, Moreton's Harbour merchants used such vessels to carry freight from St. John's until around 1960. General cargo schooners were sometimes hired to bring in a wide variety of goods. Some, like the coal schooner from North Sydney, Nova Scotia, carried only a single commodity. The building trade in schooners generated its own spin off, a small seasonal lumber industry.

The schooner fishery produced many tales of harrowing brushes with death. One of these was recounted by May in a manuscript work on the French and Taylor families. The *St. Clair* was a seventy-three ton schooner built by Theophilus Taylor of Moreton's Harbour, and owned by the local firm of D. P. Osmond. In December 1902 the vessel sailed from Moreton's Harbour under Captain Abram Earle with a cargo of cod, herring and cod oil. On five December the little schooner encountered a fierce gale that drove it out into the Atlantic. Amidst the howling winds and pounding seas the crew had to throw part of their deck cargo overboard, while dealing with other dangers like a fire from an overturned cabin stove and a snapped jib boom. The *St. Clair* was carried some 480 kilometres out to sea off Cape Bonavista. By this time the crew had lost one of their water casks, and food provisions were running short.

On 8 December the storm lost some of its fury; the crew were able to make more sail and limp their way toward safety. It was not until the seventeenth of the month that the *St. Clair* made it into St. John's and landed what was left of its cargo. Though battered and hungry, all of the schooner's men were safe. With temporary repairs made at St. John's the vessel returned safely to Moreton's Harbour, where she was fully mended. May notes that *St. Clair* then spent many more years in the Labrador fishery and in hauling general cargoes.[6]

St. Clair was only one of the Moreton's Harbour vessels which ran afoul of the northeast coast's notorious weather. The infamous "Liner Breeze" gale of September 1907 affected Moreton's Harbour just as it did Twillingate. Osmond's schooner *Pauline* was in harbour preparing to discharge its cargo of fish, 600 quintals in all. Breaking its moorings, the vessel went ashore on the rocks. Although Moreton's Harbour shipping suffered less destruction than in the larger outport, quite a bit of damage was done onshore. Three stores and one residence were damaged by the gale, along with the community's Orange and Fisherman's Halls. Such occurrences, while setbacks, never derailed the people of Moreton's Harbour for long.

Aside from the fishery and (later) lumber operations, the community was home to a pair of mining concerns in the nineteenth century, neither of which was successful. George Hodder, Uncle of Sleepy Cove developer Obediah, staked out and tried to develop an antimony deposit there. In 1876 residents digging peat on the western side of Moreton's Harbour found what was believed to be lead ore (galena). Reports of the find reached Hodder who set out to investigate, meeting up with another potential developer, Baron Francis von Ellerhausen. Ellerhausen had travelled from Bett's Cove after hearing the same reports of a galena find. He soon realized that the discovery was not galena, but an even rarer mineral – antimony. Today the element is used in certain medicines and as a constituent of alloys, but in the 1870s its uses were limited. Ellerhausen returned to Bett's Cove without trying to dissuade Hodder from his interest in the site.

Along with Corbett Pittmann and John Templeton, Hodder staked a claim to the area in the early 1880s. The trio made three small shipments of antimony, being joined in the venture by William Lethbridge and A. O. Hayward. Lethbridge was English, and spread tales of the find's worth in his homeland. Through his efforts the New World Island Mining Syndicate Limited was formed in Britain on 3 August 1892, buying the Moreton's Harbour claim for around $75,000.00. A report prepared that year by Fred F. Hunt described the mine as follows:

> ...The property is situated on the west side of the harbor and comprises an area of one square mile...Its eastern boundary

> crosses a portion of the waters of the harbor which thus affords a good water frontage...Moreton's Harbor [*sic*] is admirably situated for shipping...in fact it is one of the very best harbors in Notre Dame Bay...The mine proper is situated on a point of the shore between Fawcett's Cove and the western bottom of the harbor where a good wharf has been constructed and a space cleared for dressing ore & c...Two tunnels have been driven along the course of the lode for distances of two hundred and two feet each, the lower level is situated ten feet above H.W.M. [high water mark] and the upper forty feet above this on the slope of the hill...A vertical shaft has been let down from the upper level at seventy one feet from the inner end of the drift, which intersects the lower level at thirty four feet from its end. This shaft was sunk twenty feet below the floor of the lower level but the later part is filled with water...There is a hoisting shaft over the shaft in the upper level and a rail track laid along the floor of the lower level, from the shaft to the end of the wharf...The ore itself is...of a mixed character...It is on the whole however of a fairly good quality and I have been informed will average about forty five % of metallic antimony. Some of the pockets contain ore of a much richer quality said to have assayed 84%...As near as I can ascertain some hundred and fifty tons of ore in all have been mined and shipped to date, and there are at present in the inner part of the lower level and piled up outside some eight to ten tons of excellent ore...[7]

The Directors expected a good return on their investment, but were disappointed. Still, the initial venture did involve some short-term benefits for the community – in the 1891 census nine residents listed their occupation as mining. Only six years later the syndicate was swamped with debt and could not pay Hodder and the other original owners the full purchase price. They re-assumed control of the mine for only $500.00 when it came up for public auction on 26 June 1897. In 1905 the Newfoundland Antimony Company of New York agreed to purchase the mine for $50,000.00. Like the second owners, the New York company was unable to make full payment. Having received only $13,000.00, Hodder and his associates took the Newfoundland Antimony Company to court in 1912 and won back control of the deposit again. There was no reversal of fortune for the antimony mine. Hodder and his partners soon lost interest in a site that produced less than 200 tons of ore over twenty-three years of operation. In June 1915 the *Twillingate Sun* reported that

W. A. McKay and William Cook of North Sydney would reopen the Moreton's Harbour mine and construct an electric smelter at Botwood. The scheme apparently came to nothing, and in 1916 the site was abandoned for good.

The other Moreton's Harbour mining venture originated with an arsenic deposit on its eastern side at Little Harbour. This was found in 1896 by John R. Stewart of Little Bay. Stewart hired four men, and sank a shaft into the deposit. In 1897 125 tons of ore were mined from this deposit and shipped to Nova Scotia. Sadly for Stewart and his employees, their buyer went out of business and they were never paid for the arsenic. That seems to have been the end of this mining venture. Neither the arsenic nor the antimony deposits made a long-term impact on the economy of Moreton's Harbour. That being said, something might yet come of the industry. Reputedly, the ore from both mines contained about fourteen grams of gold per ton, maybe an incentive for future prospectors on New World Island.

"...one of the very best harbors in Notre Dame Bay."
The steamer Virginia Lake *at Moreton's Harbour, early 1900s*

While mining proved to be a short-lived feature of life in Moreton's Harbour, other institutions had more permanence. In terms of their religion, the population of Moreton's Harbour was mainly Protestant. Twelve Roman Catholics were recorded as living there in 1836, but they were gone by 1891.

The first settlers were mostly Methodist. The Salvation Army arrived in 1891, and the Pentecostal Assemblies came in 1935. To cater to these denominations Moreton's Harbour boasted a number of churches and schools. An Anglican church was built in 1823 close to the shore in Bartlett's Cove. The first school at Moreton's Harbour was established by Joseph Bartlett around the year 1840. By 1845 fifteen students were attending school at Moreton's Harbour. A Methodist church was built as early as 1836, and a school ten years later. The present United (Methodist) church was erected in 1897. Its principal designer was Joseph Blaine Osmond, who created most of its fancy woodwork. Thomas French added its bell tower in 1903, and a new parsonage was constructed around 1940.

Education standards in Moreton's Harbour were always high, and there was never a problem in providing a teacher. At least two of these teachers gained outside notoriety. Celebrated poet Edwin John Pratt (1882-1964) taught at Morton's Harbour from 1902-5. Author/professor David Pitt (b. 1921), who taught at Moreton's Harbour in 1941, produced a two-volume biography of Pratt, *The Truant Years* and *The Master Years*. The first faculty member appointed to the new Memorial University of Newfoundland in 1949, Pitt won the University of British Columbia Medal for Canadian Biography for the first part of his work on Pratt, and was named Artist of the Year by the Newfoundland and Labrador Arts Council. Pitt and Pratt weren't the only famous educators from the community. Memorial University College's first President, Albert George Hatcher (1886-1954), was a native of Moreton's Harbour. A university residence at St. John's is named after him.

Though Moreton's Harbour cultivated citizens of renown, it suffered from a problem common to many of Newfoundland's small settlements – isolation. This situation was partly remedied in the late nineteenth century when the community received its own post office. Its first Post Master was Mark Osmond. In 1908 the Newfoundland postal service established a telegraph station at Moreton's Harbour. A man named Hennebury ran the line, which was connected to Farewell Crossing at Beaver Creek and Port Albert. The town's first telegraph office was in a small frame building not far from the Church of England Cemetery. In later years the station was run from the post office. It remained in service until about 1965. Lloyd Jennings was the community's last telegraph operator. The Moreton's Harbour office was a repeating station for all of New World Island. Telegrams would be copied by morse code and phoned to eight other offices on the Island. A limited telephone system arrived in 1920, established by the postal service to connect its local office to Osmond's store and a number of important residences. Nearby Tizzard's Harbour was connected the following year, followed by Summerford in 1924 and Bridgeport in 1929.

As of 1998 Morteon's Harbour's population was around 228. With its economy based on a faltering fishery, Moreton's Harbour has seen a marked population decline in recent years, with the number of residents having fallen to 136 by 2011. Many homes in Moreton's Harbour are now Summer residences or occupied by retired locals. Some fishers remain, but in shrinking numbers; a good many residents now commute to work outside the community. Tourism is now becoming part of Moreton's Harbour's economy. There are a number of bed and breakfasts in operation, and the community is home to one of the only museums on New World Island.

....

Newville

Newville is located just south of the main tickle separating Twillingte from NWI on the east side of Friday's Bay. Located at Burnt Arm, until the 1960s Newville was called Burnt Cove. On charts it was identified as Byrne Cove. Nearby Little Burnt Cove was likewise given as Little Byrne Cove. Originally the area was frequented by fishermen out of Twillingate and Tizzard's Harbour (just across Friday's Bay) for Winter woods work. This was in the 1840s, and it was at about this time that the first settlers arrived at nearby Black Island. A family of Keefes were settled at Newville from Twillingate by the 1860s. Soon afterwards Burts from Tizzard's Harbour, along with Tarrants and Mehaneys from Black Island settled in the community.

In its early days the settlement was concentrated at the point between Little Burnt Cove and Burnt Cove, an area called Peter's Head. There a Church of England chapel was built. Other residences were located on the north side of Burnt Cove. Later a Methodist school/chapel was built between Newville and Indian Cove to the north. A larger United (Methodist) church was erected at Little Burnt Cove in 1938.

The inshore cod fishery was important in the community's early days, while the eastern side of Friday's Bay and the Main Tickle were renowned for their catches of bait species like squid, and for lobster. When Newville first appeared in the census it was given under the general heading of Friday's Bay. It was not until 1901 that the community was recorded separately, when the population was given as sixty-four. Aside from the inshore fishery, residents of Newville also participated in that to Labrador, and dealt with merchants at Twillingate or Herring Neck.

Seaside vista at Newville

Newville's population did not rise above 100 until the mid 1960s. At that time the road and causeway network was completed, linking New World Island with the mainland. Several families, mainly Rices, moved in to Little Burnt Cove from Black Island around the same time, and the town acquired its modern name. In 1971 the population stood at 138 and Newville was home to a new elementary school. By the 1990s only a few fishermen remained active at Newville. Many other residents were employed at fish plants outside the community, or in Summerford and Virgin Arm, NWI's main service centres. In recent years a Rural Development Office was run out of Newville, along with a Provincial tourist information centre, though their headquarters has now been transferred to private ownership.

....

Parkview

This small community, with a population of about 100, is located in the central portion of New World Island. Considered part of nearby Virgin Arm for most of its history, the settlement was first named Dark Hole. In recent years it was decided to rename the community as Parkview. The new name, though less colourful than the old, is a fitting description of the little town, which is adjacent to Dildo Run Park. With the adoption of its new name in February 1991 Parkview was officially recognized as a separate community.

From an early period logging was important in the area. Although only a kilometre or so removed from Virgin Arm overland, the two settlements were a considerable distance away by sea, which was the most efficient way to transport lumber. When a sawmill was built in the 1940s, a tramway was also constructed. Running from Track Cove, Virgin Arm to Dildo Run, the track and trolley system was used in transporting timber products. The Burt family built a sawmill at Dark Hole in the 1960s, and by the early 1970s a number of saw mills were operating locally. In recent years many of the people living at Parkview have had the surname Burt, or were related to the family by marriage.

....

Pike's Arm

A fishing community at the northeast end of New World Island, Pike's Arm was often considered part of Herring Neck. The communities are only two kilometres apart across Goshen's Arm when travelling by sea. Using modern roads the drive is a distance of twenty kilometres. Pike's Arm stretches over a narrow point of land which separates its harbour from Goshen's Arm. After Confederation a channel was dug across this isthmus for small boat transit.

Pike's Arm was most likely settled in the early 1800s, but it is hard to separate the area from Herring Neck in the old records. The central portion of today's Pike's Arm was often called Clerk's or Clarke's Cove before 1900. By the 1820s the Dalley and Stuckey families were already living there. In 1836 thirty-three people were recorded as residents.

The Arm was a good base for fishers, with a sheltered small boat harbour close to productive cod grounds. Setters with the names Blandford, Cutler, Liscombe, Richards, Stone and Watts arrived by the 1860s, most likely from Bonavista Bay. The Gilletts and Squires settled at Cannister Cove, closer to Herring Neck, but this area was later abandoned. The name Cannister Cove could have originated from the residents' practice of going there to obtain drinking water from the Cove's wells.

A Labrador fishery started at Pike's Arm in the nineteenth century, and was supplied by Duder's at Twillingate. The number of residents travelling to Labrador to fish rose after 1900, although an inshore fishery continued. After the Duder bankruptcy Herring Neck merchant George Carter was the main supplier to Pike's Arm fishers.

With the community located so close to Herring Neck, it is not surprising that the Fisherman's Protective Union, founded there, also influenced Pike's Arm, as it did many towns on the Isles. Pike's Arm residents set up one of the first FPU locals in 1908, and after the union established its own trading company at Herring Neck in 1912 many of the community's fishers took their business there.

In the early settlement period Church of England residents crossed the Arm to Herring Neck for Sunday worship and to attend school. By 1901 the outport had its own Anglican church, St. Paul's, situated between Pike's Arm and Green Cove; there was also a small school. Pike's Arm's Methodist community, twenty-one of 156 residents in 1901, also worshipped at Herring Neck. Esau Blandford, a planter at Pike's Arm, was said to have co-founded the Methodist congregation.

Many families left Pike's Arm for work in the lumberwoods, or moved to larger communities, as the fishery declined over the twentieth century. In 1940 the population was 140, and this had dropped to 124 five years later. By the 1960s many familiar surnames had disappeared from Pike's Arm, and a good many residents were seniors.

....

Summerford

The incorporated community of Summerford is just over 100 years old. Although a fairly new town, it is the major service centre for New World Island. Summerford has a relatively deep harbour, made up on its north side by New World Island, and framed to the south by Farmer's, Scrub and Strong's Islands. It was originally known as Farmer's Arm. The locale was frequented from the 1870s on by winter crews from the island's older settlements, particularly Tizzard's Harbour, who built schooners for the Labrador and French Shore fisheries. Thomas Wheeler and James Boyd (himself married to a Wheeler) settled at Summerford in 1892. Over the next few years many settlers with names like Anstey, Bulgin, Jenkins, Compton, Elliot, Maidment, Pelly, and Troake arrived from Twillingate, along with the Watkins from Indian Cove, and the Burts and Gates families from Tizzard's Harbour. The former Twillingate residents likely arrived in search of greener pastures following the 1894 bank crash that wiped out Duders and other fishery suppliers. With ample fishing, hunting and forest resources, the area was a natural draw for these settlers. Farmer's Arm was originally enumerated in the 1901 census, and had a population of 183. This number grew quickly, and ten years later the population stood at 246. In 1912 the community was renamed Summerford to avoid confusion with another Farmer's Arm, at Durrell, Twillingate (also renamed as Gillesport). It is thought that a local Methodist minister played a role in having the name changed.

During the first two decades of settlement, Summerford residents built about twenty schooners. Around half this number was produced by skilled builders Elijah and James Boyd. Other local builders included Frank and Arch Boyd, Fred Burt and Thomas Watkins. Summerford locals soon cleared most of the land in the area, but it was still a good base for lumbering and shipbuilding. Many local men worked seasonally as loggers for the Horwood Lumber Company, either at their sawmill in Horwood, or their Campbellton pulp mill, the latter of which closed in 1916. By the 1920s Summerford's experienced loggers found employment at central Newfoundland lumber camps supplying product for AND's paper mill at Grand Falls. About this time the Labrador fishery was in decline, and the local inshore fishery was made up mainly of Spring herring and lobster catches. In recent years long liners from Summerford have returned to the old French Shore and the coast of Labrador.

All was not toil for early Summerford residents, and a few notable events broke up the day to day routine. Harvey Bulgin relates that the first aircraft, a biplane, was seen over the community on 2 April 1921. Residents believed the plane was flown by British aviators John William Alcock (1892-1919) and Arthur Whitten Brown (1886-1948), although this was two years after their historic Atlantic crossing.[8] Perhaps the misunderstanding was caused by the isolation still gripping some Isles communities, though Summerford's links to the outside world were soon improved. On 23 October 1922 a local named Mrs. Small was party to Summerford's first telephone conversation with a caller from Moreton's Harbour.

Alcock and Brown's Vickers Vimy biplane lifts off on its historic trans-Atlantic flight, June 1919. Some Summerford residents believed that the first aircraft sighted over the community in 1921 was flown by the duo (inset)

Another break from the daily routine was the local lodge. Many early settlers from areas like Twillingate, Tizzard's Harbour and Moreton's Harbour belonged to the Loyal Orange Association. Naturally, they decided to start a new chapter in their adopted home. The Orangemen felt they needed their own building, and in March of 1931 began cutting logs on Chappel's Island. This rough lumber was mainly used to frame up the building, and was cut using a pitsaw. This type of saw was about two metres long, and worked by two men who placed their timber over an open pit – hence the name. Most of the finishing material like clapboard came from Gander Bay. Construction started in November 1931 and finished in 1936. Summerford resident John Howard Wheeler supervised the building work, which involved 6,000 man-hours of free labour! Upon completion of the lodge hall most community functions were held there, replacing an old one-room school. The LOA Hall stood in Summerford for more than seventy years but was recently torn down.

Although other days of the week were given over to functions like LOA meetings, Sunday was always reserved for church. The first Methodist (United) church was opened and dedicated in Summerford by Reverend S. S. Milley on 20 January 1918. On Christmas eve, 1921 the church received a bell which was then rung for the first time. A second United church, measuring ten metres by twenty-two metres, was built at Summerford in 1953. It is located on the grounds of the first church and, like the original, was built mainly with free labour. Much of the work, especially the interior, was carried out by master carpenter Gilbert Gates. Early in the twentieth century the Salvation Army founded a Citadel at Summerford, and their most recent community church opened in October 1978. In 1949 the first Pentecostal church opened in Summerford, with Hazel Young as its Pastor. Another Pentecostal church was later built under Pastor Young, while a third was constructed in 1975. Today the Pentecostal Assemblies are the town's largest religious denomination.

Along with their church, Summerford Methodists also built a one-room school. In the early days this was Summerford's only public building. It was used for everything from court proceedings, to Sunday school, to theatre productions. Enrollment increased over the years, and South Side (Strong's Island) residents were not pleased at having to row their children to school each day in boat. The Winter situation was even worse, as children had to cross ice that was often unsafe. School Board Chair J. H. Wheeler lived on the South Side. He contacted the Board of Education in St. John's for the go-ahead and funds to build another one-room school on Strong's Island. Since there was already one school in the area the request to build another was initially turned down. Wheeler and his team re-submitted the request, noting there was no school on Strong's Island. Strong's Island was presented to the Board in St.

John's as a separate community, and the request for a school was granted. The first South Side school was built in 1929, and a second opened in 1950. One of the first teachers on South Side was Fred Lacey from Carbonear. Mr. Lacey drowned tragically on 30 July 1937 while returning by punt from Dildo with a load of grass for hay.[9]

The Summerford United Church

The successful effort to build a school for Strong's Island resulted in it and Summerford being considered separate communities until incorporation of the Local Improvement District of Summerford in 1971; the town became an incorporated municipality in 1976. About a year after incorporation Summerford residents formed a volunteer fire brigade of twenty-six men, and a 2,270 litre pumper fire truck was provided by the government. In recent years the brigade has received new equipment, providing fire fighting services for all of New World Island. The closest additional fire departments are at Boyd's Cove/Harbour and Twillingate.

344 people called Summerford home in 1921. By the beginning of the 1940s Summerford had a population of 437. In the 1950s a few new settlers arrived from the Bay of Exploits. Still, the town did not take off as a service centre until completion of the roads and causeways made Summerford a more central location on New World Island. Since then many NWI services (like the fire brigade) have been located either in the town or just outside. The local fire hall building also houses Summerford's council chambers and a public library. The town's 2011 population stood at 853, but numbers have been declining in recent years.

....

Tizzard's Harbour

A fishing community about six kilometres northwest of Twillingate. The harbour was frequented by early Twillingate fishers, and Tizzard was one of the first surnames recorded in the "Capital of the North." Even so, no Tizzard's were among the settlers who first made their homes at the harbour in the late 1790s to early 1800s. In 1811 seven fishing rooms were reported at Tizzard's Harbour, owned by John Bide, John Forward, Andrew Locke, William Lacey, Philip Wiseman (after marrying the widow Spencer), and Thomas Colbourne. As of the 1836 census nineteen families, comprising a population of 121, were resident at Tizzard's Harbour. By this time the surname Bide or Boyd was the most common at Tizzard's Harbour, along with Burts, Forwards, Lockes and Smalls, all of which are still found in the area. The population grew quickly, due in no small measure to its good harbour near Friday's Bay, and a bountiful bait fishery. This was not to mention a large hinterland for hunting and timber. As of 1874 Tizzard's Harbour's population reached 298. Settlers were by then involved in the Labrador, French Shore and Horse Islands fisheries, some residents constructing their own schooners. In the late 1880s Tizzard's Harbour, like a number of other Isles communities, had its own lobster canning facility. In 1887 the *Twillingate Sun* reported on the product produced at Tizzard's Harbour. The editor wrote that,

> Two lobster factories have been started here, or one at Twillingate and the other at Tizzard's Harbour, the two owned by one and the same firm, Messrs. T. French and W. Baird. They are now in active operation and doing good work for the short time engaged in it. Not long since we were favoured with a specimen of the tins of lobster put up by this firm at Tizzard's Harbour, which appeared to be all that could be desired. The cans are very neatly made and carefully sealed, while the contents evidenced that the utmost care and cleanliness were exercised in the process of preparing them for consumption. First-class workmen are employed and no pains spared to turn out a No. 1 article which, we believe this firm will place in the markets, and we wish them every success in their new speculation.
>
> The introduction of this enterprise will be the means of affording employment to a good many people, and we only hope that capitalists would invest more largely in local industries, which would prove a source of revenue to others,

instead of so many having to be confined almost exclusively to the cod for a subsistence.[10]

Having originated through settlement from Twillingate, Tizzard's Harbour also sent settlers to other parts of New World Island like Fairbank, Hillgrade and Summerford. For many years Tizzard's Harbour maintained its connection to Twillingate, with many fishers being supplied out of the larger centre. In the early 1900s a pair of local merchants opened for business, Robert Boyd and Robert French, French having arrived from nearby Moreton's Harbour circa 1894. The community's commercial life declined in later years, though, and Tizzard's Harbour became reliant on Moreton's Harbour for many services, with Osmond Brothers the primary fishery supplier.

Osmond Brothers' store

At the beginning of the twentieth century Tizzard's Harbour and Twillingate maintained more than commercial ties. Around the time Boyd and French opened their doors for business the two communities were linked through a passenger ferry service with its Twillingate terminus at Gillard's Cove. The service was run by John Gillard, who had lost an arm when his muzzle-loading gun exploded at a wedding (It being the custom to fire off guns at traditional Newfoundland nuptials).

In the late 1800s some residents of Tizzard's Harbour travelled to western Notre Dame Bay for work in the mines at Little Bay and Tilt Cove. After 1910 lumber work in central Newfoundland became an important source of income for some of the community's young men. By the 1940s the population was down to 210, and today stands at around fifty people. Tizzard's Harbour is a fairly minor fishing centre, with many residents leaving on a seasonal basis for work. Some of the remaining old homes, and a church much larger than needed for current population levels, remain as signposts to the beautiful town's heyday.

....

Too Good Arm

This community lies opposite Green Cove. By the mid 1800s the Hurley family seems to have been established at Too Good Arm's northern end. Shortly thereafter a few more families arrived on the heels of an expanding migratory fishery out of Herring Neck. Church records from the 1870s contain the first written reference to the name Too Good Arm. The first family names recorded at the arm were George Hurley, John Gillett, Samuel Russell and their families.

Although the area was mainly Protestant, the Hurleys were originally Roman Catholic, but certain branches of the family later converted to Methodism. The Russells and Gilletts were Church of England, attending services at Green Cove. Later the Salvation Army arrived, making some converts and building a citadel.

The community's fishery was mainly schooner-based and conducted outside Too Good Arm, especially on the French Shore, up to the 1880s. After this date the Labrador fishery grew in importance. The Too Good Arm and Herring Neck areas were natural centres for this activity, providing good shelter for schooners. George Carter, based at Sunnyside, Herring Neck, emerged as the major fishery supplier for Too Good Arm after 1894. In the 1920s the Labrador fishery declined. Logging became an important source of income for Too Good Arm residents, just as it was for many men at Tizzard's Harbour. A few locals were also employed at the Cobb's Arm limestone quarry.

Today Hurley and Russell are still among the most common names in Too Good Arm. There is an inshore fishery conducted from small open boats and longliners, with many other residents finding work outside the community.

....

Landing stage and harbour at Valley Pond

Valley Pond

A fishing settlement on the northwest side of NWI. The community is built around a narrow cove, and former names for the town – Whale's Gulch and Salt Pond – were derived from portions of this cove. The head of the cove is known as Saltwater Pond, or just "the Pond." This area was not navigable, so fishing premises were traditionally located on either side of the entrance.

Valley Pond's location made it a prime cod fishing centre, being near herring and salmon stocks in the Bay of Exploits. The fishery off Valley Pond has been ongoing since the late 1700s, first utilized by English migratory fishers based at Twillingate. One fishery servant out of Twillingate, Richard Rideout, decided to settle at Valley Pond, and by 1818 had established a considerable fishing business there. In 1836 the first census was taken at Whale's Gulch, as it was then known, showing a population of eighteen. These residents were all Rideouts, the families of Richard, David, James and Henry, the latter settling at the cove northwest of the Pond. Throughout its history the majority of Valley Pond residents were Rideouts. Other family names recorded were Fudge and Jennings. One early settler was Charles White, who made his home in Hayward Cove at the southeast end of the Pond.

From 1845 until 1884 residents of the Valley Pond area were considered part of nearby Western Head for census purposes. In 1884 the population, which stood at 102, was recorded separately once more. In 1901 the community was enumerated under its separate parts. Eighty-two persons resided at Salt Pond, sixty-three at Whale's Gulch (probably taking in both the Cove and Hayward's Cove), and Moreton's Cove was listed with four residents – the only time it was noted as being settled. By 1940 the population of Whale's Gulch was listed as 114. It is unclear if this number also included Salt Pond.

Most of these settlers were members of the Salvation Army, which set up its own school on the path between Valley Pond and Moreton's Harbour. Valley Pond was noted as a centre of Salvationism on New World Island. Clarence Dexter Wiseman (1907-85), whose parents were stationed with the Salvation Army at Moreton's Harbour, was actually born at Valley Pond (Some sources say Moreton's Harbour). After serving in a variety of roles with the Salvation Army, including chaplaincy work in World War II, Wiseman went on to be the world-wide head of the faith from 1974-7. The author of two books, this Son of Valley Pond was made an officer of the Order of Canada in 1976, having already been awarded a honorary doctorate by Memorial University. Following his death the Salvation Army established the Wiseman Centre for the Homeless in St. John's.

Though less accomplished on the world stage than Clarence Wiseman, most Valley Pond residents were no less hardworking. Aside from their involvement in the shore fishery, locals also participated in the Labrador, French Shore and Horse Islands fisheries. The growth of this industry was restricted by the size of Valley Pond's harbour, which could not handle larger schooners. Catches in the community's early days were often sold to Twillingate, and later to the Moreton's Harbour firm of Osmond Brothers. Starting around 1910 the men of Valley Pond were also employed seasonally in the central Newfoundland lumberwoods.

....

Virgin Arm

Virgin Arm is situated at the head of Friday's Bay on the north side of NWI. Its name may have come from nearby stands of virgin spruce trees, or because the narrow arm remained unsettled until the 1870s. Though no one called Virgin Arm home at the time, the area was used for decades by Twillingate and Tizzard's Harbour fishers for Winter woods work and schooner construction. 1871 saw the first official record of settlement at what is now Virgin Arm. John Smith, a fisherman, was listed as a resident, and the total population was ten. Smith must have moved on fairly quickly, or passed away, as he was not recorded at Virgin Arm after this date. Local tradition tells us that the first permanent settler at Virgin Arm was a Curtis of Snellin's Cove, Twillingate; William Curtis was certainly resident there by 1876. In 1882 John Hicks and the Nicholas family (also from Twillingate) were resident in the community. At the turn of the twentieth century the Burts from Tizzard's Harbour, Gleesons, Hanns, Ings and Prices were also living at Virgin Arm. The community was first enumerated separately in the 1901 census, when it had a population of seventy. Since the community was located a fair distance away from the best inshore fishing grounds, the Labrador and French Shore fisheries were the most important to Virgin Arm's early settlers. The most profitable nearby fishing was for bait fish and lobster at Friday's Bay and Dildo Run. Located at the narrowest part of NWI (about a kilometre wide), a tramway was built across Virgin Arm in the early 1900s to connect the bodies of water for transporting fishing boats and lumber. Woods work always played an important role in the area's economy, a role which increased when the schooner fisheries declined in the 1920s-30s. Many men went to work cutting pulpwood, or supplying nearby sawmills. The population grew quickly in this period, rising from 178 in 1940 to 225 in 1945. The 2011 census count (which includes nearby Carter's Cove), gave the number of residents as 622.

Virgin Arm in Winter

With the completion of the road/causeway network in the 1950s and 1960s Virgin Arm South became a service centre for the local area, home to such facilities as a regional high school (Coaker Academy), and the New World Island Medical Clinic (See Chapter Thirteen). Today a new multi-grade school located between Virgin Arm and Summerford replaces Coaker Academy, which has now been torn down.

4

Fogo Island

The largest of Newfoundland's offshore islands, Fogo was one of the earliest settled portions of Notre Dame Bay. Of all the bay's regions none, even venerable Twillingate, has a longer history of European settlement than the island of Fogo. Records of European activity off the island extend back into the 1500s (Eric Witcher notes that early European accounts often used the toponym Fogo interchangeably when referring to Fogo Harbour, later the town of Fogo, and the island itself). The fishing grounds off Fogo Island were some of the earliest discovered and exploited by Europeans in the New World. The Portuguese, Spanish and French all sent vessels within a few decades of 1497.

Sometime after 1500 the Portuguese term *y del fuego*, or island of fire, became associated with the island. Soon corrupted to Fogo, the name's exact origin is unclear. The appellation was certainly in use by the 1520s, appearing on a 1527 Portuguese map. It is possible that Fogo was named by Gaspar Corte Real, after a settlement on the Cape Verde Islands. Fogo might also refer to forest fires that beset the island's northern corner – such fires were documented in 1867, 1875 and 1896 (Another forest fire, in August 1885, seriously damaged the main road from Fogo to Seldom-Come-By). There is also a suggestion that it harkens back to Native campfires observed by the early explorers, or even the heavy fogs that often blanket the area. Another suggestion is that Fogo could derive from the same root as "funk." This name was given to another group of islands, now protected as the Funk Islands Seabird Sanctuary. Both Fogo and the Funk Islands are bountiful nesting grounds for seabirds like gulls, murrs (turrs), and puffins. These birds all leave copious amounts of droppings, or guano, hence the name "funk" – bad smell.

However the term originated, from fire, fog or funk, "Fogo" has been passed down through the generations as the island's official name. This wasn't the only name the island was known under in the early historical period. In 1534 Cartier made anchor on a landmass which he named *Aves* (Bird) Island, that may well have been Fogo. As late as 1729, a British map showed Fogo as "Gory" Island, a name used on an Italian chart thirty years later. Around the time this Italian map appeared the place we now call Fogo Island was home to a number of Anglo-Irish settlements, giving them a historical pedigree of around 300 years.

....

Prehistory

We should never forget that the arrival of Europeans with their written records marks only the latest chapter in a story of human habitation many thousands of years old. Like Twillingate and New World Island, Fogo Island is no exception to this rule. To date less archaeological evidence of stone-age peoples has been found on this island than at Twillingate, but new finds are still being made – there is no doubt that Native peoples called the island home for many generations before Briton, Breton, or Basque ever fished our shores. The first of these groups were the Maritime Archaic (See Chapter Two).

Significant Maritime Archaic archaeological sites have been found at Port au Choix, in the Exploits River Valley, on North Twillingate Island, and at the Beaches, Bonavista Bay. Fogo Island has no sites of such importance, at least none that have been excavated so far. However, some ancient material has turned up. A large biface tool found in the town of Fogo may have come from a nearby quarry which is alongside a cobble beach and freshwater stream, features often associated with Maritime Archaic sites. A Maritime Archaic gouge has also been discovered at Fogo, possibly from nearby Seal Cove. No major living or burial sites have been located, though it is fairly certain that the Maritime Archaic were the first people to use Fogo as a base, or perhaps to call it home.

Though well-adapted to Newfoundland and Labrador's environment, the Maritime Archaic disappeared from the Province's archaeological record by 3000 BP. There is little hint of what happened to the Maritime Archaic, and no evidence of conflict between them and any later group. Why Newfoundland's (and Fogo Island's) first inhabitants vanished remains a mystery.

The next people to inhabit the island of Fogo were the Palaeo-Eskimo culture known as the Groswater people. The people now called Palaeo-Eskimos were of a different race and spoke a different language from the Maritime Archaic. Palaeo-Eskimo culture seems to have originated in Alaska around 4,000 years ago. In the Newfoundland and Labrador context Palaeo-Eskimo culture is generally divided into early (3800-2200 BP) and late (2500-500 BP) phases. The first phase overlaps with the second, but there is disagreement as to whether one derived from the other.

According to archaeologist James Tuck, the very first of Labrador's early Palaeo-Eskimo peoples bear a strong resemblance to Greenland's Independence I culture, while those in the period from 3500-3000 BP are often referred to as "Pre Dorset." A common feature of the Palaeo-Eskimo peoples were their tool forms. They used many of the same materials to make tools for similar purposes as the Maritime Archaic, but apart from their uses, early Palaeo-Eskimo tools were very different from those of the people they replaced. Most of their remaining material is stone, as many other substances decay in Newfoundland's acidic soil. Made from a fine-grained, colourful stone, these objects are noted for their fine workmanship and small size, the second feature giving rise to the descriptive term "microblades." The two groups may have shared some of their technology, with the Eskimos giving the Indians the bow and arrow, while the toggling harpoon was passed along in the other direction.

Evidence shows that around 3000 BP Newfoundland and Labrador experienced rapid population growth. This trend heralded the emergence of the Groswater people, named for Groswater Bay, Labrador. Archaeologist Ralph Pastore asserts that the Groswater tool tradition is similar enough to that of the Province's earliest Palaeo-Eskimos to assume that the new arrivals derived from the older group.

A 1997 archaeological survey of Fogo Island, conducted by Donald Holly, revealed an impressive Groswater site that may have been used for Spring seal hunting and for birding, although it lacks hard evidence of dwellings. The Groswater people probably made more intensive use of the island than the Maritime Archaic did; they may even have used Fogo Island in the Fall and Winter months. By about 2200 BP the Groswater people, like the Maritime Archaic before them, were gone. The Groswater people were followed by the Dorset culture. No conclusive evidence of the Dorset has been found on Fogo Island, though they were certainly resident at nearby Twillingate. With the passing of the Groswater people, the next group known to have used Fogo Island as a base were the Beothuk, whose story we will take up in Chapter Six.[1]

....

Barr'd Islands-Joe Batt's Arm-Shoal Bay

Barr'd Islands and Joe Batt's Arm are among the oldest communities on Fogo Island, while the smaller settlement of Shoal Bay was established much later. In 1972 Joe Batt's Arm and Barr'd Islands were incorporated as a rural district. A few years later the two communities and Shoal Bay were officially consolidated, making the town of Barr'd Islands-Joe Batt's Arm-Shoal Bay the largest on Fogo Island until all of its communities amalgamated in 2010. In 2001 the combined populations of the three towns stood at almost 900 but, reflecting the common employment problems in the region, this number dropped to less than 800 five years later.

Barr'd Islands is the second-oldest settlement on Fogo Island. The exact derivation of its name is not clear. Benson Hewitt relates a tradition of its connection to the explorer Corte Real. The name most likely comes from a number of islands, or narrow fingers of land, making up the settlement's harbour and acting as a breakwater. Barr'd Islands was not inhabited by Europeans until sometime around 1700, long after Corte Real's voyages, and then only during the Summer fishing season. Hailing from Poole, England and Waterford, Ireland, these first arrivals were harvesting cod, turbot and flounder along with Conception Bay fishers by the time of the Treaty of Utrecht (1713). According to Eric Witcher, the evidence places the first permanent settler families at Barr'd Islands in the mid eighteenth century, perhaps as early as Captain Vanbrugh's 1738 visit to Notre Dame Bay. Slade company records note eleven fishers operating at Barr'd Islands in 1800. Two years later the Cull, Forster and Primmer families were officially recorded as permanent residents. By 1816 the population was recorded as ninety persons. Barr'd Islands' first settlers were also involved in sealing and the fur trade. A 1987 *Decks Awash* article notes that Barr'd Islands was a desirable locale due to its close proximity to good northeast coast fishing grounds.

The early settlers dealt with the Slades until their Barr'd Island operations were bought out around 1850 by English West Country businessman James Rolls (1818-84/5). Born at Sturminster Newton, Rolls was reportedly descended from Quakers, and may have been a relation of the Whites, a wealthy Poole merchant clan. Rolls' premises were located on the inner side of Barr'd Islands' Big Harbour. They included a general store, cooper's shop, salt warehouse, a sawmill and a cod liver factory. Rolls also opened a branch store at nearby Joe Batt's Arm.

Rolls married Rachel Wells of Barr'd Islands, the Daughter of planter John Wells (1779-1851), reportedly wounded in an attack by the Beothuk at Shoal Bay. In 1860, following Rachel's death the previous year, Rolls wed the Widow Lucretia Winter. Among Rolls' children was a Daughter who became one of Barr'd Islands' first teachers, in a school house built by her Father in 1858. Another child was James Rolls Jr. (1843-1902), who married Maria Rouse, Daughter of Rev. Oliver Rouse (1820-1869) of Devonshire. The younger Rolls acted as a Fogo agent for Edwin J. Duder, and served as MHA for Fogo District from 1885 to 1893.

The town schoolhouse was not the merchant's first bequest to the community; he sponsored Barr'd Islands' original church five years earlier. The Rolls family were much loved at Barr'd Islands for their honest and cordial dealings with local fishers – unlike their successors, the family made their home in the town. An example of their community spirit was noted in the *Twillingate Sun*, where it was reported that, "...the female portion of the congregation has raised, through the energy of Mrs. James Rolls, sufficient funds to procure an elegant Brussell's [*sic*] carpet for the chancel, cocoa-nut matting for the aisles, and three beautiful chandeliers..."[2]

James Rolls

There is more than one version of how the Rolls business came to an end. ENL and *Decks Awash* say that the business was bought out by Henry Earle and Company in 1883. According to Witcher, in 1886 the Rolls enterprise was acquired by Edwin John Duder, who hired Thomas Anthony as manager. When the Duder company went bankrupt following the 1894 bank crash Henry Earle assumed the reigns. Unlike Rolls, Earle did not reside at Barr'd Islands, but the link between his family and the community was long-standing, lasting until the firm closed out its local operation in 1967. By that time James Rolls Sr. was long gone. Witcher says this was at his St. John's retirement home, Mount Dorset, while *ENL* gives his place of death as Barr'd Islands.[3]

Differences concerning the finer points of his career aside, there is little doubt that James Rolls, and his successors, supported a (generally) prosperous fishery. An 1874 census recorded that residents had landed 2,570 quintals of cod the previous year. By 1911 the settlement was home to more than 170 fishers who caught 2,672 quintals of fish, valued at over $18,500.00 – on Fogo Island only Joe Batt's Arm and Tilting brought in a greater value of cod that year. Barr'd Islanders were no doubt helped in their commercial endeavours by the adoption of the codtrap, and the Labrador fishery. In the twentieth century residents were active lobster and herring fishers as well. These hardy settlers were more than just fishers, however. In 1874 residents had their own saw mill, and a small sealing fleet of three vessels that took 450 animals. Barr'd Islands' prosperity was reflected in a rising population, the number of permanent residents increasing from 208 people in 1857 to 403 in 1891, and then to 453 in 1911.

From 1901 to 1945 the community's population remained fairly stable, and Barr'd Islands had a number of well-established institutions to serve its populace. The early settlers established a school soon after the area was first settled permanently – the Anglican school house boasted forty-two pupils by 1911. Religious instruction was also provided, although not until a generation or two after the first immigrants arrived.

The majority of Barr'd Islanders were Anglican, their first formal religious instruction coming in the form of Anglican missionary T. G. Laugharne, who visited Barr'd Islands in the Summers of 1821 and 1823. Not long after Laugharne's pastoral visits the community built its own church, St. James, named after Poole's Anglican church. Located on Foster's Point, St. James was only the second Anglican church on Fogo Island after St. Andrew's at Fogo. When St. James closed about 1870 its parishioners joined the congregation of St. John the Evangelist, located between Barr'd Islands and Joe Batt's Arm, with whom they had shared a cemetery (See below). By 1891 two-thirds of the community worshipped at St. John the Evangelist, while the remainder were Methodists with their own church, also built between the two settlements.

Methodism was established at Barr'd Islands in the 1860s, although some Methodist services were recorded as early as 1843, when a couple were married by a Methodist clergyman. A formal congregation came into being when Reverends Thomas Fox and Charles Ladner arrived in the 1860s. The first meetings were held in private homes, but a chapel, also serving Joe Batt's Arm, was built in the late 1870s. With a growing Methodist population – 139 of 403 residents in 1891 – the original church soon became too small for its parishioners, and a combined church/school was built in the 1890s. It was named after Rev. Jeremiah Embree (1844-90), for whom the town of Embree is also named. A third church, made of stone, was started in the 1930s. Named for Rev. William Mercer, who perished tragically in 1924 (See Chapter Fourteen), the new building was beset by the financial problems of the 1930s and was not completed until 1951. The Mercer Memorial Church remained in use until 1997 when a new United church was built at Fogo Island Central to serve the entire island.[4]

Barr'd Islands' churches not only provided religious instruction, but some of the formal education received by residents over the years. Witcher notes that there is no evidence that the Anglican SPG provided any education at Barr'd Islands, but he feels it likely that Rev. Laugharne may have distributed some teaching materials during his visits.

In the community's early years education was not provided by the churches, but largely through the efforts of local fisherman-planter Isaac Haggett. Haggett founded Barr'd Islands' first school in the 1830s, and he became the settlement's first teacher. This school, operated with some financial backing from the Colonial Government, was one of the first to open in Notre Dame Bay. By 1847 Haggett had forty-seven students, and this dedicated man continued instructing the children of Barr'd Islands until he retired in 1866. During his last years of service Haggett taught in a new school built in the late 1850s.

From 1865-6 Haggett was assisted by Eliza Rolls (1849-72), Daughter of the local merchant. After Haggett's retirement Rolls was joined by Alice Winter of Fogo, the pair teaching together until Rolls, now Mrs. Horace Herbert, died prematurely after the birth of a Daughter. Throughout the nineteenth century other individuals took up the task of educating Barr'd Islands' children, including James Candow, Eliza Meek, and Dorsetshire native James Rowsell. During this period enrollment numbers increased, and Rowsell taught seventy pupils in a one room school during his tenure from 1873-4. By the 1890s the problem of overcrowding in the school was becoming more severe.

It was at this point that the churches became more directly involved with Barr'd Island schooling. The Methodists built their own school to accommodate students from both Barr'd Islands and Joe Batt's Arm; it remained in operation until the 1950s. The Anglican school board built its own one-room school near Anthony's Hill sometime in the period 1911-21, while another operated at the Lookout. This school was eventually torn down in favour of expanded facilities at the Anthony's Hill school. By the 1930s the Anglicans and Methodists, the latter now part of the United Church, oversaw two classrooms each, with a total of ninety-two students. These schools were closed in 1954, replaced by two United Church schools at Barr'd Islands and Joe Batt's Arm, plus St. George's Anglican School situated between the two communities and serving both. In 1968 the last school located in Barr'd Islands was closed, and all local children have since been bussed to other parts of Fogo Island for their education.

Through whomever they were educated, and however much education they had, there can be no doubt that Barr'd Islanders possessed that gift for hard work common to most Notre Dame Bay settlers. By the 1930s, if not earlier, farming made up no small part of the community's economy. As early as 1891 Barr'd Islands was recorded as producing 136 kilograms of butter. In 1935 the town produced over 10,000 litres of milk, 25 kg of butter and over 1,300 dozen eggs.

The *Decks Awash* article speculates that this industry may have played a role in the formation of the Iceflo Co-op Society Limited in 1946. This enterprise was initiated in Little Harbour, Barr'd Islands at the residence of Nehemiah Combden. In 1951 this effort spun off into another venture, the Bardland Consumers Co-op, which served Barr'd Islanders for the best part of two decades. This Co-op operated its own retail stores, the second of which included a wharf for vessels to load and unload goods. A Co-op branch store, later sold to Eliol Lewis, operated in the early 1950s near the Primmer-Blake Cove Lookout.

Barr'd Islands

Spurred by vigorous activity like the Co-ops, Barr'd Islands' population remained over the 400 mark into the 1950s, despite earlier out-migration prompted by forestry work in Lewisporte and Birchy Bay. The good times did not last. Soon after Confederation problems began to plague Barr'd Islands' fishery. By the mid 1960s the town's population had fallen to only 274, although the numbers rose slightly through to the early 1970s. However, the overall population trend at Barr'd Islands from 1945 to 1976 was one of decline, as families were encouraged to settle in larger communities like Lewisporte. Even the pioneering Co-op was gone by 1970, a result both of out-migration and the death of some of its staunchest supporters. By the mid 1970s the population of Barr'd Islands stood at only 188, although fish plants had opened in nearby Joe Batt's Arm, providing some employment. By the 1980s the community's economy was based mainly on the longliner and lobster fisheries, along with some lumber work.

Joe Batt's Arm Roman Catholic Church

Joe Batt's Arm probably has the most famous name in a Province renowned for colourful nomenclature. It has long been the subject of good-natured jest. Many years ago the English humour magazine *Punch* even printed a Newfoundland advertisement that read "Wanted: a Nurse for Joe Batt's Arm." Presumably the original ad was meant in all seriousness. Many of Fogo Island's toponyms have mysterious origins, and this famous example is no exception. Archbishop Howley said that he had been unable to discover the origins of the name. A possible derivation of Joe Batt's Arm comes from a crew member of James Cook. This Joe Batt was supposedly Cook's own Brother-in-law, but deserted the explorer's vessel in 1763 and settled on Fogo Island two years later. The scant information available on this man indicates that he may later have become a trapper on the Gander River. *Decks Awash* notes that workers digging foundations for a fishplant in 1943 discovered a rough coffin containing the remains of an individual wearing leather seaboots – local tradition holds that this was none other than Joe Batt himself! Another possible origin for the town's name may be one Joseph Batt of Bonavista who, according to scholar Edgar R. Seary (1908-84), was punished at Bonavista in 1754 for stealing a pair of shoes.

The community's interesting name was almost lost in the early twentieth century. Around the year 1901 Joe Batt's Arm was renamed Queenstown, most likely a nostalgic tribute to the late Queen Victoria (1819-1901), who had just died after more than sixty years on the throne. Perhaps it was for the best that the new name never caught on – the former Queenstown remains Joe Batt's Arm to this day.

However the community got its unique name, there is no doubt that its European settler population goes back many years. The first permanent inhabitants arrived from Barr'd Islands sometime around 1780.[5] These early arrivals, with the surnames Brett, Freke (Freake), Taylor, Thomas and Wells, mainly settled that portion of the harbour closest to their former community. By 1845 Joe Batt's Arm boasted 329 inhabitants, about a third of whom were Roman Catholic. The first residents were all West Country English, but an upturn in the fishery created by the Napoleonic Wars led numbers of Irish, including the Hackett and Higgins families, to immigrate to Joe Batt's Arm. These new arrivals mainly settled on the south side of the community. Joe Batt's Arm's population increased through the nineteenth century; in the mid 1870s it was home to 569 residents, and was the island's largest settlement after Fogo – it even had its own doctor.

The 1874 census records only a Roman Catholic church, most likely since the community shared its Anglican and Methodist churches with nearby Barr'd Islands. St. John the Evangelist Anglican Church was located between the two communities. The church and cemetery were consecrated in 1853, while Witcher notes that the church was built in 1849. The cemetery was apparently in use prior to 1836, with funerals held at St. James, Barr'd Islands. Patterned after St. James Church in Poole, the original St. John the Evangelist Church was used until 1880, when it was replaced by another structure. This church served Joe Batt's Arm and Barr'd Islands until 22 January 1928, when was it lost to fire. When news of the fire reached the local chapter of the Society of United Fishermen, its membership extended an offer to Reverend Goodland to use their meeting hall for worship. The offer was accepted, and Anglican services were conducted at the hall for nearly thirty years. The third St. John the Evangelist was begun in 1930 on the site of the second church, but was not fully completed until 1957. In 2007 the church, now deconsecrated, celebrated its Golden Anniversary.

The United Church built a house of worship at Joe Batt's Arm in 1949. By 1964 the Pentecostal denomination had made significant progress, building their own church in the town. Joe Batt's Arm had a pair of schools with a total of eighty students as early as 1891. Twenty years later all three major denominations – Catholic, Anglican and Methodist – had their own schools. A multi-denominational school – St. George's – located in between Joe Batt's

Arm and Barr'd Islands, was built in 1954. St. George's served the community until 1972, when a new school opened in the centre of Fogo Island.

Churches and schools were only a few of the facilities serving Joe Batt's Arm. By 1911 a telegraph office had opened there, and a lighthouse was in operation. The lighthouse is a reminder of the industry that sustained all communities on Fogo Island, the fishery. Like their neighbours in Barr'd Islands, the fishers of Joe Batt's Arm were first outfitted by the Slades, then James Rolls, and finally by the Earle firm. In the early 1890s seven schooners were outfitted for the Labrador fishery, returning with over 1,800 quintals of fish. In 1911 residents landed 4,748 quintals of cod. Valued at over $24,000.00, Joe Batt's Arm's catch was the most valuable on Fogo Island that year. A quarter century later the town boasted seven schooners and more than 100 motorboats fishing off its shores. Keith Ludlow reports that the community even boasted its own form of small schooner, the "Joe Batt's Bully." Immortalized in a song by Change Islands' native Arthur Scammel, the Bully was used in the Fall fishery to the Offer Eastern Grounds.

Over the years Joe Batt's Arm's important cod fishery led to a considerable investment in infrastructure and innovative ideas. A bait depot opened in 1933. By World War II Fishery Products Ltd. had opened a fresh-fish plant on the community's south side, although this venture closed in 1946, reopening for another four years in 1953. Much earlier the community had embraced the Fisherman's Protective Union with its Fisherman's Union Trading Company Store – more on this in Chapter Ten. In a letter to the magazine *Newfoundland Fisherman*, Joe Batt's Arm resident Charles Brett was among the first to suggest the benefits of a co-op. The initial attempts at such a venture failed, but the idea was renewed with great success in the 1960s. By this time the island's fishery was facing widespread problems, including closure of the Earle business, and the threat of resettlement. The solution, a new co-operative venture, saw the fish plant reopened and a middle-distance fishery founded, based on longliners. For a time Joe Batt's Arm fishers had been taking their catches to Twillingate, but found the distances too great for a convenient fishery. By 1971 a number of new species were being harvested to supplement cod, including redfish and halibut (We will return to the Co-op theme later in this chapter).

That the cod fishery was of the greatest importance to Joe Batt's Arm is beyond doubt. This doesn't mean that locals put all their eggs in one basket. A salmon fishery supplemented earnings from cod. Even in 1911, with the highest cod landings on Fogo Island, thirty-two Joe Batt's Arm residents considered lumbering their primary occupation. Like their neighbours at Barr's Islands, locals made a significant investment in farming. In 1935 residents owned a variety of livestock including cattle, goats, pigs, poultry and sheep.

These animals provided their owners with more than 21,000 litres of milk, 422 kilograms of butter and 2,100 dozen eggs, an output topped only by Fogo.

Modern longliners at the wharf in Joe Batt's Arm

The daily toil of work in the fishery and on their small farms was only part of the lives of Joe Batt's Arm's people. Like most other settlements on the northeast coast, Joe Batt's Arm was home to a number of community organizations that provided residents with a welcome diversion from their labours, especially during the long, dark Winter months. Many of these organizations, including the Loyal Orange Order and various women's church groups, were also found in adjacent communities like Barr'd Islands, and throughout the Isles. A number of these groups served both Joe Batt's Arm and Barr'd Islands. The Protestant Orange Association, for example, formed a Barr'd Islands branch in 1908 and subsequently drew on Joe Batt's Arm for a portion of its membership. In recognition of this fact the Orangemen built their hall in between the two communities in 1914. As Witcher notes, the Orange Order, boasting more than 100 members by the 1950s, was especially associated with the towns' Methodist populations.

The Barr'd Islands/Joe Batt's Arm LOA Hall

More closely associated with the Anglican Church was the SUF, whose history was briefly recounted in Chapter Two. The Joe Batt's Arm/Barr'd Islands chapter of the SUF was begun in the late 1800s with seven charter members, including local merchant James Rolls. Meetings were first held in the local school or at Rolls' own premises, with a proper SUF Hall started in 1909. The official opening was set for April 1917 but was delayed due to the tragic deaths of several local men at the seal hunt – their story is told in Chapter Fourteen. The new SUF Hall had many functions, not least hosting "times" and wedding receptions. For almost thirty years the building was even used for church services (See above). SUF membership at Joe Batt's Arm/Barr'd Islands increased through to the 1950s. Witcher notes that in the following decades SUF enrollments declined as government programs and services took the place of the community self-help envisioned by society founder George Gardiner.

The SUF, with its emphasis on fishers helping one another, was found in many Isles communities. This is not surprising. ENL notes that Joe Batt's Arm shares a common commercial history with the rest of Fogo Island, and in the second half of the twentieth century the town acted as a link for many of the island's settlements and the outside world. Joe Batt's Arm was the home port of Harvey Cobb's vessel, the *Fogo Flyer*, used in a scheduled passenger service from the community to Lewisporte, via Dildo Run. Cobb's service also picked up passengers in Barr'd Islands, Fogo, Change Islands, etc.

At about this time the population of Joe Batt's Arm was on the rise.

This trend reflected a generally prosperous fishery, and some in-migration from resettled communities like Little Fogo Islands. In 1935 Joe Batt's Arm was home to 199 families, or just over 900 souls. As *Decks Awash* notes, these numbers were just short of Fogo's population, and more than double the number living in any other settlement on Fogo Island.

By the 1960s the population began to decline as the fishery ran into trouble. In 1971, four years after the closure of the Earle business, Joe Batt's Arm's population fell to under 900 persons. The 1991 census showed a population of 1,164 for the combined town of Barr'd Islands-Joe Batt's Arm-Shoal Bay, making it the largest municipality on Fogo Island. The strong link between the community and the fishery is reflected in census data since 1991. 1992 saw the implementation of the northern cod moratorium. Five years later Barr'd Islands-Joe Batt's Arm-Shoal Bay had lost more than 100 residents. By 2001 the number of residents had fallen to only 889, and to a mere 685 in 2011. These statistics point to the challenges facing the community, and all those on the Isles, at the dawn of a new century.

This being said, developments like the twenty-nine suite Fogo Island Inn, launched by Joe Batt's Arm expatriate Zeta Cobb and the Shorefast Foundation, may point the way to a more prosperous future. Today, the nearly 4,000 square metre Inn, designed by architect Todd Saunders, provides employment for dozens of Fogo Islanders and is a showcase for Isles tourism.

<u>Shoal Bay</u> is a smaller community than either Barr'd Islands or Joe Batt's Arm. It is located on the east side of a 7km long inlet – Shoal Bay – from which the settlement takes its name. Never a large community, Shoal Bay's population has always stood at less than 100 persons, reaching a high of ninety-six in 1935. Numbers of residents have fluctuated over the years. There were eighty-eight persons resident in 1874, but this dropped to only fifty-eight in 1891. Twenty years later the population rebounded to ninety-one, a number that did not change significantly until 1971, when Shoal Bay's population dipped to only sixty-three souls.

The community was founded in the 1850s with the arrival of the Brown and Pope families. By the 1857 census fifteen people were recorded as living at Shoal Bay. New arrivals with surnames like Bull, Pelley, Tarrant and Wells soon enlarged the population. All of these early settlers were Protestant, most of them Church of England (Anglican), with the remainder practising the Methodist faith. By 1911 the Anglicans maintained a school at Shoal Bay with an enrollment of eleven pupils.

In common with its neighbours, fishing (along with small-scale farming) played an important role in the economy of Shoal Bay, although *Decks Awash* asserts that the industry was of only "minor importance" in the mid 1930s. As early as 1891, however, Shoal Bay was noted as having fifteen fishers who landed 198 quintals of cod. In the 1930s a small herring factory was based at Shoal Bay, supplied by Notre Dame Fisheries. In 1953 the town was home to sixteen fishers, who mainly worked grounds off Little Fogo Islands.

With the foundation of the Fogo Island Co-op Shoal Bay gained a new commercial pillar, although only in the short term. Helped by Provincial Government funds and the support of the new Co-op, Shoal Bay became the centre of a small-scale shipbuilding industry employing local labour. The Shoal Bay shipyard focussed on longliners ranging from about fourteen to eighteen metres in length, at a cost of $40,000.00-$90,000.00 each. The yard produced nineteen vessels in its first four years, its entire production amounting to more than thirty longliners. Buyers came from a number of communities including Rose Blanche, Cottles Island and Harbour Grace. After expenses the new yard made a small profit in its first year of business, but total sales figures dropped thereafter. The Shoal Bay shipyard closed in 1974.

Shoal Bay is the closest community on the island to Fogo Island Centre, located to the southwest of the town. Here are found the island's stadium, high school and health centre, along with a number of private businesses. In recent years some Shoal Bay residents have found employment in service industries here, and at the fishplant in nearby Joe Batt's Arm. Many of Shoal Bay's current residents have the surname Cull, with the names Brett and Osmond also common.

....

Deep Bay

Deep Bay was first populated in the early 1800s by English settlers, whom ENL contends may have been brought there as fishery workers by the Slade merchant house. Located southwest of Fogo on the western side of Fogo Island, Deep Bay is found on the shores of a deep water bay called Hare Bay. When first settled the community took its name from its home bay, and was also called "Hare Bay." The town of Hare Bay was renamed in 1956, as there was another community of the same name in Bonavista Bay (For convenience sake the town will be referred to throughout as Deep Bay).

Seary noted one William Harebin (Harbin) as resident at Deep Bay in 1841. Harbin was followed by a Jane Kennedy in1847 and James Nippard ten years later. The first official mention of Deep Bay was in the census of 1845, at which time twenty-three persons, all of the Anglican faith, were recorded. As of 1857 Deep Bay's population stood at seventy, or fourteen families. The population rose to 107 in 1869, and by this date the original Church of England families were joined by a number of Roman Catholics. Aside from the settlers noted by Seary, other surnames associated with Deep Bay in this era were Coates, Cole, Downer, Eason, Harbin, Kennedy, Mullens, Nippard, Painter (Paynter), Snow and Waterman. By 1911 the population had dipped somewhat to eighty-seven residents.

According ENL, Deep Bay's location was an advantage in pursuing both the inshore and Labrador cod fisheries, and for sealing. With their harbour providing a fine anchorage, Deep Bay residents owned one sealing vessel as early as 1845. Eight of the early settlers were fishers. By 1869 five locals travelled to the Labrador fishery aboard Fogo vessels, while the inshore fishery brought in 134 quintals of fish, along with herring and seals. In 1911 Deep Bay fishers did even better, with 392 quintals of fish landed. Both the Labrador fishery and seal hunt lasted until the 1930s, though the inshore fishery continued to be a mainstay of the community's economy. As *Decks Awash* reports, all the families of Deep Bay had some involvement with the cod fishery. In the coming decades they diversified into other marine species like lobster and salmon, landing 1,979 kg and 2,268 kg of these species, respectively, in 1952. The salmon was sold to Notre Dame Fisheries of Comfort Cove.

As noted, these fishers and their families were mainly of the Anglican faith, with some Roman Catholic neighbours. A Church of England school was in operation in the community by 1891, with the Good Shepherd Anglican Church built some years later. By 1911 a new church school had been built and had ten pupils registered.

Unlike most Isles' communities, Deep Bay did not suffer from a declining population in the late twentieth century, with numbers remaining fairly constant, despite the resettlement of ten families (mainly to Fogo) from 1966 to 1975. Deep Bay's population, which stood at 106 in 1956, reached 150 by 1976. In this period a motel served residents and visitors, while a small multi-grade school was located in the community, though both were closed by the 1980s. At the same time fishing and work at the local fishplant, opened by Notre Dame Fisheries in 1978, provided most employment. In common with many communities on Fogo Island, Deep Bay once had its own co-operative organization, and by the late 1980s the local plant was being run by the Fogo Island Co-operative Society as a collector plant. Deep Bay has been impacted by the problems of the northern cod fishery, and its 2011 population stood at only eighty-five persons.

....

Fogo

Geography. Fogo can be found on its namesake's northwest corner, and was home to the island's first permanent European settlers. Fogo is one of Newfoundland's oldest communities north of Bonavista. In one sense Fogo's early settlement is a bit surprising, since its main harbour was always a challenge for seafarers. Encircled by shoals, craggy headlands, and many small islands – Barnes and Simms Islands among the largest – Fogo Harbour is difficult to enter in high seas or a thick fog. Still, the passage could be made if proper care was taken. As early as 1826 surveyor Thomas Smith's guide to mariners noted that, using caution, vessels could navigate Fogo Harbour in most winds, excepting south to southwest. Once inside the harbour conditions were much better, with Harbour Rock providing shelter and a good anchorage. Fogo's second harbour, Seal Cove, has always been easier to navigate, providing a sanctuary when winds made entering the main harbour treacherous. Even so, both harbours are often frozen from January to April, and pack ice is sometimes a problem until May or June. Drawbacks aside, both Fogo Harbour and Seal Cove were deep enough to accommodate schooners, the workhorse vessel of many North American fisheries until the mid twentieth century. Fogo Harbour and Seal Cove are joined for small boat traffic by a canal constructed in the 1800s.

Brimstone Head

Upon entering Fogo Harbour one's attention is inevitably drawn to Brimstone Head. Although not the harbour's highest point – at 103 metres, Fogo Head claims that distinction – Brimstone Head is certainly Fogo's most recognizable natural feature. At one angle appearing as an elongated, Sphinxlike ridge, from another Brimstone Head looks like nothing so much as a huge dome. The origin of its name is obscure, but Andrew Shea provides a possible explanation. Mr. Shea has said that, when split, some of the rock making up Brimstone Head has a distinct, sulfur-like smell. An old term for sulfur was "brimstone," perhaps giving the formation its toponym. Towering eighty-four metres above sea level, Brimstone Head is considered one of the four corners of the world by the Flat Earth Society. A number of legends have grown up surrounding Brimstone Head. It was once believed the feature was a volcano, and an old story holds that lead dropped into a certain "bottomless" hole on the water side of Brimstone Head will melt. Pirates were believed to have buried treasure in nearby caves (Does any old Newfoundland town lack its tale of pirate gold?). Today Brimstone Head lends it name to the town's popular folk festival, founded in the 1980s by a pair of school teachers. Held near the hill's base, the Brimstone Head Festival is a three-day offering of musical performances, delighting tourists and locals alike every year in early August.

Early Settlers. Geographic features like Brimstone Head have long fascinated visitors to Fogo, even if some, like Bishop Feild, weren't impressed with their more rugged aspects. Fogo Island's people made a good impression well before its natural beauty was fully appreciated. Feild's view of the settlers he met in 1846 was positive:

> The people [of Fogo Island] of course are all fishermen, or in some way connected to the fishing trade...[and] they seldom lose sight of snow and ice during the whole year. But if you were to think of the people, as in like manner strange and different in their thoughts and feelings...from your poor English neighbours, those particularly of Dorset and Devonshire, you might err and do them wrong. There are upwards of 1200 church-people in this Mission, the poor of the world indeed, but as capable of instruction, and generally as willing to receive it, as the like number of any of your rich and fruitful and quiet parishes. Their misfortune is, that being so scattered in different bays and creeks, and even, in this one mission, on different islands, they can but seldom receive the visits of their missionary, or attend the services of the church.[6]

The ancestors of Feild's poor fishers first arrived at Fogo around the turn of the eighteenth century. One of the earliest reports of Europeans at Fogo (and Twillingate) was provided by the Frenchman Abbé Jean Baudoin. Born at Nantes, Baudoin was one of many interesting characters with a link to Fogo.

Educated in his hometown, Baudoin had been a soldier before taking holy orders in 1685. In 1688 he arrived in Acadia (Nova Scotia) to perform missionary work. In 1697 Baudoin travelled to Newfoundland as chaplain to a military foray against the English. His detailed journal is a rare and valuable account of conditions in late 1600s Newfoundland. Concerning Fogo, Baudoin reported the area's use as a fishing station at the time of the French expedition.[7]

ENL notes that Fogo Harbour had a permanent settler population by 1728 at the latest, and Baudoin's account points to Summer use well before that date. From the beginning the fishery provided the main impetus to settlement, with fishers from older settlements like Bonavista migrating north following a poor shore fishery. At this date Fogo formed part of the "French Shore," a lengthy stretch of coast awarded to the French by treaty for their exclusive use in fishing. This provision was largely ignored by potential colonists, with Fogo and Twillingate marking the northern boundary of English settlement in the early eighteenth century. A Fogo census of 1738 revealed a Summer population of 215, with 143 of these settlers overwintering.

Fogo's first settlers were from England's West Country, but in the 1830s and 1840s numbers of Irish began arriving via Conception Bay. From that point on Fogo's two major faiths were Anglicanism – the English – and Roman Catholicism, the religion of most Irish. Starting in the 1860s another faith, Methodism, gained a significant following in the community.

Unsettled Times. With a rising population, Fogo attracted unwanted attention. In 1755 a Fogo resident named Christopher Bradley reported that forty French vessels were active on the northeast coast. Although fishing vessels, the craft were heavily armed and seemed to be surveying local harbours. This same Fogo resident likewise noted the capture of French spies on the island. These French activities probably had some relation to the larger situation in North America. Although the mother countries were not officially at war, British and French forces had clashed in America's Ohio country in 1754-5. In 1756, for the third time that century, the two nations formally declared war, the conflict becoming known as the Seven Year's War – the "French and Indian War" to the American colonists. The war only ended in 1763, with the last North American actions fought on the Island of Newfoundland. Fogo did not escape the effects of the conflict, and was harassed by French raiders.

The Seven Year's War dealt France a crushing defeat, but King Louis had his chance for revenge in 1775 when Britain's own American colonies rose in revolt. On the outbreak of war American privateers began cruising the waters off Fogo, with merchant-officer Jeremiah Coughlan preparing defences against them. The American Revolution finally ended in 1783 with the signing of the Treaty of Versailles. For the time being the Americans were no longer a threat, at least until war erupted again in 1812. At this time Coughlan's old canon batteries were revived, though it seems the town remained at peace.

Fogo Merchant Houses. Under the terms of Versailles, Fogo was no longer part of the French Shore, boosting British immigration. Another spur to settlement was provided by Fogo's merchant houses. Founded largely to prosecute the fishery, these merchant businesses maintained branches in a number of Isles communities, forming an important link between them in the days of the truck system. By the 1750s the resident population of towns like Fogo was on the rise, and the merchants best placed to benefit from this settled labour force were those willing to set up branches in the outports, rather than just sending ships to fish during the Summer season. Fogo first became a merchant base at the end of the Seven Year's War, when Jeremiah Coughlan, the same man who later defended the town from the Americans, set up shop. Coughlan is one of Fogo's true pioneers; we'll take a closer look at him and his alleged Daughter, Lady Pamela Fitzgerald, in Chapter Seven.

Although one of the first merchant houses established at Fogo, Coughlan's business was not its most important in the years before 1900; that distinction goes to the Slade family of Poole. Fogo became a base for John Slade the Elder in the 1760s, the town's importance to him increasing after Coughlan went bankrupt. In the early years Slade brought in many of his workers – mariners, coopers, carpenters, fishers, bookkeepers, etc. – from Britain and Ireland, with these "servants" signing on for different lengths of time depending on their occupation. Many Slade employees went home after their term of service expired, but a good many others took their chances on Newfoundland's rugged shores. It was with these settlers that Fogo's population grew in earnest.

With Slade the Elder's death in 1792 his Nephews assumed the reigns of the family business. A number of firms grew out of the original company, although they usually maintained close ties with one another and with the main business, John Slade & Company, based in Poole. One branch of their enterprise was located on the north side of Fogo harbour. This had its origins sometime before 1760, when Poole merchants Jeffery and Street bought the fishing room formerly owned by Pains and Durrells. The property was later acquired by another Poole merchant, Benjamin Lester, whose main Newfoundland interests were at Trinity, and then by George Garland. Also a native of Poole, Garland inherited a portion of Lester's business in 1801, and took full control of the enterprise four years later. An indenture of 26 December 1816 saw the Fogo property transferred from Garland to Robert Slade Jr. and John Slade Jr. for the nominal sum of five shillings.

Fogo North Side, c.1906. A branch of the Slade business was operated in this area

In 1870 John Slade & Company, then headed by Thomas and David Slade, sold all of its holdings at Fogo and Twillingate to John W. Owen, who in 1860 had signed on as Twillingate agent and attorney for Thomas' and David's Father, Robert Slade. The conveyance notes that Thomas and David had:

> ...contracted and agreed with the said John Woodhouse Owen to sell to him the said freehold premises [at Twillingate]...and all other personal Estate belonging to them at Newfoundland...for the price or sum of Five hundred pounds...[including]...all that Fishing Room or Plantation...near the Harbour of Fogo...[8]

In the 1890s the Fogo establishment was acquired by Owen's former partner, Henry J. Earle, becoming known by its familiar name, the Earle Premises. These buildings survived until the 1970s, and included a two-story nail store thought to have been built by Jeffery and Street in 1759. There was also a cooper shop and fish store constructed by George Garland in 1800 and 1802, along with structures built by the subsequent owners.

Another Slade with an important connection to Fogo was John Slade the Elder's Nephew Thomas (d. 1816). Starting out as a ship captain for his Uncle, Thomas later went into business himself, partnered with a relative named William Cox. Their firm traded at Fogo and other locales as Slade & Cox. As well as collecting and exporting fish, Slade and Cox also imported retail goods for sail to locals. Only three years into his merchant venture Thomas died unmarried. His significant fortune of £64,000, and control of his share in the business, went to a Nephew and a second Cousin, both namesakes of their late relation. The firm was later known as William Cox & Company, or simply Cox & Company, giving rise to both the Waterman and Hodge enterprises.

Bleak House. Built during the Winter of 1826-7 for David Slade. Its name comes from a Charles Dickens' novel

Robert Standley (or Studley) Slade, younger Brother of John Slade, MHA, had his own ties to Fogo. Robert Standley acted as manager of the family's Fogo operations until his death in 1846. Another Brother, also called Robert, then took over the Fogo business and served as the Magistrate for Fogo District. Robert Slade died on 1 January 1864 at what was, for the Slade men of the day, the ripe old age of sixty-eight. By the time Robert died Slade's Newfoundland operations were being wound down. As we have seen, their Fogo and Twillingate interests were sold to Owen in 1870. In 1867 another of Fogo's direct ties with the Slades had been severed when William Cox and Company closed, leaving the town's fish trade to a new crop of merchants.

Robert Standley Slade is interred in the cemetery of St. Andrew's

Anglican churchyard in Fogo, along with relative John Hayter Slade. Their graves, monuments, and their old homestead, Bleak House, are Fogo's only physical reminders of the important role the Slade family played in the community's development.

The "new" merchant houses that succeeded Slades are not well-known today, but must have had a significant impact on Fogo's economy in their time. Lovell's Directory for 1864, the year Robert Slade died, listed a total of nine merchants operating at Fogo. Like the Slades, Fogo's other early merchant houses hailed from England, mainly Poole. Men like Benjamin Lester and George Garland have all have earned a place in Fogo's commercial history.

An important merchant firm with a Fogo connection was founded by Edwin Duder Sr., who also established a large operation at Twillingate. Duder's Fogo premises, first owned in partnership with Robert Muir, were located south of Pickett's Cove. Consisting of piers, dwelling houses and a number of mercantile buildings, the property was purchased from the estate of one William Skinner of Twillingate in 1861.

A noteworthy member of the Duder family, with close ties to its Fogo operations, was Thomas C. Duder (1850-1912). Born at St. John's, Thomas became an accountant, working for his Cousin Edwin Duder Jr. In 1874 Thomas went to Fogo as the Duder firm's agent in the community, a position he retained for fourteen years. By the 1890s Thomas had set up his own business at Fogo, and went on to pursue successful political and judicial careers. Henry Mott described him as "a "shrewd and capable man in whatever he undertakes."[9]

Duders' original Fogo branch didn't fare as well as Thomas himself, running into the same difficulties as the family's Twillingate operation. The Duder enterprise was wound up after the great bank crash of the 1890s. On 24 May 1895 all the Duder company's holdings on the northeast coast were seized. The Fogo premises were bought from Duders' creditors by another merchant, Henry J. Lind, who gradually sold off parts of the property beginning in 1901.

A contemporary of Duders was the Waterman business. The successor to William Cox & Company, Watermans may have been the largest merchant firm on Newfoundland's northeast coast, paying out more duties than any of its competitors. By the 1880s the company outfitted more than forty fishing schooners a year. Letters sent out by Charles Edmonds, Cox & Company's agent at Twillingate and Fogo in the 1850s and 1860s, frequently mentioned, or were addressed to, William Waterman. Edmonds never specified Waterman's exact role with the company, but ENL describes him as an "agent and partner" with the firm. A letter to Thomas Cox, 12 September 1866, noted that Waterman and Edmonds had frequently discussed Cox's determination to wind up his Fogo operations in the Fall of 1867. By September of that year Edmonds was referring to the "new firm," Messrs W. Waterman & Co. In a letter of 9 October Edmonds noted that casks of oil shipping on the *Nymph* were marked W.W. & Co. Mr. S. Evans was charged with ensuring that the bill of lading and other shipping documents specified the oil as shipping under the auspices of the Waterman company. Although its main branch was later relocated to Twillingate, Fogo was the first centre of Watermans' operations.[10]

Fogo, pre 1905, with Wigwam Point at left. The residence, used by Hodge company managers, was called Wigwam House

From the 1870s on, the Watermans were partnered with Thomas and Richard Hodge, Thomas having been William Waterman and Company's Fogo agent. The Edmonds letters make clear the fact that members of the Hodge family were an integral part of Cox & Company from the 1860s on, working alongside William Waterman. As of 1871 Thomas had set up premises on Wigwam Point, now the site of Fogo's Co-op fish plant. Later, another member of the family, John Wheadon Hodge, the company's agent at Tilting, bought out the firm's assets on both Fogo and Change Islands. John W. Hodge ran the enterprise until 1918 when, on the death of his two Sons, he retired to Toronto.

St. John's entrepreneur Joseph Long purchased Hodge's Fogo branch in 1918, and that on Change Islands in 1922. Long renamed his new acquisition the Newfoundland and Labrador Export Company, and the firm was engaged for many years in the West Indian salt fish export trade. Members of the Layman family managed the firm's Fogo operations for a number of years, and in the community the Newfoundland and Labrador Export Company is often remembered simply as "Laymans." The company was one of the last of the old merchant firms operating in Fogo, only closing its doors in 1958.

Henry John Earle

Another long-lived Fogo merchant establishment, and the one most familiar to older residents today, was that run by the Earle family. The Earles originated in the English town of Dartmouth, County Devonshire. The first member of the family to live in Newfoundland was Henry Earle, born circa 1809. According to author Cyril Poole, Henry came to the Colony sometime between 1835-40 to work as a tailor to the British Army garrison in St. John's. With the disbanding of the garrison in 1870 Earle set up his own tailor shop near the city's waterfront. Earle's Wife Catherine (nee Noseworthy) died two years earlier, but not before the couple produced a large family. The eldest of this successful brood was named Henry John.

The Earle family's connection with Fogo began with Henry John Earle. Born at St. John's, young Henry was educated at the Church of England Academy (Later known as Bishop Feild College). His first career was that of a piano teacher at Twillingate. Switching occupations, the ambitious youth became a bookkeeper. One source reports that his first job at Fogo was bookkeeper for Slade and Company. In 1869, about the time Slade's local assets were being sold off, Henry formed a partnership with John W. Owen, the company's former attorney/agent. Named Owen & Earle, this enterprise lasted nearly a quarter century; it was only dissolved in 1893. In that year Owen assumed control of the partnership's Twillingate operations, while Earle acquired their Fogo assets. By the early 1900s Earle was operating his own Twillingate branch, with others at Herring Neck and Change Islands.

Like many stories associated with this region, there is more than one account of how Henry Earle started his business career. Another slant on his early life asserts that Earle's first bookkeeping job was with John Owen himself, not the Slades. In this version young Henry travelled to Fogo as Owen's manager, the two men becoming partners after Earle bought shares in Owen's establishment. In 1897, so the story goes, Owen retired to England. Earle then bought out Owen's remaining business interests along with his dwelling, Bleak House, which Owen had acquired from the Slades. From that point on Bleak House became the Earle's main residence.

Henry wed Amelia Rolls, a Daughter of merchant James Rolls of Barr'd Islands. In 1912 the Earle business was renamed Earle, Sons & Company, as a new generation assumed more responsibility from their Father. Five years later the business was incorporated as Earle Sons & Company, Ltd., with Henry's Son Harold (1884-1954) as manager. Like most Newfoundland merchant firms, Earles was heavily involved with the salt fish trade, but in keeping with predecessors like Slades, did not limit their enterprise to this one commodity. Besides exporting salt cod the company was involved in the production of cod oil, lobster, salmon and seal products. In 1946, during Harold's tenure as manager, the Earles expanded into freezing and canning fish. The firm had their own line of partridgeberry (lingonberry) jelly, and pet food marketed under the brand name "Happy Cat," which sold in Canada and the United States for twelve cents a can. Although the Earle company established branches in other Isles communities, including Barr'd Islands, Joe Batts Arm, Tilting, Change Islands and Twillingate, their main base of operations remained at Fogo.

The family had a long business tradition and boundless energy, but competition from motorized fishing draggers, the relocation of Fogo fishers, and declining fish stocks led to a rethinking of their merchant ventures. The company's Change Islands branch was closed as early as the 1950s, followed by those at Joe Batt's Arm, Tilting and Barr'd Islands in the mid 1960s. In a 1967 interview with the *Evening Telegram*, company President Brian Earle said the firm would close down its salt fish plant and general store at Fogo by the end of the year. According to Earle, production at their Fogo salt fish plant dropped from a peak of 60,000 quintals to only 4,000 quintals in 1966. Earle Sons & Company, Ltd. ceased to exist in 1968, taking with it around 125 jobs in the fish plant and cannery, plus another fifteen in the retail store.

In the pre Confederation era merchants like the Earles were an important cog in the development of Fogo, and all other Isles communities. This does not mean that relations between the firms and locals were always smooth. Rev. Charles Pedley noted that in 1805, the heyday of the Slade business, Fogo Islanders complained to Governor Sir Erasmus Gower (1744-1815) about the discrepancy in prices between goods paid for in fish catches, and those bought with cash or bills of exchange. There was also a significant difference between fish prices paid in St. John's and those in the outports. The people of Fogo wrote to Gower that,

> through the impositions of the merchants or their agents in the said island by their exorbitant prices on shop goods and provisions, they were from year to year held in debt, so as not daring to find fault, fearing they might starve at the approach of every winter...[and further] that the said merchants arrogate to themselves a power not warranted by any law, in selling to us every article of theirs at any prices they think fit, and taking from your petitioners the produce of the whole year at whatsoever price they think fit to give...In short, let it suffice to inform Your Excellency that they take it on themselves to price their own goods, and ours also, as they think most convenient to them.[11]

Feeling the matter to be of some urgency, Gower drafted the following reply:

> Whereas I am informed that a practice has prevailed in some of the outports of this island among the merchants of not informing their dealers of the prices of the supplies advanced for the season, or the prices they will allow for the produce, until they are in possession of the planter's voyage, whereby the latter are exposed to great impositions, the merchants are hereby required to make known to their dealers before the 15th day of August in every year, or at the time of delivery, the prices of provisions and other commodities sold by them, and the prices they will give for fish and oil, and to fix a schedule thereof in some conspicuous part of their respective stores ; and in case any merchant shall neglect to comply with this useful injunction, and a dispute shall arise between him and any dealer respecting the prices charged on such

> merchant's account, and such dispute shall be brought into a court of justice, the same shall be determined according to the lowest price charged for such goods, and the highest price given for fish and oil by any other merchant in that district. And the judge of the Supreme Court, the surrogates and the magistrates, are hereby strictly enjoined in all such cases to govern themselves by this regulation. Given under my hand, September 12, 1805.[12]

This correspondence shows that the truck system could easily work to the detriment of fishers. Even so, it was a solid, though disliked, foundation of outport life for generations. The loss of the Earle business ended Fogo's direct connection with the old merchanting firms and the way of life they represented, but their presence can still be felt. The traditional English fish merchant houses like Slades, and their successors, were a factor in the early growth of Fogo. To seventeenth and eighteenth century merchants Newfoundland was a fishing station, nothing more. Promoting permanent settlement, or the growth of an American-style colony was never their goal. Still, it was through their activities, and the occasional desertion from the Royal Navy, that the first settlers found their way to Newfoundland's rocky shores, making homes in places like Fogo. By the second half of the eighteenth century Fogo was already a large population centre, at least compared with most of Notre Dame Bay. As of 1836 the community's permanent population was 588.

The Fogo Fishery. Although they were a part of the process, the merchant companies were not exclusively responsible for attracting settlers to the Fogo area. Settlements like Lion's Den, Locke's Cove and Eastern Tickle grew up near Fogo when Conception Bay residents, faced with declining fisheries in their home outports, settled in the 1830s and 1840s. By 1869 the resident population of Fogo and the small villages nearby stood at 976. The most common surnames of this era were Downer, Dwyer, Farrell (Farewell), Oake, Pickett, Randell, Torrwill (Torraville) and Waterman. The family name Ludlow was found at Back Cove, while Leit (Leyte) and Paine appeared in Eastern Tickle.

Eastern Tickle, c.1900

Like their predecessors, the new settlers came to fish – Fogo's reason for being has always been the fishery. Fogo residents owned an average of twenty to thirty fishing craft per year from 1772 on. In those days the Fogo fishery was exclusively inshore, and nearly all shipping using the port were fishing vessels. The populations of Fogo and nearby Bonavista were similar in this era, but it is reported that many more vessels called at Fogo during the fishing season.

During the century to come another fishery important to Fogo was that off Labrador. Historian Shannon Ryan believes that this fishery grew out of the traditional northeast coast fishery, with vessels sailing north to Labrador in years when catches on their usual grounds were poor. The Labrador fishery expanded after the 1814 Treaty of Paris restored parts of Newfoundland's northern fisheries to French control. By 1820 the number of craft travelling to Labrador to fish had greatly increased. This fishery was important to Fogo throughout most of the nineteenth century, and twenty-five schooners were outfitted for the voyage to Labrador in 1891. By this date Fogo's Labrador fishery was already waning. Comparing 1890 to 1910, Ryan noted that landings of Labrador fish at Fogo had dropped by half.

With the Labrador fishery in decline from the 1890s on, economic hardship was felt by many small Newfoundland settlements. Even so, Ryan believes that this fishery, along with the Spring seal harvest, was a key factor in the survival of many Newfoundland outports; this was certainly the case at Fogo. The names of men like Patrick Miller and Ambrose Payne, along with the schooners they captained, are still synonymous with Fogo's Labrador fishery in the early twentieth century. Fogo merchants were actively engaged in the Labrador fishery, with the Slades, Duders and Thomas Hodge all sending schooners north in search of cod. The distress caused by the declining Labrador fishery was real enough, but Labrador cod remained important to the community through the 1940s. Even today a few longliner crews fish off "the Labrador," but their catches are small compared to the heady days of the 1890s when as much as 20,000 quintals of Labrador fish might be landed at Fogo.

Though the Labrador fishery was important to Fogo residents, the harvest most associated with the community, and with most Newfoundland outports, was the "shore" fishery. Conducted from small, open boats, using simple gear like hooks and lines, the shore fishery was a hallmark of the industry from the eighteenth century on. With a number of productive grounds on the nearby Fogo Shelf, the island was well suited to the role of inshore fishing centre. As early as 1728 residents of Fogo Island produced 19,000 quintals of salted shore fish. The shore fishery remained the bedrock of the Fogo fishery for more than two centuries. In 1874 inshore fishers based at Fogo Harbour were recorded as landing more than 7,000 quintals of cod, while nearby settlements like Eastern Tickle and Lion's Den brought in a combined 4,820 quintals.

These figures sound impressive for a pre modern fishery, but they should not lead us to think the industry was always reliable. The shore fishery relied on the seasonal migration of cod from their offshore breeding grounds, a process that could easily be affected by temperatures and tides. Starting around 1720 Fogo experienced a prolonged decline of inshore fish landings, although catch numbers rebounded after 1745.

Oftentimes, the greatest want was felt in late Winter when supplies ran low, especially if the previous year's fishing had been poor. Fogo residents experienced a particularly difficult year in 1867, harkening back to 1832-3 at Twillingate. In his letters Charles Edmonds recorded some of the difficulties facing local fishers, and their desperate response. On 5 March he noted that "[t]imes are miserably dull here, and poverty and misery increasing daily on all sides. The Establishments of Duder and Scott, are issuing weekly rations of...meal and molasses..."[13] On 24 March Edmonds observed that at Fogo conditions were "...frightfully bad, hundreds bordering on starvation since Govt aid has ceased. There is not a bag of bread to be purchased in the place, and but a little flour remaining."[14] By this time Cox's retail store had been broken into three times, and provisions – butter and pork – stolen. The thieves had gained entry to the store by going up through the floor boards, and Duder's establishment had also been robbed. While admitting the desperate plight of many people at Fogo, Edmonds believed that in many cases this was brought on "...through dishonesty and laziness."[15] This was a typical Victorian reaction to working class unrest. No doubt the poor inhabitants had toiled as hard as they had in years of plenty, with far less reward.

While times were certainly hard, starvation was by no means the norm. Over the years inshore fishers, at Fogo and elsewhere, were greatly aided by new technological developments, especially the appearance of the cod-trap (a box-like net), and marine steam engines in the mid 1800s. Even so, the fishery remained a fickle mistress; in the 1890s Fogo's shore fishery declined compared with that based off Labrador. By 1911, however, the attention of local merchants had turned away from Labrador and back toward the local grounds. That year only 800 quintals of Labrador cod was taken by Fogo vessels, compared with 7,118 quintals of shore fish.

While the cod fisheries remained the pillar of Fogo's economy, some diversification was attempted. In 1891 Fogo, with a population of 1,133, had its own lobster factory, employing twenty-two persons. Twenty years later the factory was still in operation, but had suffered a downturn. In 1911 the factory had only four employees, and packed a mere twenty-two cases of lobster, compared with 400 cases in 1891. Like the lobster factories on New World Island, this venture had little long-term impact on Fogo's economy.

Of greater importance to the town of Fogo was the seal "fishery." For generations this harvest was vital to Newfoundland's economic well-being, both in rural areas and the capital, St. John's. In the eighteenth century Notre Dame Bay's most important seal harvest was carried on in the Winter months, and for many years a portion of the catch was taken in nets. By the early 1770s residents of Twillingate and Fogo Districts earned an average of £1,700 a year from the Winter hunt, with Fogo used as a base for the industry.

Within a few years the first vessels set out from St. John's to engage in a new Spring seal fishery. In 1804 hunters from Fogo district harvested more than 22,000 seals during the Spring and Winter hunts. Eleven vessels were used in the Spring hunt that year, by which time Winter seal catches were declining. In the 1840s, a time when half the men of Notre Dame Bay were employed in the Spring hunt, Fogo had its own vats for rendering seal fat into oil.

The seal hunt experienced many ups and downs. In letters written in the Winter of 1866-7 Edmonds lamented that "...I regret to say very few seals [have] been taken...up to this date [24 December]...[T]his is a regular duffer of a place for catching seals in net."[16] With the appearance of steamers late in the century the cost of conducting a seal hunt rose, and only a few owners could afford to maintain sealing fleets. This development saw the industry concentrated at St. John's. Outport fleets like Fogo's were soon a memory, and by the late 1800s it was common for outport sealers to travel to the capital in search of work at the ice each Spring.

After the First World War seal prices fell, and steel icebreakers introduced before the war were withdrawn from the hunt. In the post 1945 era most large sealing vessels were owned outside the Province, while an unregulated hunt saw seal numbers decline markedly. By the 1960s the anti-sealing movement, which continues to this day, had been born. Even so, Fogo hunters continue to pursue the seals onto the ice flows each Spring, today often from small, open boats.

Justice. Despite the uncertainties of its various fisheries, and the seal hunt, Fogo residents were able to eke a living from the sea through to the late twentieth century. Stability was reflected in local demographics; from 1891, and into the early 1900s, Fogo's population remained fairly constant. As the largest settlement in the area, Fogo was often regarded as the unofficial capital of its district, and services tended to concentrate in the community. Fogo had a number of coopers like the Layman family, and blacksmith shops, of which Lem Anthony's is the best known today. Fogo was also the base for one or more doctors from the nineteenth century on (See Chapter Thirteen).

Like Twillingate, its neighbour to the west, Fogo became a centre for justice in the pre Confederation era. As early as 1821 Fogo had its own police Constable in the person of John Ludlow, who emigrated from the town of Warminster, Wiltshire a few years before. During his career Ludlow also acted in the capacity of Sheriff's Officer and Inspector of Pickled Fish. Ludlow had one of the longest law enforcement careers ever in a single Newfoundland community. In 1865 a local Grand Jury made a presentment to Supreme Court Justice, and former Prime Minister, Hugh Hoyles (1814-88) on Ludlow's behalf. The jurors noted that, having served Fogo for forty-four years, Ludlow had "...become from infirmity of age unable to perform his duty [and that] in consideration of his long services as a public servant we respectfully recommend him to your favorable[*sic*] consideration and influence to procure for him a retiring allowance."[17] It appears this was not granted, and Ludlow continued to serve his adopted home until around 1872, when he was in his late seventies. In that year Ludlow, who made his home at Back Cove, described his trade as "retired fisherman." This suggests he was a Special Constable who pursued another occupation, with policing as a part-time career. John Ludlow died in 1875 at the age of eighty, and for a time his Son William assumed the role of Special Constable.

Newfoundland Constabulary in full dress uniform at Fort Townsend, St. John's, 1937

In 1871 the Newfoundland Constabulary had been reorganized under a new Police Act, and by 1879 Fogo received its first full-time Constable, Thomas Russell. Like most of the Constables who succeeded him, Russell's time at Fogo was fairly short. At least two of these had a longer tenure at Fogo's one-man detachment. Born at Harbour Buffett, and joining the Force in 1883,William Shave arrived at Fogo around 1899, remaining in the community until the mid 1920s. With his long connection to Fogo, Shave was considered as one of their own by locals. When the Great War erupted in 1914 several of his Sons enlisted for service, with at least one paying the supreme sacrifice. Fogo's last Constable was John Harvey, who served from 1935 to 1947. When Harvey became seriously ill in the Summer of 1947 it was decided to transfer the jurisdiction of Fogo from the Constabulary to the Newfoundland Ranger Force. Harvey was replaced by Ranger Allan G. Anstey (Regt. No. 100), who became Fogo's first RCMP officer in 1950. This force provides police services on Fogo Island to this day.

Policing was but one component of the judicial system. For many years Fogo had its own court house, which was also the town's public building. The Fogo Court House had its origins in 1865 when residents petitioned Chief Justice Hoyles, noting that "...considerable inconvenience is felt in this part of the District from the want of a suitable Court House and Lock-up..."[18] The facility did not materialize right away, but in 1872 the Colonial Government bought a parcel of land from James Rowsell for £160, and a court house was in operation on the site the following year. By 1908 the "old and dilapidated" court building was sold to Patrick Miller at public auction for the sum of $115.00, on the condition that Miller had it moved. A new court house, similar to one at Burin, was then built on the same site. The structure had two fronts, one facing Fogo harbour, and the other facing the main road. The court house served a number of purposes. It had police and Magistrate's offices upstairs, with telegraph and customs offices, living quarters, and a jail downstairs. Even in 1949 the exterior was considered well maintained, though both the living quarters and jail left something to be desired.

Fogo's court house witnessed sessions of the Supreme Court when justices like Hoyles would arrive on circuit, usually in the Fall, to hear the most serious local cases. Other judicial proceedings were normally carried out under the auspices of a Stipendiary Magistrate. Fogo had six of these through to the 1930s, the first being James Fitzgerald of Tintern, Ireland. Fitzgerald came to Newfoundland in 1826, working with Slade & Company. Appointed in the 1870s, Fitzgerald served as Fogo Magistrate until his death in 1891 at age seventy-nine. Another notable Magistrate was Thomas Malcolm, who was also Fogo's resident physician (See Chapter Thirteen). Nehemiah Short, who served from about 1925-32, became Newfoundland's Chief Electoral Officer during the Confederation referendums of 1948, a position he held with the Province until 1963. He also served as Deputy Minister of Economic Development.

Social Life. Though heady matters like the law were important, they made up only a small part of life at Fogo. As at Twillingate and New World Island, the long days of backbreaking work still left some time for socializing. The court house was sometimes used for social activities, like a dance in 1910. Fogo was home to many organizations familiar in other communities of Notre Dame Bay, like the Knights of Columbus and the Orangemen

One society whose lodge still stands at Fogo, though in an altered form, was the Society of United Fishermen. The SUF has been discussed in connection with its Twillingate branch; that at Fogo was probably granted its charter in 1874, only a year after the SUF was founded. It is likely that Fogo's SUF Hall was built that same year, with a "gambrel" roof construction. According to the work *Ten Historic Towns*, this type of roof was ideal for structures like the hall, in which a large amount of headroom was needed. With its curved peak the gambrel roof was difficult to build and was rarely used in constructing houses. Sadly, this feature of the old hall does not survive today.

Fogo South Side, c.1900. The Miller house is near the centre of the picture

Through to the Present. Just as all Isles communities had their social organizations, so too did each endure the hardships of the twentieth century's World Wars, a story detailed in Chapter Twelve. Fogo was no exception. With the end of World War II many Fogo veterans came home. Things returned to normal in some respects, but from that time on the town was increasingly replaced as a commercial centre by Twillingate and another nearby town, Lewisporte. Even so, the community remained a busy place. From May to January coastal boats like the *Glencoe* and *Clarenville* connected Fogo Island with the mainland, though many goods were still carried by schooners.

A notable trader was Patrick Miller, mentioned above, whose schooner carried coal and general goods, which Miller landed at his own wharf in Little Harbour. A historic house long owned by the Miller family stands today at Fogo. Constructed for merchant Robert Scott in the late 1800s, the Miller house is noted for its elaborate decoration, including pagoda-style roofs on its square bays. Today, Miller and another mariner, Fred Chaffey of Change Islands (See Chapter Five), are commemorated through the MV *Veteran*'s Chaffey Miller Lounge. During the years that Patrick Miller flourished small passenger boats made trips from Fogo to Lewisporte, while the town was an important transshipment point for freight bound to other Fogo Island communities.

Fogo witnessed many ups and downs in the second half of the

twentieth century. A cottage hospital was built in 1952 (See Chapter Thirteen), but has been replaced with a new facility. This was not located in the town of Fogo, but in the centre of Fogo Island. Like many rural Newfoundland communities, modern Fogo has faced economic difficulties. The Earle Company's closure left fishers, already experiencing lower inshore catches, with no supplier. Fogo Islanders faced the possibility of resettlement, but with some outside help and an island-wide effort, a Co-op was founded that proved to be the salvation of Fogo Island. A downside for Fogo, noted by ENL, was that the new Co-op was headquartered at nearby Joe Batt's Arm (now at Seldom), diminishing the town of Fogo's economic importance on the island. Nonetheless, new facilities were also built at Fogo.

With the future of the fishery still in doubt after the 1992 cod moratorium, the fate of Fogo – town and island – is also in question. Like other rural Newfoundland communities, Fogo has seen many residents leave to work on the Mainland in recent years. From 1,030 residents the year before the fishery moratorium, Fogo's population stood at only 658 in 2011. Still, if history is any guide, Fogo residents are a resilient group, moving confidently with the changing tides of fortune. It is a safe bet that their full story is yet to be written.

....

Island Harbour

Found on the western side of Fogo Island, Island Harbour takes its name from Island Harbour Head, an island which helps protect the harbour from North Atlantic seas. A slightly different account of the name comes from the *Travel Central Newfoundland* website. In this case the name, also given as "Harbour of Islands," is said to derive from the town's lay-out, which stretches over three kilometres along a shoreline bordered with many small islands.

A *Decks Awash* article gives the date of first settlement as 1857, although the town's entry in ENL says only that it was settled around 1860. Many of the earliest inhabitants may have been Irish, but these were followed mainly by English immigrants. The encyclopedia notes that the influx of settlers around 1860 was connected to migration from the northern portion of Fogo Island and Conception Bay. Island Harbour first appeared in census records in 1869, at which time there were forty-three people living in the community. Five years later the population had risen to fifty-one, the number more than doubling to 114 – twenty-four families – as of the 1891 census. Early surnames in the community included Hart, Barnes, Clundin, Simms and Fooks. Later arrivals included the Bailey, Butt, Ford, Heath, McKenna, Squires and Thistle families, with Harts and Barnes still resident.

In its early years the religious makeup of the community shifted significantly. In 1874 all but one family at Island Harbour were Church of England, but over the next ten years considerable numbers of Roman Catholics arrived; by 1884 they formed the majority of the population. As of 1891 Catholics still outnumbered Anglicans at Island Harbour by nearly two to one. At this date there were also a small number of Methodists resident. The nearby communities of Paine's Harbour, settled sometime before 1884, and Black Head Cove, were Church of England. The former locale was counted as part of Island Harbour from 1901, while the latter was abandoned in 1911.

Island Harbour's Catholic population had a one-room school house built in 1888. As of 1891 it was recorded as having room for fifty pupils, though none were in attendance over the Summer. By 1911 the Church of England had established its own school in the community, which served eleven students.

Whatever level of education these students obtained, many of them (the boys, at least) went on to pursue a career in the fishery. In 1911 two schooners left Island Harbour for the Labrador fishery. That same year inshore fishers took 632 quintals of cod. Lobster was also an important catch for Island Harbour fishers. Like Seldom, and a number of communities on New World Island, Island Harbour had its own lobster factories – two – in 1911, which together packed twenty-seven cases of product. Though the era of the lobster factory was long gone in 1953, lobster catches were still a valuable part of the community's economy. In that year Island Harbour's forty-eight fishers landed 6,128 kg of the crustaceans. Salmon was also noted as an important catch. According to *Decks Awash*, many locals fished off Little Fogo Islands in this era, particularly in the Fall, selling their catches at Change Islands.

In the twentieth century Island Harbour experienced population fluctuations similar to those of many Isles communities. The population declined to only ninety-four persons in 1901 but this trend reversed through to the end of World War II when the number of residents stood at 226. By 1953 260 persons called Island Harbour home, with numbers rising to a high of 331 in 1971. Generally, numbers have dropped since that time, with the 2011 census recording a population of only 160.

In the later twentieth century local fishers were aided by a Provincial Government initiative which saw the construction of a community stage on Island Harbour Head, and later by a causeway connecting the island to the main settlement. By the early 1990s, and the eve of the moratorium, Island Harbour fishers were still reliant on the inshore fishery for their primary livelihood, in this period selling their catches to the island's Co-op. Today the little community is still home to a number of services including a pair of churches, a post office, a playground and the Black Head Cove hiking trail and picnic area.

....

Seldom-Come-By & Little Seldom

Seldom-Come-By. Located on Fogo Island's southern shore, the town of Seldom-Little Seldom, is comprised of the communities of Seldom-Come-By and Little Seldom. Seldom-Come-By is one of many communities on Fogo Island with a fascinating, if not to say mysterious, name. ENL proclaims Seldom-Come-By as one of the most cited of the Province's colourful place names. An early version of the name Seldom-Come-By was Seldom-Go-By. Speculation has it that this name derives from the difficult navigational conditions prevailing south of Fogo Island – Stag Harbour Run, to the west, was an especially dangerous passage in bad weather. For this reason mariners would rarely bypass the harbour at Seldom, often putting into the small port for the night, especially in high seas. Many vessels from the outports of Bonavista, Conception and Trinity Bays would stop at Seldom-Come-By on their way north to the Labrador fishery. Archbishop Howley believed the name was an English corruption of a French term. In the early twentieth century Seldom fishers often referred to their home as "Silly-Cum-Bay." Archbishop Howley noted that a community near New Perlican in Trinity Bay was called Scilly Cove (Changed to Winterton in 1912. Now home to the Provincial Wooden Boat Museum). An early mention of Scilly Cove came from Abbè Baudoin in 1697, when he labelled it "Celi-Cove." There are also the well-known Scilly Isles off Lands End in Britain. Howley theorizes that Seldom had much the same derivation. Today Seldom-Come-By is often called "Seldom" for short. This change is not welcomed by all. In his *Lewisporte Pilot* column Benson Hewitt discusses the origins of the name, and notes that by itself "Seldom" has nothing unique about it, unlike the full version.

Whatever form of the name one prefers, anyone who studies the history of Seldom will agree that it has a fairly lengthy pedigree, at least by the standards of European settlement on the northeast coast. Not as old as Twillingate or Fogo, Seldom was first permanently settled in the 1820s. A man named John Holmes arrived from Dorsetshire in 1828. It appears that Holmes may have been escaping family troubles back in the mother Country, changing his surname to Hodinott to avoid detection. A *Decks Awash* article places settlers at Seldom earlier than Holmes' arrival, pointing out that an Anglican school existed in the community early in the 1800s. The first person reported to have died at Seldom passed away in 1760, although this individual could have been a migratory fisher and not a settler.

The community made it into the official record in 1836, when twelve people – the Hodinott and Roberts families – were listed as making their homes at Seldom-Come-By. An influx of settlers from the crowded harbours of Conception Bay occurred in the 1840s. Many of the town's modern surnames, including Anthony, Collins and Rowe, are also prominent in Conception Bay. As of 1845 seventy-four persons called Seldom home. About thirty years later the population had grown considerably; in 1874 the town could boast 234 residents. For the next few years Seldom enjoyed something of a population renaissance, with numbers rising to 364 people in 1884 (Little Seldom included). From this time on, however, a declining Labrador fishery took its toll on the community's demographics. By 1891 the population stood at 223 – forty-five families. Even taking into account Little Seldom's 1891 population, the area still experienced an overall decline. Although Seldom's population rose to 296 at the 1911 census, by this date many people were lured to communities like Horwood for work in the lumber industry.

Thus, when the fishery declined so did the population. As in all Isles communities, the fishery was the reason for Seldom's existence. Perhaps its main problem, as *Decks Awash* notes, was that its harbour, while easily navigable, was far from the traditional fishing grounds. By the mid nineteenth century Seldom fishers were active in the Labrador and inshore fisheries while also pursuing cod to the Wadhams and Funk Island. In 1874 they landed 2,357 quintals of fish and harvested 219 seals. Nine years later Seldom fishers were recorded as owning six schooners, plus a number of small craft like skiffs. They were catching salmon using nets, and cod in traps. The early twentieth century saw a decline in fish landings at Seldom, with only 959 quintals of inshore and Labrador cod taken by local fishers. In this era Seldom still witnessed the arrival of schooners bound for Labrador, but the outport was becoming better known as the centre of an inshore trap fishery conducted from small motorboats. Most residents of Seldom shared in the experience of fishing. Other industries, like sawmilling and berry picking, were conducted on a fairly small scale.

Cod was the mainstay of both the inshore and Labrador fisheries, and few other marine species were taken at Seldom in any great number. One exception was lobster. In 1878 the settlement saw the establishment of one of Notre Dame Bay's first lobster factories. By 1911 Seldom was home to three of these factories, which employed seventeen people. Even so, a mere fifty-seven cases of product were packed that year, a number that may help explain the disappearance of lobster canneries from this part of the northeast coast.

Seldom, with the former Union Trading Company store at centre right

As we've seen, the Newfoundland fishery was conducted through the medium of the merchant firm – Seldom was no exception to this rule. The firms serving Seldom were well-known names on Fogo Island. The Waterman/Hodges concern ran a local branch, managed by former school teacher Philip Newell. Thomas C. Duder ran his own merchant store at Seldom until his election as Fogo District's MHA in 1893. In 1913 William Coaker's FPU opened a Fisherman's Union Trading Company store, an operation that bought most local fish product for the next fifty years.

Like its industry, Seldom's faith was fairly homogeneous. From the time Seldom was founded nearly all locals, with a few exceptions, were members of the Protestant Anglican or Methodist faiths. The religious makeup of the town in 1874 stood at 133 Anglicans, eighty-five Methodists, plus thirteen Roman Catholics. We might recall that a Church of England (Anglican) school was an early part of Seldom's infrastructure, at least according to *Decks Awash*. ENL dates Seldom's first church school from around 1874, with Philip Newell as teacher. Though Anglicans made up a large part of the population, only the Methodists had a community church as of that year. It would take the best part of two decades, but Seldom's Church of England residents finally had their own place of worship in 1891. In that year the Church of England school provided instruction to thirty pupils.

Twenty years later two church schools – Methodist and Anglican – served ninety students.

The Wesley United Church, Seldom, built in 1910. Now an art gallery

As of 1935 Seldom's population had dropped to 271, and by the 1950s some families began settling off Fogo Island to the forestry town of Botwood. All was not lost, however, as an influx of families – Combdens, Eveleighs, Harnetts and Morgans – from nearby Wild Cove helped to partly counter the exodus. An important boost came in 1962 when Seldom was made the terminus for a ferry service running from Carmanville. Unfortunately for Seldom, this development was not permanent. The terminus was shifted to Man o' War Cove near Stag Harbour, with a connection to Farewell, in the mid 1980s. In 1956 a salt fish plant was opened in the community under the auspices of the Provincial Government. By the 1960s this facility was taken over by the island Co-op, and infrastructure was installed to process alternate fish species like flounder, greysole and turbot. More improvements were made in 1971, and fishers from a number of towns on Fogo Island began sending their landings to Seldom for processing. Since the 1992 fishery moratorium population statistics show the same downward trend common to most Isles communities; in 1991 the combined community of Seldom-Little Seldom was home to 590 residents, a number that had dropped to only 427 in 2011.

Little Seldom was first recorded as a settlement in 1857, when twenty-three people were recorded living there. First called Little Seldom-Come-By, the community's name was soon shortened to its current form. Like Seldom, Little Seldom expanded with the arrival of Conception Bay fishers, the surname Penny being especially associated with the new arrivals. By 1874 Little Seldom was home to sixteen families, or eighty-one persons in all. The population rose to more than 100 by 1891. Along with Seldom-Come-By, Little Seldom was affected by a declining Labrador fishery. The number of residents dropped considerably by 1911, when the population was only thirty-eight, or six families. The population rose again in 1935. By 1966, following in-migration from Indian Islands, 141 people called Little Seldom home. In more recent years numbers have declined again, a trend starting as early as 1971.

Little Seldom's religious makeup was much like its larger neighbour, most residents being of the Anglican and Methodist faiths. A Methodist school operated at Little Seldom in the 1870s, and by 1911 its capacity was noted as twenty-five students, although none were in attendance at the time of the census.

Although farming played a role in Little Seldom's economy – the community's dairy cows produced over 26,000 litres of milk in 1935 – its mainstays were fishing and sealing. Participating in both the Labrador and inshore fisheries, locals landed 632 quintals of cod and took sixteen seals in 1874. Fishing was still important in the 1930s, but in 1935 Little Seldom fishers were recorded as owning only four motorboats and a single dory. With the introduction of longliners after 1949, and a Funk Islands grounds fishery, a marine centre was established on the road linking Little Seldom with Stag Harbour to the southwest.

....

Stag Harbour

Located on the southwestern tip of Fogo Island, Stag Harbour is the island's newest community. It was founded largely through the relocation of people from the nearby settlements on Indian Islands. Residents of Notre Dame Bay had long frequented Stag Harbour for logging purposes. The harbour also served as a convenient Winter shelter for Indian Islands' schooners. ENL reports that there were no settlers noted at Stag Harbour until the 1921 census. In that year a single family of eight called the harbour home. *Decks Awash* notes that in 1920 Cornelius Sheppard, an eighteen year old mariner from Eastern Cove, eastern Indian Island, built a number of structures at Stag

Harbour. Sheppard stayed on permanently following two major storms that destroyed property on Indian Islands. The first of these storms, known locally as "The Washout," occurred in 1922. Fishing premises and a number of homes were destroyed at Eastern Cove, forcing some locals to overwinter at the more sheltered Stag Harbour. A saw mill was built, and eventually most residents of Eastern Cove relocated to Stag Harbour.[19]

There is disagreement as to exactly when the last families left the Indian Islands for Stag Harbour. One source contends that most of the remaining families had left Eastern Cove for Stag Harbour by the 1950s, with others moving there from Perry's Island, the more westerly Indian Island, by the 1960s. A second source says that all the remaining population of the Indian Islands had left by 1945. In any case, the resettlement process appears to have been completed sometime in the twenty years after World War II.

By 1953 Stag Harbour's population stood at 267, a number that increased to 379 in 1966. For several decades the new immigrants pursued a successful fishery at Stag Harbour, with locals landing more than 9,000 kilograms of lobster in 1953. Like many other locales on Fogo Island, the community experimented with a consumer co-operative in this era, theirs being one of the more successful. As long as this prosperity lasted the local population continued to grow, with the Anglican, United, and Pentecostal faiths all maintaining churches in Stag Harbour. From the late 1960s through to the 1970s, however, the town's population consistently decreased, with many youths relocating for work. As *Decks Awash* reports, the community experienced some renewed growth starting in the mid 1980s. It was in this period that the island's ferry service was relocated from its Seldom-Come-By terminus to Man O' War Cove, about 2.5 kilometres from Stag Harbour, which is now the first (and last) community travellers see when making a round trip to and from Fogo Island. Still, the overall demographic trend has been downward, with only 161 persons – less than half the 1966 population – calling Stag Harbour home in 2011.

....

Tilting

A puzzle connected with many localities on Fogo Island concerns the origin of their colourful names; as we've seen, this is true of both Fogo and Joe Batt's Arm. Tilting, one of the older settlements on the island, has its own toponym mystery. Dr. Robert Mellin reports that the name may come from the places where fishers would head, split and salt (i.e. "tilt") their fish. Some sources claim that the name Tilting comes from the wooden shacks or "tilts" constructed by early European fishers, and that the community's name was first given as "Tilt Town." A *Decks Awash* article asserts that there is little proof of this derivation – the settlement was called Tilton Harbour as early as 1757. Mellin disagrees, stating that Tilting was the area's original name, Tilton being no more than a nineteenth century corruption. Archbishop Howley's research supports this view. Howley came into possession of the will of one Daniel Bryan of "Tilting Harbour," dated 1820. Likewise, an agreement between Bryan's Sons, John and William, dated 1856, also names the community as Tilting Harbour. John Bryan's own will, from 1860, refers to his hometown as "Tilton Harbour." It was from this period, Howley contends, that the name began to change from its original spelling. In 1905 Tilting was officially agreed upon as the community's name, as there was another Tilton in Conception Bay.

However its name derived, there is no doubt that Tilting, located near a number of good fishing grounds, has had a long attraction for peoples of many nations. The area does have its pitfalls, however. It lies on a stretch of coast that James P. Howley (1847-1918) labelled one of Newfoundland's most dangerous shores. Partly divided into an outer portion called "The Harbour," and an inner area known as "The Pond," Tilting's harbour is protected from fierce North Atlantic gales only by Pigeon Island at its mouth. As Mellin reports, navigation always presented a problem, probably insurmountable without Pigeon Island's uncertain shelter. Even with the island for protection, vicious storms, such as occurred in 1935, have caused extensive property damage.

Still, where there is fish there are fishers. Tilting was used by the French in the early 1700s, and they are even thought to have built onshore facilities at Garrison Point. Evidence of French occupation of Tilting has been found near Green's Point, on the east side of Tilting Harbour. The French were not the first to appreciate Tilting. Beothuk were reported in the area as late as 1819, when a man named Turpin was killed by them at Sandy Cove, a story recounted in Chapter Six.[20] A small number of English settlers made Tilting their home in the eighteenth century, perhaps as early as 1729, but by the second half of the century Tilting was firmly an Irish enclave.

Most of the Isles' population are Protestant, and of West Country English descent. Tilting has an altogether different character, being one of the few communities on the northeast coast with a largely Roman Catholic population. Tilting is also one of the most "Irish" communities in the entire Province, and Mellin notes that before Confederation most residents held allegiance primarily to Ireland, rather than Newfoundland. In fact, one of Tilting's earliest permanent settlers was an Irishman, Thomas Burke (b. 1722), a native of Dungarvon, who arrived in 1752. Burke's descendants were a very learned clan by contemporary outport standards, and a number of the Burkes kept journals and diaries. The family was known for its shipbuilders – along with Daniel Bryan, the Burkes were building sealing schooners at Tilting by 1800. They also produced a fair share of master mariners, like Skipper William Burke of the *Daniel O'Connell.*

The Burke's fellow shipbuilder, Daniel Bryan, came to Tilting from Ferryland in 1786, marrying one of the Burke clan, Bridget. Bryan built a sealer named the *Success* in 1812, and a number of other vessels, including *Enterprise*, *Harmony*, and *Triumph*, in partnership with his Sons, through to 1838.

Tilting's original Burke, Thomas, was soon joined by other settlers with the surnames Keefe, Lane and McGrath. Later arrivals included the Broaders, Dwyer, Foley, Greene, Mahoney, Reardon and Hurley families. At the dawn of the twenty-first century these names still resound at Tilting. ENL points out that Tilting became an important fishing outpost from an early date, and by 1812 was home to 184 persons, all but twenty-three of whom were Roman Catholic. The population increased significantly over the next two decades, reaching 327 in 1836. By 1874 Tilting supported seventy-three families, or 430 persons, all of whom were Roman Catholic. With this strongly Catholic population there was clearly a need for formal religious instruction, and such had been initiated beginning in the 1830s.

In 1835 the community's first parish priest, Reverend Martin Joseph Bergin, arrived from Dublin. Father Bergin died at Tilting in 1841. The appointment of a parish priest was soon followed by the construction of a church. This structure may have been completed as early as 1838, or as late as 1842 – it was certainly in use by 1844. The Catholic Church also operated a school at Tilting, and by 1890 a new facility was in the works for the growing number of children in the community. Perhaps the plan for a new school followed in the wake of an 1889 report by James Wickham, Fogo's superintendent of Roman Catholic schools. Although he had some critiques of other schools on the island, Wickham found nothing but praise for the efforts of Tilting's teacher John Sargent and his predecessors, Allan Dwyer and Stella Burke. At the time of the superintendent's visit the school served more than forty pupils, who apparently studied a broader range of subjects than taught by most Newfoundland schools of the day. By 1911 practically all of the town's children were students of the community's two-room school house.

ENL notes that Tilting quickly became one of the more important fishing settlements on Fogo Island. By the turn of the nineteenth century the community was sending vessels to the French Shore fishery. This fishery continued through to the late 1800s, supplemented by involvement in fisheries at Little Fogo Islands and to Labrador. In 1874 Tilting was home to 128 fishers, who owned nine schooners and 130 smaller craft. In this era only Fogo and Joe Batt's Arm had larger fisheries, despite the limits placed on the industry by the small size of Tilting's harbour. By the time of the 1891 census, Tilting had a total of 149 fishers, out of a population of just over 400. By this date the town's inshore fishery was much more important than that to Labrador, with 3,332 and 180 quintals of cod taken, respectively. Twenty years later Tilting's resident fishers numbered 174, although their combined catch was less than in 1891 – 2,599 quintals. Even so, the value of fish landed stood second only to Joe Batt's Arm, bringing almost $19,000.00 into Tilting's economy. In more recent years Tilting fishers benefited from the introduction of fresh-fish processing at Joe Batt's Arm. Like other islanders, Tilting residents were involved in the establishment of the Co-op amidst the threat of resettlement, and by the time of 1992's fishery moratorium had an important longliner fishery.

Traditional fishing stage at Tilting

Merchants were at the centre of all Isles fisheries, and Tilting was no exception to this rule. In the mid eighteenth century crews employed by Jeremiah Coughlan, based at Fogo, and Trinity's Benjamin Lester were actively pursuing the fishery at Tilting. In the early 1800s the only English names found at Tilting were Forsythe, at Sandy Cove, and Horton, whom ENL presumes were agents of the Fogo and Trinity merchants. Rochfort's *Directory of Newfoundland* lists a single merchant at Tilting in 1877. By the turn of the twentieth century the community had two merchant houses, with both the Earles and Hodges operating branch stores at Tilting run by company agents. In 1953 Earle Sons and Company were still active at Tilting, while the Fisherman's Union Trading Company had its own store.

Despite the long association between the merchants, the fishers, and the planters of Tilting, friction between the groups was by no means unknown. Perhaps this sprang from the traditional discord between the Protestant English – most merchants – and the Catholic Irish, Tilting's fishers and planters. Disputes between the two nations went back into the middle ages, and were only intensified by the Irish famine of the 1840s. On the other hand, many writers have noted the exploitative nature of the truck system under which Newfoundland's traditional fishery operated. It is likely that any grievances noted at Tilting had as much to do with the economic structure of the industry as to any "racial" antipathy. First recorded at Tilting in the eighteenth century, these disputes seem typical of many early Newfoundland communities, even those where merchants and settlers were of the same religion.

In his book *The Irish in Newfoundland 1600-1900*, Mike McCarthy records three early instances of such friction.[21] One involved an Irish planter named Patrick Murphy. Murphy became indebted to his supplier, William Keene. Owing Keene just over £102, Murphy was ordered to repay the full amount. Murphy's misfortune occurred in 1759, the same year that another Irish resident of Tilting, Francis Fleming, lodged a complaint against his master, one William Chalk. In the complaint Fleming alleged that Chalk had paid him in fish rather than bills of exchange. Governor Edwards ordered that Chalk repay his servant just under £16 compensation, the amount of Fleming's account. The third case of settler versus supplier occurred three years later, and was adjudicated by Governor Thomas Graves (1725-1802). In this case William Sullivan complained that he had worked as a fishery servant for John Power at Tilting from September 1761 to August 1762, but had been forced to leave Power's employ due to lack of provisions. In fairness to his master, which Power may not have deserved, Sullivan offered to deduct the time lost from wages he was owed. Power turned the offer down, at which point Sullivan presented his petition to Graves. Unlike the Fleming case, the Governor did not make a decision, instead referring the matter to a Justice of the Peace.

New troubles surfaced in the nineteenth century. In 1805 eight Tilting fishers petitioned Governor Gower to complain of their treatment by the merchants. The missive contended that Fogo Island merchants had placed "exorbitant" prices on their provisions and retail goods, keeping the fishers constantly in debt and wondering if they would make it through the Winters without starving. The merchants, the petitioners contended, were able to set whatever prices they wanted for fish catches, regardless of market conditions. In short, the people of Tilting were getting a raw deal. We may recall that during his tenure as Governor, Gower tried to root out abuse of the truck system by forcing merchants to post the prices they charged for goods, along with what they were paying for that season's landings. Perhaps the Tilting petition had some impact on Gower's thinking in the matter.

Only twenty years later Tilting residents seemed to have the merchants on the defensive. In 1825-6 three prominent Fogo firms – John Slade and Company, its offshoot Cox & Company, and Robert Scott – wrote to the authorities complaining of the belligerence of Tilting residents. It appears that the inhabitants of Tilting were prepared to come en masse and take supplies and provisions from the merchants' stores. This was no simple case of an unruly mob turning to theft. The Winter of 1825-6 was an especially hard one for residents of Bonavista and Tilting. The new Governor, Sir Thomas Cochrane (1789-1872), who arrived in October 1825, was soon forced to begin relief efforts, putting inhabitants to work on projects like road building. Although their actions were born out of dire necessity, Cochrane could not let Tilting settlers seize whatever they wanted from the merchants. He ultimately despatched a Royal Navy vessel, HMS *Scrub*, to Fogo Island to keep order over the Winter. Nevertheless, it appears that Governor Cochrane did have some sympathy for the poor fishers, as his relief efforts testify.

Difficulties did not end after 1900; the twentieth century was no less challenging for Tilting than it was for other Isles communities. The fishery suffered a decline in the 1930s, but this was partly offset by a rise in agricultural production and animal husbandry. Keeping both cows and sheep, Tilting's output of products like milk and butter were the highest on Fogo Island in 1935. The 1891 census recorded a population of 413, but with the decline of the Labrador fishery Depression-era Tilting was home to only 393 residents and a single business. The number of residents had fallen again by 1953, although this rose to 444 by 1966. As we have seen, Tilting made common cause with other Fogo Islanders in battling the threat of resettlement, but the post moratorium years have impacted on Tilting no less than its neighbours. Its population stood at 379 the year before the moratorium was imposed, but by the census of 2011 this was a mere 204.

For Tilting the future may be closely bound with its past. As early as 1984 the Tilting Expatriates' Association (TEA) was formed at St. John's with the intention of preserving Tilting's history and promoting community development – the group even produced its own newsletter and journal. The Tilting Recreational and Cultural Society (TRACS), based in the community, was founded in much the same spirit. The importance of Tilting's Irish heritage, and continued links between the community and Eire, was recognized in 2008. That year the Provincial Government awarded Tilting $15,000.00 for a study on the feasability of establishing a centre for Newfoundland/Irish studies in the town, an important component of Tilting's 2006 economic plan.

The award-winning Dwyer Premises

Tilting is likely to become an important lure for tourists eager to experience a vanishing way of life. Tilting may be unique in Newfoundland and Labrador in the degree to which historic residences, land use and folkways have been preserved. A number of communities on the Isles have a local museum, but Tilting is practically its own living heritage display. This fact has been recognized by the town's classification as a National Historic Site of Canada, and as the Province's first Registered Heritage District. A further honour was bestowed by the Historic Sites and Monuments Board of Canada, which designated Tilting a Cultural Landscape District. In 2005 the community received the Manning Award. Presented to recognize excellence in preserving public historic sites, the award honoured Tilting's work on the Dwyer Premises.[22] Constructed by one Vincent Bryan in the early 1870s, this small complex includes a house, stage, store, wharf and numerous fish flakes. This was not the first honour for the premises, which in 2000 had received the Newfoundland Historic Trust's Southcott Award, presented for "built heritage preservation." As Mellin reminds us, however, Tilting is not simply a collection of preserved heritage structures. Even in Newfoundland's post moratorium era, it remains a living, working fishing community. If the key to a secure future be effort and perseverance, few of our old fishing communities will have a brighter tomorrow than Tilting.

....

The Resettled Communities

It is a well-known, and oft-lamented fact of Newfoundland history that many small, isolated settlements were abandoned from 1954 through the early 1970s under the Smallwood Government's sponsored resettlement programs. What is less well-known is that Fogo Island, itself physically separated from the mainland by Sir Charles Hamilton Sound, was once home to numerous tiny communities that now lie abandoned. Perhaps even more interesting is that fact that most of these communities were resettled prior to, or immediately after Confederation, simply through the desire of their inhabitants to make a better life in larger centres.

Lion's Den, c.1900

Some of Fogo Island's most well known resettled communities lay along what is now the five km Lion's Den walking trail just outside the town of Fogo. The trail takes its name from one of these small communities. The other settlements included Locke's Cove, established in 1874, and Eastern Tickle. Lying about two km from Fogo Harbour, Lion's Den was first settled by Irish fishers from Conception Bay in the early 1800s. The name Lion's Den is obscure, but could relate to the Biblical story of Daniel, reflecting the hardships faced by locals. First recorded in the 1836 census, Lion's Den had a population of around thirty to fifty, including some Protestants by the 1930s, for much of its history. Eastern Tickle stood at the entrance to Fogo Harbour, and was also settled in the early 1800s, probably by fishers working for the Slades. The community was somewhat larger than Lion's Den, its population peaking at 145 in 1884. Eastern Tickle even had its own Church of England school that could accommodate seventeen students. By the 1940s the populations of both Lion's Den and Eastern Tickle were in decline as people moved away to be closer to services. *Decks Awash* states that both communities were abandoned by 1945, although the last householder to leave Lion's Den was reportedly Ambrose Squires sometime around 1960.

Another old Fogo community with a colourful name was Shagg Rocks, a small cove sandwiched in between the communities of Shoal Bay and Barr'd Islands. It was settled around the 1850s by Charles Keats of Dorchester, England. Following his marriage to Elizabeth Hagget, Keats established his own fishing enterprise at Shagg Rocks and practised subsistence farming. Eric Witcher notes that the couple sent their children to school at nearby Barr'd Islands. Two Sons, William and Isaac, stayed on at Shagg Rocks, where they raised their families. By the 1950s their own children had all moved away to nearby Barr'd Islands or other locales, leaving the cove deserted.

Other resettled communities on Fogo Island included Wild Cove, near Seldom, inhabited from the 1870s through to 1945; Blackhead Cove, established prior to 1857, which was home to four families in 1884 but abandoned by 1911, and Cape Cove, a Roman Catholic community founded in the early 1800s and abandoned by 1953 due to isolation and the decline of traditional fisheries.

Some resettled communities were found not on Fogo Island itself but on some of the smaller islands off its shores. One example was established off the north coast of Fogo Island on Little Fogo Islands. Aside from the main island, Waterman's Harbour Island (about 1.25 km long), this group includes the smaller Easter and Penton's Islands. Only the largest island was home to a permanent community, first recorded in 1857. A Roman Catholic settlement supplied by the Waterman firm, Little Fogo Islands once had its own church and school house. 120 people made their homes at Little Fogo Islands in 1884, but the population fell quickly thereafter, with the community not appearing in the 1921 census.

Off the opposite shores of Fogo Island, southwest of Stag Harbour and Seldom, are the Indian Islands. The two largest Indian Islands – the only ones ever permanently settled – are Western Indian Island, about 6.5 km long, and the four km Eastern Indian Island. The islands are described by Don Downer as being generally flat, and covered with grass and brush. The name is said to derive from Summer usage by Natives. The settlement's founder was William Cull, noted for his dealings with the Beothuk (See Chapter Six). ENL says he arrived around 1840, though Downer gives the date as 1810. Settlers from locales like Harbour Grace were soon drawn by the islands' fisheries, and as of 1874 the Indian Islands had a population of 238, all Anglicans and Methodists. The inhabitants were spread out over several communities, Perry's Island on Western Indian Island, along with Eastern Cove, Indian Island, and Chalkish (or Chalky's) Cove on Eastern Indian Island. The encyclopedia, which also gives "Southside" as a community name on the islands, says that the combined population peaked at 433 in 1921. Downer contends that the peak was 372 residents in 1911. Whichever figures are correct, Indian Islands had passed its apex by the 1930s. Inhabitants of the low-lying islands suffered losses due to storm damage in the 1920s, and a number of families resettled at Stag Harbour (See above). By the mid 1940s the population of Indian Islands was down to only 141, and many of the remaining residents departed for Stag Harbour and Lewisporte. By the end of the 1950s the last Indian Islanders were gone.

Over the coming years, encouraged by government, many other small outports followed the lead of these Fogo Islanders, leaving behind all they had known in hopes of a better life for their families. Though the physical bonds were broken, the sentimental attachment felt by former residents is best reflected by the well-attended reunion organized by Indian Islanders in 1988. Filmed by the CBC, the reunion was the basis for an episode of the popular programme *Land and Sea*. The reunion also inspired Downer, who was actively involved in its planning, to write his 1991 account of life on the islands, *Uprooted People*. Whether people made the choice to move enthusiastically, or with profound sadness, Downer's choice of title was certainly apt.

....

The Fogo Island Process & the Founding of the Co-op

Some aspects of Fogo Island's history are held in common, and can't be properly discussed as part of only one community's story. The best example is the remarkable tale of how Fogo Islanders came together in the 1960s and 1970s to save their island from resettlement. In the process they founded an organization that has been a model of what Newfoundlanders and Labradorians can accomplish when they put their minds to it.

As Newfoundland and Labrador became Canada's tenth Province in 1949, Fogo Island fishers were experiencing serious problems. In response to declining catches on the Fogo Shelf, the local industry attempted to diversify. A fresh fish plant had been built at Joe Batt's Arm during World War II, and found a renewed (though brief) life in the 1950s. In the same era the Smallwood Government funded the construction of a new salt fish plant at Seldom-Come-By.

Neither initiative was a long-term success. From the 1950s through to 1967 Fogo Island's economy was still firmly based on the salt fish industry, although the island's fishers now took a broader range of marine species. Along with cod, they harvested salmon, lobster and mackerel, with herring, squid and caplin landed for bait. Cod remained king, with landings in the town of Fogo alone standing at 5,000 quintals in 1953. At this time two of Fogo Island's traditional merchant companies, the Newfoundland and Labrador Export Company, and Earle Sons and Company Ltd., remained prominent in supporting and supplying the local fishery, especially at Fogo.

Still, this was a time of major change in the fishing industry. Fogo Island's Labrador fishery had collapsed, and the Provincial Government increasingly turned away from the traditional salt fish industry in favour of a fresh frozen product. In the midst of these shifts, the Newfoundland and Labrador Export Company ceased operations in 1958, with Earle Sons and Company, Ltd. gone less than a decade later. These collapses left many Fogo Island fishers without a supplier just as the fishery was taking a turn for the worse, and Smallwood's Administration began implementing one of its series of resettlement schemes. As an island, suffering through a serious fishery crisis, Fogo seemed a likely candidate for resettlement; Premier Smallwood said as much during an official visit in 1966.

This plan did not sit well with many Fogo Islanders. The groundwork for a solution to the island's problems – one that did *not* involve resettlement – was laid a few years earlier, in1964. In that year expatriate Fogo Islander Fred Earle travelled to the island as a fieldworker with Memorial University's Extension Service. As a relative of Fogo Island's most prominent merchant family, it was hoped that Earle could act as a liaison between the island and the government in St. John's. The Fogo Island Improvement Committee grew out of a series of discussions involving Fred Earle and locals. The Committee's mandate was to find solutions to Fogo Island's economic difficulties, apart from resettlement. The Committee began its field work in 1966, at which time its membership stood at thirty-six.

Other developments were also underway. From September 1966 to September 1967 researcher Robert L. DeWitt lived in the town of Fogo. DeWitt's fieldwork was originally meant to study religious behaviour on Fogo Island, but the issue of resettlement was so pervasive that he elected to examine this issue instead. In his 1969 report, DeWitt noted that many residents were not opposed to resettlement *per se*, but this attitude was founded on the premise that staying on Fogo Island meant *no* development. A majority of Fogo Islanders wanted to see local development, preferring to remain if this condition were met. In publically airing their discontent, islanders hoped to influence political decision making. Their message to the politicians: development of Fogo Island was far preferable to resettlement.

With the aid of MUN's Extension Service, the Fogo Island Improvement Committee set up a fisheries conference in March 1967. Out of this conference a partnership grew between locals, the MUN Extension Service under Don Snowden, and Canada's National Film Board (NFB). The NFB played a crucial role in the process. Their involvement began when Challenge for Change producer John Kenny engaged respected film-maker Colin Low to produce a series of films on Fogo Island. Low and his film crews arrived on the island in the Summer of 1967 and worked closely with Fred Earle.

Low eventually produced a series of twenty-eight short films recounting the difficulties facing Fogo Islanders, and their hopes for a more prosperous future. The crews only filmed with the permission of Fogo Islanders, who then previewed the footage and could have anything removed that they didn't like. According to John A. Niemi, this made for better interviews, as people were not afraid of making mistakes.

A total of twenty hours of film was shot, edited, and shown around the island. In the beginning the primary issue discussed was resettlement, but the films eventually encompassed a broad range of issues. Their titles reflect some of the topics dealt with by the NFB: *The Fogo Island Improvement Committee*; *Dan Roberts on Fishing*; *Tom Best on Co-operatives*; *Some Problems of Fogo*; *A Woman's Place* and *Discussion on Welfare*. Through viewing such films, Fogo Islanders better understood the common issues facing all communities on the island and, Niemi notes, gave fishers a good deal of confidence in dealing with their problems.[23] Likewise, the NFB films gave these people a platform from which to air their concerns. The films were also shown to

Cabinet Ministers, and meetings were later arranged between the Ministers and islanders.

This pioneering use of film as a forum for community discussion is remembered as the "Fogo Process." The Fogo Process did more than simply generate discussion, as it fostered a new spirit of co-operation among islanders. A public meeting was convened in December 1967 involving local community representatives and Newfoundland Co-operative Services. This meeting helped lay the groundwork for the Fogo Island Shipbuilding and Producers Co-operative Society (Co-op). Earlier that year future Co-op President Don Best, and several others, travelled to St. John's, hoping to convince a broker to sell Fogo Island's salted cod. Deciding to take a risk, the broker built up a successful working relationship with the Fogo Island Co-operative. The new Co-op soon enrolled 125 members and had $625.00 in share capital. By 1968 Co-op membership reached 575, a number that stood at 835 four years later. By this date share capital had also grown exponentially, amounting to a full $120,000.00.

Historically, the Co-op processed groundfish species like cod, turbot and halibut, along with shellfish and pelagic species, at five different locations on Fogo Island. Salt fish production was an important plank of the enterprise into the 1980s, with the Co-op – boasting sales of almost $5,000,000.00 – supplying twenty per cent of all salt cod marketed by the Canadian Saltfish Corporation in 1980. In 1987 *Decks Awash* reported that being a Co-op gave the organization a social mandate, dictating a real concern for the needs of islanders. Although operating only one facility would have made more sense from a purely profit-driven standpoint, the existence of five fishplants provided more employment, and easier access to processing, for members throughout the island. At the time of the *Decks Awash* article the Co-op made it a practice to buy everything its members could land.

Though a boon to Fogo Island over the years, the Co-op has navigated its share of troubled waters. The Co-op faced near-bankruptcy in 1972, just as the important long liner fishery – employing 200 of 450 Fogo Island fishers – was experiencing difficulties. This was not all. In its early days an important part of the Co-op's operations was a shipyard at Shoal Bay, geared toward the construction of fifteen metre long liners, but this facility closed in 1974. Things were looking better at the start of the 1980s, when the Co-op once again found itself on a sound financial footing. The Co-op weathered another fishery downturn in that decade, though the most serious crisis was yet to come.

With the imposition of the 1992 cod moratorium fishers attempted to switch to new catch species, or gave up their traditional livelihoods, many of them migrating out of the Province. As of now (2015) the fishery has not fully recovered. The effects still reverberate throughout Fogo Island, and the Isles in general. Even so, the Co-op remains a centrepiece of the Fogo Island fishery, a true model of what Newfoundland communities can achieve when faced with adversity.

5

Change Islands

The Town

Change Islands lies a few kilometres to the west of its larger neighbour, Fogo Island. Like Twillingate, Change Islands is made up of a group of islands, including two large ones which are home to the modern town. Today the incorporated community stretches along the shore line of the narrow tickle separating the two main islands, with the larger number of residents making their home on the bigger South Island.

One of the many interesting facets of the town's history is not its written, *human* history but the geological record left behind from ages past. Change Islands has been studied by geologists since the 1960s. According to Dr. Thomas Eastler, as recounted on the community website, the islands contain some of North America's oldest rock formations. The islands are comprised of three distinct formations, including – from youngest to oldest – the South End Formation, the North End Formation and the Change Islands Formation. The Change Islands Formation is noted for the presence of trace fossils, and Dr. Eastler's findings included the discovery of tracks left by an ancient animal known as an Eurypterid. The story of Change Islands' rich geological past is preserved today in the local interpretation centre.

Although its geological pedigree is impressive, Change Islands' human habitation is fairly recent, even by the standards of Newfoundland's northeast coast. Though Native peoples occasionally visited the area, Change Islands was uninhabited through most of the eighteenth century, when it formed part of the French Shore. In this era French fishers visited Change Islands to prosecute the northern cod fishery, but did not settle. The roots of European settlement on Change Islands can be traced back to 1783 when the boundaries of the French Shore were shifted, leaving the islands in British territory. With this new status Change Islands saw the arrival of the first English fishers, sent out by merchants from Poole and Bristol. Much as in other areas of the Isles, the arrival of the migratory fishery led to some permanent settlement, although few people lived on the islands year-round until the mid nineteenth century.

In 1845 the number of permanent settlers on Change Islands stood at 316. By 1884 their numbers had grown considerably, with 934 persons residing there. The numbers remained fairly stable in this period, with just under 1,100 people resident at Change Islands in the first two decades of the twentieth century. In common with all Isles communities, demographic growth was fostered by a prosperous fishery – nearly a third of all residents in 1845 were fishers. Apart from an inshore harvest, the early inhabitants also travelled north to the Labrador fishery, and by 1874 the community had become a centre of the traditional Winter seal hunt, conducted from the land. By the early twentieth century Change Islands served as a port of call for the coastal boats. The community also welcomed foreign vessels landing salt and supplies, which then returned to Europe and South America laden with Newfoundland salt cod. At this time Change Islands was home to important branches of the Bay's large merchant firms. Prominent among these was Earles, profiled in our section on the town of Fogo. A real sense of local pride was evident when Change Islands residents became some of Newfoundland's first fishers to welcome Coaker's Fisherman's Protective Union in 1908 (See Chapter Ten). These hardy residents did not simply rely on the fishery for sustenance, however; they also cultivated gardens with crops like potatoes.

St. Margaret's Anglican Church. Change Islands' oldest place of worship

As in all Isles communities, a central focus of life in Change Islands was the churches. The first denomination to arrive on the island was the Church of England. Today, St. Margaret's Anglican Church, opened 16 June 1892, is the oldest church on Change Islands. This building, named after an English saint, was not the first Anglican church serving the community, however. Records indicate that an earlier place of worship, St. James the Apostle, once stood at the North End of the settlement. A bible presented to the congregation of St. James the Apostle by the Bishop of Newfoundland in

1853 is still on display at St. Margaret's.

The Methodists first arrived at Change Islands in 1841, when a minister from Trinity held services in a private home. A chapel was opened in 1847, with the first church erected in 1861. A new church was begun in 1896, opening for worship on 18 October 1897. Still standing, this building's interior features hand carved patterns done by Joey John Taylor. The first Methodist minister stationed at Change Islands full-time was Reverend Patterson in 1900, although a parsonage was not completed until 1906.

A third denomination to make converts amongst Change Islanders was the Salvation Army. Salvationist meetings were first held at Edgar Fancy's store, South Island, in February 1916. A Salvation Army citadel opened for worship in March 1917, although it was unfinished at the time. A new citadel was built in the 1970s, with the present church opened in 1995. The Pentecostal faith was introduced to Change Islands in 1968, with services conducted at parishioners' homes. The community's first Pentecostal church served about a dozen families. The present structure, called Bethel like its predecessor, dates from 1978.

Old United Church, Change Islands. Opened in 1897

Along with places of worship, the denominations founded church schools to educate Change Islands' youth. The Methodists established a school on Change Islands' South Side at an early date. This school served as a place of worship during construction of the new church in 1896. The Salvation Army likewise established a school, which was renovated as late as 1972-3. The tradition of schooling on Change Islands is carried on by A. R. Scammell Academy, named after one of the town's most prominent native Sons (See below). The school started life as Change Islands Integrated School in 1980, and was renamed ten years later. Serving grades kindergarten to twelve, and housing a public library, the school's enrollment has been impacted by out-migration in recent years – in 2005 four students graduated from A. R. Scammell, with a only single pupil completing grade twelve the following year. At the start of the 2011 school year about twenty-five students were enrolled.

The change from church-run to integrated schooling has been but one of many transformations impacting Change Islands since Confederation. As we have seen, Change Islanders were among the first to heed William Coaker's call to organize against the power of the fish merchants. In the 1940s, with a World War raging in Europe and the Pacific, local fishers established their own cooperative fish store as a more equitable alternative to selling to merchants. The process is detailed in a publication celebrating the fiftieth anniversary of Change Islands' incorporation. As early as 1941 the Seaway Cooperative Society, with its own Board of Directors, began operations with its head office at Main Tickle. The Seaway Cooperative had a fish exporting branch, located on the South Side, that operated for around ten years. A new organization, the Northeastern Cooperative Society Limited, later assumed control of this operation, adding a fish dryer to its infrastructure. Unfortunately, this venture lasted for only a year. On the other hand, the Seaway Cooperative continued operating retail stores on both islands. It eventually expanded into fish buying, and initiated the Viking Credit Union.

With the 1949 Canadian union even more changes impacted the community. As the town anniversary work notes, other Newfoundland communities had begun the process of incorporating as municipalities, providing inspiration to some Change Islanders. In consultation with the Smallwood Government, meetings were organized to gauge public support for the formation of a council. The town was canvassed, and residents encouraged to contribute a small fee – $5.00 – in support. On 16 October 1951 Change Islands became an incorporated community, and soon elected its first town council.

E. S. Spencer Causeway, Change Islands

The following years saw improvements arrive in Change Islands at a rapid pace. Only five years after the town's incorporation a new post office opened, replacing an older structure. Following renovations, the new post office doubled as a council hall until 1967. In that year a new town hall, housing a public library and medical clinic, was built as a Canadian centennial project. As an island, the community was linked by Canadian National (CN) steamers like the *Springdale*, and in 1965 a new Federal wharf was constructed to better accommodate the vessels. The CN boats' role in transporting passengers and goods was soon taken over by a new ferry service which inaugurated automobile carriage, and also served Fogo Island (See below). Around the time the Federal wharf was built Change Islands received its first public electrical services, provided by a large diesel plant located on North Island. This arrangement serviced the island for nearly a quarter century, until September 1988, when the town was brought under the Provincial power grid. Other infrastructure begun in the 1960s included new roads, and a steel "Bailey" bridge, connecting North and South Islands for automobile and pedestrian traffic. Named the E. S. Spencer Causeway in tribute to then-Minister of Finance and MHA for Fogo District, Hon. Edward Samuel Spencer (1893-1973), the causeway opened in 1965. Dial telephone services arrived the following year, with improvements continuing into the 1970s and through to the present.

Not all of Change Islands' recent history has been positive. By the 1980s the community was home to both long liner and small boat fisheries, with residents landing lobster and participating in the Spring seal hunt. At the time a local fish plant was in operation, owned by the Province but run by B. C. Packers. While the fishery continues to play an important role in the economic life of Change Islands, the town has no more escaped the effects of the northern cod moratorium than has any other Isles community. As we have seen, the population hovered around the 1,100 mark in the early twentieth century, but residents began out migrating in search of better opportunities as early as the 1930s, when more than 100 persons left. By 1991 the population was down to a mere 524. In 2011 only 257 persons remained.

All is not lost for Change Islands. The bedrock of the local economy remains the fishery, and there have been calls in recent years for secondary processing at the local fish plant. After being closed for some time, the plant was re-opened in 2005. Today, the Change Islands' fish plant is managed by the Change Islands Fisherman's Improvement Committee, with one of its most important products being sea cucumber, sold as a delicacy on the Asian market.[1]

Despite the continued importance of the fishery to Change Islands, tourism now forms an essential pillar of the town's new economic reality. Change Islands has endeavoured to preserve its way of life by sharing its traditions with fascinated visitors. The interpretation centre, mentioned above, was but one of several initiatives undertaken by a Town Tourism Committee. The Committee also set about building several hiking trails which showcased the beauty of Change Islands. A number of private tourist ventures have been initiated, like the Olde Shoppe Museum, and the community is home to a Newfoundland Pony refuge. The town formed an Economic Development Committee consisting of two councillors and other members of the community, whose primary goal was to secure a business venture for Change Islands to stop out migration through job creation. Other ventures are on-going.

Like Tilting, Change Islands is especially rich in traditional architecture, particularly fishing stages and stores. In fact, the Change Islands' town website notes the community's claim to be "the fishing stage capital of the world." There are some firm foundations on which to base this claim. Change Islands is home to around 200 fishing stages and stores, of which many remain in use. Of particular note is the Walter Torraville property, which stands near the Spencer Causeway. Including a stage built in the late 1800s, and a cottage dating from the 1930s, the property was designated a Registered Heritage Structure on 2 May 2004. It has also been presented with the Southcott Award in recognition of the extensive restoration work carried out on the premises.

Aside from the unusual curved shape of its roof, the Torraville stage has the distinction of having served as the town's original car ferry terminal, the boats connecting Change Islands to Cobb's Arm, New World Island. Operated by Fred Chaffey, the service ran from November 1968 till December 1979, when it was replaced by a new service, also operated by Mr. Chaffey. This second service connected the South End of Change Islands with Farewell, and ran until 1988. Fred Chaffey's service consisted of three vessels, the original ferry, the 56 ton *Botwood*, a second ferry named the *Agnes & Anne* (113 tons), with a freighter, the fifty-six ton *Barbara Darlene* (A passenger lounger on the ferry MV *Veteran* is named in tribute to Capt. Chaffey). For a number of years the site of the original ferry service, the old Torraville property, was home to the Burgundy Squid Café.

Change Islands, early 1900s

The restoration of the Torraville property is but one project of Change Islands' Stages and Stores Foundation, whose mandate is the restoration and preservation of such historic structures in the town. The foundation came into being following the destruction of a century old fishing stage in the community during the Spring of 2000. Stages and Stores has undertaken numerous restoration projects on Change Islands, examples of which can be found on the organization's website. At one time Stages and Stores Inc. even published its own newspaper, *The Main Tickle*, during the tourist season from June to September. Named to commemorate the channel which bisects the community, the paper first appeared in 2004, covering a variety of community-oriented news.

While Change Islands faces the problems common to all Isles communities in the post moratorium era, its residents have likewise shown the determination to meet these challenges head-on, both through initiatives like tourism and a commitment to the community's traditional base in the fishery.

....

Its Famous Sons

Though its population has never risen much over 1,000 souls, and now stands at much less, the town of Change Islands has produced a number of individuals whose accomplishments are celebrated throughout the Province. We might ask why this is so. Perhaps no one can give a definitive answer, but Cyril Poole's introduction to his biography of Canon George Earle (See below) provides some interesting observations. An outport neither too big nor too small in the overall scheme of things, as Canon Earle has said, Change Islands was a very prosperous fishing and sealing settlement from the mid 1800s through to the Great Depression. In those days Change Islands bred confidence and optimism amongst its inhabitants, who became some of Coaker's first stalwarts in his new FPU. Likewise, as Poole notes, Change Islands seemed especially blessed with those local "characters" whose wit and humour were a byword. Cultivating a tremendous sense of affection in residents and expatriates alike, Change Islands seems a fertile soil for greatness.

One of the first Change Islanders to leave his mark on the outside world was Joseph Edmund Elliott. Those most knowledgeable about the Newfoundland fishery are aware that the cod trap, a large, box-like form of net, was invented by Captain William H. Whitely in the Strait of Belle Isle in the year 1865. What is not so commonly known is that another version of the cod trap was independently developed by Elliott, a Change Islands native, two years later. ENL reports that Elliott was inspired by a church sermon on a miraculous catch of fish!

Newfoundland crew hauling a cod trap, c.1900

Although Joseph Elliott is all but forgotten today, three other Change Islanders still loom large for their contributions to Newfoundland and Labrador culture. The first of these was Arthur Reginald Scammell, born at Change Islands in February 1913. An author and educator, Scammell taught both in his native Newfoundland and later at Montreal, retiring from the profession in 1970. Displaying the characteristic Change Islands' wit, Scammell produced many humourous short stories and poems. His published books include *My Newfoundland* (1966), *From Boat to Blackboard* (1987) and *Newfoundland Echoes* (1988). In 1945 Scammell was a co-founder of the *Atlantic Guardian* magazine, acting as an associate editor and making frequent contributions to the publication.

Whatever his other accomplishments, in many peoples' minds A. R. Scammell will always be associated with a song. His composition, the *Squid Jiggin' Ground*, is considered one of Newfoundland's most beloved ditties. Scammell actually wrote the song when aged only fifteen and fishing with his Father at Change Islands. The work was inspired by Scammell's roots. Poole notes that the author and his friend George Earle both insisted that the colourful characters featured in the *Squid Jiggin' Ground* were all real. The song was later written down by businessman/publisher Gerald S. Doyle (1892-1956), and finally recorded by Scammell in 1943. Far from a "one hit wonder," Scammell produced other noteworthy Newfoundland tunes, like *The Newfoundland Come Home Song* (1966) and *A Sealer's Song* (1977).

A. R. Scammell

Scammell's contributions to Newfoundland folklife and culture have been widely recognized. In 1977 he was awarded a honorary Doctorate by Memorial University, and in 1985 the Newfoundland and Labrador Arts Council created an annual writer's award in his honour. Two years later Scammell was elevated to the Order of Canada. Finally, in 1990, Change Islands' local school was renamed the A. R. Scammell Academy in tribute to this accomplished Son. Likewise, the observation deck on the Fogo-Change Islands ferry, MV *Veteran*, is named in his honour. Arthur Scammell died in 1995.

A year after Scammell's birth another Change Islander marked for greatness first saw the light of day. Unlike Scammell, the Son of a fisherman, this Change Islander was a member of one of the region's great merchant families, though he was destined to make his mark in other endeavours. George Halden Earle was born in 1914, a direct descendant of merchant house founder Henry J. Earle. Although Henry's main business was located at Fogo, his youngest Brother Frederick Charles (b. 1855) was sent off to mange the firm's Change Islands' branch. Frederick Charles was George's paternal Grandfather, and established that family branch's connection to Change Islands. Though George Earle moved to Fogo with his family while a teenager, he always considered himself a Change Islander.

George Earle received a solid education, graduating from Queen's College in 1938. The next year he was ordained as an Anglican deacon, taking up parish duties in St. John's. During the years 1940-57 Earle served as a priest at various locales in England, while earning his Bachelor's and Master's degrees in arts. In 1957 Earle returned to Newfoundland, becoming Provost of Memorial University's Queen's College, a post he retained until 1979. During this period (1971) he was made Canon of St. John's Anglican Cathedral. Canon Earle was active in many organizations, including the Kiwanis Club, the Canadian Mental Health Association, the Corporation of Queen's College and, in later years, the Wessex Society of Newfoundland, which promotes ties between Newfoundland and western England.

Despite his many accomplishments as priest and community leader, Canon George is best remembered as a humorist, writer and public speaker. Upon his return from England Earle was much in demand as an after-dinner speaker, and believed that he had given more than a thousand such speeches over the years. Canon George spoke to a wide variety of groups, with little reward other than the appreciation of his audiences and the chance to spread his take on Newfoundland folklore, "old foolishness" as he called it. Like Arthur Scammell, Earle was greatly influenced by the humour and characters he remembered from his boyhood days at Change Islands. Though much of his humour was appreciated only by his audiences, in retirement Canon George was able to translate some of his humourous folklore into print, when Harry Cuff Publications released his work *Old Foolishness or Folklore?* in 1987. The book, including some new material, went into a second edition the following year as *Foolishness & Folklore*. Earle also contributed a series of articles to the *Newfoundland Herald* on the Province's traditional words, and some of his work appeared in the *Newfoundland Quarterly* in 1989-90.

In the 1980s Earle gained new fans, and instant recognition in the Province, when he was cast as the loveable slacker Jethro Noddy in a CBC television adaptation of Ted Russell's *Tales from Pigeon Inlet*. Like Art Scammell, Earle was recognized for his contributions to Newfoundland culture by the award of a honorary Doctorate in 1979. In frail health during his last years, Canon George Earle passed away in May 2000.

Another talented Change Islander was Gerald Leopold Squires, born in November 1937. Unlike his predecessors Scammell and Earle, Squires' celebration of Newfoundland did not come through the medium of humour, but instead that of art. In 1949 Squires moved to Toronto with his parents, and went on to study at the Danforth Technical School, where it was suggested that he concentrate on landscapes. Travelling to Mexico in 1958, Squires studied painting, drawing and printmaking under Carl Lewis Pape (1900-1998). Following a stint as an editorial artist with the Toronto Telegram, in 1969 Squires returned to Newfoundland with his family. Two years later they took up residence in an abandoned lighthouse at Ferryland, where Squires remained for a dozen years. Here he produced three major surrealist landscape series, "The Boatman," "The Ferryland Downs," and "Cassandra." Squires maintained a prolific output, including everything from portraits, to religious themes, to sculpture. In 1998 Squires was commissioned by the Beothuk Institute to create a bronze sculpture, "The Spirit of the Beothuk," for the Boyd's Cove historic site, and in 2007 gave a presentation on the creation of the work at the Beothuk Interpretation Centre.

Based at Holyrood starting in 1983, Squires made significant contributions to the art world apart from his body of work. He helped found Oshawa's Robert McLaughlin Gallery, and the Artists' Coalition of Newfoundland & Labrador. Squires served on the Newfoundland and Labrador Art's Council, was a jurist for the Province's Art Procurement Program and the Canada Council for the Arts "B" Awards, and adjudicated St. John's annual Arts and Letters Competition. Gerald Squires was also a longtime art instructor at Memorial University.

Renowned for portrayals of Newfoundland life, people and vistas, Squires received numerous accolades. Like Arthur Scammell, he was a member of the Order of Canada, and like Scammell and Earle, received a honorary Doctorate from Memorial University. In 1984 Squires was presented with the Ted Drover Award by the Newfoundland and Labrador Arts Council. In 1987 the Canada Council for the Arts recognised Squires with its "B" Award. In 1999 he became a member of the Royal Canadian Academy of Arts. Well established in his lifetime as one of Newfoundland & Labrador's greatest artists, Gerald Squires died on October 3 2015.

It is unlikely that another outport of comparable size to Change Islands can claim three honorary Doctoral recipients as native Sons! Equally impressive is the fact that at least two other well-known Newfoundlanders have ties with the small community. Humourist Ted Russell (1905-77) married a Change Islands native, journalist Dora Oake, and for a time taught school at nearby Fogo Island. A one-time politician and cabinet minister, Russell is best known for his Pigeon Inlet stories, chronicling Newfoundland's most beloved fictional outport, and featuring characters like Uncle Mose. Russell received many honours of his own, including a Newfoundland and Labrador Arts Council award named after him. Incidently, Russell was also the recipient of a honorary degree from Memorial University.

Russel's Daughter, Elizabeth Miller, is a professor of English at Memorial University, and has edited volumes of her Father's works. Russell's Son Kelly is a distinguished musician, a member of the band Figgy Duff, and the founder of a recording company, Pigeon Inlet Productions.

We've seen that Russell's *Tales from Pigeon Inlet* television series starred George Earle as Jethro Noddy. A friend of Earle's, Otto Tucker, starred alongside him in the role of Pigeon Inlet elder, Grampa Walcott. Born at Winterton in 1923, Tucker at one point taught school at Change Islands. For a number of years Tucker combined the role of Salvation Army officer with that of educator, before concentrating more fully on the latter field. He taught at both the University of Toronto and Acadia University before moving to Memorial University's Faculty of Education in 1971, where he served until his retirement in 1995. Like Earle, Tucker was known for his after-dinner speeches, and published the books *From the Heart of a Bayman* (1984) and *A Collection of Stories* (1987). More recently a new collection of stories from Tucker has appeared titled, *That Nothing be Lost. Recording Elusive Memories of Otto Tucker.*

The founding President of the Wessex Society of Newfoundland, Tucker was presented with the Canada 125 Medal, the Heritage Award of the Newfoundland Historical Society, and the Silver Cross of St. George by the publishers of *This England* magazine. In 1994 he was inducted into the Baccalieu Chamber of Commerce Hall of Fame. As one might expect from this distinguished group, Tucker received a honorary Doctor of Laws degree from Memorial University. Dr. Otto Tucker passed away in October 2015, aged ninety-two.

6

The Beothuk Presence

Beothuk Culture

One of the most fascinating (if tragic) aspects of Newfoundland history, and one with a close connection to Notre Dame Bay, concerns the aboriginal people now known as Beothuk. Encountered by the earliest European explorers, they were considered extinct by 1829. The Beothuk, who occupied portions of Notre Dame Bay when the first English settlers arrived, had a long connection with the Island of Newfoundland. It is entirely possible, but not proven, that the Beothuk may descend from the Maritime Archaic. Researchers are more confident in tracing Beothuk ancestry to the Recent Indian population, which arrived in Newfoundland from Labrador around 2,000 years ago. Groups believed to be direct ancestors of the tribe were inhabiting the Island by 400 AD, if not before. The earliest group from whom archaeologists confidently trace Beothuk ancestry are known as "The Beaches" culture, after the place in Bonavista Bay where much evidence of them has been found. They were succeeded around 1000 AD by the "Little Passage" people, who are generally considered the prehistoric phase of Beothuk culture.

Sketch of Beothuk camp by John Cartwright

The normal social organization of the Beothuk was into bands of fifty or less persons, and the group's total numbers on the Island were probably less than two thousand at any given time. In the past some estimates put Beothuk numbers much higher, contributing to the idea that they were massacred in large numbers by white settlers.

The Beothuk employed a variety of house forms, their general word for house being *mamateek.* For much of the year the Beothuk lived along coastal areas in small, single-family structures, similar to the dwellings we know as "wigwams." These small houses were made of wooden poles overlaid with birch or fir bark, and included sleeping areas hollowed out in the earth, a feature practically unique to the Beothuk. In Winter the bands retreated from the coast, moving into larger multi-family dwellings.

The Beothuk were hunter-gathers and lived off a wide variety of foods. These were caught using a range of weaponry, including toggling harpoons, spears, and the bow and arrow. Sea mammals such as seals were important, as were fish like salmon. Birds also formed an important part of the Beothuk diet. The now extinct, flightless great auk was especially valued by the Natives. The Beothuk travelled sixty kilometres to the Funk Islands, using their uniquely-shaped birch bark canoes, in search of the birds and their eggs. In Winter the main source of protein for the bands was the caribou. The Beothuk waited for herds of the animals at specific locations along their migration route, building a type of fence to funnel the deer into one area where they could be brought down more easily. For many years after the Beothuk left the area, downed trees making up the fences could still be seen along rivers like the Exploits. Caribou skins were put to a wide variety of uses by the Beothuk, not least of which was the manufacture of clothing.

Archaeology has taught us much about the material context of Beothuk life, but unfortunately tells us little about their belief and value systems. There is evidence the bands participated in a ceremony similar to the Innu *mokoshan* feast, where caribou marrow was consumed to honour the spirit of the animal and to ensure good hunting in the future. One important aspect of Beothuk life was their use of red ochre to coat their implements, bodies and the remains of the dead. The Beothuk extracted red ochre from local iron deposits, which were subsequently mined by Europeans. Later, colonists used the ochre as paint, mixing it with linseed oil. During the early years of English settlement Twillingate was noted for the use of this red paint on buildings like fishing stages, a practice observed on Fogo Island by Bishop Feild in the 1840s. A major source for the ochre was Fortune Harbour on the tip of the Fortune Harbour Peninsula, only thirty-two kilometres across Notre Dame Bay from western New World Island. The colour red seems to have played a role in

Beothuk tribal identity, and disgraced band members might be ordered to remove the colouring as a form of punishment. We don't know for sure, but it is very likely that the red hues had spiritual overtones for the people.

Of Beothuk religion we also know little. It seems they believed that when a person died his/her spirit travelled to a "Happy Island" to be with the Good Spirit. Like the Christian Heaven, getting there depended on meeting certain moral qualifications. Not least among these was a refusal to make peace, or communicate, with Whites, who were said to come from the Bad Spirit. This belief probably formed early in the Beothuk relationship with Europeans, and may partly explain their avoidance of trade contacts with settlers.

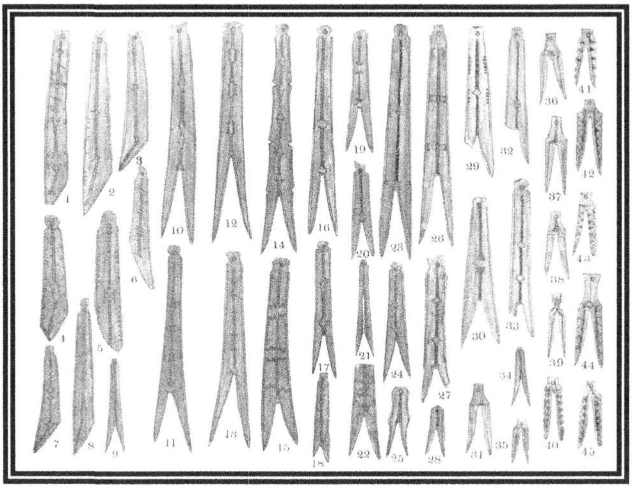

Beothuk pendants

....

Beothuk & Europeans – Early Encounters

It is hard to know when Europeans first encountered the Beothuk. When the Scandinavian Vikings visited Newfoundland around 1000 AD they met, and fought with, Natives whom they named *Skraelings*. These people may have been Beothuk ancestors, but that has never been proven. By the seventeenth century the Natives were already reluctant to meet with Europeans, and may have been mistreated by fishers who had been coming to the Island for a century. In a 1768 letter to Governor Palliser, Lieutenant John Cartwright (1740-1824) reported a tradition current among the English settlers that relations between themselves and the Beothuk had originally been friendly. Information given by Newfoundland fishermen led Cartwright to believe that hostilities were primarily due to the behaviour of the English. He saw the Beothuk avoidance of Europeans as stemming from a just resentment of wrongs committed against them.

One of the first confirmed instances of European-Beothuk interaction, and one of their few *friendly* encounters, took place in 1612. In 1610 merchant adventurer John Guy set out for Newfoundland with a party of settlers intending to found a colony in Cuper's Cove (Cupids), Conception Bay. Guy only stayed until 1613, and his colony eventually failed, although some of his settlers helped found Bristol's Hope, which became Harbour Grace. During his stay in Newfoundland Guy engineered the one known peaceful encounter with the Beothuk. Setting out with a party of men in two boats to try and establish contact with the Natives, he finally located a group of them in Trinity Bay, probably in Bull Arm near the modern town of Sunnyside. Descriptions of the Natives' distinctive half-moon shaped canoes and extensive use of red ochre confirms their identity as Beothuk. The two parties exchanged gifts, danced, and shared a meal. Guy apparently hoped this would lead to a yearly trade between the two peoples. By the time the Beothuk returned to the meeting place the next Summer Guy had left for England. Instead, the band encountered a fishing craft whose captain had no knowledge of Guy's trading venture. Alarmed at the sudden appearance of "Savages," he fired a shot at them and the Beothuk fled. In future there would be little or no friendly interaction between the two peoples.

For the next two hundred years the Beothuk dealt with the European presence in their midst by retreating from the newcomers and refusing to trade or interact with them. The expansion of English settlements and competition with another of Newfoundland's Native groups, the Mi'kmaq, gradually confined the Beothuk to the Island's northeast coast, and eventually to the area of Red Indian Lake.

No one is sure why the Beothuk refused to interact with Europeans. Settlers certainly treated them brutally, as Cartwright noted, but this had happened to mainland Canadian Natives. Despite this, the Canadian Indian nations established military and trade relationships with European colonists. Perhaps the Beothuk belief that Europeans came from the Bad Spirit was a factor, or they may simply have felt they did not need to trade. Although the Beothuk prized materials like iron and canvas, they could get all they needed from fishing premises vacated over the Winters. This tendency only made things worse between the settlers and the Natives, as it was considered "pilfering" by the Europeans. In the end interaction consisted of little more than retaliation and counter-retaliation for perceived wrongs. By the time the first permanent English settlers arrived at Twillingate and Fogo Island in the early 1700s the coastline and islands of Notre Dame Bay were the Beothuk's major retreat. French and English crews fished the Bay in this period, but encounters with the Beothuk were rare at that time.

....

Boyd's Cove & Other Beothuk Sites

One of the Natives' last secure refuges was not actually located on the Isles, but very close by, at modern Boyd's Cove, just across the causeways that link Twillingate and New World Island with the main island. The Boyd's Cove site was occupied from about the years 1650 to 1730 by a band of thirty to forty Beothuk who lived in eleven separate dwellings. They also maintained a presence on nearby Inspector Island. Screened behind small islands and shoals, the site was ideal for Native canoes, but dangerous for larger European craft. Evidence suggests Boyd's Cove was a safe haven for many years. The situation changed with the foundation of Fogo and Twillingate, the latter only twelve kilometres away by sea. The Beothuk were now exposed and vulnerable. The European presence had a direct impact on Native food resources, especially the crucial salmon. With English competition for essential riverine salmon stocks, the Beothuk position in the area became precarious at best. The Beothuk killed a number of salmon fishers, but could not drive settlers out of the area. In time competition for this resource, vital to the Natives, became fierce among the English themselves. Eventually the stocks were almost wiped out. The establishment of an English salmon station at Dog Bay, just east of Boyd's Cove, may have been the last straw. It is no coincidence that English settlement of the region and the Beothuk retreat occurred at almost the same time.

The Boyd's Cove site is located in a clearing on a high glacial moraine, just behind a beach. There is a good stream flowing to the sea nearby. The area was used by Newfoundland Natives for many generations. Before the Beothuk habitation Dorset Palaeo-Eskimos used Boyd's Cove. There is also evidence of occasional prehistoric Indian visits to the area. Occupation of the site was sporadic for many years, as it is not the best location for obtaining certain food resources. In prehistoric times harp seal herds arriving off Newfoundland in the Spring would have been an important dietary component. Located away from headlands and the open sea, Boyd's Cove was not well suited to this hunt.

Beothuk village site at Boyd's Cove

The Beothuk settlement at Boyd's Cove was re-discovered in 1981, and first excavated from 1982-5 by Ralph Pastore. The area has provided some of the best artifactual evidence for the relationship of the historic Beothuk to the prehistoric Little Passage people. There is also evidence of the Natives' dietary habits, with the remains of caribou, harp and harbour seals, birds, bears, fish and shellfish being found. During one's year's excavation at Boyd's Cove 2,900 bones and teeth, along with twelve kilograms of shells, were uncovered. None of this material was gnawed by animals, indicating that at Boyd's Cove at least, the Beothuk did not keep domesticated dogs. The faunal material excavated at the site indicates that the camp was mainly used from early Spring through to the late Fall. The Beothuk normally retreated to the interior, especially the Exploits River and Red Indian Lake, to hunt and trap during the height of Winter. Boyd's Cove would have been especially useful in this regard, situated fairly near the Exploits River caribou migration route.

Other material remains discovered at Boyd's Cove include 1,700 metal items, particularly nails, which the Beothuk were quite skilled at turning into arrowheads. Pastore cites this, and the presence of items like fish hooks, as evidence that the historic Beothuk acquired much of their European material through pilferage, especially of fishing premises. Beothuk sites occupied later than Boyd's Cove still contain a high percentage of metal items, but a smaller proportion is made up of nails, presumably because overwintering of settlers made obtaining the nails more difficult.[1]

There were about 700 dark blue and translucent white trade beads found at Boyd's Cove. These may have had spiritual significance for the Beothuk. Although conclusive evidence linking the beads to trade has not been found, they may have been left by Europeans trying unsuccessfully to establish amicable relations. It is also possible the beads were traded to the Beothuk by the Native Montagnais (Innu) who visited Newfoundland as late as 1788, trading furs to the French. There are records of the French employing the Montagnais as intermediaries in trade with the Beothuk, as Francois Martel de Brouage did in 1718, but no definite indications of success. A Beothuk woman named Shanawdithit – more on her later – spoke of "good Indians" living on Newfoundland's other (west?) coast. This is far from conclusive, but it could indicate contact between the two groups. There may be no firm evidence, but it is fascinating to think that ancestors of today's Labrador Innu may have visited the Beothuk at Boyd's Cove.

Boyd's Cove is the most important Beothuk archaeological site in the area, but it is not the only one. A Beothuk burial and small quarry sites have been located on New World Island. The burial was found at Spirit Cove, Farmer's Head, by Scott Wheeler and Lloyd Watkins in 1936-7. This burial contained the remains of one individual, and consisted of a rock-wall erected on a cobble beach. The wall was about one metre below the beach, having a heavy rock structure at one end. The remains of poles approximately five centimetres thick were found by a side wall. These likely held up a covering of bark on which beach cobbles were piled. Burial sites have also been found on a small island in Indian Island Tickle, and on two islands off Comfort Cove.

Another burial was reported from Fogo in 1887. While constructing a road near the Fogo Harbour canal a man named Thomas Farrell found a quantity of birch bark. Intrigued, he lifted the bark covering. According to the *Twillingate Sun*, Farrell discovered,

> ...a tomb about thirty inches deep, of equal width, and between six and seven feet long. It was covered with large flagstones resting on the smooth walls. The birch bark gave evidence of exceedingly fine sewing, as good as could be done by any of our most improved sewing machines, and was placed above the flagstones in the shape of a light covering over the sepulchre...[2]

In a cavity underneath the flagstones Farrell found human remains, including a skull with some of its scalp still attached. The body had been shrouded in seal skins, and was accompanied by grave goods including bone handles and two knife blades.

....

Hostile Relations

Unfortunately, physical remains are about all the information we have concerning most Beothuk activity in Notre Dame Bay. Such relations as did exist between the Beothuk and the Bay's first colonists were tenuous at best. To protect themselves Twillingate's early English residents were forced to carry firearms whenever they travelled the several kilometres between settlements. Contact between the first settler families was thus very limited. T. D. Scanlon reported to Alexander Parsons that one of these settlers, Moore of Back Harbour, normally carried two pistols, one in each hand, whenever he ventured to South Island. According to Scanlon's account, Mr. Moore frequently discharged his pistols at the Natives to scare them off, whether killing any of their number Scanlon did not say. Moore's contemporary, the Jenkin's Cove settler surnamed Bath, admitted in his old age that many years earlier he fired his musket at what he thought were Beothuk. Even at that point in time, Parsons reported, Bath could never be persuaded to admit what the results of his shot were.

In his classic study of the Beothuk, James Howley noted a number of traditions about Native-settler animosity in Twillingate. Some of these he obtained from Thomas Peyton, whom Howley described in 1907 as "...about the only really reliable authority [on the Beothuk] now living..."[3]

In the early 1700s Hart's Cove, on the south side of Twillingate harbour, was the usual stop-off point for ships coming from England. One day a boy going ashore there for water was killed by the Beothuk. Two boys from another vessel went to Kiar's Pond on a Sunday to wash their clothes. After they ran late a party of men went to look for them only to find the two boys' bodies, and a number of Natives making off about 1.5 kilometres away.

Not all traditions concerning the Beothuk at Twillingate had tragic endings. One of the oldest stories of Beothuk-settler interaction there appeared in a December 1915 issue of the *Twillingate Sun* newspaper. The event supposedly happened exactly two hundred years before. If true, it would confirm the tradition of the first settler families arriving on the islands around 1700. One of these families was named Young, and a member of this clan was one of the main protagonists in the encounter. The incident also indicates the presence of caribou at Twillingate. If so, the large mammals have not been recorded there for many, many years. As the story goes, Mark Young and his dog were spending Christmas week alone in their tilt at Young's Point. Apparently, his garden had been ravaged by frosts and Native incursions – in the story the Natives were never specifically identified as Beothuk. The only animal Young had recently caught was a doe caribou at Kiar's Pond. Putting out Arctic hare snares to supplement his meagre rations, Young heard a faint moaning noise. He was startled to see the hand of a Native child sticking out of the snow. The boy, no more than a young teen, was taken back to Young's tilt, wrapped in caribou skins and given some hot food. Soon the youth was sleeping peacefully. Going outside to gather wood, the man was waylaid by three Natives who bound him and took him back inside the cabin. Young must have thought his end was at hand. The trio ransacked the tilt, but soon the boy arose, talking and pointing excitedly at Young, tied up on the floor. Apparently one of the three men was the boy's Father, and was overjoyed to see him alive. At the same time, it being Christmas Eve, the Natives' attention was drawn to a picture of the Christ Child in the manger lying on Young's table. The men pointed at it several times, exclaiming "Kismas." The Natives replaced Young's belongings as they found them, leaving the humble dwelling and repeating "Kismas, good man." Young's selfless deed in saving the youth was returned in kind.

If authentic, this tale would be one of the few positive encounters recorded between Natives and Europeans on the Isles, but there are a few problems with it. At this date (1715) it is likely that Natives in the Twillingate area would have been Beothuk, rather than another group like the Mi'kmaq. This being said, for the three aboriginal men to have been moved by the Christmas spirit, and to have spoken some words in English, implies contact with Europeans, especially missionaries. As far as is known such contacts did not exist in the Beothuk case. Perhaps there is some truth at the core of this story, but embellishments were probably added over the span of two hundred years. Even in the case of better authenticated contacts, the truth often became distorted over time.

A case in point – one with more hostile overtones – revolves around a family named Stuckly (Stockley or Stuckey?), living at Herring Neck. One day when only the Mother and a Daughter were home some Beothuk men apparently tried to kidnap the younger Stuckly. The Mother was then supposed to have hit one of the Natives with a clothes pole and the party ran off. This was one of the cases where a story about the Beothuk was certainly exaggerated. In later years a Stuckly descendant related that the Beothuk hadn't even closely approached the house, much less tried to carry anyone off. It seems they were frightened away by the family's dogs. Even the location of the incident was reported incorrectly – the Natives paid their visit at South Twillingate Island before the family moved to Herring Neck.

Nevertheless, the Beothuk did make their presence known at Herring Neck. On one occasion local fishers finished a day's work and went home to their dwellings. A number of Beothuk had concealed themselves under the residents' fishing stages (something they are reported as doing elsewhere), and came out when the coast was clear. The Natives sliced up the sails on a fishing boat, along with the fishers' lines, and damaged other property. The settlers discovered the Beothuk, but the Natives made good their escape.

Similar tales of conflict abound from Fogo Island, though material remains of the Beothuk are relatively scarce there. Donald Holly's 1997 archaeological survey provided no firm evidence of how often the Beothuk may have visited Fogo Island. Holly believed it was primarily used for birding and other activities not conducive to year-round settlement. Therefore, the Beothuk probably lived on Fogo Island only during the Summer months. As we saw in Chapter Four, the toponym"Fogo" may even originate from fires the Beothuk lit to smoke fish and meat.

Reports of Native-settler contacts in the Fogo area, with the invariable litany of mutual assaults, are not hard to find. In 1785 British naval officer George C. Pulling (1766-1819) visited Newfoundland for the first time, becoming interested in the Beothuk and their plight. He visited the Island's northeast coast in 1792 under orders to investigate relations between the Natives and settlers. Pulling's report mentions that Fogo Islanders had their boats cut loose by the Beothuk almost every year. A story making the rounds at the time Pulling visited came from a Fogo merchant named Clark. According to Clark, he and a partner named Hancock sent a boat to Shoal Bay to collect ballast. Anchoring their schooner near the shore, the nine-man crew landed in a small boat. Just as they began to disembark the men had arrows fired at them by two Beothuk concealed on the cliffs above – five of the nine men were wounded. Apart from this attack on his employees, Clark had other negative dealings with the Beothuk, losing a net to them.[4]

Howley reported on another encounter near Shoal Bay, which resulted in the wounding of John Wells of Joe Batt's Arm. Wells was one of six men travelling from their home town to Fogo by boat, when forced to put ashore in Shoal Bay by adverse winds. While trying to take a shot at a sea bird, the party were surprised by a Beothuk man who fired an arrow at them. The missile pinned Wells' hand to his oar. The injury never fully healed, and Wells was said to have died from complications (Albeit many years later).

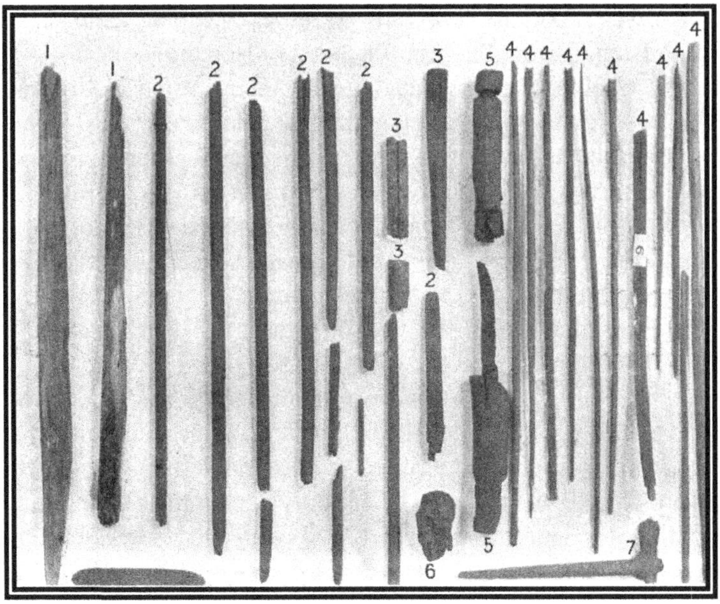

Beothuk implements, including (2) sections of arrow shafts and (3) pieces of bows

One of the most well known stories of the Beothuk attacking settlers on Fogo Island comes from the town of Tilting. As the legend goes, an Irish-born resident named Michael Turpin was working near Sandy Cove beach on 9 June 1809. Mike McCarthy asserts that Turpin was one of several men planting their gardens; a version given by Sean Broders in *Downhome* has Turpin accompanied by one Thomas Murphy. As there had been no confrontations with the Beothuk on Fogo Island for some years, the men were unarmed. Their sense of security turned out to be unfounded. Confronted by a group of Beothuk hunters, the men fled toward Tilting. According to Broders' account, Murphy and Turpin split up, with Murphy continuing on in the direction of the settlement. On the way he met up with an old woman digging potatoes. The intrepid senior raised her hoe as though it were a musket, scaring off the Beothuk. Michael Murphy lived to tell the tale, although he had taken an arrow in the side.[5] Broders tells us that Turpin was not so lucky. He swam out to a schooner anchored off Sandy Cove, hoping its crew would save him. This was not to be – the vessel's compliment had all gone to Tilting for the day. Turpin could not make it up the vessel's side, and was captured by some of the Beothuk men who had taken to their canoes. Near a large rock on shore, still called Michael Turpin's Rock, the Beothuk beheaded their hapless prisoner. It was reported that Turpin's head was last seen mounted on a pole near the Exploits River. Apparently this was a typical Beothuk ritual after they killed a European. In a notebook from around 1902 Thomas Peyton noted that "[w]henever the Red Indians kiled[*sic*] a White man they always cut off his head, and most always stuck it up on a pole."[6] In McCarthy's account Turpin had kept on running but sought refuge on the rock when his escape route was cut off. Whatever the precise details of the encounter, there is little doubt that Turpin met his death at the hands of the Beothuk. He was one of the last settlers killed by the Natives.

Reports of such grisly events shouldn't give us an unfair picture of the Beothuk. They were normally a peaceful people, something noted about the tribe since the time of John Guy. When they did take hostile action it appears largely as a result of the threat they felt from the settlers, or when an injury had been done to one of their own. On the other hand, reports of settler assaults on the Beothuk span the gamut of early Newfoundland history. Some incidents were justified by their perpetrators as retaliation for the Beothuks' own depredations, while others appear totally unwarranted.

It was said that after the attack on Clark's crewmen a group set off from Fogo in pursuit of the assailants. Fogo Island chronicler Benson Hewitt surmises that the men were heavily armed, and a bloody revenge might have been expected had any Beothuk been found. Around the year 1790 a Tilting planter named John MacDonald reportedly attacked a group of Beothuk near the Funk Islands. It was said that in the unprovoked assault MacDonald fired his musket directly into one of their canoes, but seems to have killed no one. From the Beothuk perspective this was not the most deadly incident. Shortly before Pulling visited the island it was reported that a Fogo settler named Hooper had killed a Beothuk man.

Accounts of attacks on the Beothuk come not just from Fogo Island, but from all over the Isles. While at Twillingate in 1768 John Cartwright reported that he had been approached by a settler from Trinity expecting a reward for his part in the killing of a Beothuk woman and the abduction of her young child. The woman was apparently shot and mortally wounded by a party of fishermen who then fled with the infant, having seen two Beothuk men nearby. Cartwright's indignation at this crime was only increased by the fact that the poor orphan was later taken to Poole and exhibited as a curiosity for a charge of two pence. One Twillingate furrier named Rogers boasted that he had personally killed sixty of the Natives, including nine at one time. According to Ingeborg Marshall, Twillingate's Reverend Laugharne may have been referring to the same man when he told Royal Navy surgeon James Dobie that a man had once boasted to him of killing ninety-seven Beothuk, and wished to make it an even 100. These claims were probably exaggerated, given the small numbers of the tribe, though the murder of Natives was a well-established fact. In 1807 Governor John Holloway (1747-1826) made the Government's position explicit in a proclamation warning that the injury or murder of Beothuk would be punished like that of any other of King George's subjects. In short, the offender would hang!

We should be careful about the old adage that the Beothuk were slaughtered wholesale by Europeans. In his work *Shanawdithit's People*, Pastore notes that the Beothuk decline resulted from a combination of many factors. Thus, we should avoid simple and sensationalist arguments that Newfoundlanders were sadists who killed Beothuk "for fun." Nevertheless, the evidence of Cartwright's narrative, and reports like that from Rev. Laugharne, indicate the callous attitude certain Whites had toward our Island's indigenous peoples. This derisive opinion is best summed up by a man named Richards, who told Howley that "...the Red Indians were nasty brutes and stank awfully."[7]

....

Tom June & John Cartwright

Newfoundland's Beothuk Indians maintained their unhappy co-existence with Europeans for over 300 years. One source of Native mistrust was certainly the European habit of abducting aboriginal people. We have no accounts of Beothuk reaction to this callous practice, but it could have done nothing to make them think better of Whites. In 1500 Corte Real brought back fifty-seven Natives from Newfoundland to use as slaves, though all soon died from European diseases. In later centuries the British authorities authorized the capture of more Beothuk – all women and children – in misguided attempts to use them as "ambassadors" to their people.

One Beothuk captive had a close connection to Fogo, a man known in later life as Tom June, after the month of his capture. June was apparently taken by Irish hunters in 1758 when he was around nine years old. As per usual, the incident grew out of a desire for revenge, the hunters believing the Beothuk had stolen fishing gear and traps. Finding a Beothuk camp, the hunters lay in wait with their muskets, killing a Beothuk man and a boy as they emerged from their mamateek. Another boy, the future Tom June, was taken prisoner. After his capture June lived for many years at Fogo, where he was noted as an expert fisher. June's employer was a planter and furrier named John Cousens (d. 1790). Originally from Wimbourne, England, Cousens later made his home at Fogo. His association with the young Beothuk led to June's nickname – "Cousens' Indian."

Tom June was kidnapped when old enough to remember something of his people's beliefs and customs. Sadly, little use was made of June's knowledge – apparently he could speak his native language for some time. A tradition exists that June regularly visited his relatives in the country, but the reports are all third-hand or were circulated years later. Many now doubt the stories of June's visits to his Native family.

John Cartwright

The only European to employ Tom June's knowledge was John Cartwright, the same officer approached for a reward following the murder of a Beothuk woman. John's elder Brother was George Cartwright (1739-1819), a trader and explorer whose name is closely linked to Labrador. Although somewhat overshadowed by his sibling, John Cartwright was a fascinating character in his own right. Born at Marnham in Nottinghamshire, John entered the Royal Navy in 1758. The young officer was present at the capture of Cherbourg, and participated in the 1759 naval battle of Quiberon Bay. In 1766 Cartwright was appointed as surrogate for Governor Palliser in the Trinity and Conception Bay Districts, and served five years as deputy commissary to the

Colony's Vice-Admiralty Court. In 1768 John explored the Exploits River along with Brother George. Cartwright returned to England in 1771 suffering from poor health. In his later life he championed the cause of the American colonists, and always fought to advance British liberties and Parliamentary reform. Charles Wendell Townsend noted that these activities did not endear Cartwright to His Majesty's Government. Only his impeccable reputation allowed Cartwright to avoid imprisonment on a charge of sedition in 1820 – he was still fined £100. John Cartwright passed away at Hampstead five years later.

His 1768 expedition to the Exploits cemented Cartwright's association with the Beothuk. Directed by Governor Palliser, Cartwright mounted the expedition in hopes of establishing friendly contacts with the tribe. John Cousens was hired as a guide, with his Indian (Gills) Point establishment serving as headquarters for Cartwright's expedition before their departure and upon their return. As a prelude to the trip Cartwright interviewed Cousens' employee, Tom June. Marshall feels that June would have made a perfect guide, and speculates that Cartwright may have extended such an invitation to the young man. She wonders if June, or Cousens acting on his behalf, refused the offer. In any case, June gave Cartwright a description of the body of water now called Red Indian Lake, which the officer named Lieutenant's Lake. Cartwright was very impressed with June's recollection of geographical details. In tribute to his informant, Cartwright named an arm of the lake "June's Cove," today's Millertown. June provided Cartwright with precise details of where to find his childhood village, and the expedition located the site exactly where the Beothuk man indicated. Unfortunately, the locale was long abandoned. Cartwright failed to find any recent trace of the Beothuk. This might prove that the stories of June's visits to his people were wishful thinking or pure invention by later writers. On the other hand, June had seen first hand what Europeans might do to Beothuk still living their old life in the bush. Perhaps he didn't fully trust Cartwright, and deliberately steered the party away from his people's current villages.

Whatever the truth of the matter, the 1768 expedition marked the last contact between June and Cartwright. For two or three decades after their meeting, Tom June continued fishing at Fogo. J. P. Howley asserts that June drowned when his fishing skiff overturned while entering the gut leading into Fogo Harbour. The exact year of this fatal mishap is not clear, but it probably occurred between 1788-97. After Cartwright no other Europeans attempted to question June about his people and their culture.

....

Beothuk Encounters – William Cull

The uncertainty surrounding the date of Tom June's death is a reminder of just how sketchy is our knowledge of the Beothuk as individuals. June's story is one of only a few fortunate survivals. Most of the Beothuk who ever lived are now completely lost to the historical record. The only way we know the Beothuk at all is through archaeology and the stories of Europeans like Cartwright, who interacted with them. One of the most famous, or infamous, persons in the second category is William Cull (*fl.* 1803-23).

ENL lists Cull as an "Indian Hunter," although this term does not do the man full justice. Cull has been a focus of attention for many years; he figures prominently in Howley's classic study of the Beothuk, appears in the work of academics like W. Gordon Handcock and Ingeborg Marshall, and most recently in the writings of Fogo Island chroniclers Eric Witcher and Benson Hewitt.

Cull may have been born at Barr'd Islands sometime in the 1760s, his family among the first to permanently settle the community. Another tradition has it that Cull was not a native of Barr'd Islands, but emigrated from Poole, Dorset. What is not in doubt is that by the 1790s William Cull was a prominent Notre Dame Bay entrepreneur. In 1796 Cull worked as a furrier for John Peyton, himself closely associated with the Beothuk. Cull later had dealings with the Slades, selling them everything from cod and salmon to sealskins and timber. It is recorded that by 1821 Cull and Wife Mary had seven children baptised at Barr'd Islands by missionary John Leigh. In the thirty years before this date Cull became noted for his dealings with the local Native people.

By the mid 1700s reports were reaching the colonial authorities of mistreatment of the Beothuk by settlers, and the fear grew that the group might be dying out. Such fears prompted the authorization of Cartwright's expedition and Pulling's 1792 investigations. In both cases the aim was to make contact and open peaceful trading relations with the Beothuk. One aspect of this strategy, alluded to earlier, was the attempt to capture individuals who could be taught English and return to their people as liaisons. Anyone who could accomplish this goal was offered a reward, first of fifty then 100 British pounds. Cull was the first person known to have made an attempt at the reward in 1803.

It is not certain how Cull found out about the reward, but once he had done so he vowed to do everything he could to open relations with the Beothuk. We may wonder if Cull's enthusiasm for the cause was motived by any sense of philanthropy or simply by a desire to get the reward money, which he did, in fact, receive. Cull had been one of Pulling's informants in 1792, and the naval officer believed the settler had few compunctions about killing the

Natives. Whatever his motivation, in 1803 Cull captured a Beothuk woman. As Handcock notes, the circumstances surrounding this event are sketchy – even the woman's name was never recorded. By one account the woman, described variously as "young," or as being aged fifty or older, was captured by Cull as she paddled her canoe looking for bird's eggs. Cull took the woman to St. John's to collect his reward. After remaining there for some time, and being given presents, the Beothuk woman was taken back to Fogo Island by Cull, who had been instructed to return her to her people as a goodwill ambassador. After keeping his charge with him on Fogo Island for about a year, Cull and a small party of men headed up the Exploits River with her in 1804, leaving the woman to meet up with her people. Her fate remains unclear. Cull returned to where he'd dropped the woman off a few days later, and assumed she had returned to her tribe. On the other hand, there were reports that the woman returned to the coastal settlements on her own. The author/explorer William Epps Cormack (1796-1868), a passionate advocate on behalf of the Beothuk, doubted she ever rejoined her people.

Though Cull and his captive had gone their separate ways, his involvement with the Beothuk was only just beginning. In 1809 Cull was engaged by Governor Holloway to head an expedition to the Beothuk Winter territory, Red Indian Lake. Cull set out on new year's day, 1810, accompanied by six Notre Dame Bay settlers and two Mi'kmaq. Four days into their trek, nearly 100 kilometres up the frozen river, the party found a large Native dwelling made of wood, covered with bark and skins. Inside were venison and skins, plus three tea kettle lids that may have been given as presents. Another structure stood on the opposite bank of the Exploits, though Cull and his men did not investigate it. Two Beothuk were sighted but, discovering the interlopers, they fled; Handcock believes they warned other Beothuk in the vicinity. Cull's expedition reported on the deer fences the Beothuk used to capture caribou, but this was about as much as it accomplished, other than leaving a few trade goods in exchange for some skins. At this point a disagreement arose among the party, perhaps over fear of attack, upon which Cull and his men withdrew.

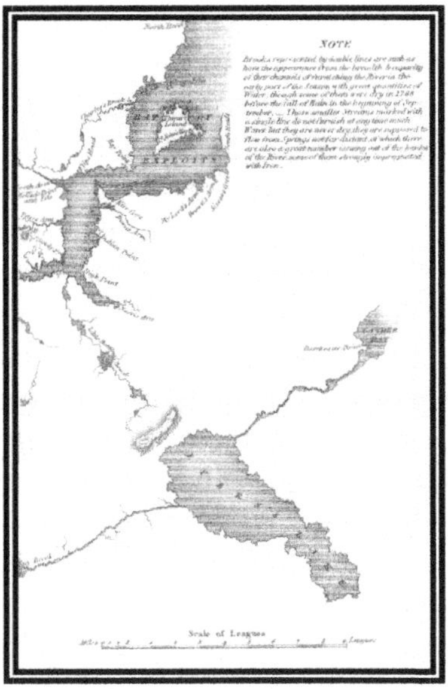

Cartwright sketch of Lieutenant's (Red Indian) Lake

The next year Cull was called upon to join another expedition at the behest of Governor Sir John Thomas Duckworth (1747/8-1817). This venture, headed by Lieutenant David Buchan (1780-c.1838), was the closest anyone came to establishing good relations with the Beothuk since John Guy. Unfortunately, this golden opportunity went tragically wrong. Cull was appointed chief guide to Buchan's ambitious expedition, which departed up the Exploits on 13 January 1811. Despite a difficult progress, Buchan's party found an old Beothuk camp and, soon after, recent tracks made by the Natives. On the banks of a frozen lake they made contact with a group of Beothuk, including men, women and children. After a meeting of several hours that seemed to go well, Buchan and most of his group, accompanied by four Beothuk men, left to gather presents the expedition had been obliged to leave behind. Two of Buchan's men, both marines, stayed behind to repair broken snowshoes. The next day many of Buchan's party, still accompanied by one of the Beothuk, returned to the Native camp. All were perplexed to find it deserted, though there was no indication of violence. The Beothuk man remained with the group, which now bedded for the night in the Beothuk camp. The group left after distributing gifts among the mamateeks, planning to return in two days. The Beothuk man went with them but abruptly stopped and ran off. The reason soon became clear. Buchan and the others found the bodies of the marines who remained with the Beothuk – both had been beheaded. Years later the Beothuk woman Shanawdithit recounted why the men had been killed. After Buchan's departure the group became fearful that they would all be captured and carried off to the coast. One of the men who accompanied Buchan for a short distance – a chief – returned, arguing that the two Europeans should be put to death. Although some of the others resisted the idea, the plan was eventually agreed upon. The marines were shot with arrows and decapitated. Fearing attack, Buchan and his men returned to the coast. A later expedition led by Buchan failed to find the Beothuk, and the best chance for peace between the Natives and Europeans was lost.

It has been suggested by Handcock that taking men like William Cull, considered by some as bitter enemies of the Beothuk, on the expedition was a mistake by Buchan. Perhaps the sight of those furriers who had so often been their foes unnerved the Natives. Overall, Cull's career is reflective of the missed opportunities of establishing a genuine relationship of trust. Though Cull received his fifty pounds for capturing the Beothuk woman in 1803, and was even said to have learned some of her language, he did little to promote better relations through his captive. Naturally, one private citizen like Cull could not have resolved matters on his own. Ingeborg Marshall places much of the blame on the British authorities. Although well intentioned, they made little real attempt to learn what specific grievances the Beothuk had, or what the best way might have been to improve Native-settler relations. Of Cull himself, little is known of his later years. By the time he died, around 1831, the Beothuk had been pronounced extinct.

....

Demasduit, Shanawdithit & John Peyton

Some of the most well known incidents involving the Beothuk centre around two Native women, Demasduit (Mary March) and Shanawdithit (Nancy April), and an English merchant, John Peyton Jr. (1793-1879). Peyton's Father, John Sr. (1747-1829), first came to Newfoundland from the family's home of Christchurch, Hampshire in 1770. The elder Peyton was a close friend of John Cousens, and it was Cousens who persuaded him to come to Newfoundland. Peyton travelled from England accompanied by George Cartwright. The pair landed at Fogo before moving on to the Labrador coast. Peyton worked for Cartwright for two Summers. Thereafter, Peyton Senior traded in fish at Fogo, and later ran salmon-fishing stations on the Exploits River, where his goods were frequently pilfered by the Beothuk. Peyton was reportedly harsh in his retaliation on the Natives; he was said to have killed an elderly Beothuk man by beating his head in with the remains of a stolen trap. At one point it was even suggested he be expelled from the Bay of Exploits. Peyton Senior stayed on, however, and in 1812 his Son joined him in Newfoundland.

John Peyton, Jr. took well to the Newfoundland outdoor life. Peyton's Son Thomas later wrote that his Father "...never seemed so happy as he did when he was tramping through the snow on snow shoes with a bundle of steel traps slung up to his back..."[8] Like his Father, John Jr. experienced losses at the hands of the Beothuk, but was more humane in his approach to them. After losing a boat loaded with salmon at Lower Sandy Point in 1815 Peyton resolved to get back his goods, but also decided to establish relations with the Natives. Peyton thought he might even persuade them to trade rather than continue stealing his property.[9]

He was only successful in capturing one Beothuk, the woman named Demasduit. During the capture her Husband, Nonosabasut, was killed by Peyton's men while trying to rescue her. Evidence indicates that the party also killed another Beothuk man, though Peyton himself denied this. Now a widow, Demasduit was also the Mother of an infant child. Left behind with her people, Demasduit's baby later died as there was no milk to feed it. Demasduit was renamed Mary March after the month of her capture, much like Tom June. She resided at Twillingate for a time before being moved to St. John's. At Twillingate Demasduit became the charge of Reverend John Leigh and helped him compile a list of more than 200 Beothuk words. A copy of the list can be viewed at the Provincial Archives, and contains terms such as *mamshet* - beaver; *bukashamesh* - boy, and *thine* - thank you.[10] Peyton hoped, perhaps foolishly after having caused her Husband's death, that Demasduit could be an ambassador to her people. This plan came to nothing, as Demasduit died of tuberculosis in January 1820. A party of men, including Peyton, then returned her body to her people's old camp at Red Indian Lake, but no contact was made.

The second Beothuk woman, Shanawdithit, was found by furriers in 1823, along with her Mother and older Sister. The leader of this group of furriers was none other than William Cull. By this time the numbers of Shanawdithit's people had been greatly reduced by deprivation, disease, and the incursions of White settlers. The Mother and Sister soon died, but Shanawdithit spent a number of years living amongst the Whites. She became a part of John Peyton Jr.'s household at Exploits Island in a capacity similar to a servant, and was much loved by the Peyton children.

Despite the troubled relationship between the Beothuk and Whites, many of the latter took an enlightened interest in the Natives' well being. William Cormack gathered information from Shanawdithit not only on her language, but on Beothuk cultural and spiritual beliefs. It is unfortunate that this material is not more extensive, as it is the most detailed information we have concerning these people. Like Demasduit, Shanawdithit was eventually taken to St. John's. This move was well meaning but cruel in a sense, as the Peytons were the closest thing she now had to a family. Sadly, Shanawdithit shared Demasduit's fate, dying of tuberculosis in June 1829.

Beothuk women Demasduit (left) and Shanawdithit

....

Twilight?

Cormack also tried to help the Beothuk when he founded the Boeothuck[sic] Institution. Its first meeting was held at Twillingate's Court House on 2 October 1827. Through the Institute it was hoped to foster good relations with the Beothuk and to introduce them to the benefits of European civilization. The second aim might seem misguided to us, but in those days it was considered a worthy goal. According to Howley's history of the Beothuk, thirteen men were made corresponding members of the Institution at its first meeting. Their number included six from Twillingate. John Peyton was a member, but gave Exploits as his address, as this was his primary residence at the time. Other prominent names associated with the Institution included its patron, Anglican Bishop John Inglis (1777-1850), honorary vice-patrons, University of

Edinburgh Professor Robert Jameson, Governor Cochrane's aide-de-camp John Dunscombe, and Admiralty Secretary Dr. John Barrow (1764-1848). Merchants Thomas and David Slade of Fogo were also members. Despite the noble intentions of these high-powered benefactors, the Institution may have come too late. Traditional wisdom holds that Shanawdithit was the last member of her tribe. With her death, only two years after the formation of the Boeothuck Institution, her people are generally considered to have become extinct.

Santu

This may not be the end of their story. Many people, including some from the Isles, claim partial descent from the Beothuk. One of the more interesting accounts of such descent comes from ethnologist Frank G. Speck (1881-1950). In 1910 Speck interviewed a Mi'Kmaq family encamped near Gloucester, Massachusetts. The family matriarch, Santu Toney (c.1837-1919), said she was born near Red Indian Lake, Newfoundland. Her Father was apparently a full-blooded Beothuk who married a Mi'Kmaq woman. According to Santu, her Father's Beothuk name was "Kop," after a red root growing in the lake, and his people called themselves *Osa'yan•a*. Kop left

Newfoundland for Nova Scotia with Santu when she was ten. While J. P. Howley was inclined to discount Santu's story, after many interviews Speck concluded that her tale was plausible.

Santu's is not the only tradition of Beothuk survivors with a Mi'Kmaq connection. Mi'kmaq oral tradition tells of at least two remaining bands of Beothuk, one of which went to Labrador and joined the Innu people, something mentioned by Santu. John Peyton befriended J. B. Jukes during his 1840 geological survey – the two men ascended the Exploits River together as far as modern Grand Falls. Peyton recounted the tradition of surviving Beothuk bands to Jukes. According to Jukes, Peyton heard that men in red deer skins had been recently seen in Labrador, this ten years after Shanawdithit's death. Contemporary reports also expressed doubt as to whether the Beothuk were really gone. E. Slade, who helped Peyton capture Demasduit, was convinced that as of 1829 there were still many Beothuk survivors. The Slade Company's Twillingate agent, Mr. Salmon, reported abundant signs of the Beothuk in Notre Dame Bay during an 1844 trek to St. John's. It is possible these signs were fifteen to twenty years old, but Salmon's description indicates a more recent occupation. A story recounted in a 1986 *Decks Awash* article alleges that Robert Woolfrey, paddling his boat near modern-day Lewisporte, was shot in the back with an arrow fired by a Native man ashore. If correct, the chronology supports the idea that Beothuk lived on long after 1829 – Woolfrey's mishap apparently occurred in 1870! The Native man could have been Mi'Kmaq, but they were living at peace with the English by this time, and had long been using firearms. After visiting Shanawdithit at Exploits Island, Bishop Inglis remained doubtful she was the last of her nation.

There was apparently some foundation for Inglis' opinion. Only a few years after his first visit to Newfoundland, a report concerning the Beothuk appeared in an 1834 issue of *The Star and Conception Bay Journal.* The unsubstantiated article indicates that the Beothuk may have visited Newfoundland's northeast coast for some years after Shanawdithit's death. The paper reported that:

> A person recently returned from fishing at Seldom Come By informs us that a party of Boeothics or aboriginal inhabitants of this island, to the number of ten or twelve, attacked some grass cutters from Fogo, some time in the last month [August 1834], at Western Arm, about four or five leagues distant from the first mentioned place. – The latter were obliged to make a precipitate retreat, and being covered by a high beach reached their boat without receiving any injury from the

> arrows of their assailants. – Shortly after they took their guns and went on shore in pursuit of the savages, to some distance inland, but no trace of them could be discovered. It is supposed that this remnant of a race, supposedly to be wholly extinct, have found an opportunity of revisiting their old and favourite part of the country...[11]

While many contemporaries of Bishop Inglis, like most modern scholars, were convinced that the Beothuk died out with Shanawdithit, the *Star and Conception Bay Journal* story suggests encounters with the group after 1829, some reported as late as 1878. Doug Jackson deals with the issue in his book, and the subject is taken up by Gerry Wetzel in his MLA thesis, "Decolonizing Ktaqmkuk History." Some of Wetzel's later research dealt with Kop and Santu, and a possible Beothuk connection to Piper's Hole (Swift Current) in southeastern Newfoundland.

Bishop John Inglis

Evidence for Beothuk intermarriage is not confined to Santu's account. Howley relates a story passed along indirectly from a Nova Scotia Mi'Kmaq woman, Nancy Jeddore. Jeddore told of a party of Mi'Kmaq hunters who came across a Beothuk camp and trailed its fleeing occupants, hoping to establish friendly relations. The trio of hunters overtook one woman who came to live with their band. Marrying a Mi'Kmaq man, she bore him a number of children. Jeddore's Father was personally acquainted with the Beothuk woman, who probably lived around the turn of the nineteenth century.

The idea that a distinct band of Beothuk survived well past 1829 is given further credence by accounts from Conne River residents Michael John and Melvin Jeddore, as related to them by their Grandfathers. In one case a band of nine persons was encountered, and in the other a lone male. John's description in particular indicates that these individuals were certainly Beothuk. According to Jackson, neither encounter could have occurred earlier than 1840. The areas where these meetings occurred suggest that the Beothuk survivors, or at least some of them, made their way south from Red Indian Lake, not north as is often suggested. It is possible that separate bands of Beothuk migrated in different directions from the 1820s on. Richard Dahl's account of the shooting of a "Red Indian" man by a Mi'Kmaq hunter sometime after 1814 places the Beothuk near Piper's Hole in that era, further suggesting a southward migration. To Jackson the southward route was a natural one for the Beothuk as caribou migrate in the general direction of Red Indian Lake, on to Pipestone Pond, and finally to Long Harbour River.

All of these accounts are interesting, and might lead us to take a second look at declaring the Beothuk completely extinct. Whatever the true story, it is a fact that no confirmed encounters between the Beothuk and European settlers occurred in the Isles region following the capture of Shanawdithit, her Mother and Sister. In the years after 1829 what should have been a shared heritage with Newfoundland's Beothuk became that of European descendants alone.

7

Jeremiah Coughlan & Lady Pamela

Jeremiah Coughlan.

In the 1690s Fogo Island was already an important Summer fishing station, but it had no merchant houses of its own for many years. Although merchants from communities like Trinity probably made use of the island in the period 1730-60, it was only from 1764, just after the Seven Years War, that a Bristol merchant named Jeremiah Coughlan (Coghlan) made Fogo Island his main base of operations.

Bristol, Jeremiah Coughlan's hometown, eighteenth century

During the 1750s Coughlan captained a number of Bristol merchant ships, trading to the Mediterranean, the West Indies and North America. He first visited Newfoundland in 1756 in command of a trading vessel. In 1762-3 he sailed to Newfoundland in his own vessel, the twenty-five ton *Lovely Joanna*. With a crew of five, the little craft was named after Coughlan's Wife (Johanna Davis), with whom he had five children.

During the Summer months Coughlan employed men in the codfishery, while his crews engaged in sealing and furring during the Winter (Coughlan normally spent Winters in Bristol, where he kept a large residence on Trinity Street). Coughlan was also active in the Springtime salmon harvest.

He was noted as an importer of clothing, fishery supplies and provisions into Newfoundland, an important function in a colony producing few, if any, manufactured goods. At the height of his business Coughlan sent anywhere from eight to ten ships to Newfoundland and Labrador per year, bringing supplies and returning with colonial produce.

Coughlan was certain that Labrador's fish stocks offered great commercial potential, and that Fogo Island, lying well to the north, would make an excellent base for exploiting this resource. Coughlan's Fogo enterprises may have been based at Wigwam Point, in Fogo Harbour. One account contends that Coughlan first operated at Fogo on his own behalf and later represented other Bristol-based companies as their Newfoundland agent. Another source maintains that Coughlan was primarily an independent trader, forming but one partnership during his career.

George Cartwright, onetime business partner of Jeremiah Coughlan

In 1769 he went into business with another Bristol merchant, Thomas Perkins. The two entrepreneurs bought an eighty ton schooner which they used in trading between Poole and the island of Fogo. Later, the soldier/explorer George Cartwright and naval Lieutenant Francis Lucas were added to the partnership. This combination lasted only until Lucas was lost at sea after a trading expedition to the Inuit. Having Incurred considerable losses, Coughlan and Cartwright ended their partnership in 1770, the year of Lucas' death. The pair then divided northern Labrador into commercial spheres of influence. Coughlan and Perkins dissolved their own partnership three years later.

With Fogo as his headquarters, Coughlan concentrated on establishing his independent business in Labrador, operating coastal fur-trading and fishing premises. In a 1777 letter to Governor John Montagu (1719-95), the businessman asserted that he (Coughlan) had started a sealing operation at Chateau Bay, Labrador in 1765. According to Coughlan's own account, this enterprise was the first of its kind in the region. Coughlan sent two or more ships to Labrador each year, starting in the 1770s – among their number were the vessels *Admiral Montague* and *Young Joseph*, sent out in 1777. Upwards of 250 men worked for Coughlan on that portion of the Labrador coast from Chateau Bay to modern Cartwright, inland to the Mealy Mountains.

Coughlan's experiences with this venture illustrate some of the problems that might be encountered by early entrepreneurs. His employees gave Coughlan considerable trouble, frequently disrespecting his rights in regard to property and profits. In 1777 John Peaton (Peyton) was working for Coughlan as a "servant" (manager) at a post in the Mealy Mountains. Without authorization, Peaton assumed control of the operation himself. Coughlan then appealed the matter to Montague, who promptly reasserted Coughlan's lawful claim to the post. Another case saw Coughlan's employees, who had agreed to split the revenue from that season's trapping and fishing with him on a 50/50 basis, refusing to turn over Coughlan's share of the profits.

While they were not always known for their loyalty, Coughlan's men were first-rate in another respect, their military training. Coughlan's role as a trader was complemented by more martial duties. In 1769 Coughlan was appointed naval officer reservist for the port of Fogo and the region adjacent to Bonavista District by Governor John Byron (1723-86). By 1776 Coughlan was Governor Montagu's principal Lieutenant on Newfoundland's northeast coast, performing a number of important tasks, including the enforcement of customs duties and the transport of criminals to St. John's for trial.

The previous year, 1775, Britain's thirteen American colonies rose in revolt, launching a struggle that lasted for eight years. The war ended in defeat for the mother country, and presented Coughlan with headaches of his own – as the Governor's surrogate he was forced to take on new responsibilities. He actively recruited for volunteers to oppose a rebel invasion of Lower Canada (Quebec) in the opening months of the war. In 1778 an American privateer under one John Grimes sacked Coughlan's Chateau Bay establishment. Grimes attacked Coughlan's posts on the Alexis River, capturing one of his ships. The privateer then meted out a similar treatment to Coughlan's business rival, John

Slade.

With privateers like Grimes active in the area, Coughlan Feared a direct attack on Fogo. The merchant-officer met with his competitors in an effort to form a defence force, or militia. With his fellow merchants unenthusiastic about supplying men, Coughlan drew on his own resources and armed his largest ship, the *Resolution*. In support of Coughlan's efforts Montague sent a pair of naval vessels in pursuit of Grimes, but the privateer escaped after destroying George Cartwright's premises in Sandwich Bay, Labrador. Thanking Montague for his aid, Coughlan redoubled his efforts to organize an informal militia at Fogo. Sixty-seven volunteers were mustered with Coughlan as their "Colonel-Commandant." In 1779 and 1780 the new Governor, Richard Edwards, sent Coughlan muskets and cannon to defend the port. With these resources, Coughlan constructed forts at Garrison Point and three other locales around Fogo Harbour. He was also given funds to raise an official militia from among Fogo fishermen. This militia kept a round-the-clock watch for suspicious vessels entering the eastern or western tickles. In 1779 the four-gun privateer *Centipede* attacked Twillingate, but was deterred from a similar assault on Fogo by Coughlan's militia and forts.

Despite this success, Jeremiah Coughlan's prosperous years didn't outlast the American Revolution. Toward the end of the war rumours began circulating that Coughlan's business was in trouble, and his eldest Son brought a petition for redress before Edwards at St. John's. The reports of Coughlan's insolvency, fuelled by testimony from former associates like Cartwright, were proved to be unfounded and malicious. Only one year later (1782) Coughlan really did go bankrupt, perhaps proving that the rumours were in fact true. On the other hand, the allegations may have undermined confidence in Coughlan, and were the real cause of his troubles, as Professor William Whiteley suggests.

With the ruin of its most prominent merchant Fogo was thrown into chaos. A naval Captain was despatched by the Governor to resolve the matter, promptly seizing Coughlan's effects to pay outstanding debts and wages. With Coughlan's downfall opportunities opened up for new merchants at Fogo, John Slade in particular.

....

Nancy Simms, Lady Pamela Fitzgerald.

Although he was Fogo's pioneer merchant, a Labrador trailblazer, and rendered an important military service to Fogo Island, Jeremiah Coughlan may be best remembered as the (alleged) Father of a woman named Nancy Simms, later famous as Lady Pamela Fitzgerald.

The baby that grew up to become Lady Pamela Fitzgerald was reportedly born in a Winter tilt at Dog Bay, adjacent to Fogo, in 1773. At birth the child's name was apparently Nancy Simms, though she was not officially christened, there being no priest in the area at the time. Since her Mother's name was also Nancy, everyone called the youngster "Little" Nancy. The future Lady Pamela is one of the great mysteries of the Isles, though we have a fair bit of information about her life generally. Even the "fact" that her original name was Nancy is not certain. As was common in those days, her surname was spelt a number of ways, while her marriage certificate referred to the young woman as "Anne Caroline Stephanie Sims." Her Mother's name has likewise been given as both Mary and Nancy. To avoid confusion between Mother and Daughter we will call Little Nancy by her later name of Pamela.

Newfoundland Winter tilt (cabin)

We know very little about Pamela's early life, and several men have been named as her Father. A French seafarer named Guillaume – William – de Brixay (also spelled de Brixey or DeBrizey), a man named Seymour, and even Louis Philippe Joseph, the French Duke of Orléans (1747-93) are all candidates. One "William Berkeley" was supposedly listed as Pamela's Father on her marriage certificate. Reverend William Pilot, author of a biographical article on Lady Pamela, noted that de Brixay was named as such on the certificate, thus Berkeley was simply an Anglicized version of de Brixay.

The tradition that Pamela's Father was Jeremiah Coughlan was recounted to Rev. Pilot sometime in the 1870s by Pamela's Cousin, septuagenarian fisherman Henry Simms of Fogo. Simms was Nancy's Nephew through her Brother. According to Simms, Nancy had worked for Coughlan as a servant. The merchant became smitten with his young employee, and by the time Coughlan returned to Bristol for the Winter Nancy was pregnant with his child. With Coughlan away, his former servant and lover moved back into the Simms family tilt, where her Daughter was born. By virtue of its source, Pilot was convinced that the story was true – Jeremiah Coughlan *was* Pamela's Father.

Lady Pamela biographer, Rev. William Pilot

Henry Simms provided Pilot with further details. When Pamela was aged about three or four Coughlan arranged for the youngster and her Mother to sail for England on a ship carrying salt fish. Calvin Coish's short biography of Lady Pamela, and Simms' own account, reveal that Nancy was shipped as the Wife of the vessel's skipper, the Frenchman de Brixay; the mariner was likewise named as Pamela's Father. This fiction served to avoid a scandal for Coughlan, who was married and had other, legitimate, children.

After their vessel arrived in Poole Coughlan seems to have abandoned Nancy, who ended up in Christchurch, earning a subsistence living doing skilled needlework.[2] On the other hand, in a letter to Nancy's Brother, Coughlan argued that he continued providing for his Daughter. Perhaps, but from this point in Pamela's story there is no further mention of Coughlan.

Madame de Genlis

Sometime between 1779 and 1782 Pamela went to live in France, accompanied by a man named Forth, agent for the Duke of Orléans. Though France and Britain were officially at war, the Duke sent Forth to England horse buying and, while there, the agent was instructed to look for an English-speaking companion for Orléans' children. Struck by Pamela's beauty, Forth secured her Mother's permission to take the child across the Channel. Duke Philippe's governess – probably his mistress – Stéphanie Félicité Ducrest de St-Aubin, Comtesse de Genlis (1746-1830), soon renamed the little girl. Thus it was from de Genlis that the name Pamela originated. Madame de Genlis grew very fond of her young charge, and supposedly paid Nancy Simms £25 to give up all contact with her Daughter. According to Nephew Henry, Nancy wrote to her Brother saying that she was unable to provide for Pamela, and that the she had parted from the child, who had gone into "foreign parts."

Here is where more of the mystery surrounding Pamela creeps in. By some accounts Madame de Genlis was far more than Pamela's governess and protector. She was actually rumoured to be the young girl's real Mother, implying that Philippe himself was the Father. If this be true, the whole tale of "Little Nancy" from Fogo was only a cover story to disguise her real parentage. It was Madame de Genlis who named Mr. Seymour as the Father. Another "smoke screen" to cloud the truth behind the girl's birth? Gerald Campbell, a biographer of his kinsman – Pamela's future Husband – Lord Edward Fitzgerald (1763-98), felt that the question of her parentage might never be resolved. Campbell was inclined to believe that the Duke and de Genlis were Lady Pamela's true Mother and Father, citing among other evidence, a physical resemblance of Lady Pamela's Grandchildren to members of the Orleans family.

On the other hand, good evidence exists supporting the idea that Pamela was actually a Simms of Fogo. The French poet/author Victor Hugo (1802-85) once noted that Madame de Genlis had been wrongly named as the Mother of children who were not hers. Contradicting her claim about the man Seymour, de Genlis' own memoirs list Fogo as Pamela's birthplace, and her parents as Captain de Brixay and a woman named "Sims." Author Paul O'Neill found further evidence to support the belief that Pamela was indeed Little Nancy of Fogo. This story appears in his 1982 publication, *Breakers. Stories From Newfoundland and Labrador.* While visiting Scotland in 1972 to research a history of St. John's, O'Neill found an 1836 letter from clergyman John Chapman amongst the papers of Sir Thomas Cochrane. At the time Chapman was stationed at Twillingate, and his letter indicated that he had interviewed two Fogo residents who remembered Nancy "Syms." Chapman asserted that many of the town's oldest inhabitants could recall both Nancy and her child, whom he refers to as "Ann," as on her marriage certificate. Chapman was in no doubt that this was the same child who was taken to Christchurch and went on to become Lady Pamela Fitzgerald.

Whatever the truth of her origins, Pamela spent the next few years in France, attending school at Belle Chase, where princes and princesses were her classmates. Pamela was known for her beauty and intelligence, becoming so proficient in French that she later used the language for correspondence.

After the outbreak of the French Revolution in 1789 Pamela returned to England in the company of her surrogate Father. In the beginning Duke Philippe supported the French Revolution and its ideals, assuming the name *Citoyen Égalité* (Citizen Equality). The Duke had gone so far as supporting the execution of his Cousin, King Louis XVI (1754-93). Such credentials did not guarantee safety in the turbulent world of revolutionary France. With the country divided into many factions, those in power one day might find themselves under arrest the next. Pamela's entry in ENL presents the trip to

London as more of a social visit, but Coish states that the Duke sent his family to England (where they lived in near-poverty) for their safety. He was probably right to do so. Like many of the Revolution's early supporters, especially aristocrats, "Citizen Equality" met a violent end. Égalité was beheaded in 1793, the same year as King Louis' own execution.

While in England Pamela became acquainted with the renowned Irish playwright-politician Richard Brinsley Sheridan (1751-1816). She and Sheridan were engaged, Pamela apparently resembling his late Wife, but the two never married. The reasons behind the couple's split are another mystery of Pamela's life. This setback may have distressed the young lady, but Pamela soon encountered the most important romantic figure in her life. Returning to Paris, the young woman met the Irish aristocrat Lord Edward Fitzgerald.

Lord Edward Fitzgerald

The fifth Son of James, first Duke of Leinster, Lord Edward fought with the British Army during the American Revolution, and was wounded at the 1781 battle of Eutaw Springs. On his return to Ireland Lord Edward, supported by his Brother, the second Duke, was elected to Parliament as MP for Athy and Kildare (1783). Completing his military education at Woolwich, Fitzgerald travelled to Spain before sailing for New Brunswick as a Major with the 54th Regiment.

Returning to Britain, the young aristocrat turned his back on his former political and military allegiances, becoming involved with factions sympathetic to the French revolution. As the situation in France became increasingly unstable the British authorities were in no mood to tolerate its influence at home, and Fitzgerald was expelled from the Army. On the heels of this disgrace, the young Lord travelled to Paris in October 1792, living with revolutionary author Thomas Paine (1737-1809).

While in Paris Fitzgerald and a friend attended the play *Lodoiska*, and chanced to see a young beauty sitting in another theatre box. Enchanted, Fitzgerald arranged a meeting with the girl, and the two were inseparable from that point on. The young lady was Pamela, now returned to France from England. The couple wed at Tournay on 27 December 1792, less than a month after their first meeting. They headed to London in January, moving to Dublin shortly thereafter. Letters written by Lord Edward to his Mother reveal the bliss shared by the two newlyweds, and the delight they felt in one another's company. Their happiness did not last long.

The English had settlements in Ireland since the Middle Ages, and controlled portions of the country. Differences between the two realms increased after England became Protestant, and Catholic Ireland suffered under the excesses of men like Lord Protector Oliver Cromwell (1599-1658). Large land transfers left many native Irish landless and, though the island had its own Parliament, it was constituted only of the minority Protestants. By the 1790s, with Britain embroiled in a war against the new French Republic, the situation in Ireland was reaching crisis point.

A patriot, Lord Edward joined the Society of the United Irishmen, whose goal was the establishment of an independent Irish republic. In 1796 the Fitzgeralds travelled to Germany, from where Lord Edward made a side trip to Switzerland, advocating an invasion of Ireland by the French. Papers later found at Lord Edward's residence, Leinster House, indicate that Lady Pamela played an active role in her Husband's activities, but the full extent of her involvement is not clear. Pilot and Campbell contend that all of Lady Pamela's intimates believed her innocent of actual treason.

Though his Wife's involvement may have gone no farther than hiding him from the authorities, Fitzgerald advocated violence and assassination. This commitment to force converted one Thomas Reynolds from a sympathizer into a government informant. Acting on a tip from Reynolds, several conspirators were captured on 12 March 1798 at the Dublin home of merchant Oliver Bond. Reynolds may not have totally recanted his loyalty to Lord Edward, whom he warned of the impending arrests.

Going into hiding, it was said that Lord Edward spent some time with his Wife at their various family residences – the last time the pair saw one another. Eventually Fitzgerald was betrayed by a barrister named Magan, who anticipated a £1,000 reward. When the authorities arrived to seize him Fitzgerald put up a ferocious struggle and was shot, either in the shoulder or arm. Taken to Newgate Prison, Lord Edward Fitzgerald died on 4 June 1798 of an infection resulting from his wound. Though Lady Pamela and her in-laws appealed that she be allowed a final meeting with her Husband, the request was rejected by the authorities.

Lady Pamela Fitzgerald and her Daughter Pamela

Soon after Lord Edward's death, Lady Pamela was implicated in her Husband's revolutionary activities. In July 1798 a posthumous Bill of Attainder was issued again Lord Edward, and Britain's Privy Council ordered Lady Pamela to quit Ireland. She travelled to Hamburg in 1799, taking up residence with her childhood protectress, Madame de Genlis.

Although cut short by Lord Edward's death, the Fitzgerald marriage produced three children, Daughters Lucy and Pamela, and Son Edward (Pamela eventually married General Sir Guy Campbell, while Lucy wed Captain J. F. Lyon; Edward became a British Army officer). While living at Hamburg Lady Pamela married a second time, to Mr. Pitcairn, the city's American Consul. Though it ended in divorce, this marriage produced another Daughter for Pamela. Sadly, Pamela was denied an active role in her children's futures. With the dissolution of his marriage to Lady Pamela, Pitcairn took their child to the United States, where she was raised. Likewise, when she was forced out of Ireland, Lady Pamela left her two eldest children with their Fitzgerald relatives, where her second Daughter later joined them. The Pitcairn marriage apparently angered the aristocratic family, who then assumed full custody of Pamela's children.

Lady Pamela's fortunes took an upturn in 1812, when Emperor Napoleon Bonaparte (1769-1821) granted her permission to return to France. Settling in Montauban, she hoped for a state pension when her childhood playmate, Orléans' Son Louis-Philippe (1773-1850), became King of France in 1830. Although they were raised almost as Brother and Sister, and may have been so in truth, the "Citizen King" took little notice of Lady Pamela. She retired to a convent, where she died in poverty on 9 November 1831, her wish for recognition and support unfulfilled. Perhaps Louis-Philippe, who attended Pamela's first wedding, was troubled by his neglect of her. In the end the King arranged a proper funeral for his erstwhile companion, and was said to have often visited her grave.

Though he did not provide for his friend in her later life, Louis-Philippe did provide us with further evidence that Lady Pamela was truly the former Nancy Simms of Fogo. In 1847, near the end of his reign – he was overthrown the following year – the King sent a letter to Reverend John Chapman, formerly the Anglican missionary at Twillingate. As we have seen, Chapman conducted his own inquiries about Lady Pamela a decade earlier for Governor Cochrane. In King Louis-Philippe's letter he inquired about Pamela's family, the Simms, and made particular mention of the companion he later ignored. Chapman forwarded the letter to the Simms family at Fogo, but Coish notes that they never did send a response. The reasons why remain among the mysteries of Lady Pamela's life. It is not every day that a Newfoundland fisher family gets a letter from the King of France – they might have thought the correspondence was a hoax. Perhaps the real reason was even more straightforward. Henry Simms, who saw the note, told Pilot that his Father failed to answer the letter as he was not a "knowledgeable" man.

King Louis-Philippe of France

Even in death it took a while for Lady Pamela to find peace. Her grave was originally at Montmartre Cemetery in France, but it was seriously damaged when the Prussian Army besieged Paris in 1870. At one point Lady Pamela's remains were on the verge of removal when an Irish gentleman living in Paris, one J. P. Leonard, offered to house her body in his own family tomb. Lady Pamela's Grandchildren later arranged to have her remains transferred to St. Nicholas' Churchyard at Thames-Ditton, near London, in August 1880. A number of Lady Pamela's descendants attended the re-interment ceremony, and pieces of her original tombstone were used in constructing the new monument to this fascinating lady. She was laid to rest alongside her two eldest Daughters, Lady Campbell and Lucy Lyons, and Lady Sophia Fitzgerald, Lord Edward's Sister, who had raised her two Nieces.

Lady Pamela's final resting place, Thames-Ditton, was the longtime home of Lord Edward's Brother, Lord Henry Fitzgerald, and his Son Lord Ross. At the time Pilot wrote his biography several of Lady Pamela's Great-grandchildren still called the village home. Standing on English soil, St.

Nicholas' Cemetery, Thames-Ditton, was the closet "Little Nancy" would ever get in returning to Fogo, her native home.

8

The Twillingate Sun

"Well Mixed"
Printer's ink, when mixed with brains,
Has no limit to its gains;
It spreads its glory far and near,
And business stirs throughout the sphere,
But ink and type and paper fair
Serve only thought and skill and care.[1]

Twillingate Sun *office, Path End, early 1950s*

....

History

For more than seventy years Twillingate was home to its own newspaper. Despite its name, the *Twillingate Sun* was not just a paper for the residents of one town; its readership encompassed the greater area of Notre Dame and Green Bays. The paper's first issue appeared on Thursday 24 June 1880, under the title *Twillingate Sun and Northern Weekly Advertiser* – this was shortened to its more familiar name in 1912.

Jabez P. Thompson

The Sun's founder was Jabez P. Thompson, a onetime manager and foreman printer with the *Harbour Grace Standard*. Thompson was born at Harbour Grace in 1857, Son of Elizabeth (nee Curtis) and Henry Thompson. Educated in his home town, Thompson later married Sarah A. Salter. He moved to Twillingate in 1880. A supporter of William Whiteway, J. P. Thompson was elected MHA for Twillingate and Fogo District in 1882. Three years later he lost his seat while running as an independent Whiteway supporter. This was despite a petition of 14 October 1885, signed by more than 100 supporters, urging Thompson to seek re-election in the district, and expressing their satisfaction with his representation. Thompson's next run at politics was more successful; he became MHA again in 1889 and was re-elected in 1893. He was named Surveyor-General in 1894, and served as a cabinet minister in the short-lived Administration of Liberal Daniel J. Greene (1850-1911). Whiteway resumed leadership of the Liberal Party in 1895, appointing future Prime Minister Robert Bond to the Executive Council. Thompson resigned his seat in favour of Bond, and was then appointed Stipendiary Magistrate for Brigus. Leaving Twillingate and his editorship of the Sun in late 1895, Thompson moved to Conception Bay. Three years later he started a new paper, the *Vindicator and Brigus Reporter*. For the next two years Thompson combined the roles of proprietor, editor and publisher. He tried to make a political comeback in 1900, running as the Liberal candidate for Port-de-Grave, but was unsuccessful. J. P. Thompson retired as Magistrate in 1934, and died at Brigus in January of 1938.

When Thompson originally moved to Twillingate in 1880 people in the outlying Bays and communities of Newfoundland lacked even basic information about important events. It was true that the Island's oldest communities, like St. John's and Harbour Grace, did have newspapers. In those days, however, mails had to be carried by coastal boat, and the papers' news would be several days out of date by the time they reached places like Notre Dame Bay, if they arrived at all. The situation was even worse in Winter. Thompson believed a need existed in Newfoundland's northern communities for a newspaper of their own. Although Twillingate was isolated from centres like St. John's in those days, it was an important regional *entrepôt*, and the hub of its Bay. Thompson resolved to start his paper there, an effort he hoped would be a means of "diffusing rays of intellectual brightness." In 1887 Thompson published an editorial which was a sort of mission statement for the *Twillingate Sun*. Many Victorian authors were known for flowery speech, and Thompson was no exception. His "mission statement" read:

> To all our subscribers and patrons, who since the inception of the enterprise, have assisted us in any way, in our endeavours to provide a public benefactor, which a properly conducted newspaper in any community cannot fail to prove, we tender our heartfelt thanks. In the career of any journalist there are times when duties are to be performed that may not be very pleasing to himself, but which in the public interest he is compelled to undertake, even though it should prove, as it has in many cases, at the sacrifice of personal gain. But in any course that may have been pursued by us, we have aimed to avoid personal and abusive references to individuals, and while at times criticizing and condemning their actions in respect to public matters, we may have been rather pointed in our remarks, it has not arisen from any antagonistic views or feelings on our part, but entirely in the interest of the public, in whose behalf we trust the SUN may long be continued to shine. We are thankful we again repeat for the liberal recognition heretofore extended, which we might have been able to boast even more of, if home or native industries as a rule were better encouraged by businessmen, who prefer sending printing orders out of the country.[2]

Thompson had a staff of two, and all his print was hand-set. He used an old Washington press which produced about 200 copies of the paper an hour, but which needed the attention of all three staff. No one is sure where the Sun's paper came from in these years since the Colony only began making newsprint under AND in 1916. The paper was normally four pages in length, with the first given over to outside advertisements; the inside contained news centring on the town and local area. This included church news, shipping movements, weddings, socials etc. Its original price was three cents an issue. The paper sold for the same three cents a copy for its entire seventy-three year run – its main revenue came from advertising.

George Roberts

In 1896 Thompson sold the paper to George R. Roberts (c.1845-1920), a vessel owner and trader based at Twillingate. The paper claimed to be politically neutral, but both Thompson and Roberts were supporters of William Whiteway, and sat in the House of Assembly as Liberal MHAs. Roberts was first elected in 1900 as a follower of Robert Bond. He was re-elected in 1904, 1908 and 1909. In 1919 he was appointed Stipendiary Magistrate at Twillingate, replacing William J. Scott. In this role Roberts was noted for his fair, if sometimes severe, judgements. George Roberts was described by *Twillingate Sun* biographers Yvonne Stuckless and Norma Jennings as "...a clever and ambitious man to all who knew him...He penned his articles with impeccable life and meaning."[3]

Roberts had more than a touch of wry wit about him, a trait he demonstrated in an 1899 letter to the Governor, Sir Henry Edward McCallum (1852-1919). It seems that Government House elected to cancel its subscriptions to a number of newspapers, including the Sun. Apparently, customers could pay their bill – one dollar – at the end of the year. They had been receiving the paper for eleven months, and it is clear from Roberts' letter that Government House hoped to be excused from paying for the final month of their subscription. In response, Editor Roberts wrote directly to Governor McCallum on 6 July:

> Dear Sir Henry
> ...assuming that [the Deputy Colonial Secretary] was acting upon your instructions in this matter, I shall address my resp[onse] to the Fountain Head – Your Excellency...[Roberts noted that]...in cases where the subscribers are destitute and unable to pay in full I am always very lenient...Possibly it is through stress of circumstances that your Excellency is forced to drop the "Sun" so, giving you the full benefit of my sympathy I shall...[charge you]...only for the time you have taken the paper since the date of last payment...I hope your Excellency won't always be so "hardup" for spendables, but on the contrary will soon be able to earn enough money to subscribe constantly...The bill enclosed, then, is for 11 months at $1.00 year 91 ⅔ cents...
>
> Before saying adieu, permit me to add that I was only recently...told that your Excellency has had...an increase in salary of $3000 a year, making a total of $10,000. In view of that I was half inclined to hope that our good Governor would have compassion on the poor and instead of discontinuing the "Sun" would send an order for an extra copy – For some friend in Africa. But it was silly of me to thus hope, for what can a man, even an economist, do on only $10,000 a year in a country like this where whiskey, cigars, and "dancing pumps" pay such a high tariff & where state paupers are as thick as flies around a "lassy" puncheon...

Trusting your Excellency will live long & see better days.

I have the hono. to
Be sir yours truly
George Roberts
Prop^{p}. Of T'wgate Sun[4]

Roberts may have ruffled some feathers at Government House, but this does not seem to have hindered his career in journalism. He went on to head the Sun for another decade, selling the paper to its third editor, William B. Temple, Son of Canon Robert Temple, in 1910.

During Temple's tenure at the paper the Sun had its own office dog, "Bobs." A forward thinker, Temple played a role in bringing the first telephone service to Twillingate (See Chapter Two), helped form a fire insurance company, and was involved in founding Twillingate's hospital (Chapter Thirteen). He was also forward looking in his operation of the paper, replacing the outdated Washington press that produced the Sun for three decades. In a 1917 editorial Temple noted the importance of the new press, and another technological innovation he proposed:

> When I assumed control of the SUN in 1910 I realized that the most necessary improvement was a more modern type of newspaper press. The SUN, then only five columns, was printed on an old Washington press which could not print more than 200 copies (one side) an hour, requiring a man and two boys for the operation. By dint of economy I was able to install in 1911 a cylinder press on which the SUN is at present printed. This press cost me over four hundred dollars. It is run by a gasoline engine, can print about 1000 sheets (one side) an hour, and a boy can manage it...
>
> But I was not satisfied. Hand labor[*sic*] in setting type is to[o] slow. Moreover type wears out rapidly and, as you can see, many letters are broken and a new dress is needed. But type costs today a tremendous amount of money. I therefore began to investigate the matter of a type setting machine or rather a slug machine. I have been able to get hold of one of these machines at a price that puts it within my range; and it is already somewhere on the way from Toronto, and I hope to have it working by the end of November...[5]

The innovative Temple went on to an assistant editorship with the St. John's *Daily News*, and in August 1921 Stewart Roberts, Son of former owner George, took over the newspaper. The younger Roberts guided the paper for a quarter century, taking it through the lean years following World War One and the Great Depression.

New Twillingate Sun *office hauled up Path End in 1928, during the editorship of Stewart Roberts (inset)*

The Sun office was located at Path End, near the Customs Office (Women's Institute building). In 1928 Stewart Roberts purchased a new building from Edward Roberts. In March of that year this structure was hauled onto the newspaper property and the equipment was transferred into it. A second small building was used as a business office, and the original Sun office was later torn down. As diarist Stephen Loveridge reported, "Stewart Roberts has former shop of Edward Roberts hauled close by present Sun Office - this to replace office now used. The shop was hauled along by our back door and up through late George Roberts' land on which it now remains."

Aside from owner/editor Roberts, one of the *Twillingate Sun*'s most important employees in those days was Andrew Lunnen, a journeyman printer and compositor. Lunnen joined the staff in May 1888 under Thompson. Apart from a break of four years, Lunnen served with the paper continuously until his death at age seventy on Candlemas Day 1945. In a newspaper interview Roberts' Daughter Muriel (Mercer) reported that, although Lunnen was not large in stature, he was able to set and distribute type faster than a machine, and was quite meticulous in his work.

Ms. Mercer noted that most Twillingate school children in those days used exercise books, or "scribblers," produced by the Sun. As a sideline, Stewart Roberts even provided a barber service for some of the many men who dropped by the Sun office for a chat! When Roberts died the Sun's future was uncertain, and a notice of sale was published in its own columns.

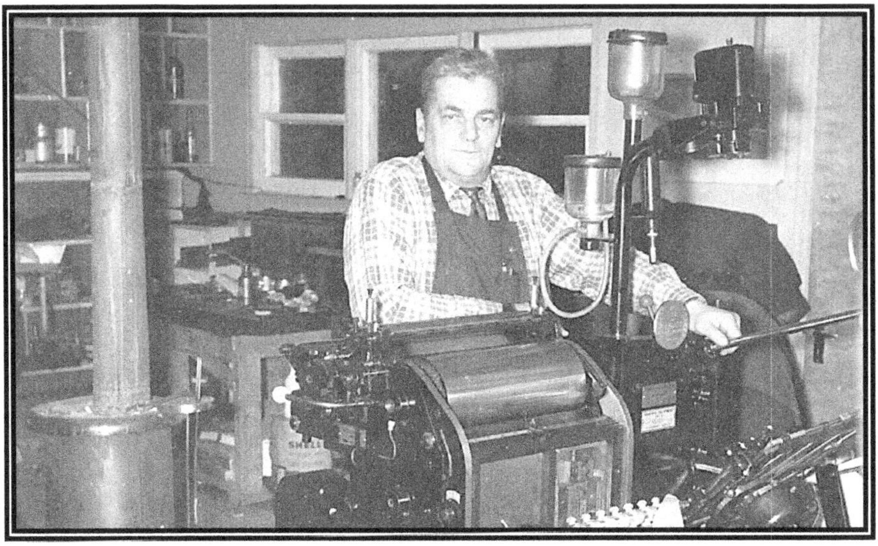

Ernest George Clarke

In 1947 the *Twillingate Sun* was acquired by its final editor Ernest G. Clarke (1917-67). Clarke served for a number of years with the Newfoundland Ranger Force before taking over the Sun. In later years he ran a movie house at Twillingate, and was a charter member of the Twillingate Lion's Club branch in 1953. Clarke was also involved with municipal politics, and sat on the Board of the NDB Memorial Hospital. In 1948 John Loveridge noted that Clarke's editorials were known "...for their forthrightness, and the unbiased opinions expressed have been quoted over the radio and in the press."[6]
As proprietor of the Sun, Clarke employed five men, all of whom were typesetters. One of these was Harold Roberts, son of the former editor, whom Loveridge described as Clarke's "right-hand man." Although using his more modern press for the newspaper, Clarke still found work for the ancient Washington press in "job printing," which involved such items as flyers, letterheads etc. Paper for the Sun in this era was provided by AND of Grand

Falls, and was shipped to Hodge's store in Twillingate via coastal boat. The Sun's last issue appeared on 31 January 1953. At the time it was one of Newfoundland's oldest published weekly papers, and the last in Canada to be hand-set. In 1956 former editor Clarke moved the old Sun equipment to a new building across the street where he continued job printing. After his death in 1967 his Widow Ada (nee Minty) continued job printing for some time. Over its seventy-three year history the *Twillingate Sun* only suspended publication once, from 16 January to 15 February 1947, during the transfer to Clarke's ownership. In recent years the paper has been revived annually for the Twillingate/New World Island Fish, Fun and Folk Festival. Well-known Newfoundland writers Ronald and Marilyn Pumphrey were closely involved with the re-launch.

....

Articles

Many of the *Twillingate Sun*'s old stories still make interesting reading, and two of these are reprinted below. The first recounts how tourists from other parts of Newfoundland travelled to the Twillingate area in the late 1880s.

> A few remarks on our trip to Twillingate and back may perhaps interest your readers; at any rate it will help to fill up, and will prove a little light reading amongst the heavy parliamentary debates which still occupy your columns.
> We left this place [Bonavista] about 3 a.m. on the 11th inst.
>
> King's Cove was first port of call, celebrated for its riot over the public wharf in the Spring, but more especially and honourably, for its Roman Catholic chapel which, being on a commanding site and of beautiful architecture, readily attracts the eye and elicits admiration from all travellers. In the old grave yard close by, the old Parish Priest, after many years of toil in Trinity and Bonavista Bays, was laid to rest. A handsome stone slab raised a few feet above the ground on a wall of the same kind of stone marks the spot, but we were sorry to see that it was falling into a state of disrepair, and that the fence around the ground was down in several places. Surely the good people of King's Cove have more respect for the good old man than to let his grave become a ruin for lack of a little attention.

Methodist "church without a spire" at Greenspond, c.1900

Salvage was touched en route and the steamer "lay to," under the shadow of its high perpendicular cliff, which those who see will not forget readily from its peculiar appearance. Away then from Greenspond, past islands to right and left, Little Denier with its fine light house, and the beautiful bold and rocky scenery thereabouts. We past [*sic*] Puffin Island, with its old stone light house, to an anchorage in Greenspond harbour, and then ashore to inspect the sights &c. The name itself is suggestive, Green, because green trees and grass are about the scarcest things there, and pond because fresh water is about the next scarcest. Following this incongruity comes our Methodist property with its church without a spire and its Central hall with one. The latter building is the result of [the] Rev...'s foresight and energy, and is spacious, handsome and easy of access, being right on the public road...Other public buildings worthy of note are the Episcopal Church and hall, and the Orange Lodge, a peculiar low building which prompts every passenger to ask "What building is that?"

Off again for Fogo, passing Cabot Island, with its light house...Arrived at Fogo we lay alongside the wharf...to land freight, and there our steamer took the liberty of reclining on the soft, muddy bottom when the tide fell, compelling us to await the rising which was six hours away; some of us went on shore for a few hours social intercourse at a friend's, before we turned in for the night. The narrow entrance to the harbour where the "Somerside" came to grief a few years ago, was of course the object of remark for all strangers, and on shore perhaps the most striking building is the school house...which is quite ornate in design and construction. Fogo boasts a Post-master who keeps the steamer or rather the mail for two hours, i.e., he will not deliver the Northern mail to the steamer until two hours after he receives the Southern, and vice versa; for that reason he is not popular with the travelling public.

Herring Neck was soon reached; this is a beautiful spot, islands and arms of the sea producing a most fascinating loveliness. Here we received intelligence that we would be quarantined at Twillingate, only passengers for the port being allowed to land. This spread dismay amongst those who were not bound there, as a public wharf to land at gave all a chance to go ashore and have a walk on terra firma.

However we reached Twillingate in good time and those who had travelled a little and "knew a thing or two" simply walked ashore without any questioning, while those who asked permission had to stay on board for a little while longer.

Here we landed the ministers who had come from the various southern ports for their district meeting...All were pleased with their stay at the Notre Dame Bay Metropolis. Apart from the kindness of the friends who made us all so comfortable, there is much in Twillingate to be admired, its public wharf, and fine streets, its bridge and canal, its court-house (whose cells by the way we found empty, swept and clean, and withal comfortable enough for any occupant – long may Twillingate gaol want a prisoner) and fine drives around Back Harbour, Wild Cove, and the light-house on one side, and the Arm with its coves and settlements on the other, are all objects which we are sure on fuller acquaintance would prove more interesting; but then we only had a limited time to take stock of all these things and yet they impressed themselves on our memories. The dwelling houses, business premises and Churches are also deserving of remark.

Twillingate is dear to us Methodists, for resting in the South Side cemetery are the remains of Rev. Wm Marshall, our pioneer minister in these parts, who, after a life of faithful service, lay himself down to die far away from his old home and friends, yet "safe in the arms of Jesus"...

Sunday was a high day in Twillingate. Sermons at 7 a.m., 11 a.m, and 6:30 p.m., in both our churches, and also Sunday School meetings in each at 3 p.m. The Conscript arrived at 11 a.m., but at the request of the District she was allowed to remain until midnight; accordingly at a few minutes past twelve we steamed away with pleasant recollections of our visit to your town.

Our homeward trip is remarkable because we made the run from Fogo to Greenspond in five hours, and forty minutes being the quickest trip on record, running twelve knots by the log.

Shortly after we left King's Cove we were mustered in the saloon to spend an hour or two in singing. We had good singing, good hymns, good tunes; we fancy those on board will not soon forget it. We were therefore very sorry when we arrived at Bonavista and had to go ashore, the only time in our lives when we were sorry our sea voyage was over...[7]

....

One of the most poignant editorials in the Sun's history was its last. It was written by Ernest Clarke as a send off to the paper on its final issue in January 1953. It was fittingly titled, "Sunset."

Today we have written "finis" to a long and honoured chapter in the history of Twillingate. That which was conceived nearly three quarters of a century ago to serve the people of this town and its surrounding district, to which devoted men gave of their best in mind and body through the decades, fighting grimly for survival against the relentless pressure of illiteracy, isolation and depressions, now passes into history.

The Twillingate Sun has fought the good fight. It has finished the course. In the great scheme of things it has played its part for good, given unsparingly of its columns for every worthwhile cause, lifted its small voice in protest against evil and now passes on the torch to methods of communication undreamt of at its birth.

The Twillingate Sun has not outlived its need, though in honesty we must confess it may have outlived appreciation of the need. There is still a part for it to play, perhaps as great as any in its past but it is mechanically incapable of filling the role. Better that it should pass into oblivion now than continue with steadily faltering pace for another decade. Equipment geared to a press patented in 1864 cannot be expected to continue indefinitely to fill the demands of the twentieth century. In a town and district which with every year sees the great majority of its annual crop of young adults move on to other centres to find a permanent niche, it would be sheer folly to seriously contemplate modern mechanization running into many thousands of dollars.

The Twillingate Sun will be missed, despite its many typographical errors, mainly due to its battered type being almost impossible to proof, it has served to bring you a fairly accurate picture each week of just what is going on in the town. Our fine old subscribers who live abroad will have lost their treasured link with the homeland and to them, more than to any others, we now express our gratitude for the support and encouragement through the years, and our sincere regret we can no longer span the gap.

To one and all, our advertisers, both local and mainland, our many subscribers including those somewhat delinquent in their payments (but good souls nevertheless), our readers including the many hundreds whose names do not appear on our subscription list, to each and every one of you Twillingate Sun sends its last greeting, its farewell and its thanks for the pleasure of serving you.

And now the last editorial is written, the last column is filled, the press has finished its run and silence descends.[8]

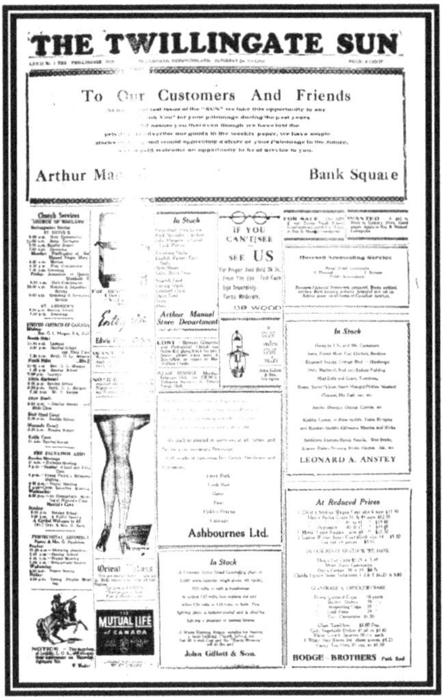

THE TWILLINGATE SUN

To Our Customers And Friends

Arthur Ma... Bank Square

Church Services

In Stock

IF YOU CAN'T SEE SEE US

FOR SALE

WANTED

Arthur Manuel Store Department

LOST

NOTICE

In Stock

LEONARD A. ANSTEY

Ashbournes Ltd.

At Reduced Prices

In Stock

John Gillett & Son.

BODGE BROTHERS

MUTUAL LIFE of CANADA

NOTICE

Cover page of the Twillingate Sun*'s final issue*

9

Georgina Stirling, Nightingale of the Isles

"Mme. Toulinguet"

At the turn of the twentieth century a Daughter of Twillingate was lauded as one of the great stars of the operatic world. She was a child of the early Twillingate medical practitioner Dr. William M. C. Stirling and his Wife Ann (nee Peyton). Georgina "Georgie" Stirling was born at Twillingate on 3 April 1867, the youngest of ten children. John Peyton Jr. was her maternal Grandfather. In fact, Ann Stirling was most likely one of the children Shanawdithit helped raise during her time in the Peyton household. Georgina's paternal ancestry was Irish. William Archibald Stirling emigrated from Ireland to Harbour Grace, where he married Emma Mayne of Bonavista; the couple had eleven children. Stirling Senior practised medicine at Harbour Grace until 1853, dying at Twillingate in August 1858.

Dr. William Stirling

The younger Doctor Stirling encouraged an appreciation of music in all of his children, buying them two pianos, a violin and a flute. Life was generally good for the family, but in 1882 Ann Stirling died. The following year William went abroad, sending Georgina to the Toronto Ladies' College where her studies included music. About 1885 she returned home and became a founder of the Dorcas Society which made clothes for the needy. This work was commendable, but Georgina's destiny lay elsewhere. She showed promise as a singer from a young age, and frequently entertained locals with her musical talents. Mme. de Alberti, a music connoisseur in St. John's, felt Georgina's voice was best suited to ballads and oratorio. However, Georgie had her heart set on soprano opera, and the strong-willed young lady had her way in the end. There was no local training available, but as the Daughter of a doctor Georgina was able to travel to Europe in1888 to hone her skills. She studied in Paris at the school of Mathilde Marchesi, an acquaintance of renowned composer Franz Liszt (1811-86). It was while performing under Marchesi that young Georgina was invited to become part of an Italian opera company, and she may have debuted at Milan's La Scala opera house around 1890. After a year in Italy Georgie returned to her Parisian studies with Madame Marchesi.

La Scala opera house, Milan, by Giovanni Dall'Orto, 20 Janaury 2007

1892 saw the neophyte opera star return home for the first time in four years (Her Father had passed away in April 1890). While in Twillingate, Stirling sang at both St. Peter's and St. Andrew's Anglican Churches.

Georgina left home for Europe again in October, on the way entertaining parishioners at St. John's Roman Catholic Cathedral with Bishop Power attending. Stirling made her Parisian grand operatic debut in 1893, the last year she worked with Madame Marchesi. It is said that during a performance in France she sang Britain's martial naval anthem, *Rule Britannia*. At the time the two nations were not on the friendliest of terms, but such was the power of Georgie's talent that her performance, including Rule Britannia, got rave reviews and won over the audience.

Georgina Stirling, Mme. Toulinguet, the Nightingale of the North

Following her Paris debut Georgina returned to Newfoundland, stopping first at St. John's. While in the capital she sang at the Methodist College Hall. The next year the soprano performed in England, touring there during the 1894-5 season. During a break in her schedule Georgina returned home to Twillingate, giving a number of performances at St. John's on the trip back to Europe. It was in this period that Stirling took the stage name Mme. Marie Toulinguet in honour of her hometown. Georgina's singing talents also earned her the nickname "Nightingale of the North" from her many fans.

From 1896, until it collapsed due to competition with the New York Metropolitan Opera House, Georgina toured the United States as prima donna in Colonel J. Henry Mapleson's Imperial Opera Company. On her way to New York Mme. Toulinguet again stopped at St. John's, and was part of Gower Street United Church's dedication service. The singer was paid $150.00 for each performance with Mapleson's Company, plus her travelling expenses, a goodly sum in the late 1800s. Nonetheless, the company's mid season closure left Stirling stranded, along with its other performers. A number of singing engagements in the eastern United States put the Nightingale of the North back on track, and she soon returned to Newfoundland.

While there, in 1897, Marie Toulinguet took part in the quadcentennial of John Cabot's landing in Newfoundland. That year was also the sixtieth anniversary of Queen Victoria's accession to the throne, and in St. John's the celebrations were combined. Bishop Michael Howley designed a Cabot Memorial which was eventually finished in 1900 as Cabot Tower, although the design was simplified. In June 1897 a crowd of 5,000, including dignitaries and naval officers, assembled on Signal Hill for the Tower's dedication ceremony. Georgina Stirling was front and centre for the event, singing "God Save the Queen" for the assembled masses. Georgina arrived with her friend and fellow singer Marie du Bedat of Dublin, who also performed at the Cabot/Jubilee celebrations. From there the two friends journeyed to Georgina's hometown where they spent the Summer.

In October Marie Toulinguet debuted with the Scalachi Operatic Company, run by Sophia Scalachi, a former member of Mapleson's troop. The new unit travelled widely over the United States where they were given rave reviews, Georgina Stirling's performances being singled out for the greatest praise.

The following year (1898) Stirling became a member of the Grand Italian Opera Concert Company. She spent most of the next two years touring Italy, singing in Milan at the La Scala opera house with the Italian Royal Family in attendance. For another Italian performance Stirling received a standing ovation. Following her rendition of *Night of Honour*, live canaries were thrown to the soprano, along with heaps of flowers. Such tokens were fashionable on the Italian stage, but only for performers of rare and outstanding talent. During these years her many fans at home took an avid interest in Miss Georgie's career, and the *Twillingate Sun* published updates on several occasions.

The many friends of Miss G. Stirling, youngest daughter of the late much respected Dr. Stirling, will be pleased to hear that this talented young lady has recently been one of the performers on two select occasions in Paris...She is ranking amongst the world's most famous singers, and from time to time is very highly complimented in the leading newspapers of Paris as well as in Italy...Miss Stirling has lately been visiting Paris and displaying her talented and cultured voice before audiences composed of the very best of society. It must be very pleasing to her numerous friends and acquaintances to hear of her marked success, and we are proud to congratulate her upon the rare talents and extraordinary attainments in the world of song.

An agreeable surprise was afforded the friends of Miss Janet and Miss Georgina Stirling by their unexpected arrival from Europe on Tuesday afternoon last, having come direct in the steamer *Rhiwderin*...,bound to Tilt Cove, and which put into port that afternoon for the purpose of landing her lady passengers. The *Rhiwderin* had rather a nice time crossing the Atlantic, and made the passage from Cardiff in ten days.

It affords us much pleasure to welcome the return of these young ladies to their native town after so many months absence, particularly Miss G. Stirling who has been away for four years, residing for the greater part of the time in Italy and Paris where she has been undergoing a course of tuition in the art of public singing under the training of the most celebrated professors of the age. The superior alto and soprano voice which Miss Stirling possesses, having perfect command of the compass of these two difficult and opposite parts, has called forth most favourable criticisms from the leading press in those large cities where she has appeared occasionally in public...She has come back, accompanied by her sister, to enjoy a few weeks' rest, which no doubt she so much requires after labourious studies and excitement of populous city life, and then she will return to Paris to complete her tuition. It has been gratifying to learn of Miss Stirling's success from time to time and there is no question but she possesses rare talents, which are destined in the near future to rank her amongst the few of the world's most noted and gifted singers. We trust she

> will enjoy her visit and return invigorated to resume her arduous studies.[1]

Unfortunately, the Nightingale of the North's singing career was cut short. In the early 1900s Georgina's voice was permanently damaged by the rigours of her operatic performances, though no one is sure what her condition actually was. As Paul Butler and Maura Hanrahan report in their book *Rogues and Heroes*, few then knew the extent of the singer's ailment. Living in London, and supported by Sisters Janet and Lucy, Georgina even arranged to keep on performing, although choosing less strenuous numbers. Georgina went home to Newfoundland in 1904 where her fans assumed she was still performing opera. In October a planned recital at St. John's was cancelled at the last minute. The Nightingale managed two more successful concerts – her last public performances. The end of her career brought on a depression, and Georgina began to abuse alcohol. She moved back to England, and on Janet's advice took up residence at the Duxhurst Farm Colony for Women and Children in Surrey. The Colony was started in 1895 by Lady Somerset to benefit women recovering from alcoholism. Georgina lived at Duxhurst intermittently for the next twenty years, also residing with Janet and a third Sister, Susannah Stirling Temple. By 1929 both Sisters had died. Lonely and short of funds, Georgina returned home to Twillingate.

In an era when most women married and raised families, the majority of the Stirling Daughters, including Georgina, did not. Butler and Hanranhan note that no evidence has been found that Marie Toulinguet was ever involved in a romantic relationship, although she did at one time attract the attention of a young lawyer.

For the remainder of her life she and another Sister, Rose, lived together in the old family home. Being animal lovers, Georgina and Rose had a number of cats, and Georgina even had a pet piglet. Georgina Stirling was long remembered working in her beautiful garden and performing charitable works. She returned to volunteering with the Dorcas Society, and at one point gave away one of her dresses to a poor woman who came selling to her door. Georgina also sang at Hustler's Club concerts, raising money for a hospital at Twillingate. Such generosity was nothing new for Georgina Stirling. While at the height of her career profits from Marie Toulinguet's performance at St. John's Methodist College Hall, and concerts in Twillingate, were given to the poor.

The Stirling family home at Twillingate, 1905

Stirling's best performing years fell in the age before musical recordings were commonplace. Few songs performed by her are believed to exist – one recording thought to be of Stirling can be heard at the Twillingate Museum & Craft Shop. This was made in 1904, after her voice began to deteriorate. Even if the recording really *is* Georgina Stirling, our generation will likely never experience the full scope of her talent.[2]

The Nightingale of the North died of cancer on Easter morning 1935, a respected member of her community, but in relative obscurity compared to her days on the stage. She was buried on a snowy day, and a diagram was needed to locate her family plot in St. Peter's Anglican Cemetery. No room being left in the plot, Georgina was laid to rest nearby.

The singer's resting place was unmarked for many years, but in 1964 a memorial was erected to Miss Georgie at her grave site. A fund for its construction was begun by St. Peter's incumbent Reverend Raymond Brett, and on 19 July the church held a special memorial service for the Isles' most famous Daughter, followed by the monument's dedication.[3] It is inscribed:

> In memory of Georgina Stirling. Mille Marie Toulinguet Prima Dona. Died April 21 1935 age 68 years. Songstress of Newfoundland. The Nightingale of the North sang fairer than the larks of Italy. She entertained royalty by her voice and the poor by the kindness of her heart. Erected by an admiring

public 1964.

Grave site of Georgina Stirling

....

Epilogue

Before leaving Mme. Toulinguet's story behind altogether, we should note that Georgina was not the only interesting member of the Stirling clan – her paternal Grandfather had quite the career of his own. William Archibald Stirling was born in 1786, probably in Ireland. According to Nigel Rusted, he came to practice at Harbour Grace around 1808. Stirling may have taken over the practice of his late Brother John, a Navy surgeon. Active locally, Dr. Stirling was a founder of the Conception Bay Benevolent Irish Society, and was appointed Health Officer for Harbour Grace in 1832. He also served as local Magistrate. Afflicted by blindness in his later years, Stirling retired to Twillingate where his Son William, Georgina's Father, was then practising.

In 1834, during Dr. Stirling's tenure at Harbour Grace, a man named Downey was hanged for murder. According to one source, while the body was being readied for burial someone with a macabre sense of humour re-hung it on the gallows. Pinned to the corpse's chest was the note, "Doctor, Doctor, can you cure Downey from Gibbett Hill?"[4] Friends of the dead man then carried his body to Stirling's doorstep, requesting that the doctor have it buried as soon as possible!

Dr. Stirling was also involved in what we might call the "Winton Affair." Henry David Winton (1793-1855) was editor of Carbonear's *Public Ledger*. After 1832 he became a vocal opponent of future Premier John Kent (1805-72) and another Newfoundland political reformer, Dr. William Carson (1770-1843). This stance made Winton numerous enemies in the Colony; in December 1833 a riot was narrowly averted outside Winton's home after the journalist supported candidate Timothy Hogan again Carson. Travelling by horseback from Carbonear to Harbour Grace in 1835, Winton was attacked by men in disguise. These men mutilated Winton's ears, which they stuffed with dirt. The editor survived despite much loss of blood, thanks in no small measure to the medical treatment he received from William Stirling. A large reward was posted in hopes of apprehending the assailants, but they were never identified.

In her biography of Georgina Stirling, Amy Louise Peyton (nee Anstey) relates a number of interesting stories connected with the singer's family, one of which we'll recount here.[5] This particular tale does not so much concern the Stirling family itself as their former residence. Located on Twillingate's North Island, it lay only a kilometre or so away from Georgina's final resting place. Though she passed on in the 1930s, it was reported that Georgina may not have left the site of her old home. In 1937, two years after Georgina's death, her Sister Rose also died. Thereafter the residence was rented to Magistrates and their families. It was said that the old Stirling home was haunted, and unexplained noises were often heard there. This was reported on in a brief work on Georgina Stirling by Canadian recordings expert Edward B. Moogk (1914-79). The old dwelling was later torn down and replaced by a new Magistrate's residence, so we may never know the truth behind the ghostly legend.

10

Coaker and the FPU – Isles Connections

William Coaker – The Early Years

An important chapter in Newfoundland labour history has an intimate connection with the Isles. To begin the story we must briefly leave the northeast coast and head to Newfoundland's capital, St. John's. It was here that William Ford Coaker was born in October of 1871. His Father was a carpenter by trade, and served on sealing vessels as a master watch. The elder Coaker was supposedly a bayman who married St. John's native Elizabeth Ford, the couple residing in the city. Another source alleges that the elder Coaker and his Wife came from Devon, and first settled at Twillingate before moving to St. John's. In any case, young Coaker grew up near the city's Southside Hills, just alongside St. John's busy waterfront. Almost every trade involved with the Colony's fishery and seal hunt was practised there, and the setting would have given William the chance to see the social and economic divisions between merchants and the labourers they employed.

Merchant warehouses and fish flakes. St. John's waterfront, pre 1892

Coaker attended the General Protestant Academy and Presbyterian Finishing School, but left sometime between the ages of eleven and fourteen. From there young Coaker worked on the waterfront at a warehouse owned by

Job's, one of Newfoundland's most important fish exporters. Just two years later the boy, who had been hired as a fish handler, assumed a heavier load when he led the other boys in a strike. Coaker and his colleagues demanded, and won, wage parity with workers at rival fish company Bowrings. It was the young Coaker's first experience of the strength of the organized working man.

Coaker later took a job as clerk for the firm McDougall and Templeton. He must have impressed his employers. At the tender age of sixteen Coaker was sent to manage the firm's store at Pike's Arm, often counted as part of Herring Neck. So began William Ford Coaker's connection with the Isles. The youth managed the store each Summer for four years, returning to St. John's in Winter. In the capital he worked days, and at night resumed his studies under the tutelage of William Lloyd (1864-1937), later Prime Minister of Newfoundland. At age twenty Coaker decided to buy out his old employer's store on New World Island and go into business as an outport merchant. This venture didn't last long. After only four years Coaker's enterprise was ruined by the 1894 bank crash, the same debacle that finished the Duder Company in nearby Twillingate and Fogo.

This was a setback for the young man, but undaunted he turned his great physical strength to farming on an uninhabited island on Dildo Run near Herring Neck, which he named Coakerville. Before long the energetic and able Coaker turned his island into one of the Colony's most successful farms. He was probably helped in this by a short tenure at MacDonald College, near Montreal, where he studied practical farming.[1]

Coaker also did some fishing and lobster canning, but his greatest contribution to the area in those years came in the Winters. Since the men could not fish during this time of year Coaker opened a night school to teach subjects like reading. He also opened a community branch of the Orange Lodge. Always looking for a challenge, Coaker became involved in politics, and was a supporter of Sir Robert Bond, canvassing Herring Neck on Bond's behalf. This support earned him a number of government jobs in the Winter months, such as telegraph operator and Chair of the local Roads Board. With a Conservative election win in 1897 Coaker lost the jobs, but regained them when the political tide turned in 1900. He was also made a postmaster and collector of customs. In keeping with his early commitment to labour, Coaker formed a telegraph operators' union which published its own newspaper. Before long Coaker's superiors came to view his union activities with suspicion. By this time Coaker had become disenchanted with Bond, supporting a splinter party in the general election of 1905. With Bond's electoral victory he resigned back to his farm at Coakerville before he could be fired.

....

FPU – Isles' Roots

William Coaker's next move was even more radical than the telegraph operators' union, and has forever linked a tiny Isles community with organized labour in Newfoundland. Reflecting on his own setbacks, Coaker became more aware of the plight of fishers at Herring Neck, whom he felt were treated little better than serfs. After the 1908 fishing season brought especially bad prices (half that of the previous year), Coaker decided to organize fishers into their own union. This wasn't going to be easy. Prospective members were spread over hundreds of miles of coastline in many isolated communities. A large number could neither read nor write, and they were not wage earners, often hopelessly indebted to merchants under the truck system. Still, Coaker would try.

His idea was that fishers would stop buying from the merchants, whom Coaker believed were only looking out for their own interests, and purchase fishing supplies from union-owned stores. Cash would be used for transactions, and with even a little money one could start on the road to freedom from merchant credit. Another thing Coaker wanted to change was the servant-like attitude most fishermen displayed towards merchants and authority figures, another by-product of the system. Finally, Coaker hoped to increase educational standards among the fisherfolk, making them better able to stand up for their rights.

On 2 November, at the Orange Lodge in Herring Neck, Coaker called a meeting of fishermen. In a two hour speech – typically unpolished, but powerful – the would-be labour leader told his audience they could take charge of their own destinies, breaking the hold of merchants over them. About 250 people attended the meeting, but Coaker was able to sign up only nineteen of their number to form the first union council. Those few were the first members of the Fisherman's Protective Union, following its simple and democratic constitution, drawn up over a three year period by Coaker himself. Determined to make a go of the union, Coaker gave another speech at Herring Neck the following night, despite the toll the first took on his voice.

He was soon off to a nearby community recruiting more FPU members, being taken by horse courtesy of one of his newly-unionised fishers. Coaker spent the Winter of 1909 canvassing Notre Dame Bay, often on snowshoes, to enlist support. Before long the organizer's reputation preceded him, and in the Spring fifty union councils, encompassing about 1,000 members, were in place. These members paid a fee of twenty five cents to support local, district, and the supreme councils. In the days when fishers saw very little cash for their labours this was no small amount, and reflects well on the commitment of early FPU members.

Herring Neck Loyal Orange Lodge, birthplace of the FPU

For once encouraged to be proud of themselves, FPU members wore regalia much like a fraternal order and had their own newspaper, the *Fisherman's Advocate*, every word of which was written by Coaker himself. The union motto was *suum cuisque*, "to each his own," reflecting the fact that Newfoundland fishers did *not* get their fair share of benefits. In these years the northern fishers held Coaker in considerable awe, writing him numerous letters on every type of subject. Just as he did with the newspaper, Coaker wrote his replies personally – a full 2,500 in one year alone!

To break the hold of the credit system over fishers, FPU locals began taking orders for fishing supplies from members. These were bought in St. John's and sold at cost. Soon Coaker formed the Union Trading Company (UTC), in which union members purchased shares. By 1919 the FPU operated forty cash stores, doing more than $3,000,000.00 in business that year. The UTC was successful in raising the prices paid to fishers for their catch. In 1910 Coaker acted as their agent, and many refused to sell until a union-set price was matched. Coaker also used union revenue to start new enterprises like the Union Exporting Company to sell members' fish abroad.

One place where the FPU took firm root was Fogo Island, and the union's connection to the community of Barr'd Islands was retraced by author Eric Witcher. Witcher noted that the union's first secretary at its Herring Neck foundation was a schoolteacher, Dorman Fennimore, originally from Barr'd Islands. Soon after the inaugural meetings Coaker journeyed to Fogo Island, where councils of the FPU were quickly formed.[2] Regular union gatherings were held at Barr'd Islands, where a UTC store was founded at Lewis's Point, directly across from the Earle merchant establishment. Managed by Victor Rowe of Seldom, the operation consisted of a two-story building used to sell general merchandise and for storing fishing supplies, along with a schooner wharf. The Barr'd Islands' store operated for less than fifteen years. Witcher traces the failure to several factors, not least of which was the good relationship the Earles and their predecessors, the Rolls family, had built up with locals.

The Marine Interpretation Centre, Seldom. Formerly the local UTC store

Other FPU enterprises on Fogo Island were more long-lasting. A FPU local was started at Seldom-Come-By in 1909, soon after Coaker's visit to the island. Four years later a Union Trading store opened in the community, and remained Seldom's major fish buyer into the 1960s. Today the old store still stands. It has been converted into a museum preserving the history of the local fishery and the important role played in the region by Coaker and his Fisherman's Protective Union.

....

New Horizons

Although the Isles were the birthplace of the FPU, the union soon spread to other parts of Newfoundland. One of the FPU's boldest moves was the foundation of a model community in 1916 – Port Union, on the Bonavista Peninsula, not far from Notre Dame Bay. The town was one of the first in Newfoundland with electricity, plus it enjoyed modern innovations like fish-dryers and a soft-drink bottling plant. Port Union became the centre of the FPU's activities, although an office was retained in St. John's. Later the Congress Hall was built, patterned after St. Paul's Cathedral, which served as the union's home base and convention centre. The town was also home to the Union Publishing Company which turned out newspapers from its own commercial printing plant. In 1920 another important landmark opened at Port Union, the Anglican Church of the Holy Martyrs. It commemorated locals who had given their lives in the Great War. There were ten of these, aged from eighteen to twenty-five years, and their memory was preserved in ten stained glass windows. The church, and much of Port Union, was destroyed by a fire on 3 March 1945. Holy Martyrs and Port Union were soon rebuilt, though the modern town has been hard hit by the fishery crisis, while remaining a popular tourist destination.

As the driving force behind the labour movement, its stores, and finally Port Union, Coaker became known as the "Messiah of the North." He visiting isolated coastal communities in his small yacht, the *F. P. Union*, to the accompaniment of salutes fired from sealing guns and displays of hand-knitted mats emblazoned with union slogans. The quasi-religious nature of the FPU was probably no coincidence, since Newfoundland society was dominated by the church, whether Catholic or Protestant. Coaker intended that the union be non-denominational, and it was at first. The goals of the FPU, which seemed aimed at upsetting the traditional order, drew fire from the established churches. The Anglican supported Society of United Fishermen told members to steer clear of the FPU, and the Roman Catholic establishment did the same with its parishioners. The Protestant Churches didn't have as much authority over their flocks, and the FPU continued growing in northern districts. In the largely Catholic southeast of the Island the admonishments of the Bishops had more effect – the union never did have much strength in the region. The failure to enlist *all* the Dominion's fishers may have played a role in its ultimate failure. In an early work on the FPU, future Premier Joey Smallwood contended that Coaker's greatest mistake was taking the FPU in a new direction before the union was firmly established in all parts of Newfoundland.

That direction was politics.

Despite strong opposition from the established churches and the merchant interest, the FPU prospered before 1914. Even so, Coaker felt that his goal of breaking the truck system could not be met by a union alone; it required mastery of forces like quality control, reduction of harmful competition between exporters, and development of new markets. All these things could only be done by government, but the established political parties didn't seem to be listening. Coaker was determined to form a political arm of the FPU, a strategy outlined at union conventions on Change Islands in 1909, and at Bonavista in 1912. The FPU entered a seat sharing arrangement with the opposition Liberals. Coaker hoped to defeat Prime Minister Sir Edward Morris' Conservative People's Party, which had reneged on many promises to fishermen. Coaker felt the Liberals, in combination with his own party, were the best hope for positive reform. Unfortunately for the FPU, the Liberals did badly in the 1913 election, losing most of their districts and allowing Morris' return to power. In the north, where the FPU ran candidates, they won eight of nine seats, including one for Coaker.[3] The new MHAs were not typical Newfoundland politicians, drawn from the Island's professional and business classes. Among their number was a boatbuilder, a tinsmith, two clerks, a school master, and of course, three fishermen. It was a tribute to how the strength of the union had grown. Through the House of Assembly, union newspapers, and regular letters, Coaker fought against government corruption and mismanagement. He even travelled to the Spring seal hunt, observing working conditions on board the steamers.

As part of the governmental system the FPU might well have achieved its aims, but then in 1914 the Great War erupted. Although he was an ardent reformer, and unhappy with the way Morris handled the outbreak of war, like many Newfoundlanders Coaker supported Britain and its empire. Although he was over forty years old Coaker considered enlisting for active duty, but was talked out of the idea by supporters. With the backing of Britain's Colonial Office, in 1917 Morris decided to extend the life of his government for a year to see out the war crisis. This left the opposition, including Coaker, in a bad position. When Morris offered concessions for them to join a national coalition government, the union and the Liberals agreed. A portion of the union platform was suspended until the war was won, but measures including a bill to reform conditions for sealers and loggers was passed with no amendments. On the downside, as part of the government Coaker and his supporters were forced to share in unpopular decisions, including conscription. Compulsory military service was popular in St. John's but reviled in the outports. Coaker first promised to resist conscription, but in the end his patriotism won out at the expense of union solidarity. The effects of the war had grave repercussions on the union. The reforms sought by Coaker and his co-unionists in the early days were within reach during the artificial prosperity created from 1914-19, but wartime expediency outweighed their immediate implementation. A golden opportunity was lost.

William Ford Coaker, c.1919

In November 1919 Newfoundlanders went to the polls for the first time in six years. This time the Liberal-Union alliance, now under Richard Squires (1880-1940), and called the Liberal Reform Party, won the government. Squires' tenure began just as the wartime boom ended. Unemployment grew, and up to 1,500 people were leaving the Dominion annually. People demonstrated in the streets of St. John's, and rioting erupted at the House of Assembly in 1921. Coaker now held one of the most important government portfolios, Minister of Fisheries, and it seemed within his power to set things right. The Administration tried to implement a regulated fishery including government-backed research, grading and inspections, a system of foreign trade agents, information services (for weather and market reports), plus regulation of merchant marketing practices. International forces took the initiative out of government's hands. Scandinavian competitors, absent during much of the war, re-entered the market. Prices fell, creating chaos among local exporters, who then circumvented the new regulations, selling fish at rock-bottom prices. Neither the government nor the union were to blame for the market troubles, but the introduction of the reforms at the same time led many to point fingers. Merchants vigorously opposed the reforms and were successful in having them revoked. This failure even led many fishers to doubt their union's program – the truck system hadn't been eliminated. Coaker still thought big, however, supporting a pulp and paper mill project on the Humber River which seemed like a solution to debt and government relief programs.

....

End of the FPU

The mill aside, from this point on the FPU's glory days were well and truly finished. Coaker felt he was taking on too much with his political career, union presidency, and managing the union's business holdings. In 1923 he accepted a knighthood sponsored by Squires. Three years later he resigned his post with the union, and in 1932 retired from government. Coaker and the union were absolved in a 1924 scandal that revealed Squires' complicity in embezzlement, but the tarnish from Coaker's other activities weren't so easily removed. From 1923 on, Coaker's main interest was the union's business enterprises. Ironically, the man who once pledged to break the credit system now ran his businesses more and more like a traditional merchant. Ventures launched by the FPU became little more than limited companies in which union members had no real say. Before the war Coaker intended to challenge the traditional system by offering fishers cash for their product. By the late 1920s the Union Trading Company was one of Newfoundland's largest creditors, and Coaker instructed managers not to take fish if they had to pay cash. Coaker grew wealthy, and the union began its long, terminal decline. The distinction between the Liberals and the Union Party gradually blurred until the latter was absorbed.

Coaker passed away a few years after he retired in 1932. He is buried today at Port Union. The FPU left a mixed legacy. Coaker's business practices in the 1920s soured his reputation with some unionists. The UTC continued operations until the 1970s, but little had been done to cement a union movement among Newfoundland fishers – that had to wait until the 1960s. Likewise, Newfoundland's strict class structure and the credit system remained intact. Any gains made to that end were destroyed by the Great Depression of the 1930s.

Still, Ian McDonald feels that something positive *was* accomplished. The great range of activities the union engaged in destroyed the notion that common Newfoundlanders weren't fit to rule themselves. For over fifteen years union members were occupied with everything from legislative activity, to running union locals and social functions. Their willingness to accept a figure like Coaker, from outside Newfoundland's political establishment, demonstrated a spirit of independence and a willingness to entertain novel solutions to their own ills. At the very least, Coaker's movement gave pride and self-respect to a generation of Newfoundland fishers who had been fully at the mercy of the merchant class. By supporting progressive legislation to conserve timber stocks and seal herds, plus introducing a strict grading system for cod, union members displayed a good understanding of their own economic self-interest, which even the merchants appear to have lacked. As McDonald argues, it was not that Coaker never did enough, but that the Island had too few leaders like him and Robert Bond. The FPU's tangible achievements may be limited but they are real, and originated in a small community on the Isles!

11

The Fogo Wireless Relay Station

First conceived in the nineteenth century, the telegraph was the world's original form of electronic communication. The electromagnetic telegraph was developed in 1832, while the world's first commercial electrical telegraph was used in Britain in 1839. Another type of telegraph was developed independently by American Samuel F. B. Morse (1791-1872) . Today the inventor is best known for his "Morse code," a form of communication using a series of "dots" and "dashes" – long and short "blips" – which represented letters. The Morse Code was intended for use with the new telegraphs, a medium for which it soon became the *lingua Franca*. The first telegraphs were connected by cables, and by the 1830s land-line cable networks linked points in Great Britain, Europe and North America.

Cyrus W. Field (left) and Alexander M. Mackay

....

Newfoundland's First Telegraph Network

The Colony of Newfoundland owed its first land-line telegraph network largely to the efforts of English engineer Frederick N. Gisbourne (1824-92).

Gisborne hoped to construct a telegraph line to open communications between St. John's in the east and Cape Ray on Newfoundland's southwestern tip. With the help of American financier Cyrus W. Field (1819-92), work on the line started in 1853. By 1856 Field had successfully laid a cable across the Cabot Strait, completing the St. John's to Cape Ray telegraph that same year. On 1 October the first message was sent from Cape Breton to St. John's. Another key player in the construction was Alexander M. Mackay, who rebuilt the entire line. Starting in 1859 the Associated Press stationed a vessel at Cape Race, Newfoundland. With the Colony now linked by telegraph, the Associated Press ship would collect messages from passing steamers, which were then telegraphed to mainland North America.

This practice became obsolete on 27 July 1866 when a trans-Atlantic cable was successfully laid, connecting the European and North American telegraphic systems. The western terminus of the cable was landed in Heart's Content, Newfoundland by the giant steamer *Great Eastern* and a smaller vessel, establishing the first rapid communications link between east and west. To initiate the service US President Andrew Johnson (1808-75) and Britain's Queen Victoria exchanged greetings. Field, attending the inaugural ceremonies at Heart's Content, was said to have wept with joy.

....

Marconi & Wireless

With the extension of land-line cables across the globe, the next major development in electronic communications was the introduction of "wireless" telegraphy. Wireless involved the transmission of telegraphic signals through the atmosphere without the need for land-line cables. Although many individuals played a part in the wireless revolution, it is most closely associated with the man whose system became the most widely used, Italian inventor Guglielmo Marconi (1874-1937), the "Father of Radio."

In Marconi's day conventional wisdom held that radio signals could only travel along the line of sight. Marconi was convinced otherwise; he was sure that radio waves could actually travel vast distances, following the Earth's curvature. To prove his contention, Marconi proposed to transmit a wireless message across the Atlantic Ocean. The inventor first set up a transmitter at Poldhu, Cornwall. Marconi then travelled to St. John's and assembled a receiver at Signal Hill. Each day Marconi and his assistants raised an antenna using a kite, although its time aloft was limited by high winds. Daily, at a prearranged time, Marconi's staff in Cornwall sent him a signal, the letter "S," selected for its simple Morse code signal, three dots. On 12 December 1901,

Marconi (apparently) received the signal, which would have travelled more than 2,700 Kilometres and bounced off the ionosphere twice. Since that time some experts have cast doubt on Marconi's achievement, but there is no dispute that by the following year his wireless equipment was receiving complete messages from as far as 2,500 kilometres away. By 1903 his Marconi Company was transmitting regular trans-Atlantic news broadcasts.

Marconi, the "Father of Wireless"

Following his Signal Hill experiment Marconi became convinced that a wireless station at Newfoundland's Cape Race was a practical idea. Sadly for Marconi, there was a major roadblock in his path. In return for installing Newfoundland's first land-line networks, the government granted Field's Anglo-American Telegraph Company (AAT) a fifty year monopoly over all the Colony's telegraphic communications, a stipulation that remained in effect until 1904. No sooner had Marconi announced his experiment's success than a lawyer representing AAT threatened a lawsuit if the inventor received any more communications in Newfoundland. Marconi complied, temporarily shelving his plans for a Cape Race wireless station. Although

Newfoundlanders generally supported the introduction of wireless, Marconi avoided a confrontation with AAT by constructing his station at Glace Bay, Nova Scotia.

This did not mean the Newfoundland Government had given up on the idea of developing wireless communications in the Colony. On 29 November 1902, more than a year before the AAT monopoly was due to expire, the Marconi Wireless Telegraph Company, London (UK) and the Bond Administration concluded a draft agreement. It stated that the Company, later represented by its Canadian subsidiary, agreed,

> ...to install wireless telegraph stations as may from time to time be required in Newfoundland and on the Labrador and to supply for such stations all necessary apparatus station furniture and all tools as specified in the schedule hereto (the Government providing poles and rigging) and such electricians as shall be reasonably required in the installation of the said stations and in training the Government's staff thereat.[1]

In 1904, with the AAT monopoly no longer in force, Marconi finally built his wireless station at Cape Race. Over the next few years he continued exploring the capabilities of wireless. Marconi later developed short-wave radio technology, and a worldwide radio telegraph network for the British authorities. He shared the Nobel prize for physics in 1909. The only real stain on Marconi's reputation was his ardent support for Italian Dictator Benito Mussolini (1883-1945), though he did not live to see the tragic outcome of his nation's Fascist experiment.

....

New Communications Links

Though AAT's Newfoundland monopoly created problems for entrepreneurs like Marconi, it still allowed some elbow room for expanding the Colony's telegraph network into the outports. The first telegraph lines on the Island were meant to connect St. John's to other centres, with the eventual goal of integrating Newfoundland into the North American communications network. According to D. W. Prowse, Cyrus Field had little interest in Frederick Gisborne's project of building a limited Newfoundland line. Field was more interested in connecting Europe and North America by submarine cable. Within a year of the trans-Atlantic cable's completion St. John's, Carbonear,

Trepassey (with branches to the Cape Race and Cape Spear lighthouses), Heart's Content, Old Perlican and Placentia were all linked by AAT land-lines.

The original agreement signed with AAT allowed the Colonial Government to rescind the company's telegraph monopoly in 1874, after twenty years in operation. Obviously pleased with AAT's performance to date, the Carter Administration decided to maintain the original agreement. Before this period all of the Colony's telegraph infrastructure and maintenance had been undertaken privately. Britain's other North American colonies had expended large sums of money on local service. Prior to 1877 Newfoundland, in Prowse's words, "...had not spent a farthing on telegraphs beyond the Carbonear line, which was taken over at par by Mr. Field."[2]

Under the terms of the original 1854 agreement, the Newfoundland Government could initiate telegraph services to any regions AAT considered unprofitable. As Robert Cuff notes, this basically meant anywhere in Labrador or on the Island off the Avalon Peninsula. In 1876 Carter's Government announced its intention to extend telegraph services into rural Newfoundland. AAT remained the experts in telegraphy, and they were contracted to install the new lines. The first communities were connected in 1877 under Alexander Mackay's supervision. Another series of government lines followed in 1878. Despite this good start it was another seven years, during the premiership of Robert Thorburn (1836-1906), before any further lines were laid.

....

The Fogo Telegraph Office.

One of the lines installed during the Thorburn Administration linked Fogo Island to the outside world, and saw the establishment of a telegraph office in the town of Fogo. The *Twillingate Sun* detailed the background to this development, and the importance of the service to Fogo Island in the late 1800s:

> ...[T]he respected representative for Fogo District, JAMES ROLLS...has brought the subject of Telegraph communications for Fogo prominently before the Government, advocating the measure so effectually that its extension to that community may now be considered an accomplished fact, for which the hon. member deserves to be complimented...
>
> Fogo is an important place...In point of commerce there are but three or four outports which exceed it, and while

> every settlement around the island of Newfoundland of any significance whatever, can boast of telegraphic communication with the outside world, Fogo up to the present has been out in the cold...In these times of keen business competition, the lack of such a boon to a community, while all others enjoy it, must place...business men at disadvantage...But the extension of the telegraph system to Fogo will not only benefit that immediate locality, but will serve several of the surrounding settlements, such as Barr'd Island[s], Tilton Harbour, Seldom-come-bye, etc., in each of which considerable business is transacted. It is particularly desirable that the last named settlement should be accessible by means of telegraphic communication, as it is a renowned port of refuge for craft going South and coming North, and frequently during the year, when overtaken by storms, and they have to seek shelter in Seldom-come-bye, much anxiety would be saved on the part of all interested to be able to ascertaining [*sic*] their whereabouts...
>
> ...we are pleased to note that this subject has been under the consideration of the Government, of late, and we trust that a favourable issue will be the result...[3]

A "favourable issue" did indeed result. Fogo Island and Change Islands, along with several other communities, were finally linked to the world by telegraph on 31 October 1887. The steamer *Favourite*, Captain Walsh, laid the cable to Fogo Island, with the entire process taking around two weeks (An interesting sidebar to this work concerns a man named Scanlan. Part of a crew working on the Fogo telegraph extension, Scanlan took the remains of the Beothuk man found by Fogo resident Thomas Farrell back to St. John's for display in a museum. The exact whereabouts of the Native's grave goods, and his remains, are currently unknown).[4]

Located in the community court house, Fogo's telegraph office opened for business as soon as the cable was laid. Celebrations followed the opening, and the Sun reported that "a display of bunting" was hung by locals to hail "the inception of so great a boon at that old and important settlement."[5] The telegraph station's first ever message was sent to St. John's on behalf of the local Magistrate and citizens, who congratulated both the government and A. M. Mackay on the achievement. Emily and William Duder had the honour of sending Fogo's first personal telegram, passing along greetings to a family member named Henry.

Fogo court building, home of the local telegraph office, 1953. Decorated in celebration of Queen Elizabeth II's coronation

Soon after AAT's monopoly expired the Fogo office was absorbed into Newfoundland's system of postal telegraph offices, created by the Colonial Government in 1905 as a branch of the Department of Posts and Telegraphs (DPT). The plan was to consolidate all of the Colony's postal, telegraph and telephone services under one umbrella. According to ENL, the DPT sent and received more than a million telegrams in 1929 alone; ten thousand of these were public service messages like weather reports and notices to mariners. In that same year DPT operated almost 250 telegraph offices, servicing 347 communities – fifty-five of its stations were wireless, with eleven situated on the Labrador coast.

Fogo's postal telegraph office served the community, and island, for the best part of a century, only ceasing operations in the 1970s; by this time new means of communication had made it redundant. Several operators manned the station over the years. One of these men was Ron "Grump" McLean, a familiar figure in Fogo during the telegraph office's later years of operation. Near the end of Grump's tenure he was joined by Dick Hynes, who remained at the Fogo telegraph station until it closed. Kay Manuel of Lewisporte also worked at the office in this era as a relief for the regular telegraph operators.

The Fogo Wireless Relay Station

The establishment of a telegraph office put Fogo Island in instant contact with the outside world, thrusting it into the modern age. This rapid communications link was of great importance to the island, but it provided an indirect benefit as well. Fogo's telegraphic link was an important factor in the decision to establish a wireless station there in 1911-12. Combined with the island's strategic location well out in the North Atlantic, the established land-line connection made Fogo an ideal locale for a wireless relay station.

....

The Station.

Fogo's wireless station was a vital link between the island, the larger Colony of Newfoundland, including coastal Labrador, and ships at sea. In 1904 Prime Minister Bond told Ewart J. Watts of the Marconi Company (UK) that,

> ...the Government's aim in establishing the Marconi system on the Labrador [and later at Fogo] was to connect the various fishing settlements with each other, and with St. John's via the Canadian Telegraph system...[U]nless the fishing population scattered along the coast are enabled to communicate with their principles, to order supplies, and to ascertain the value of the fishing product very much of the value of the system will be lost to the trade.[6]

The Fogo station was the only facility of its kind along the many hundreds of kilometres of wind-swept coastline between Cape Race and Belle Isle. The establishment of a wireless station on Fogo Island was no matter of chance; the island lies about eleven kilometres off Newfoundland's northeast coast at its nearest point. As we've seen, the island's position well to the north, and out in the Atlantic, was a primary consideration in building a wireless station at Fogo. Likewise, the decision to build at Fogo would not have been made had the community not been linked to the early twentieth century's "information highway" through its land-line telegraph office.

Fogo Island's wireless station was built at the request of Newfoundland's Colonial Government. The Marconi Company signed agreements with the Newfoundland authorities in 1903 and 1906. Under the terms of these agreements the firm built wireless facilities at various locales in Labrador, including Battle Harbour, Venison Tickle, Seal Island, Domino, Grady, Indian Harbour, Cape Harrison and Makkovik. In 1912 a new contract was agreed between the Newfoundland Government and the Marconi Wireless

Telegraph Company of Canada Limited. This document stated that:

> The Company agrees to erect and maintain at its own cost and expense a Wireless Station at Fogo with sufficient power and capacity to transmit and receive business to and from the Company's Wireless Station on Belle Isle. The said Station shall be open and ready for business upon every day from 8 a.m. to 8 p.m., Sundays included. The said Station shall be the property of the company and shall not...be liable to the tax of $4000.00 imposed on Wireless Stations...The Company agrees...to maintain an efficient and satisfactory service between the Station at Battle Harbour and the Station at Fogo.[7]

According to the 1912 agreement, rates between the Labrador stations and Newfoundland (i.e. Fogo) were set at not more than thirty cents for messages of ten words or less, with two cents for each additional word. Addresses and signatures were free. Press messages were set at half the regular rates, while government communications were transmitted free of charge.

The Newfoundland Government expected that the Fogo station would be "...erected and in operation by First March."[8] At first all went according to plan. Marconi representative Alexander Reoch wrote Deputy Colonial Secretary Arthur Mews (1864-1947) on 5 January 1912, informing him that the last consignment of goods for the station left North Sydney on 30 December. Reoch hoped that these components had reached St. John's in time to ship to Fogo by the steamer *Fogota*. It was soon apparent that not everything was on schedule. Mews noted that twelve packages and a coil of wire were received, but delayed by weather conditions *en route*. This material was eventually shipped onboard the *Stella Maris*, but due to heavy ice she could get no farther than Catalina. Reoch reported that as of 29 February the Fogo station was nearly complete apart from "...the machines which have not yet arrived there. These machines are essential for the operation of the station."[9] By 21 March, three weeks after the government's intended opening date, the winds changed, clearing the ice from the land. *Stella Maris* finally made it to Seldom, and the components were shipped overland to Fogo. This was not the last time weather played the deuce with the Fogo wireless station.

For the moment other matters occupied those connected with the new facility. In May the authorities approved the installation of a land-line linking the station to the government telegraph office at Fogo. In the interim a messenger boy was hired to relay ice and weather reports. In June the company requested that the government build a road to the station as the ground was bad, making for difficulties in transporting materials and supplies. By 12 August $250.00 was allocated for the road, and the sum placed in charge of station operator Norman Gosse.

Fogo wireless station and outbuildings, with the mast in the background, c.1920

A final piece of business concerned the land on which the wireless station was built; at first this did not belong to the Marconi Company. The Company requested an allocation of eighteen acres of land. The request was approved in July, but a grant of 6¼ acres was deemed sufficient. Costing Canadian Marconi a mere $3.10 for both the property and the grant fee, this allotment was located on a hill rising more than ninety metres above the south side of Fogo. A common feature of wireless stations in this era was that, where the signal was weak, they were built on the highest accessible point of land, height being necessary to get a good signal using contemporary technology.

To extend the wireless station's range even further, a forty-six metre tall mast was constructed near the living quarters. Atop the mast was an ariel for transmitting and receiving messages using a switching arrangement. The pole was constructed from three lengths of British Columbia fir, its sections joined by metal clamps and anchored in place with a series of guy wires; the ring bolts for these remain at the station site. Painted a brilliant white, the mast was intended to stand out even from a great distance. Upkeep of the mast, including painting, was carried out by two locals, Ambrose "Bo" Pickett, and his neighbour Joe Pickett. Keeping the mast intact proved to be one of the major challenges in operating the station.

The Fogo Marconi station was larger than the one-man posts the company built along the Labrador coast, but was still fairly simple in layout. The station building was a small, one and a half story structure, with its main entrance through a porch on its southern end. An extension projected from the opposite side. The Marconi equipment room occupied the western portion of the building, which faced roughly in the direction of the mast. The station did double duty, serving both as a wireless station and as a family home. The second function was a necessity, as all of Fogo's primary wireless operators had families.

A short distance east of the main station was a power house, measuring about five metres by three metres. Housing a single cylinder, ten horsepower Morse gasoline belt drive engine, powering three DC generators, the foundations of this structure can be seen at the site today. Also on the site were a small battery charging room and a coal shed. About thirty metres north of these buildings was a root cellar, restored in 2006 as part of a "Green Team" student project. The cellar was used to store the family's vegetables, either bought locally, or grown in garden plots behind the station. Even with their own gardens, most of the supplies needed by the wireless operators and their families had to be brought in by horse; this was a full-time job, and a local man was hired for the task.

On 23 March 1912 Marconi engineer John Cann cabled Colonial Secretary Robert Watson (c.1868-1930) to report that the Fogo "station [was] in operation yesterday evening communication established this morning with Bellisle." On 26 March 1912 a Marconi telegram to Watson announced "Fogo station now open for communication Bellisle pointamour battleharbour..."[10]

The Fogo wireless station was assigned the call sign VOJ, Britain and its imperial domains having the call sign designations VAA-VZZ, the "V" prefix thought to commemorate the late Queen Victoria. Newfoundland, then a sovereign territory of the British Empire, was granted the call signs VOA-VOZ. The Marconi stations at Cape Ray, Cape Race and Belle Isle were advertized as Canadian, and had Canadian call signs – VCR, VCE and VCM, respectively. The Canadian Marconi Company apparently gave all of its independently-built stations in Newfoundland and Labrador Canadian call signs. In cases where the company was contracted by the Newfoundland Government to build stations, as at Fogo, Newfoundland call signs were used.

Even if official records muddy the nationality of Newfoundland and Labrador's wireless facilities, their importance was unquestionable. Fogo formed a key link in the chain of stations, acting as the primary communications hub between the main island (Newfoundland), and Labrador, by way of Battle Harbour and Belle Isle, a role specified in the 1912 contract. Once a Morse code message was received at Battle Harbour it was transmitted via the North American land-line network, which connected Labrador's isolated coastal settlements with the outside world.

Another valuable service provided by Fogo's wireless station was the maintenance of communications with vessels at sea during the busy sealing season. A second operator was normally brought in to assist with the many messages, or "traffic," passing between ship and shore at this hectic time of year – in the Winter of 1920 there were *three* operators at the station. A twenty-four hour watch was the norm, and a minute of the Executive Council, 8 March 1915, noted that "...the Fogo wireless station shall be in continuous operation...during the progress of the sealfishery..."[11] Sealing vessels sent in daily reports, along with other messages. In 1916 the practise of transmitting a "good night" message from each sealing steamer was inaugurated. In the wake of the 1914 Newfoundland Disaster (See below) this was intended as a safeguard, ensuring no men were left on the ice.

The wireless facility's busy period continued through the Summer months, its services a boon for the scores of Newfoundland fishers who went north in search of cod. Though their ancestors fished the Labrador grounds for generations, the advent of telegraphy marked the first time Newfoundlanders could quickly exchange messages with loved ones back home. Likewise, their employers, the merchant companies, could maintain constant communication with their vessels on the Labrador.

Another valuable service provided by personnel at the Fogo Marconi station was the collection of ice and weather data for the benefit of mariners. The weather and the Fogo wireless station were always linked, often in ways that frustrated both the government and the Marconi Company. We've seen how heavy ice flows delayed the station opening when *Stella Maris* could not get through with vital equipment. By the end of 1912 new weather troubles arose. On 12 December Reoch passed the following information along to Secretary Mews:

> ...[D]uring the hurricane last night the top gallant mast was carried away, fell to the ground and was broken in pieces.

> It will not be possible to communicate to Belle Isle with the remaining part of the mast, and we have instructed the officer-In-Charge at Fogo to obtain the services of a local rigger and have a new mast made and hoisted in position immediately.[12]

This wasn't the last time severe weather knocked the station out of commission. On 6 January 1914 a wind and glitter storm saw the entire mast blown down. Hearing of two good masts located at nearby Ladle Cove, Gosse was sent to buy the them, provided he found the masts satisfactory. On returning to Fogo Island by SS *Prospero*, Gosse could get no further than Seldom, and set off to Fogo on dog sled. The masts could neither be landed directly in Fogo nor transported across the island; they were sent off to St. John's to await the Spring thaw. In the meantime Gosse oversaw the erection of temporary spars to keep communications open, especially vital with the seal hunt about to begin. In short order the temporary masts were also downed, and jury-rigged repairs begun again.

Given his efforts at keeping the station operating, it was ironic that by March certain government officials blamed Operator Gosse for some of its problems. They believed that Gosse failed to ensure an adequate supply of vital equipment like condenser plates. The Marconi Company rushed to defend the conduct of their employee, and themselves. Writing to the new Colonial Secretary, John Robert Bennett (1866-1941), they noted that any interruption in service was brief. Fogo had been supplied with ample condenser plates for normal circumstances, but "...conditions at Fogo are not normal...[T]his company sought to obtain the very best of material and workmanship for the Fogo station...and in view of the terrible conditions...on the Northeastern Coast of Newfoundland during the present winter, we consider the criticism quite unjustified..."[13]

In the end the government agreed with the company, and the tone became more conciliatory. Another glitter storm brought the top gallant mast down on Sunday, 7 March 1915. This time the Deputy Colonial Secretary remarked that "[t]he Government fully appreciate the efforts which you [Marconi Co.] have made so that the station would be able to work in a satisfactory manner. The present circumstances seem to be such as would be outside ordinary human control."[14]

Despite its trials and tribulations, the Marconi facility was a vital part of Newfoundland's communications network for more than two decades, but by the early 1930s it was becoming obsolete. As radio broadcasting became more practical, more and more households owned their own set, and could tune in to programming worldwide. The Fogo station was equipped with the old "spark" form of transmitter, noted for very broad, overlapping transmissions used to cover the broadcast band anywhere in the station's immediate vicinity. If anyone nearby were listening to their radio a tremendous amount of interference was created whenever the station began transmitting. On New Year's day, 1934, Newfoundland's land-based wireless stations were slated to switch to tube transmitters, eliminating this interference. To make the changeover the Fogo station needed a thorough overhaul of its equipment, along with a more powerful electric generator. The expense could not be justified. As early as 1914 the Marconi Company lamented that "...from a commercial standpoint the Fogo station is already a dead loss to this company..."[15] Even were it profitable, by this date new technologies made a Fogo-based wireless station redundant.

Fogo wireless station house. Home to the primary operators and their families

The station closed permanently in August of 1933 and its last operator, Edward Myrick, was transferred to Signal Hill in St. John's. With the station's decommissioning the Canadian Marconi Company put its infrastructure up for sale. Arthur Earle purchased the main building which he sold off for lumber, while Captain Patrick Miller bought the radio mast, using the sticks on a schooner. As the wireless station was coming down, a new Star of the Sea Hall was going up at Fogo. The new structure incorporated some of the station's wainscot panelling. The Lukeman family bought the house's front extension, which they hauled away to form part of their family residence in the community of Lion's Den. Matthias Mahaney, a former "runner" or errand boy at the station, acquired its front porch, which he also incorporated into a residential home. With the dismantling of the station an era came to an end at Fogo.

....

The Operators

Serving the northeast coast for over two decades, the Fogo wireless station employed a number of people as wireless operators. One of its secondary operators was long-time Marconi employee Stanley Brazil, at Fogo in 1912. Robert Myrick, who spent his teen years at the station, reported to Patrick Pickett that a First World War veteran named Lindall assisted his Father from 1921-3. When the Myrick family came to Fogo for a second time in 1930 Leo Walsh and William J. Kelly acted as second operators. One of the Myrick Daughters, Elsie, took over second operator duties in one season when none of the regulars were available. For her work Elsie earned the sum of forty dollars a month, not bad money in those days! Besides the operators, a man named Fen Gosse was also part of the station staff.

During the Summers Fogo operators travelled to their posting on the Newfoundland coastal boats. Travel was much more difficult during the Spring sealing season, and operators had to catch a train to Lewisporte. From there they would cross the ice of Hamilton Sound to Fogo Island by horse or dog team. The men were often tired by the time they arrived at the station, as they had to do a lot of walking, or running, along the way.

From 1912 to 1933 five men filled the job of primary operator at Fogo. The station's first primary operator was Norman Gosse, who started at the station in 1912. Born at Spaniard's Bay, Gosse was the Son of a self-employed wheelwright. Following his stint as a Marconi operator Norman Gosse and his Wife operated the Empire Store in Spaniard's Bay. At this point he decided on another career change, and was soon enrolled at St. Bon's school in St. John's. Gosse then attended Nova Scotia's Dalhousie University. In 1922 he graduated as a medical doctor at the top of his class. Following the completion of his training in New York, Dr. Gosse helped found the Cancer Society of Canada. He was a part-time faculty member at Dalhousie and a practising surgeon in Halifax for the bulk of his career. Dr. Gosse continued teaching at Dalhousie, acting as head of the surgical service until age sixty-five. He continued in private practice for a number of years afterwards.

One of Dr. Gosse's Sons, Clarence (1912-96), followed in his Father's footsteps, becoming a physician and a professor of urology. Born in Newfoundland, he served with the Canadian Medical Army Corps at Normandy in 1944. The younger Dr. Gosse served a term as Nova Scotia's

Lieutenant Governor (1973-8), and was made an officer of the Order of Canada in 1978. Clarence's younger Brother Hamilton (1914-99) spent most of his life in Regina, Saskatchewan, and served as national President of the YMCA.

Primary wireless operator Benjamin Clarke Sr. at his post in Fogo, c.1919

Norman Gosse remained at the Fogo station until around 1916, at which time Benjamin Clarke assumed the reigns as primary operator. Clarke was born at Brigus on 5 August 1892, the Son of Benjamin and Catherine Clarke. He started his working career with the Reid Newfoundland Company in 1906, receiving a correspondence diploma in telegraphic studies from an American school in 1908. Leaving Reids in 1909, by 1912 Clarke was employed with the Canadian Marconi Company at Cape Ray. The next year he may have transferred to Point Riche, before moving on to Fogo.

On 20 November 1918 Clarke married schoolteacher Gertrude Downer of Eastern Tickle. Their only child, named Benjamin after his Father and Grandfather, was born at Fogo on 11 November 1919. Clarke remained at Fogo until 1920, when Herbert Hardy arrived to assume the post.

Benjamin had a Brother named Alexander living in Detroit, Michigan, and headed to the State for work. He found employment with the Ford Motor

Company, his Wife and Son following on the Red Cross liner *Rosalind* in 1922. The family moved twice, with Benjamin working both for Ford and as a telegrapher for the Detroit, Toledo and Ironton (D. T. & I) Railroad.

The Great Depression saw a downturn in Benjamin's fortunes. After being laid off around 1930 he tried to land work with several radio stations, but to no avail. Eventually he took a position managing a Shell gas station in Inkster, Michigan. The family's luck appeared to be on the upswing, but in 1936 tragedy struck when Gertrude died. Benjamin left to work on an iron ore boat while his teenage Son remained behind to operate the gas station and continue his education.

The elder Clarke returned to Inkster in 1937, buying the gas station. Just five years later America entered World War II, and Benjamin Jr. signed up as a radio operator/waist machine gunner on a B-17 bomber. Shot down over France in 1943, he spent two years in captivity. Returning home in 1945, Benjamin Jr. gave up his dream of becoming a professional radio operator to help his Father manage the service station until it was sold in 1963. Benjamin Sr. spent nearly ten years in retirement, and passed away on 21 November 1972, aged eighty.

Clarke's replacement at Fogo, Herbert "Bert" Hardy Sr., was born at Harbour Breton in November 1877. As a young man he travelled to New York where he learned telegraphy and wireless. Returning to Newfoundland, Hardy found work with the Reid Newfoundland Company. He joined the Canadian Marconi Company in 1907, and was first posted to Battle Harbour, Labrador. While at Battle Harbour Hardy met Ethel Lewis, and the couple were married in 1916 after Bert returned from a stint at Marconi's Point Amour station. Herbert and Ethel Hardy eventually raised eight children. Hardy was posted to the Fogo wireless station in Fall 1920 but returned to Labrador the following year. Aside from his landward duties, Hardy sometimes spent Springs serving as a wireless operator aboard sealers, including the *Eagle* and *Terra Nova*. After working at the Point Amour wireless station for several years, Hardy built a home at nearby L'anse Amour in 1931. He was still serving with the Point Amour station when he retired due to ill-health. Herbert Hardy passed away in 1953.

Though Bert Hardy's stay at Fogo was brief, his successor had a longer connection, being the only primary operator who served two separate tenures on the island. Edward J. "Ned" Myrick (Fogo operator 1921 to 1923; 1930 to 1933) was born at St. John's to Irish parents on 25 July 1872. His Father Patrick worked at the Cape Race lighthouse, starting a family association with the Cape Race facility lasting to the present day. Myrick went to work at Trepassey after learning telegraphy from a man named Jackson.

Myrick's next job was at Cape Broyle under Michael P. Cashin (1864-1926), later *Sir* Michael Cashin, Prime Minister of Newfoundland. Like Clarke and Hardy, Ned Myrick was employed by the Reid Company, and was night operator at Bishop's Falls. In 1905 he joined the Marconi Company, working at the Cape Race wireless station. In 1910 Myrick married Ellen Lawlor, whose family operated the telegraph office in her hometown Cappahayden. The couple later moved to New Brunswick where Ned was stationed at Partridge Island. This station was located at the mouth of Saint John harbour, and the three eldest Myrick children – Robert, Mary and Elsie – were all born at Saint John. Ned was later posted to Cape Ray, Newfoundland, where the youngest Myrick sibling, Jean, was born. After the Cape Ray station closed in 1921, Myrick was transferred to Fogo, returning to Cape Race as Officer-in-Charge in 1923. Seven years later Marconi's Cape Race facility was combined with a D. F. station operated by Canada's Department of Marine. Myrick returned to Fogo, remaining there until 1933 when the Fogo station was also decommissioned. Edward Myrick's final posting was at Signal Hill, St. John's. He died in 1958, spending his retirement years in Newfoundland, where he and Ellen lived with Daughter Mary (Healy).

The seven years in between Myrick's postings saw the Fogo wireless station manned by primary operator Michael "Mike" Walsh. Mike Walsh was born at Plate Cove, Bonavista Bay in 1894. Originally a sealer, Mike was part of the SS *Bonaventure*'s crew when a blizzard set in, nearly trapping him and his shipmates on the ice. This was the infamous sealing season of 1914. Though Walsh and his companions made it safely back to the *Bonaventure*, the crew of the SS *Newfoundland* were not so lucky – over seventy of their number perished on the icefloes (See below). Hoping for a better living, Walsh took a correspondence course in wireless operating with the assistance of his Uncle, Magistrate Joseph Long. Michael later married Catherine Mary Dwyer of Fogo Island, who was a telegrapher herself. Mike and Catherine's wedding was delayed for a year as, working for the Marconi Company, the groom-to-be was transferred to Sable Island. Their eldest child, Augustine (Gus), was born on Sable Island in 1923. Walsh transferred to the Fogo wireless station, where all five of his younger children were born, later in the year. During Walsh's tenure at Fogo operators were given the responsibility of collecting additional weather data like wind speeds. In 1928 Mike transmitted news of the first east-to-west transatlantic flight from Dublin to Labrador, the event occurring only a year after Charles Lindbergh's west-to-east solo flight. Mike Walsh retired in 1961 after forty-four years of service with the Marconi Company. Not content with the life of a retiree, Walsh was soon back to work as a wireless operator on deep-sea ships, his career continuing into in his eighties. During this time he visited ports like Honolulu, Shanghai, Tokyo and New Orleans. Remaining active to the end, Mike Walsh passed away in 1980.

....

Disasters

Loss of RMS Titanic. *News of the disaster was relayed to Fogo from Cape Race*

Being an island, tied to the sea, it is no surprise that Newfoundland's history is replete with tales of maritime tragedy. At least three significant marine disasters have a connection with Fogo's wireless station. Local tradition has it that Fogo was one of the first installations to receive the distress call sent out by the White Star liner RMS *Titanic* on the ill-omened night of 12 April 1912. That night the 46,328 (gross) ton liner was on its maiden voyage from Southampton, England to New York City when it struck an iceberg and sank in just over 2 ½ hours.

This most famous of ocean disasters, which saw more than 1,500 people perish in the North Atlantic, occurred only three weeks after the Fogo wireless station became operational. According to the local account, the vessel's distress signals were passed on to Fogo by Cape Race, the only land-based station to receive the message directly. Two other nautical tragedies, less well-known outside Newfoundland and Labrador than the *Titanic* disaster, also have a connection to the Fogo station.

Newfoundland Disaster. Commanded by Westbury Kean, Son of Newfoundland's foremost sealing skipper, Abram Kean (1855-1945), the SS *Newfoundland* was part of a fleet of vessels at the ice flows for the Colony's 1914 Spring seal hunt. Though many sealers that year were newer steel icebreakers, the *Newfoundland* was old, wooden and (significantly) had no wireless set. By the end of March Captain Wes found his tired steamer stuck in pack ice. Unable to manoeuver, Wes decided to send his men to find the seal herd across the ice flows. Though this might involve a long and arduous journey, Kean reasoned that the men could bunk for the night on the big steamer *Stephano*, captained by his Father, who was also fleet commodore. Once on board *Stephano* most of the sealers expected to stay on board until morning, or that they'd at least get a lift back to their own ship. This was not to be. After a quick "mug up" (lunch and tea), 132 of *Newfoundland*'s men were sent back on the ice to take more seals. Though no one knew it, a massive storm was bearing down on the sealing fleet from the southwest. Apparently, Captain Abram's own barometer gave no warning of the maelstrom.

Soon, *Newfoundland*'s men were battling a vicious blizzard. Westbury Kean, unable to contact his Father by wireless, was convinced his people were safe aboard *Stephano*. Captain Abram was equally certain that the *Newfoundland* crewmen had made their own vessel before the storm hit. In reality the sealers, now lost, walked for hours in search of their ship. Finally they hunkered down for shelter behind crude snow walls. By the morning of 1 April the exhausted and hungry men had spent an entire night on the ice, with another to follow. By this time many of their number were already dead. It was Captain Wes who finally spotted the pitiful survivors, suffering the full effects of two days exposure on the ice. Though several dozen men were eventually rescued, for many it was far too late.

Another sealer, SS *Bellaventure*, steamed into St. John's with the survivors and laden with a grim cargo of bodies. Seventy-seven men perished in all. The Newfoundland public wondered how such a thing could have happened, and questions surrounding the disaster swirled for many years. Abram Kean, who sent the sealers back onto the ice, bore much of the blame. The vessel owners and some of their captains were criticized for disrespecting the dead when they continued the hunt. One thing was beyond question, 1914 was the deadliest year in the history of Newfoundland and Labrador's seal industry. As if the tragedy involving the *Newfoundland* were not enough, the steamer *Southern Cross*, on its way back from the front, was caught in the same massive storm and disappeared with all hands.

Captain Wes Kean (inset), and the SS Newfoundland

The Fogo wireless station played its part in the drama by transmitting first news of the *Newfoundland* catastrophe, this information being relayed to the postal telegraphs in St. John's. Fogo also kept in regular wireless communication with those craft despatched to pick up survivors and the remains of the dead. In covering the disaster the *Twillingate Sun* specifically mentioned the important role played by the Fogo station.

Viking. Though it involved a smaller loss of life than the *Newfoundland* disaster, the *Viking* tragedy has also become ingrained in the Newfoundland and Labrador historical memory. Its events were unwittingly set in motion by American filmmaker Varrick Frissell (b. 1903). Frissell produced the movie *White Thunder*, which saluted Newfoundland sealers, and featured renowned Arctic mariner Robert "Bob" Bartlett (1875-1946) of Brigus. Frissell's international distributors thought the film lacked excitement, and suggested it needed some additional action sequences. To get the new shots Frissell would head north onto Newfoundland's Spring icefloes. One of the new scenes involved an overturning iceberg. To produce the effect on cue, large quantities of gunpowder were loaded on board the film crew's chartered vessel to generate an explosion. This craft was the SS *Viking*, which sailed from St. John's in 1931 with about 150 men on board. Built at Arendal, Norway in 1881, *Viking* had been used in the seal hunt every year since.

Having filmed several scenes, Frissell's crew were relaxing on board the vessel one night when a sudden explosion – the exact cause never determined – rocked the *Viking*, throwing men through the air and blowing off the vessel's stern. Frissell was last seen alive near this area of the ship, obviously injured. His body, and that of cameraman Arthur Penrod, were never found.

Damaged photograph of Varrick Frissell (front right) and his film crew, along with some members of the Viking*'s crew, 1931*

With their ship self-destructing and on fire, the survivors were forced onto the ice, helping injured comrades as best they were able. Under the supervision of Captain Abe Kean Jr. (1887-1958), who was among those seriously hurt, the men bravely gathered supplies from their burning ship and made their way across nineteen kilometres of rough pack ice toward the outport of Horse Islands. The first men arrived safely at Horse Islands after a harrowing sixteen hour journey, but help was urgently needed for the wounded. Unable to bring them all along, the able-bodied were forced to leave their injured comrades on the ice with two fit men watching over them.

Steamers were quickly dispatched, while volunteer searchers set out on foot from Horse Islands. Some men, badly injured, endured forty-eight hours on the ice flows. Though the disaster produced heroes who risked life and limb for their mates, many were not saved. The final death toll fell just short of thirty souls.

First word of the tragedy was received by telegraph in St. John's. As it had done during the *Newfoundland* disaster seventeen years earlier, the Fogo wireless station reported the progress of rescue vessels like *Foundation Franklyn*, *Sagona* and *Eagle*. The era's technological limitations were illustrated when communications from the *Sagona* to St. John's by way of the Fogo station were temporarily cut off due to a break in the land line. Though the Viking disaster is well-known in Newfoundland and Labrador today, the important role played by Fogo's wireless station – closed only two years later – has largely been forgotten.[16]

12

"We Will Make You Proud" – Fighting Islanders[1]

Newfoundland and Labrador was faced with an unprecedented crisis in 1914. When Britain declared war on Germany and its allies in August of that year Newfoundland found itself automatically a combatant. Although it was the height of the fishing season, men from all over the Colony rushed to enlist. Their patriotism came at a heavy price. A tribute mounted on the wall of the NDB Memorial Health Centre in Twillingate, itself a monument to their sacrifice, was erected "in memory of the men from the old electoral districts of Twillingate and Fogo who lost their lives in the Great War 1914-1918." It contains dozens of names. A monument to parishioners who fell in the war can be seen in St. Andrew's Anglican churchyard, Fogo; these are but two of many tributes in the region.

About 6,200 Newfoundland and Labrador men served with the Royal Newfoundland Regiment. More than 1,900 enlisted with the Newfoundland Royal Naval Reserve (NRNR), while around 500 joined the Forestry Corps. Data compiled by Sydney Frost suggests that almost 3,300 fought with the Canadians. Some local examples include Twillingate's Elmo Ashbourne, along with Ralph Knight and Lindy D. Brett of Moreton's Harbour, who enlisted with the Canadian Navy. Newfoundlanders and Labradorians also served with the British, Australian and American forces; author Frank Gogos believes their numbers were significant. Though we are focussing only on the Isles, it would still be impossible to tell all our stories of wartime courage in a single chapter, so we'll zero in on a few of our native heroes to represent the sacrifice made by all.

....

The Royal Newfoundland Regiment, 1914-18

Blue Puttees. Newfoundland and Labrador's most celebrated recruits were the original 500 infantrymen sent overseas as part of the Newfoundland Regiment (In 1917 the Regiment was honoured with the "Royal" prefix in recognition of its gallantry, only the third time such a distinction was conferred in wartime). A Newfoundland clergyman serving with the Canadian forces wrote that the Regiment "...has won fame for itself...as a clean, first class fighting regiment, and the dear old Colony has cause to be proud of her sons. They have done magnificently..."[2]

"It's a Long Way to Terra Nova." SS Florizel
with the First 500 on board, 1914

The Regiment came into being on 12 August 1914 at a public meeting in St. John's Church Lad's Brigade Armoury. By late September around 1,000 young Newfoundlanders had volunteered for service, just over half of whom were deemed medically fit. Tradition has it that, with proper uniforms lacking, leggings called "puttees" were acquired from a local supplier, in blue rather than the regulation khaki. In a recent work, former Lt. Governor Edward Roberts has challenged this myth, noting that use of the colour blue for the puttees was a deliberate decision, made to give the Newfoundlanders' uniforms a distinct look. Whatever the truth of the story, the first 500 were immortalized as the "Blue Puttees." They were first trained at Pleasantville in St. John's before departing for further training in Britain.

Although most of Newfoundland's original volunteers hailed from St. John's, it is a source of pride for locals that well over a dozen of their number came from the small communities of the Isles, representing Fogo, Twillingate, Change Islands, Moreton's Harbour, Seldom-Come-By and Indian Islands. Service records held by PANL (GN 19), along with materials from its McNeily Collection (MG 940), record the names of those who departed for overseas on HM Transport (the former sealing steamer) *Florizel* 4 October 1914. The Isles' Blue Puttees included: Walter J. Arnott, Seldom; Samson Bixby, Indian

Islands; Jonathan Brett, Fogo; Joseph Dawe, Twillingate; James P. Griffin, Twillingate; Francis T. Lind, Fogo; Archibald M. Newman, Twillingate; Bertram W. Oake, Fogo; Douglas M. Osmond, Moreton's Harbour; Arthur Purchase, Fogo; Leo T. Rendell, Fogo; Frederick G. Roberts, Change Islands; John H. Simms, Fogo; Hardy F. Snow, Twillingate; William B. Shave, Fogo; Frederick W. Waterman, Change Islands; Edward White, Twillingate, and Rowland Williams, Fogo. Of this group few returned to Newfoundland unscathed, while many never saw their homeland again.

A few of the Isles' Blue Puttees. Top, L-R: Ned White; Bert Oake; Fred Roberts; Doug Osmond; Hardy Snow. Bottom, L-R: John Simms; Leo Rendell; Rowland Williams; Sam Bixby; Fred Waterman

Arriving in Britain on 20 October 1914, the Blue Puttees were first posted to Pond Farm Camp, Aldershot. Hardy Snow sent the *Twillingate Sun* an account of the troops' journey to England, and the Regiment's first few weeks in camp, entitled "We Are All Ready for the Kaiser Willie." On 25 November the young recruit wrote:

> We had a fine time across on the Florizel, the sea was very smooth not one of the volunteers had an occasion of running to the rail to utter that dreaded sound Eur-ope. We were met off Cape Race by the Canadian transports about 33 in number, after falling in the rear we proceeded with light hearts.

After 11 days sailing we finally reached Devonport. On entering the harbour we were cheered on either side of the town by the inhabitants, especially the young ladies. One thing that drew my attention was the old fashioned ship in which Nelson won the battle of Trafalgar. We stayed at Devon 3 days and thence we went to the plains [Pond Farm Camp, Salisbury Plain].

Life here was not as pleasant as we all imagined it. We live in canvas tents, each tent containing seven men.

A crowd of our men have gone to lark hill in order to build huts and it is rumored[*sic*] we are soon going to move there. "Reveille" is blown at six a.m. and it is then the muttered groans are heard, mingled with the most imperious tones of the N.C.O.s, for none of us is delighted to get up early in the morning. At 8 a.m. we have bread and bacon. Then we settle down to drill till the welcome sound of the clock-house is heard, during which period the ground is alive with orderlies, and the air is full of the clash and clatter of "billys" and tin pans. In the melee which follows a very serious thing occurs – a pail of tea is upset.

Every Sunday we have open air service, a form of worship resembling the Salvation Army, for the big drum makes a terrible racket.

It is rumored we are going to the front in March. Whenever it is we are all ready for Kaiser Willie. You bet he'll get a hearty reception from us.[3]

I am writing this in the Y.M.C.A. tent. There is a wet canteen in the back of it, and some of the fellows are now dancing the tango.[4]

In December Snow and his comrades moved on to Fort George, Inverness for more training. A three month posting as the guard for Edinburgh Castle followed, until the Regiment was transferred to Stobs Camp on 11 May 1915. In August 1915 four companies of the Newfoundlanders marched to new quarters at Badajoz Barracks, Aldershot, before departing on the nineteenth of the month for their first front line duty at Gallipoli.

Gallipoli. By the Summer of 1915 a deadlock had developed on the Western Front, with the British Empire and France facing off against German armies in muddy trenches snaking across the countryside of France and Belgium.

There were few hopes of a breakthrough in the west, or a similar advance by friendly Russian armies in the east. In hopes of reversing their fortunes Allied military planners, including British First Lord of the Admiralty Winston Churchill (1874-1965), hoped to force a passage through the Dardanelles Strait. Lying at the eastern end of the Mediterranean Sea, the Dardanelles divided the Gallipoli Peninsula from mainland Turkey. The intention was to relieve pressure on Russia and knock the German-allied Turks out of the war. These high hopes ended in disaster for the Allies. A failed naval assault against Turkish positions in March was followed up by infantry landings in April. With the Turkish defenders occupying high ground, assaults by British, French, Irish, Australian and New Zealand troops soon bogged down into static warfare much like on the Western Front. By the time the Allies admitted defeat and withdrew in January 1916 more than a quarter million of their troops had become casualties. The victorious Turks suffered even more, with around 300,000 dead and wounded.

The Newfoundland Regiment joined the 88th Brigade at Gallipoli on 20 September 1915, being shelled soon after landing. On 30 September the Newfoundlanders moved into the front line for the first time, alternating between the front, and back area postings, until December. The Regiment earned its first decorations in November when a small party under Lieutenant J. J. Donnelly occupied a small knoll the enemy used for sniping. With aid from another group under Lt. H. H. A. Ross, Donnelly and his men successfully held what became known as "Caribou Hill" from counter attack – more on this below.

During this period the Isles' original recruits suffered their first casualties, though the majority were not through enemy action. James Patrick Griffin (Regt. # 577) of Twillingate was evacuated sick from the Peninsula on 27 October, and never rejoined the Regiment in the field. In 1916 Griffin was embarked for Newfoundland, where on 24 June he was declared medically unfit for service. Carpenter Edward White (Regt. # 486), also of Twillingate, was evacuated from Suvla on 7 November. He spent fifty-six days in the Third London General Hospital, Wandsworth – chosen to receive wounded Newfoundlanders in Britain during the war – from January to March 1916. An official report noted that White was suffering from enteric (typhoid) fever, "[c]aused – active service (Dardanelles) During convalescence had attack of pleurisy..."[5] He recovered, and was granted a furlough. Another medical casualty was Frederick William Waterman (Regt. # 441). The Change Islands native worked as a clerk prior to the war, and on 16 December 1915 was admitted to the 54th Casualty Clearing Station (a type of field hospital for the seriously ill or wounded) at Suvla with severe jaundice.

Some of Waterman's comrades suffered even more. A vicious storm in late November caused flooding in the Allied trenches and in low lying areas near the landing beaches. The Newfoundland trenches became miniature rivers, leaving the men sodden and exhausted. Nature had an even crueler trick to play on the Allied troops when the weather turned colder and snow began to fall. No Winter kit was received at Gallipoli, and the men suffered terribly. Fortunately, no one in the Newfoundland ranks perished. Regimental Headquarters evacuated some of the worst of its sick from the front lines before the flood hit, but even so nearly 150 Newfoundland troops were hospitalized, the majority for frostbitten feet.

Among those affected was Francis "Frank" Lind (Regt. # 541), who was evacuated on 8 December, and later admitted to hospital at Malta. Lind recovered and went back into action. Not everyone got off so easily. The very first enlistee from the Isles was Rowland Williams (Regt. # 10). Working as a stenographer at St. John's when the war erupted, Williams' family was originally from Fogo. During the terrible days of November Williams suffered severe frostbite, and was admitted to 54th Casualty Clearing Station on 1 December 1915. On 14 December he was transferred to the military hospital at Valetta, Malta. On 29 December Williams became a patient at Wandsworth, after arriving in Britain aboard H.S. *Massilia*. On 8 April 1916 Williams was attached to the Regiment's Depot at Ayr. Though he was eventually promoted to Sergeant, and became a 1st class rifle instructor, Williams never returned to front line duty.

Among the Isles contingent the most serious casualty resulting from the storm was Lance Corporal Jonathan Brett (Regt. # 537). Working as a clerk for Earle Sons & Company in 1914, Brett signed up in his hometown Fogo, along with his friend Frank Lind. Invalided to England on 17 January 1916, he was admitted to Wandsworth on the 24th. A medical officer's report on Brett notes that he,

> was in [the] trenches when the weather was very cold & then was snow storms. His toes became frozen & afterwards gangrene sit [*sic*] in. Had some amputated at Malta Dec: 17 – 1915, & re-amputated on March 23 – 16, at this hospital...There are no toes on the Rt. foot, on the left the two smallest ones are the only ones left. Cannot walk without a stick...[6]

Brett was fitted with special boots to help him walk better. After a short stint at the Pay and Record Office in London he was sent back to

Newfoundland on the SS *Sicilian*, arriving home in November 1916. The following month Brett was officially discharged as medically unfit for service. The next year Brett was accepted for training as a Marconi telegraph operator, but left his studies for other employment. In 1921 he took a job with Elliott and Company, becoming their Change Islands manager.

Though most of the Isles' casualties at Gallipoli were caused by conditions on the front lines, some were the direct result of enemy action. Twillingate's Archibald Mark Newman (Regt. # 487), a sailmaker before the war, received a shrapnel wound to the head on 1 November. He was admitted to hospital at Cairo four days later.

One of the Allied landing beaches at Gallipoli, 1915

Beaumont Hamel. The last Allied troops left Gallipoli in January 1916, with the Newfoundland Regiment forming part of the rearguard; a small number of Newfoundlanders, including Lt. Owen Steele, were among the last troops to leave the Peninsula. Returning to Europe, the Regiment was posted in April to the front line trenches in a fairly quiet sector north of the River Somme. The tranquillity was soon shattered. In June the 29th Division, of which the 88th Brigade and the Newfoundland Regiment were part, was at the northern end of the British line, opposite the village of Beaumont Hamel. An Allied assault was planned to break through enemy lines on the Somme. With thousands of French troops defending fortresses to the south at Verdun against a determined

German offensive, the Somme was primarily a British affair.

On 1 July, following a week-long artillery barrage, the detonation of a mine at Hawthorne Ridge (delayed by weather) signalled the beginning of an Allied assault on the German lines. The 88th were ordered to move up, with the Essex Regiment supporting the Newfoundlanders. As it turned out, the Essex were unable to get to the front line, so the Newfoundland Regiment went "over the top" alone on 9:15 am. Their goal was to advance on and capture two lines of enemy trenches up to 900 metres away. Unfortunately for the Newfoundland Regiment, the Germans, while shaken by the bombardment, were largely safe in concrete bunkers. To compound the Newfoundlanders' problems, the mines were blown some time before the initial British attack, while the artillery barrage had moved beyond the Newfoundlanders' first objective. Thus the initial wave of attackers were deprived of an expected curtain of fire. The well-rehearsed Germans were able to set up their machine gun units in plenty of time to receive their opponents.

"Through the Wire." Allied troops advance on the Western Front

The Newfoundland Regiment moved out in excellent order over the shell-blasted expanse of ground between the opposing trenches called No Man's Land. Expecting little resistance, the first wave set out at a walk. The men were soon caught in a murderous cross fire, and were without artillery cover. The Newfoundlanders began to drop, dead and wounded, first singly, then in groups. The Germans had easy targets, only having to train their machine guns on gaps in the barbed wire cut to let the troops pass. Those not already down made their way toward one of the few landmarks still standing, the Danger Tree. Very few made it near the German positions – many had not even made it past their own front lines. The assault ground to a halt in less than thirty minutes. For the rest of the day survivors, often seriously wounded, attempted to make it back to their own lines. Many lay for hours until rescued, while others succumbed to wounds or were shot by snipers while trying to reach safety.

The Somme offensive dragged on until November, but it was on this bloody first day that the Newfoundland Regiment immortalized itself in the ranks of the Colony's heroes. It also paid the heaviest of tolls. More than 800 Newfoundlanders went over the top on 1 July, but when roll was called next morning only sixty-eight answered. Over 700 youths were listed as killed, wounded or missing, the day's highest battalion casualty list.

Among those killed or wounded were a number of the Isles' first recruits. By this time Francis Lind was famous as "Mayo" Lind, through his series of published letters home (See Chapter Fourteen), the last written only a few days before the action at Beaumont Hamel. A short account of Lind's death was published in the *Twillingate Sun*. A correspondent from Botwood reported,

> ...that a returned soldier is sure he saw Frank Lind dead on the field on July 1st. He passed him going out and noticed he was doubled up as though he had been hit in the stomach. The same man [who] was later wounded in crawling back passed the place again and is sure there was no doubt that it was Lind and that he was dead.[7]

Of the little group of Isles recruits that sailed on the *Florizel*, Lind was not the day's only loss. Like Jonathan Brett, Douglas McNeil Osmond (Regt. # 306) of Moreton's Harbour had been a clerk before enlisting. Promoted to Lance Corporal on 3 February, Osmond was wounded during the advance. He succumbed to his injuries on 8 July at the 29th Casualty Clearing Station. His burial at Gezaincourt Military Cemetery was overseen by Rev. T. Sands. A similar fate befell Archibald Newman. Mortally wounded, he too died at the 29th Casualty Clearing Station (3 July) and was interred at Gezaincourt.

On 1 July many Newfoundlanders considered themselves lucky only to be wounded – Fred Waterman found himself among this group. Two days after the Regiment charged the enemy trenches he was at Wandsworth suffering from a gunshot wound. Leonard Rendell (Regt. # 231) was admitted to the 1st Canadian General Hospital at Etaples on 3 July suffering from gunshot wounds to the left hand and shoulder. Transferred to Wandsworth two days later, the former paper maker was discharged on 17 October. Wounded in the right thigh, William Burton Shave (Regt. # 543), the Son of Fogo's police Constable, also found himself hospitalized at Wandsworth. Another casualty was Joseph Dawe (Regt. # 328). The one-time sailor was invalided to England on 7 July, spending nearly three weeks at Queen Mary's Military Hospital, Whally Lane with a severe gunshot wound to the right buttock and another to his left wrist. Samson Bixby (Regt. # 241), who'd been hospitalized at Gallipoli, was also wounded in action.

For some the injuries received at Beaumont Hamel marked them for the rest of their lives. Change Islander Frederick George Roberts (Regt. # 440) received a gunshot wound in the left arm. The limb was removed in France about ten centimetres below his shoulder joint. Roberts spent another eight months in various hospitals, including Queen Mary's Convalescent, Roehampton where he was fitted with an artificial limb. Discharged on 29 March 1917, Roberts was briefly attached to the Regimental Depot, before sailing for Newfoundland from Liverpool aboard an Allen Line steamer in April. He was officially discharged as medically unfit at St. John's on 9 May 1917.

Gueudecourt. The Newfoundland Regiment was back in action three months after the debacle at Beaumont Hamel. This engagement, the Battle of Gueudecourt, was a measure of revenge for the Newfoundlanders. As Frank Gogos notes, it was the Regiment's "first full scale victory," and was followed by others at Monchy and Cambrai. Returning to the Somme battlefield, the Newfoundlanders would have noticed little change in the front lines from July. Though the Allies had made some progress in the Somme sector, in many areas the British advance amounted to a few hundred metres or less. In late September General Sir Douglas Haig (1861-1928) decided to renew his offensive, with the Newfoundland Regiment arriving at "Cocoa Trench," near the ruins of Gueudecourt village, on 9 October 1916. Even before going into action the Newfoundland Regiment suffered casualties from enemy shells and machine gun fire.

Just after 2:00 pm, 12 October, the Newfoundlanders went over the top toward the opposing German trench lines. A and B Companies led the way, with C and D Companies following. In contrast to Beaumont Hamel, the Regiment's advance was covered by a creeping barrage, in which the Artillery maintained a covering fire timed to advance just beyond the farthest friendly troops. This was designed to prevent the enemy from mounting a proper defence in time to ward off the attackers. By 2:30, after a fierce fight, the

Newfoundlanders seized the German Hilt Trench. By some accounts, they then stormed their final objective, Grease Trench (the Brown Line), but were forced to retreat to Hilt Trench after receiving cross fire. Gogos conducted extensive research on the action, and feels that the Newfoundlanders did not make it as far as Grease Trench. Confusion may have arisen from the placement of a Caribou memorial statue on the site of Grease Trench. Many people believe, incorrectly, that the Caribous were placed to mark the Regiment's farthest advance on a given day of battle. With Hilt trench secured two companies, some sixty men under Cecil Clift, advanced a further ninety metres in an attempt to secure a second line. Gogos believes this was their final objective, but the platoons were wiped out.

On the Newfoundlanders' left, the Essex Regiment met with success at first, but then ran into trouble and withdrew. With their left flank now exposed, the Newfoundland Regiment was left holding Hilt Trench alone against an inevitable counterattack. Preparing their defences as best they could, the Newfoundlanders soon came under German bombardment and an assault by enemy infantry. Keeping up steady rifle and machine gun fire, the Regiment held off their German attackers. Turning the tables on their adversaries, the Newfoundlanders bagged a large number of prisoners. At 9:00 pm a Company of the Hampshire Regiment and some Royal Engineers arrived to reinforce Hilt Trench, with more of the Hampshires appearing to consolidate the position around 3:00 am the next morning. Their heroic work over, the Newfoundland Regiment marched back to a support trench near Flers.

The Battle of Guedecourt was one of the Regiment's greatest successes during the war. Though its results were in great contrast to Beaumont Hamel, the day was not without its own costs – the Newfoundlanders suffered 239 casualties, almost half of whom were killed. Among the dead was Lance Corporal Hardy Snow (Regt. # 322) of Durrell, memorialized at Beaumont Hamel.

Following their action on 12 October the Regiment suffered more losses from shelling, and on the eighteenth they acted as stretcher bearers when the Hampshires and the Worchester Regiment captured Grease Trench, losing two more of their number.

Allied field hospital. Despite the efforts of medical personnel, many wounded, including Douglas Osmond and Archibald Newman, succumbed to their injuries in these stations

Steenbeek, Broembeek & Other Battles. 1917 saw the Newfoundland Regiment involved in numerous actions, including Sailly-Saillisel and Monchy-Le-Preux. Launched on 14 April, the latter engagement witnessed the highest Newfoundland casualties after Beaumont Hamel. Two noteworthy battles in 1917 were fought as part of the Third Ypres offensive. The campaign, sometimes referred to as Passchendaele, was launched on 31 July 1917 by Field Marshal Haig (Promoted on 1 January). Haig hoped to break the German Army by a massive offensive that would also lead to the destruction of German submarine bases in occupied Belgium. The battle was preceded by a massive artillery bombardment lasting ten days. As was the case at the Somme a year earlier, this did not reduce the German defenders, but did alert them to an immanent attack.

The portion of Third Ypres known as the Battle of Langemarck began on 31 July. The 88th Brigade was moved into position for an assault on the German lines in mid August. Early on the morning of 16 August the Newfoundlanders and their compatriots, protected by a creeping artillery barrage, advanced through a quagmire of mud toward three objectives, the Blue, Green and Red Lines. The various regiments set out near the River Steenbeek, from which the day's action took its name. Apart from battling the environment, the Newfoundland Regiment, along with the Worchesters, the Essex and the Hampshires, came under fire from entrenched machine gun positions, shelling and aircraft attack. Nonetheless, the attack was a success, with all three objectives reached and an enemy counterattack broken up. Both the 88th and 87th Brigades captured their objectives, making the 29th Division's assaults the only successful part of the day's wide-ranging British advance.

John Henry Simms of Fogo. Winner of the Military Medal (inset) at the Steenbeek

The Steenbeek saw many individual acts of heroism, and Newfoundlanders were the proud recipient of a number of medals, including a Military Cross for Captain Grant Patterson, and the Military Medal for Private Arthur Murray. The Isles would have its own champion on the day, Fogo's John Henry Simms (Regt. #88). Simms was a twenty-two year old fisherman when he enlisted at his hometown on 2 September 1914. An official account of how Simms became a decorated hero read:

> In the attack on the enemy near Langemarck...16th Aug. 1917, whilst in command of a Lewis Gun Section [Private Simms] showed great initiative and leadership in getting his men across a particularly bad piece of ground. He rescued one man

> under heavy shell fire who had sunk almost to his shoulders in mud. On reaching one objective he rushed forward in spite of a heavy barrage and located an excellent position for his Lewis Gun, from which good results were obtained.[8]

For his courageous actions Simms was awarded the Military Medal, but did not live to enjoy his accolades. An official telegram noted that Simms received gunshot wounds to the right leg and head. Admitted to the 4th General Casualty Clearing Station, he died there on 17 August. Of his Son, John's Father wrote on 14 July 1918 that "...it is very sad to know the bright young man he was will never return but gods[*sic*] will must be done so we must leave it in his care..."[9] As per his family's wishes, John's Military Medal was presented at Fogo by Magistrate Andrew Cook at a public tea meeting held in the local SUF Hall.

Another casualty was Joseph Dawe. Among the wounded at Beaumont Hamel, Dawe was hit at Monchy on 14 April 1917. The Steenbeek marked Dawe's third time on the casualty lists. On 29 August he wrote home to his Mother, telling her that "...I have been wounded again in the [left] leg...but its [*sic*] slight...[W]ell Mother this is the third time wounded & I tell you I am just about sick of it but I expect to spend another Winter out here..."[10] Dawe's words were prophetic, as the Newfoundland Regiment had months of heavy fighting ahead.

In the meantime, Third Ypres rolled relentlessly ahead, with Haig determined to capture Passchendaele Ridge. Just as the Newfoundlanders' fight on the Steenbeek was part of the wider Battle of Langemarck, so were the operations at the Broembeek part of the Battle of Poelcappelle. Flanked by the 4th Division and the Guards, the 29th Division was assigned to advance and capture a series of three objectives, starting at the stream known as the Broembeek. The covering barrage started at 5:30 am, 9 October. The Newfoundlanders advanced in the front attacking wave through a boggy morass, along with the Worcesters. Silencing enemy strong points, the Allies reached their first objective at 7:30 am, and by 10:00 am were at objective two. More German positions had to be silenced by the infantry, the slurry underfoot preventing intended tank support from materializing. The Newfoundland Regiment was able to reach its objective, as did the Guards Division. Their comrades were not as successful, and both the Newfoundlanders and Guards were forced to withdraw to the other Regiments' farthest points of penetration. Relieved on 10 October, the Newfoundlanders were eventually sent back for a month out of the front line.

Though the Newfoundland Regiment and the Guards Division met with some success, and an Anglo-Canadian assault took Passchendaele Village on 6 November, Third Ypres saw almost a third of a million Allied casualties, with only a few kilometres of ground captured. Among the casualties was Leonard Rendell. Injured on 9 October with a shell wound to his left hand, Rendell was invalided to England three days later, where he was admitted to the Second London General Hospital, Chelsea. He was then transferred to Ashford V.A.D. Military Hospital, Shorncliffe and N.C.D., Ripon. Rendell was discharged on 22 January 1918 and attached to the Regimental Depot at Ayr.

British tank advancing toward enemy lines

The British soon made another attempt to break through the enemy trench lines. This time the infantry were supported by masses of armoured tanks on ground more suited to their use – the Battle of Cambrai. The Newfoundland portion of the assault, launched on 20 November, is remembered as Marcoing-Masnieres. Once again our gallant band did not come through unscathed. A telegram to William Shave's Father noted that he was at the "...Fifth General Hospital, Rouen, November twenty second suffering from severe gunshot wound in upper extremity."[11] On the twenty-eighth he was invalided to England and taken to Richmond Military Hospital, Surrey. He was assigned to duty at the Depot on 27 December. A similar fate befell the thrice-wounded Joseph Dawe, who received a gunshot to the left foot, resulting in a compound fracture of the tarsal. Like Shave, Dawe was invalided to England, and then posted to duty at the Regimental Depot.

The tank tactics employed at Cambrai produced spectacular results on the first day of fighting, but this was not matched thereafter. Enemy counter attacks and a British withdrawal on 5 December saw the Germans regaining much of their lost ground. The battle resulted in some 90,000 men – Allied and German – being killed, wounded and captured, to little effect.

In the new year the Newfoundland Regiment – now "Royal" – played a role in countering a massive German Spring offensive, fighting on into the Fall of 1918. It was during this late phase of the war, while advancing near Ledeghem, that Sergeant Thomas Ricketts (1901-67) of Middle Arm won the Royal Newfoundland Regiment's only Victoria Cross, the British military's highest award for valour. The Regiment fought its last action at Ingoyghem Ridge in trying to assault strong German positions. On 26 October the Newfoundlanders were withdrawn from the front lines for the last time, and were at Cuerne, Belgium when the armistice ending the war was signed.

Other Isles Heroes. During the course of World War I more than 240 men from the Isles enlisted for service with the Newfoundland Regiment, though not all made it to the front. While our focus has been on the first contingent, we should not forget that those youths who followed were no less courageous, and they likewise paid a high price for their dedication. We would be remiss to leave the story of the Regiment without recounting the deeds of two other decorated soldiers from the Isles.

Augustus Bulgin (Regt. # 2427) hailed from Durrell, Twillingate. He attested for service 5 April 1916 at the age of eighteen. The Son of John Bulgin, Augustus was a fisherman prior to enlisting. Embarking for overseas aboard the steamer *Sicilian* on 19 July, Bulgin joined the Regiment in France 4 October 1916. He was gazetted for the Military Medal on 14 January 1918, as a result of his actions at the Battle of the Brombeek on 9 October 1917. A letter from the Chief of Staff's Office noted that "...[a]s a company runner he took a message from the 2nd objective to Battalion headquarters, through a heavy enemy barrage and reported back after having delivered the message."[12] The CSO wrote to John Bulgin that, "I wish to congratulate you on the conduct of your son which reflects credit not only on himself, but on his regiment."[13] On 19 March Augustus Bulgin was promoted to Lance Corporal, but less than a month later he was killed as the Regiment fought desperately to counter a German penetration of the British line on 13 April at the Battle of Bailleul. At first it was thought that Bulgin may have only been wounded and taken prisoner. The *Twillingate Sun* ran these optimistic lines: "...Pte. Augustus Bulgin M.M. was reported to his parents as wounded and missing. It is to be hoped that this heroic young fellow is in a German hospital, and further particulars may later be received through the Red Cross Society."[14] This was not to be. Bulgin's Military Medal was presented posthumously at Twillingate's Alexandra Hall 11 June 1919.

One of the highest awards won by a Son of the Isles was presented early in the war to Richard Edward Hynes (Regt. # 807). A native of the now resettled community of Indian Islands, Hynes was twenty-four years old when he signed his attestation papers at St. John's 28 December 1914. Formerly a fisherman, Hynes was part of the Regiment's second contingent, and embarked with his Cousin, Lemuel Edward Hynes (Regt. #806) aboard SS *Dominion* 3 February 1915. Landing at Gallipoli on the night of 19-20 September 1915, Hynes was awarded the Distinguished Conduct Medal on 11 November for his part in the action at Caribou Hill. Official documents quoted the following from the *London Gazette* of 24 January 1916:

> For conspicuous gallantry on the night of Nov. 4-5 1915, on the Gallipoli Peninsula. With an officer and six other men he [Hynes] attacked superior numbers of Turks, who were attempting to surround a small post. In spite of heavy casualties on our side Pte Hynes kept rapid fire at close range which resulted in the Turks abandoning their enterprise and enabled our party to bring in the wounded.[15]

In his work *The First Five Hundred*, Richard Cramm recorded Hynes's actions as follows:

> ...[A] large party of Turks...were rapidly surrounding our men who were holding the ridge. In the skirmish that followed only Sergeant Greene and Private Hynes escaped without being wounded. The coolness, resourcefulness and courage with which these two men managed the situation could not be surpassed by soldiers of many years active warfare experience. By their rapid fire at close range they completely deceived the Turks who greatly exceeded them in numbers. The enemy finally retired to his own tranches and the attempt to surround our original patrol was completely foiled.[16]

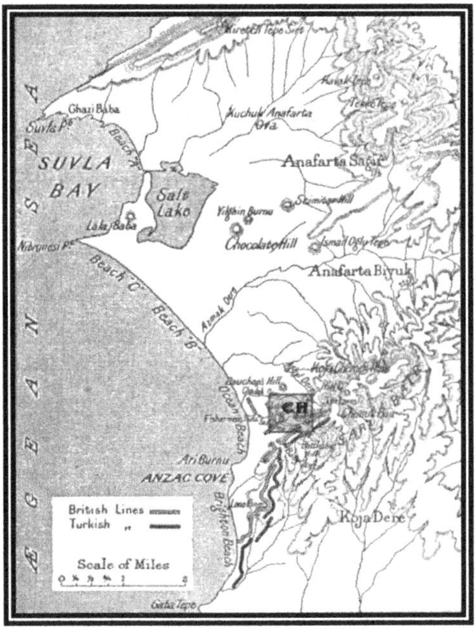

Gallipoli, 1915. "Caribou Hill" is indicated by the block at centre

It would be pleasing to report that Richard made it home to enjoy his well-deserved laurels. Instead, the young hero fell, along with Frank Lind, Douglas Osmond, Archibald Newman, and so many other Newfoundlanders, in storming the German lines at Beaumont Hamel. First listed as missing, Hynes' status was later revised to killed in action. Cousin Lemuel did not survive the war either. Lemuel Hynes was reported missing at Monchy-Le-Preux 14 April 1917, and listed as "presumed dead 17-11-17"[17]

Epilogue. The war's toll on soldiers in the Regiment was nothing short of appalling. Of the eighteen Isles Blue Puttees who sailed on the *Florizel* in October 1914, no fewer than five were killed in action. Another six suffered from wounds or sickness severe enough to cause serious impairment. In addition to Brett's lost toes, Williams' severe frostbite, Roberts' and White's amputated limbs, and Griffin's discharge as medically unfit, Frederick Waterman suffered partial deafness as a result of his wartime service, though his problems did not prevent Waterman from attaining the rank of Captain, and earning the Military Cross. Most of their comrades suffered from less serious wounds, with Joseph Dawe, Leo Rendell and William Shave all appearing on the casualty lists more than once. Of those who served through the war, only

Walter Arnott (Regt. # 458) appears to have escaped without a wound or medical condition requiring hospitalization. Neither Bertram Oake (Regt. # 509) nor Arthur Purchase (Regt. #540) saw active combat, both returning to Newfoundland when their initial six-month enlistment period expired.

In some cases the full effects of the conflict were not felt until many years later. During the war William Shave married Cassandra Gemmell of Prestwick, Ayr. In 1919 the couple and their infant Son started a new life in Newfoundland. Twenty years later William was living at Long Island, New York, and appears to have remarried. In 1940 Mrs. Ellen Shave wrote to the Newfoundland Government requesting a Widow's pension. William had apparently been sick for some four years before finally taking to his bed and passing away on 14 February 1939. Shave's doctor attributed his death to a kidney condition caused by the war. Clearly the men of the Royal Newfoundland Regiment were forever marked by the conflict – they were not alone.

....

The Newfoundland Royal Naval Reserve

Background. With our long maritime tradition it should come as no surprise that nearly 2,000 Newfoundlanders and Labradorians chose to serve at sea with the Newfoundland Royal Naval Reserve, rather than ashore with the Regiment. The Isles made their own important contribution to the Reserve, with around twenty men enlisting from the community of Fogo alone. Of the first fifty Reservists, eight came from Fogo, the third highest total of any community on the Island, St. John's included. A 1920 electoral district report noted that from 5 October 1914, 102 men from the Twillingate District had joined the NRNR, with another forty-seven enlisting from Fogo District.

For all this, the Reserve has never received quite the attention or accolades accorded to the Royal Newfoundland Regiment. In their recent work on the NRNR W. David Parsons and Ean Parsons offer an explanation. Unlike soldiers of the Regiment, Newfoundlanders serving with the NRNR were not kept together as a unit, being spread throughout the Royal and Canadian Navies. They served on everything from large battleships to small armed trawlers, and on all the world's oceans. Likewise, the Regiment was easily identified as "ours," while the widely scattered members of the NRNR could not be reported on as a unit, though individuals did attract some attention from the local media. Nevertheless, they did their duty as surely as their comrades ashore. As we will see, many paid the ultimate price.

Men of the NRNR pose aboard their training vessel, HMS Calypso, *1906*

The Newfoundland Royal Naval Reserve had its roots in 1902 when Governor Sir Cavendish Boyle (1849-1916), famed as author of the *Ode to Newfoundland*, proposed to establish a force of 600 men in the Colony. Prime Minister Sir Robert Bond agreed to an annual payment of £3,000 for ten years to support the organization. The obsolete warship HMS *Calypso* – later renamed *Briton* – was brought to Newfoundland to train members of the reserve. Enlistees agreed to train in St. John's for twenty-eight days and remain available for service for at least five years. Expenses were paid for outport reservists required to travel to St. John's. Records held at Memorial University's Maritime History Archives detail some of the pre war training received aboard *Calypso*, which was moored in St. John's harbour. For example, Fogo's Frank Hart (# 117X) completed twenty-eight days training aboard the old warship in December 1913 and again in April 1914. In each case his competency with the "great gun" and rifle, and his general conduct, were rated as Very Good. Similar results were obtained by Frederick Randell (#816X), also of Fogo, who drilled in December 1913.

When war erupted in 1914 the Newfoundland Royal Naval Reserve was Newfoundland's only formal military organization, its members called to active duty on 2 August. Despite its being the fishing season, every member of the Reserve reported for duty as ordered. The first contingent of Newfoundland Reservists sailed for overseas aboard SS *Franconia* on 6

November 1914, with another fourteen contingents departing through December 1916. In December 1914 the *Twillingate Sun* listed a number of Isles residents who had sailed with the NRNR in the opening months of the war. They included: George Coates, Fogo; Chesley Kearley, Herring Neck; James Keates, Joe Batt's Arm; Walter Ledrew, Change Islands; William P. Snow, Fogo; Jonas Watkins, Summerford; Albert Young, Twillingate, and Harold Young, Twillingate.

Three of our Naval Reservists, L-R: George Hawkins; Eric G. Woodford, and Herbert G. Osmond

Tragedies at Sea. As we've noted, Newfoundlanders were found wherever the Royal Navy had ships at sea; they even performed home duties in guarding the Admiralty's wireless station in Mount Pearl, and manning a gun emplacement at Fort Waldegrave at the entrance to St. John's Harbour. Members of the NRNR also manned three vessels used by the Newfoundland government for coastal defence. As we cannot trace their full story here, three losses suffered in Winter 1915, plus another disaster from 1917, will serve to illustrate the tremendous sacrifices made by these men, and the dangerous nature of their service. By the end of hostilities the Newfoundland Royal Naval Reserve had suffered some 180 fatalities.

More than a third of the NRNR losses occurred during a two month period in 1915, with the sinking of three armed merchant cruisers. Armed merchant cruisers (AMCs) were former civilian vessels equipped with guns to supplement the overtaxed Royal Navy. The idea seemed like a good one, but their high profiles and lack of armour made the AMCs vulnerable to enemy fire. One important use for the AMCs came with the establishment of the 10th Cruiser Squadron, which aided in a British blockade of the North Sea. Three of the vessels making up this squadron were the HMS *Viknor*, *Clan Mcnaughton* and *Bayano*. Each vessel had a dozen or more Newfoundlanders – one or more from the Isles – making up their ship's compliment. When one of the Squadron's AMCs sighted a suspicious craft a boarding officer and crew were sent to inspect it using one of the ship's patrol launches. With a legendary reputation as small boatmen, the Newfoundlanders were often chosen to make up the patrol boat crews.

SS Atrato, *later HMS* Viknor. *Lost with all hands in the Winter of 1915*

The 10th Cruiser Squadron's first two losses are true maritime mysteries. Even today no one is certain if either resulted from enemy action. At 5,386 tons, HMS *Viknor* was a former Royal Mail Steam Packet Company vessel. Built by Robert Napier in 1888, and originally known as *Atrato*, she was requisitioned by the Admiralty in December 1914. On 13 January 1915 *Viknor* was heading to port in Liverpool from patrol station in the North Sea. Its commanding officer was Commander E. O. Ballantyne, transferred from the cruiser *Arthur*. *Viknor*'s compliment included twenty-two officers and 273 ratings, most from the Royal Naval Reserve. Included among their number were twenty-five men of the Newfoundland Reserve. The cruiser was making its way through heavy weather on the morning of the thirteenth when it reported its position off Malin Head, on Ireland's north coast. Nothing further was heard from *Viknor*. For decades few traces of the AMC were found, other than bodies and wreckage washed up on shore.[18] Due to the inclement weather, and the fact that the Germans had mined the area, it remains a puzzle whether HMS *Viknor* foundered in the storm or sank after hitting a mine. All of her crew were lost, including the twenty-five Newfoundlanders. Among the dead were Seaman George Coates (# 1147X), Son of Philip Coates of Fogo, and Seaman Enos Barnes (# 1220X) of Change Islands. Of the Newfoundland dead, only John Bowen Mercer of Bay Roberts, whose body washed ashore, has a grave – the rest lie buried at sea.

Eerily similar to the fate of the *Viknor* is the story of HMS *Clan McNaughton*, formerly operated by the Clan Line. On 2 February 1915 the *Clan McNaughton*, notorious for stability problems in heavy weather, was steaming in the North Sea west of the Outer Hebrides. The vessel's compliment was 261, under Commander Robert Jeffries, RN. Among the crew were twenty-two members of the Newfoundland Royal Naval Reserve, including Jonas Watkins (# 2177X), Son of Henry and Ellen Watkins of Farmer's Arm (Summerford). Battling heavy seas, the cruiser reported losing a man overboard, and then...Nothing! Like *Viknor*, *Clan McNaughton* appeared to have been swallowed up by the sea, with only some wreckage washing ashore. Neither Jonas Watkins nor any of his crewmates ever saw home again. Both mines and severe weather were advanced as plausible explanations for the loss.

About a month after the disappearance of *Clan McNaughton* 10th Cruiser Squadron suffered another loss, though in this case the details are better known. The 5,948 ton HMS *Bayano* was built by A. Stephens & Sons Ltd. of Glasgow in 1913, and before the war was operated by Elders & Fyffes. On 11 March 1915 *Bayano* was off Carswell Point in the Firth of Clyde heading out from Liverpool to coal. Unbeknownst to the vessel's crew, she was about to cross the path of German submarine U-27, commanded by *Kapitänleutenant* Bernhardt Wegener. Spotting *Bayano*, Wegener launched a torpedo which hit the AMC, triggering a series of explosions that doomed the vessel. *Bayano* sank in under three minutes, with the bulk of her crew still asleep below decks. Approximately 180 men went down on the cruiser, with four officers and twenty-two men saved. Eleven members of the Newfoundland Royal Naval Reserve went to the bottom with *Bayano*, among their number Edmond Brown (# 815X) and Joseph Farewell (# 927X) of Fogo. Of the few who made it off the dying vessel, only one was a Newfoundlander, Isles resident Stephen Keates (# 458X) of Barr'd Islands.[19] U-27 was lost five months later in a surface action with the British Q-ship, *Baralong*.

Two years after the loss of *Bayano* the NRNR suffered another major loss of life when the HMS *Laurentic* was sent to the bottom. *Laurentic* was built in 1908 by Harland & Wolff Ltd. of Belfast. At almost 15,000 tons, the vessel was originally operated as an Atlantic passenger liner. The ship was requisitioned by the Royal Navy in 1914 for use as a troop carrier, and was part of the convoy in which *Florizel* transported the Royal Newfoundland Regiment's first five hundred in October 1914.

SS Laurentic *in a pre war image. Lost to an enemy mine, 1917*

On 23 January 1917 *Laurentic*, with a secret cargo of gold to pay for war materiel, cleared Liverpool for the Canadian port of Halifax. Following a stop-over at Lough Swilly in Northern Ireland, *Laurentic* was steaming off Malin Head in a gale of wind when it entered a minefield laid by the submarine U-80 under Alfred von Glasenapp (b. 1882). What happened next was described in the columns of the *Twillingate Sun*. The Sun noted that,

> ...suddenly the ship struck a mine and a tremendous explosion occurred amidships...Her wireless was put out of commission by the explosion and it was impossible to call for help so that it was some time before any help reached the ship. Several

> boats were quickly lowered but many of these were broken or swamped. An attempt was made to beach the ship, as she was not far from shore but this failed. Many were injured by the explosion and suffered before receiving aid...[20]

The troop carrier sunk in under forty-five minutes, taking 404 of its passengers and crew to their deaths. Among this number were twenty-one Newfoundland Reservists, either heading home for leave or back to HMS *Calypso*. Among the Newfoundland dead was Seaman Ephraim Freake (# 2213X) of Fogo, and Frederick Randell, who trained on *Calypso* in December 1913. Randell had served on HMS *Carron* from December 1914 to December 1916. Of the Newfoundland Reservists on board, only Edward Green of Little Heart's Ease, and Albert Harold Brushett from the Burin Peninsula, were saved. *Laurentic* was the twenty-fourth largest vessel sunk by enemy action in World War I.

Air Raid, 1917. In their work on the NRNR the Parsons note that service records of Newfoundland Reservists detail the shore stations at which a sailor was posted during his naval career.[21] His pay book was located at a Reservist's shore station, and followed anytime he was transferred to another base. Popularly known as "stone frigates," the shore bases were named as though they were actual warships. The Parsons point out a drawback of the NRNR records: though sailors would be assigned to seagoing ships, only their shore base might be mentioned in the service records. A Reservist's wartime career often involved many more postings than the bare-boned service records indicate.

Sometimes a high drama played out at the stone frigates, rather than on ships at sea. This was certainly the case in September 1917 at the Chatham Royal Navy barracks, HMS *Pembroke*. Construction of the barracks began in 1897 on the site of a prison, and the facility was officially opened in 1903. Named after a former base ship, the complex cost £425,000 to build. In 1912 Chatham sailors opened the Pembroke House Girls Orphanage, which they both managed and financed. In the same era Chatham became one of the Royal Navy's three manning ports, with a third of the Navy based there. Some Newfoundland Naval Reservists were based at Pembroke starting in 1914.

On 3 September 1917 Pembroke's drill hall was being used as overflow accommodation. In July HMS *Vanguard* was sunk at the Royal Navy's base in Scapa Flow, and men intended for duty on her were forced to wait at Chatham for other assignments. At the same time more men were quarantined at the base after an outbreak of meningitis. In all, some 900 men were sleeping in the drill hall. Among their number were two Isles residents. Albert Cluett (# 2222X) was born at the now resettled community of Cape Cove, Fogo Island, in 1892, and enlisted 14 October 1916. In 1917 Cluett had been serving on Defensively Armed Merchant ships (DAMS). Born in 1895, Thomas Andrew Ginn (# 2266X) was a Fogo native. His service began on 6 November 1916, and included stints on naval trawlers and HMS *Idaho*. Both Cluett and Ginn were at Chatham awaiting new assignments.

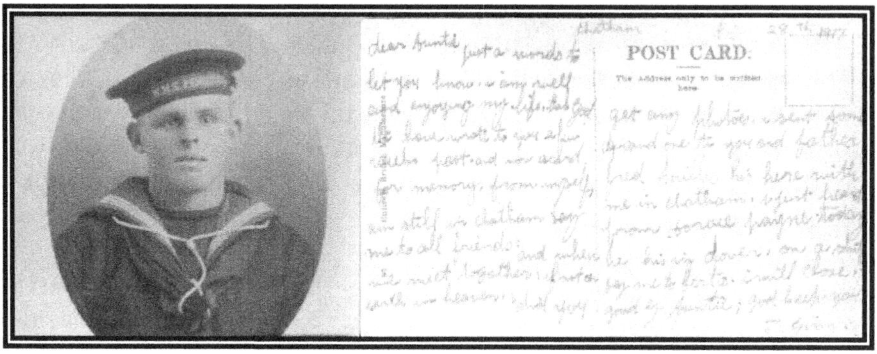

Thomas Andrew Ginn, NRNR (left), and his last letter home, a postcard to his Aunt

As the two Fogo Islanders and their comrades slept a flight of five German Gotha bombers took off from occupied Belgium. The large, two engine biplanes had three man crews and could each carry fourteen bombs. Earlier in the war Gothas and airships (Zeppelins) carried out daylight raids on England, but it was decided to switch to night attacks following heavy losses. One bomber experienced engine problems and returned to base. The other four aircraft continued on, and around eleven pm were following the River Medway toward Chatham.

This was the German's first night attack, and the town was unprepared when the bombs began to fall. The drill hall suffered a direct hit. Its partially glassed ceiling shattered, raining shards down on the sleeping men below. Many not killed when the bomb exploded were lacerated by these missiles. The drill hall's large clock stopped at 11:12, the exact time the bomb exploded. Rescuers noted that many of the dead were in an awful condition, with limbs and heads missing, or their bodies cut to ribbons by the glass. Survivors were treated on site, and a good many men expired in hospital. All told, some 136 fatalities resulted from the Chatham raid, with about forty wounded. Among the dead were four Newfoundlanders, Francis Crocker of St. Barbe, Nathaniel Gooby of St. John's, and the two Fogo Islanders, Cluett and Ginn.

Ninety-eight victims of the raid were buried with full military honours on 6 September at Woodlands Cemetery in Gillingham near Chatham, including the four Newfoundlanders. While the death of sailors through air attack became fairly commonplace during the Second World War, it was a new development in the Great War. Most NRNR casualties died at sea; these four represent the service's greatest loss of life due to enemy action on land from 1914-18.

Q-ships. During the Great War many Royal Navy ships had at least one Newfoundlander aboard, and this applied to one of the strangest of naval craft, the Q-ship. One of these, the *Baralong*, was mentioned above for its role in sinking U-27. Q-ships were a top secret part of Britain's campaign against the U-boats. The Q-ships were decoys, Royal Navy vessels outfitted to appear as tramp steamers, colliers, trawlers and other harmless merchant vessels. Prowling the sea lanes in disguise, the Q-ships would entice U-boat skippers to surface, and finish off the decoy with its deck gun – expensive torpedoes were best left for more valuable targets. Once vulnerable on the surface the submarine was confronted with a vessel that suddenly ran up the Royal Navy's White Ensign, while a motley gang of merchant mariners transformed into a professional cadre of Navy men. The sub might find itself outmatched from a hidden arsenal of depth charges, torpedo tubes and guns.

The original British Q-ship was commissioned in November 1914, although the first kill was only scored on 24 July 1915, when the converted collier *Prince Charles* sank the U-36 with her deck guns. The most famous Q-ship skipper was Gordon Campbell (1886-1953), who won a Victoria Cross for sinking the U-83 in 1917 after his own vessel, the *Farnborough* (Q-5), had been torpedoed. Although the Q-ships sunk less than twenty submarines during the war, they seriously damaged several dozen others. Though they weren't a huge success, Douglas Botting feels that between 1915 and 1917 the Q-ships were the best answer the Royal Navy had to the submarine menace.

More than a dozen Newfoundlanders served aboard Q-ships, including Benjamin Samms of Codroy, part of *Farnborough*'s crew when U-83 was destroyed. Samms won a Distinguished Conduct Medal for his role in the action. Three Isles men also served aboard Q-ships, including Seaman Chesley Miles (# 2060X) of Herring Neck, a crewman on Q-6, HMS *Zylpha*. Two Joe Batt's Arm residents, Lot Coffin (# 1906X) and William H. Brett (# 1930X), also saw service on the mystery ships.

Q-ship crewmen manning their deck gun

The Honour Roll. The Isles NRNR Contingent may have garnered fewer accolades than their compatriots in the Regiment, but they did Newfoundland and Labrador proud. As we have seen, a good many Newfoundland Reservists never saw their homeland again. Other locals who died serving with the NRNR in World War I include Arthur Baggs (# 2239X) from Twillingate, and James Mahaney (#2216X) of Fogo. Another Fogo native, gunner Harold Coates (# 2130X), died when SS *Hermes* sunk 28 April 1917.

Our look at the NRNR has focussed mainly on sacrifice, but a force that helped win the war for the Allies could look back on more triumphs than tragedies. Newfoundland Reservists won many awards and commendations in the conflict, and the Isles men were no exception. Two locals were mentioned in official dispatches from their commanding officer, an honour denoted by an oak leaf emblem on the Victory Medal. Able Seaman George Bignall (# 1831X) of Fogo was mentioned in 1915 for his services at Gallipoli, while fellow Fogo Islander Abraham Collins (# 1179X) of Stag Harbour was mentioned in 1918 while serving with the 10th Cruiser Squadron. Not to be outdone, Seaman George Cobb (# 621X) of Joe Batt's Arm received a letter of commendation dated 20 April 1917. Many Reservists were eligible for campaign medals like the 1914-15 Star, the Victory Medal and the War Medal, as were soldiers of the Royal Newfoundland Regiment. A special medal was earned by Seaman Isaac Keefe (# 1042X) of Twillingate for his long and steady service. The Long Service Good Conduct Medal (LSGC) was awarded to Petty Officers and Ratings who served more than fifteen years with the Reserve, wartime years counting as double. Keefe signed up with the Royal Navy in 1897, before the NRNR even existed. Serving aboard the battleship HMS *Iron Duke* during the war, Keefe spent an amazing twenty-one years in naval service.

Isaac Keefe of Twillingate, recipient of the Long Service Good Conduct Medal

Given its faithful wartime service, we might expect that the Newfoundland Royal Naval Reserve continued on for many years. This is just what a cash strapped Newfoundland Government hoped would happen, since employment in the Reserve brought in needed dollars. As Mark Hunter notes, the Dominion was disappointed in its expectations, as the economy-minded imperial authorities felt the Newfoundland Reserve was a waste of money. The NRNR was officially disbanded in 1921-2. When war erupted again Newfoundland would find itself without any standing military force.

....

Crisis and Change

Only two decades after World War I ended, a new generation of Newfoundlanders and Labradorians were called to arms. Once again the Colony found itself automatically at war when Britain announced hostilities with Germany, now under Nazi Dictator Adolf Hitler (1889-1945), on 3 September 1939. The twenty years after World War One saw many changes in Newfoundland. The old Colony was granted Dominion status in 1918, only to lose its independent government in the midst of severe economic and political crises in the early 1930s. In 1939 Newfoundland was governed by an appointed Commission of Government. While the budget conscious Commissioners *did* create a home guard, the Newfoundland Militia (Newfoundland *Regiment* from 1943), it saved money by not raising its own overseas contingent. Newfoundlanders and Labradorians who wished to serve did so with the British and Canadian forces. In the end some 20,000 men and women in the Colony – all volunteers – served in some branch of the military, or as merchant mariners and loggers.

Located at the eastern tip of North America, Newfoundland became the Allies' "unsinkable aircraft carrier" during the Battle of the Atlantic, and acted as a staging point for North Atlantic convoys. The war saw other changes, as the Canadian and American forces arrived. New projects like the Gander Airport were launched. The Americans, in particular, built numerous facilities in the Colony, hiring locals for their construction projects. For many it was the first time they received cash payment for their work. The mere presence of American and Canadian troops began to change social values in a land where there had been little chance to interact with outsiders. By the time World War II ended in 1945 the old ways of doing business in Newfoundland were seriously undermined. Many consider the great changes brought about by the war as the first step toward Confederation in 1949, but that is another story.

....

The Royal Navy

Background. While the Newfoundland Royal Naval Reserve was a thing of the past, the men of 1939 were no less renowned for their seafaring abilities than their Fathers in 1914. It is not surprising that more Newfoundlanders and Labradorians served at sea with the Royal Navy in World War II than with any other branch of the military. The call for volunteers went out on 24 October 1939, when Governor Sir Humphrey Walwyn (1879-1957) issued a proclamation asking for 625 men for service with the Royal Navy. Recruits came from across Newfoundland. With their strong ties to the sea, the outports were especially well represented. In some cases men enlisted in groups, as did John A. Hewitt (# DJX181205) of Joe Batt's Arm, along with two others from his community, and five men from Fogo. After a delay caused by a diphtheria outbreak the first contingent of 198 men, including Frederick J. Bryan (# D/173656) of Fogo, sailed from St. John's aboard the SS *Newfoundland* on 27 November. These first volunteers were followed by another seventeen contingents, the eighteenth and final draft arriving at Liverpool on 9 November 1941.

Some heroes of the Royal Navy, World War II. Top, L-R: Sydney Donald Wheeler, Summerford; Ralph White, Twillingate; Raymond White, Cottle's Island; Allan K. Collins, Fogo. Bottom, L-R: Wilfred Gillard; William Stephen Lloyd Linfield; Stanley Stockley, and Stephen Lambert, all of Twillingate

Like their predecessors in the NRNR, the new Royal Navy recruits did not serve together as a distinctive unit. Wherever the Navy was active Newfoundlanders could be found. From the frigid seas of the Russian Arctic convoys to the shark infested waters of the Indian Ocean, they were there. Newfoundlanders and Labradorians played an active role in the Battle of the Atlantic. This struggle saw the Allies pitted against a new crop of German U-boats in a battle that spanned the war. The longest campaign of World War II, the Battle of the Atlantic was also one of the most important. Whoever controlled the Atlantic sea lanes and the vital supply of goods to Britain would win the war.

Newfoundlanders serving with the Royal Navy helped ensure the Allied victory. They were also present for some of the most famous engagements of the war, like the sinking of HMS *Prince of Wales* and HMS *Repulse* by Japanese aircraft, and the rescue of Anglo-French troops from the beaches of Dunkirk. Perhaps the most well-known naval engagement of the war pitted the German pocket battleship *Bismark* against British naval forces. Among the many Newfoundlanders serving aboard the battleship HMS *Rodney* during the final chase was George G. Freake of Joe Batt's Arm (# 220919), a member of the eleventh contingent.

By the final victory in 1945 hundreds of servicemen from Newfoundland and Labrador had bravely served with the Royal Navy – dozens never returned. From the first draft alone fifty-five men were killed or seriously wounded. Former seaman Herb Wells notes that 345 Newfoundlanders died serving with the Royal Navy from 1939-45. The author of two works on the subject, Wells felt it would take many books to tell the full story of Newfoundlanders in the World War II Royal Navy. Likewise, to relate in a single chapter the experiences of all Isles residents who served is not feasible. As we've done with the NRNR, let us take a few stories of valour to illustrate the example set by all.

HMS *Avenger*. A number of Royal Navy vessels had large contingents of Newfoundlanders serving aboard. This would certainly have been welcome to men so far from home. With loved ones hundreds or thousands of miles away, it must have been of some comfort to talk with messmates who loved a meal of salt fish and could sing "The Banks of Newfoundland." On the other hand, when such a vessel met with disaster, this could lead to heavy losses for the little Colony, as the stories of the *Viknor* and *Clan McNaughton* demonstrate. The heaviest single loss of life suffered by Newfoundlanders in the Royal Navy occurred in 1942.

The story began in 1939 at Chester, Pennsylvania when the keel was laid for a passenger-cargo vessel launched in 1940. The vessel was requisitioned by the US Navy and converted to an auxiliary aircraft carrier. Acquired by Britain under the Lend-Lease agreement, the vessel was commissioned as HMS *Avenger* on 2 March 1942. The carrier's first active duty came in September when she was assigned to escort convoy PQ18 to northern Russia. With the convoy under attack from German submarines and aircraft, *Avenger* aided in the sinking of U-589, while her planes accounted for twenty-six enemy aircraft damaged or destroyed. The carrier was then assigned to assist in the Allied North African landings, Operation Torch, providing fighter cover for the offensive.

Herbert Stuckey of Herring Neck (left). One of three Isles residents who made the supreme sacrifice when their vessel, HMS Avenger *(right), was torpedoed on 15 November 1942*

Following its stint in North Africa *Avenger*, under Commander Anthony Paul Colthurst DSO, was assigned to protect convoy MKF1 heading from Gibralter to the United Kingdom. At 3:05 am 15 November, *Avenger* was hit by a torpedo from the Type IXC submarine U-155 commanded by Adolf Piening (1910-84). Hit amidships on her port side, the carrier's bomb room exploded, and *Avenger* went down in about two minutes. Over 500 of *Avenger*'s crew went down with her, Commander Colthurst among them. Only twelve men were saved, including Walter Russell of Bonavista. Daniel Jennings (# 180937) of Moreton's Harbour, Edward Combden (# 181404) of Barr'd Islands, and Herbert Stuckey (# 181155) of Herring Neck were among the thirty-one Newfoundland casualties.[22]

Twice Torpedoed. When school mates Harry Hyde and Francis C. R. Peckford of Change Islands set out from their hometown to enlist in the Royal Navy neither could have known what fate had in store; for one a watery grave, for the other a near miraculous story of survival. The boyhood friends set sail from Halifax on the steamer *Newfoundland*, part of convoy HX44, escorted by the AMC *Ausonia*. The Change Islanders and their comrades arrived safely in the United Kingdom, with no ships of the convoy lost.

In August 1940 Hyde (# SSx31750) and Peckford (# P/SSx31755) were serving on board the Royal Naval Sloop HMS *Penzance*. Built at the Devonport Dockyard, Plymouth, the 1,025 ton *Penzance* was a Folkestone Class sloop, commissioned in 1931. On 15 August *Penzance*, under Commander Allan John Wavish (d. 1940), was assigned as escort for slow convoy SC 1 from Nova Scotia to Britain.

Leaving North Sydney on 15 August 1940, convoy SC 1 was nine days into the voyage when it was sighted by Kapitänleutnant Victor Oehrn (1907-97), commanding the Type IX U-boat, U-37. Oehrn shadowed the convoy, but was picked up by *Penzance*'s asdic (sonar). Though he'd lost the element of surprise, Oehrn struck first, launching a torpedo into the port side of *Penzance* at position 56°16' N, 27°19' W. Hyde told Herb Wells that, after informing the Officer of the Watch of the incoming torpedo, he was hurled through the air and smashed against the deck. When he came to Hyde was floating on the oily sea near where his vessel sank. The young seaman and a few other survivors spent about an hour in the water before being rescued.

Their saviour was the British merchant vessel *Blairmore*, carrying a load of wooden pit props. Salvation was only temporary. The next day U-37 struck again, torpedoing the *Blairmore*. Oehrn then returned to base in France, leaving the stricken vessel to its fate. The survivors took to a lifeboat but it began to sink, forcing Hyde and his comrades back on board the *Blairmore*. Luckily the wooden cargo prevented *Blairmore* from sinking quickly. The survivors were able to take to life rafts, and were picked up by two lifeboats that got safely away. On 27 August the men were rescued for good by a Swedish ship, the *Eknaren*. Some ninety crew were lost from *Penzance*, while *Blairmore* had twenty-nine dead. Only seven of the sloop's crew survived the initial sinking, but all made it through the second torpedoing. Harry Hyde was the only one of *Penzance*'s Newfoundland crewmen to escape. He went on to become Executive Director of the Newfoundland Hospital Association at St. John's, while his school and ship mate, Francis Peckford, never saw his island home again.

<u>The Tale of Harry Earle</u>. In war sacrifice involves more than laying down one's life, though that is the *supreme* sacrifice. There are dozens of colourful and tragic stories of wartime service that might be recounted from the Isles, and one very interesting tale was recorded in Wells' book *Under the White*

Ensign.

Fogo resident Harry Oake Earle (# D/187480) sailed with the Royal Navy's fourth contingent of 177 men. After service on the armed merchant cruiser HMS *Corfu*, and the destroyer HMS *Reading*, Earle was assigned to the Tribal Class destroyer HMS *Zulu* when she was sunk by dive bombers on 14 September 1942 during a British raid on the African port of Tobruk. Helping to man a landing craft ferrying commandoes ashore, Harry Earle was not aboard *Zulu* when it went down. Earle was taken prisoner by Italian forces after the landing craft was also sunk. He was briefly sent to a camp near Bengasi, then sent aboard an overcrowded merchant steamer which transported him to Italy's prison camp P.G. 70. Though there were food shortages, and conditions were sometimes unsanitary, Earle remembered that the internees were not badly treated. Even so, Earle sickened due to a combination of lice and poor diet. Still suffering from this fever, he was repatriated under a prisoner exchange, arriving in Turkey by hospital ship in April 1943. Taken to a naval hospital in Alexandria, Egypt, Earle's fever was successfully treated and he was discharged. He then served on a number of other naval vessels, and was en-route to the Far East when word of the Japanese surrender was received in August 1945.

Harry Earle's overseas service included a tour of duty on one of the vessels escorting Winston Churchill from Argentia following the Prime Minister's historic meeting with US President Franklin D. Roosevelt (1882-1945). Earle was also part of the covering force for the 1944 Normany landings, participating in the sinking of at least two U-Boats while on escort duty. Following his discharge in June 1946 Earle eventually took holy orders in the Church of England and served as a minister in Zimbabwe.

....

The Newfoundland Artillery Regiments

Beginnings. While the largest number of Newfoundlanders and Labradorians served with the Royal Navy, many others entered different branches of the services. While they are not as well known today, Newfoundland can boast two of its own World War II Artillery Regiments, each a worthy successor to the Royal Newfoundland Regiment. With Newfoundland's pre war economy in the doldrums, the idea of the Colony raising its own ground force to send overseas was a non-starter. Instead, the Commissioners requested that the British government recruit Newfoundlanders and Labradorians directly into the Imperial forces. At first the British asked for men to serve for a term of seven years, but after much protest the service requirement was adjusted to the duration of the war. It was decided to form the Newfoundland recruits into one or more Regiments within the Royal Artillery, under the command of British officers and N.C.O.s (Later, some Newfoundlanders were commissioned as officers, or promoted to non-commissioned rank). On 6 February 1940, after a delay to avoid affecting naval recruitment, Governor Walwyn issued a proclamation calling for volunteers for the new units. By mid February about 400 men were accepted for service, and on 25 April the "First 400" arrived in Liverpool aboard the passenger liner *Duchess of Richmond.* Included among this first draft were Gordon Frank Harnett (# 970048) of Twillingate, and William Frank Simms (# 970049) of Fogo. Newfoundland's original Artillery contingent was soon followed by other drafts, and at the end of 1940 more than 1,400 Newfoundlanders and Labradorians, from all parts of the Colony, swelled the ranks.

166th Regiment R.A. The first formation to take shape was the 57th Heavy Regiment, Royal Artillery – "Newfoundland" was added to the name in May. After a stopover at the Royal Artillery Depot, Woolwich, the first recruits were divided into four batteries and began training. This was interrupted when word arrived of the German invasions of France and the Low Countries. Fearing imminent attack, the British authorities assigned the 57th to prepare and man defensive works on England's south coast. In June the Regiment received its first guns and, with the addition of new recruits from Newfoundland, the Regiment departed for Norfolk to guard against possible invasion of the east coast. In 1941, with a German attack on England looking less likely, the Regiment underwent a change in status and name. It was decided to convert the unit into a more mobile field Artillery Regiment, equipped with 25-pounder guns. This was a welcome change for the Newfoundlanders of the 57th, as Regiments equipped with light field guns were more likely to see action during the Allied invasions of North Africa. On 15 November 1941 the Regiment was officially renamed the 166th (Newfoundland) Field Regiment.

After another year in training the Newfoundlanders of the 166th left for Tunisia in January 1943, supporting British and Free French units. On 7 April the Regiment suffered its first casualty, Gunner J. J. Flynn of Norris Arm. In all, two dozen Newfoundlanders perished in the struggle for control of North Africa. The 166th was involved in all the major battles of the campaign, including the fight for Djebel el Ahmera – "Longstop Hill." Among the artillerymen present for this battle was the late Harvey G. Earle (# 971583) of Twillingate. Earle related his story in a pair of interviews given in 1998.

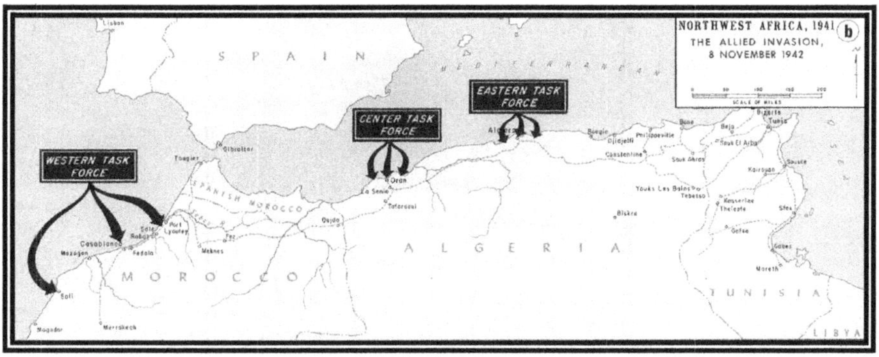

Operation Torch, the Allied invasions of North Africa, 1942

He had been working in Badger in 1941 when he decided to enlist along with a friend, Don Roberts of Triton. Roberts joined the 59th Heavy Regiment (See below), and the two did not meet up again until they boarded the troopship that took them home at war's end. Earle trained for six months at Lark Hill before departing for North Africa from Glasgow aboard the troopship *Circassia* in January 1943. The smallest man in the regiment, Earle was nicknamed "Cub."

Earle noted that at Longstop Hill he and his comrades had to cross a minefield to take up position. They then entrenched some 1,100 metres from the enemy, opening fire on the Germans around midnight. Though their bombardment lasted serval hours, the enemy was able to counterattack, driving the gunners into their trenches. The Germans were eventually driven back, and Long Stop was captured on 23 April 1943. The Axis – German and Italian – forces in North Africa surrendered in May 1943. In October the 166th was ordered to join in the invasion of Italy as part of General Bernard Montgomery's Eighth Army.

Landing in southern Italy, the Newfoundlanders formed part of the Allied drive to capture what Churchill erroneously called the "soft underbelly" of Europe. American commanders had pressed for an operation in mainland Europe, preferably France, but were persuaded to invade Italy by their British allies. Although the Italians overthrew Mussolini and changed sides, the German defence of Italy was unexpectedly stubborn. As General Montgomery (1887-1979) and his American opposite numbers slowly made their way up the Italian peninsula they were forced to overcome strongly defended German positions every step of the way.

Harvey "Cub" Earle, 166th Regiment, North Africa and Italy

Among the participants were several Isles residents, including Harvey Earle. Another comrade at Cassino was Allan Harry Roberts (# 1158176). Born in 1921, Roberts was working at carpentry in Botwood when he returned to his hometown Twillingate to enlist. In a 1998 interview with Erica Greenham, Roberts remarked of his service in Italy that he was "...frightened to death but...could not let it get the best of me."[23] Another local who served with the 166th at Cassino was Frederick George Atkins (# 971704) of Herring Neck. While most of the Newfoundlanders came through Cassino unscathed, at least bodily, more than 100,000 Allied troops and some 80,000 Germans were casualties.

"Cub" Earle was among those wounded. On 3 March 1944 he and two others were manning A Troop's No. 1 gun, a twenty-five pounder, when the trio were hit by shrapnel. One of Earle's comrades, Reginald Freeman of Norris Arm, was killed, while the other was buried alive by the blast. Earle was hit in the arm, and when found had one of his bones protruding through his greatcoat. He was taken back through the lines, and eventually to a hospital in Bolford, England, where he spent several months recovering. By the time his therapy was complete the war was over; even in his later years Earle's arm was never quite 100 per cent. Following the action Earle's parents received telegrams that he was first missing and then killed in action, before being informed that he was only wounded. In the end the sacrifice of men like Harvey Earle did not sway the outcome of Cassino; in May the Allies bypassed the German position and pushed on to Rome. Cassino was eventually taken by II Polish Corps as the Germans withdrew. The 166th (Newfoundland) Regiment remained in action in Italy until the Winter of 1944-5.

"Artillery Trio." L-R: Alfred Jenkins and Harry James Vineham of Twillingate, and Reginald John Holwell of Herring Neck

During its campaigns a number of other Isles residents served with the 166th, including John Ernest Dalley (# 971721), Cyril George Preston (# 971764) and John Thomas White (# 971322) of Twillingate.

59th Heavy Regiment. About two months after the 57th Heavy Regiment was formed a new unit came into existence on 15 June 1940, the 59th (Newfoundland) Heavy Regiment. It was first considered as a source of recruits for the 57th but, as G. W. L. Nicholson notes, the Regiment earned its own battle honours as part of the 1944-5 invasion of Hitler's "Fortress Europe."

While its Sister unit manned guns in southeast England during the invasion scare, the 59th was assigned to an infantry role at Tunbridge Wells. The Regiment remained in the area for several years. In 1942 the Regiment's training was geared more towards an offensive role, and in 1944 it was actively preparing for its part in the upcoming invasion of Nazi-occupied France.

Newfoundland artillerymen preparing to fire their heavy Howitzer

Armed with massive 155-millimetre guns and heavy 7.2 inch Howitzers, the 59th landed in Normandy with the 1st British Corps on 5 July 1944, and were in action the next day. Suffering its first wounded on 17 July, the Newfoundlanders then supported the Canadian Division in its attack toward Falaise. The 59th was later engaged in covering the Allied Seine River crossing, and were at Nijmegen during Montgomery's costly Arnhem offensive. Near the end of September the Newfoundlanders came under the command of the First Canadian Army, supporting the Canadians' offensive operations in Belgium and Holland. Late in the year the 59th was placed under the command of the British Second Army. Early 1945 saw two of the Regiment's batteries helping to stem a German offensive (the last of the war) in the Battle of the Bulge, while the other two were active west of the River Meuse. Some of the Regiment's fiercest fights came in February and March, in support of the First Canadian Army, along with the 30th British and 2nd Canadian Corps. In some of their final operations the Newfoundlanders' guns supported the crossings of the Rivers Rhine and Elbe. Their last shots of the war were fired on 2 May 1945 at Hamburg, two days before the city's German defenders surrendered.

Some Isles residents who served with the 59th Heavy Regiment in Europe included Donald Dawe (# 971278) of Seldom; Alfred E. Jenkins (# 971332), Twillingate; Wilson Allenby Manuel (# 971010), Twillingate; Stewart George Bennett (# 971270) of Fogo and Wilfred Broomfield (#

971168) of Bridgeport.

The End. Following its service in Italy, the 166th Regiment sailed for England in July 1945. The last German forces surrendered on 8 May 1945, and it was decided against sending either of the two Newfoundland Artillery Regiments to the Far East against the Japanese. The first Newfoundland artillerymen sailed for home aboard the *Lady Rodney* on 7 August. Documents held at the Provincial Archives note the travel arrangements of some of the Isles veterans.[24] For example, L/Bdr. Wilson Manuel of Twillingate and his Wife sailed on 22 November, along with Kenneth Wilson Holmes (# 971281) and his bride, bound for Seldom-Come-Bye. Others slated "for repatriation" were Gunners M. R. Burt (# 1158014) of Moreton's Harbour; R. J. Holwell (# 971971), Herring Neck; Lawrence Jones (# 970781) of Moreton's Harbour; Brendan Lane (# 971975), Tilting; Francis Mahoney (# 971847) of Fogo; Cyril Rideout (# 1158001) of Moreton's Harbour and A. H. Roberts (# 1158176) from Wild Cove, Twillingate.

The 59th (Newfoundland) Heavy Regiment was officially disbanded in August 1945, and the 166th two months later. More than 2,300 Newfoundlanders and Labradorians served with the Regiments from 1940-5, with over seventy of their number dying in service.

....

The Royal Air Force

To the Skies. Early in the war Newfoundland's Commission of Government decided that its citizens should play a role in ariel combat as well as on the land and oceans. The first step was realized in May 1940 when Governor Walwyn issued a proclamation calling for volunteers for ground service with the Royal Air Force (RAF). Successful volunteers were drawn from the ranks of skilled tradesmen such as locksmiths, electricians, instrument makers and wireless engineers. With Newfoundland then having few industries, the number of recruits was small, but the first volunteers left St. John's in June; over seventy were serving with the RAF by the end of 1942.

Some of those from the Isles who served with the RAF, either as airmen or ground crew included, James Henry Pynn (# 1346870) of Twillingate; William John Simms (# 1066439) from Change Islands; Elmo Baird (# 1345326), Twillingate; Leonard Snow (# 1356316) from Fogo; Edward Strickland (# 1356334), Fogo; Eric Wilson Pardy (# 798571) of Twillingate; Ralph S. Taylor (# 798643), Moreton's Harbour; Charles Weston Earle (# 798849) of Fogo, Brendan McKenna (# 1306315) from Island

Harbour, and Ned Simms (# 798850), Fogo. Another person who served with the RAF was Ernest Peyton (# 308257) of Gander, whose family had strong roots in Twillingate. W. J. Goodland (# J46557) of Joe Batt's Arm did his service with the Royal Canadian Air Force (RCAF).

Twillingate Royal Canadian Legion tribute to Neil W. Harnett, RAF. Memorial Wall, Notre Dame Bay Memorial Health Centre

June 1940 saw the first call for Newfoundland volunteers to train in Canada for air combat roles under the Commonwealth Air Training Plan. The first draft consisted of fifty-two volunteers, of whom half would perish on active service. Though fewer men were recruited for the RAF than either the Navy or Artillery, in the end more than 700 Newfoundlanders served with the Air Force. As the *Newfoundland Heritage* website points out, the small numbers were probably for the best. Of the Colony's RAF enlistees, a fifth never returned home, the highest attrition rate of all three services. Among the dead was Warrant Officer Neil Willoughby Harnett (# 798646). The Son of William and Annie May (Colbourne) Harnett of Twillingate, Neil attended Memorial University College before serving as a navigator/bomber with the RAF. Harnett was killed in an aircraft accident on 4 January 1945, just a few months before the war ended. He is buried in the RAF Regional Cemetery, Chester, England.

As in the Royal Navy, Newfoundland airmen and ground crews could be found in many roles, servicing or manning the aircraft defending Britain's skies, conducting bombing raids deep into enemy territory, or flying coastal patrols on the lookout for German submarines. They saw service in the skies of Europe, North Africa, the Middle East and Southeast Asia.

125th (Newfoundland) Squadron. Many Newfoundlanders serving with the RAF found themselves attached to the 125th Squadron. Like the two artillery regiments detailed above, the 125th had the name "Newfoundland" attached. The Squadron originated when the Commission gave the British government half a million dollars raised from War Savings Certificates. The hope was to use these funds to initiate a squadron of two-seater Defiant fighters manned exclusively by Newfoundlanders. This plan never came to fruition, as Newfoundland did not produce enough recruits to man the squadron by itself. The 125th (Newfoundland) Squadron RAF was composed of a mixture of Newfoundland airmen, along with comrades from Britain and other nations. It became the established tradition to pair a Newfoundlander with a non-Newfoundlander, one assuming the role of air gunner, the other pilot.

The limitations of the slow moving Defiant Mark I fighter soon led to a change of focus for the 125th. It was decided that units equipped with Defiants would be reassigned to a night fighter role. Taking on the German Luftwaffe (Air Force) at night, the Defiants proved to be one of the Allies' most successful night fighters during the early stages of the war. In July 1941 the first six Newfoundlanders to earn their wings in Canada joined the 125th. Of these six no fewer than four did not make it through their first year.

In 1942 the Squadron converted from its Defiants to the twin-engine Bristol Beaufighter. The efficient Beaufighters saw the Squadron's air gunners replaced with navigators, and the former were reassigned to bomber command. As Nicholson relates, the Newfoundlanders were almost immediately noted for their great skill in handling the Beaufighters. No. 125 Squadron engaged the Luftwaffe during nighttime raids over Britain during April 1942, damaging a number of enemy aircraft. The Squadron registered its first confirmed kill, a Junkers 88, on 27 June 1942. By November the 125th had registered eight known kills, plus a number of others damaged. On the night of 13-14 May 1943 the Squadron had an impressive night with four enemy planes downed, one probable, with another damaged.

In early 1944 No. 125 traded in its Beaufighters for the versatile de Havilland Mosquito. Over the course of three years of war the radar-equipped Mosquito night fighter accounted for 600 enemy planes and an equal number of unmanned V1 flying bombs.

De Havilland Mosquito XVIII, armed with a 57 mm Molins gun

On 23 April 1944 the 125th made its first contribution to this total, with two German raiders destroyed and another pair damaged. About two months later, 22 June, "Taffy" Grey, a Welshman with the 125th, scored three German planes, while another Mosquito destroyed two aircraft. That same night a third fighter from the Squadron damaged an enemy plane. The 125th got its first V1 in July. By the end of the war 125th (Newfoundland) Squadron accounted for forty-four enemy aircraft destroyed, with another twenty damaged. Two English officers of No. 125 scored a JU 88 on 20 March 1945, the last German plane downed over Great Britain. Nicholson notes that the squadron's kill numbers were small compared to some of the fighter squadrons that started out in the Battle of Britain. Still, they provided a vital service in guarding the night skies over Britain through several years of war.

As the war wound to its conclusion the 125th remained on station in England, and in training with new models of Mosquito fighters. By the Summer of 1945 the Newfoundland Royal Artillery units were demobilized, but the 125th and other Newfoundland airmen were being considered for service against the Japanese, a possibility that did not sit well with the long-serving pilots and ground crews. In the end Japan capitulated without the 125th transferring to the Far East. On 20 November 1945 125th (Newfoundland) Squadron RAF was officially disbanded, some of its Newfoundland recruits having returned home as early as August.

Jim Anstey, RAF Gunner. Many Newfoundlanders served with the RAF outside the 125th, as ground crews, fighter pilots, bomber crewmen and more. One of these men was Twillingate resident Archibald James "Jim" Anstey (# 1308261). Born in 1912, Anstey enlisted with the Newfoundland Overseas

Forestry Unit (See below) in 1939. In 1998 Anstey told interviewer Erica Greenham that he felt he should do more than serve with the Forestry, and wanted to join the armed forces. On 31 July 1940 he signed up for the RAF, and initially trained as a ground gunner. Feeling he could do still more, Jim volunteered for air crew training and became a tail gunner. He first served on a Stirling bomber which dropped propaganda leaflets onto Nazi-occupied France, and later on a massive four-engine Lancaster.

Jim Anstey, RAF Bomber Command

From 1942 on, RAF Bomber Command and its American counterparts were engaged in day and night bombing raids deep into German-held territory. The giant raids took a fearful toll on Germany's infrastructure and its populace, but at a high price. The crews of Bomber Command suffered some of the heaviest losses of all services in the Second World War. Among the brave aircrews taking to the skies over Germany one could often find a Newfoundlander like Jim Anstey. The perils of the service are related in

Nicholson's work, *More fighting Newfoundlanders.* Anstey reported that during a 1,000 plane raid over Frankfurt a German night fighter was tailing his Lancaster. The pilot took evasive action, putting the bomber into a steep dive, no mean feat in an aircraft not built for manoeuverability. The plane descended some 900 metres before pulling out of the dive. Anstey admitted that his stomach did not feel much up to flying the next day. He was treated for air sickness but recovered.

Anstey had worse luck on another mission when he actually passed out. Following this incident he was grounded, and assigned to Air Field Control north of London. From this point until the end of the war he worked at directing aircraft on the ground. Repatriated in late 1945, Jim Anstey ate his Christmas dinner in the mid Atlantic on his way back to Newfoundland. Despite the long odds against the men of Bomber Command, he made it home.

....

Civilians Who Served – Foresters and Merchant Mariners

Whenever the story of Newfoundland and Labrador's contributions in the World Wars is told the armed services usually grab the lion's share of attention, particularly the Royal Newfoundland Regiment of World War I. The lads of the Regiment, Navy, Air Force and artillery had a dangerous yet glamorous role to play in the dramas, fighting it out against Germany and its various allies. However, it is unlikely that the victories of 1918 and 1945 could have been won without the services of two other groups of men, many of whom were civilians – the merchant mariners and foresters.

<u>The Merchant Marine</u>. In discussing the Royal Navy we've noted the importance of the Battle of the Atlantic during the Second World War. The pattern was nothing new. Germany tried to starve Britain into surrendering during the Great War by cutting off its vital overseas supplies. In 1917, at the peak of Germany's first U-boat war, some 3,700 ships were sunk, damaged or captured. In the course of the two campaigns thousands of civilian merchant mariners, including many from Newfoundland, sailed into harm's way. Manning everything from sail fishing craft, to oil tankers and general cargo steamers, the men of the merchant navy paid a heavy toll for their devotion to duty. Hundreds died a lonely death amidst the cold, black waters of the North Atlantic. In many cases sailors survived the loss of their vessel but were never rescued, death from exposure being their only release. Some came through, but were scarred for life trying to swim through burning oil floating amidst the settling remains of their vessels.

One of the Newfoundlanders who helped maintain the flow of Allied commerce was Charles Hart of Fogo. Hart was but one of many merchant mariners to lose their lives from 1914-18. In 1918 Hart was part of a five man crew serving under Captain Edgar Kean on board the 102 ton schooner *Cecil L. Shave*. Owned by A. E. Hickman & Co. Ltd., the *Cecil L. Shave* departed Cadiz for St. John's on 16 February. Two days later the small vessel was sailing west of Gibralter when she was spotted and torpedoed by U-155 under Korvettenkapitän Erich Eckelmann (1880-1929). On 24 May word reached the vessel's owners that *Cecil L. Shave* had been sunk, but of the fate of Charles Hart and his comrades, nothing further was heard.

Six months after Hart was lost, another vessel with Isles connections was the victim of a submarine attack. In August 1918 the three masted, 203 ton schooner *Gladys M. Hollett* left Twillingate under the command of Captain Cluett. The vessel had arrived at Twillingate with a cargo of coal for Ashbournes Ltd. Loading a cargo of herring for the firm, the schooner sailed for New York. According to the *Twillingate Sun*, the vessel was about sixty-four kilometres south of Halifax, Nova Scotia when she was sighted by the U-156 commanded by Kapitänleutnant Richard Feldt (1882-1918). Feldt attacked the schooner, most likely with his deck gun, as torpedoes were too costly to expend on small sail vessels. The Sun reported that the *Gladys M. Hollett* was sunk, though the website *uboat.net* suggests she was only damaged. In any case, the crew abandoned ship and made it safely to shore. Feldt and U-156 were not so lucky. On 25 September 1918 the sub is believed to have hit a mine in the Northern Passage, taking all seventy-seven of her crew to the bottom.

Feldt's successors had a measure of revenge. The Second World War witnessed another season of suffering. In 1942 alone a further 1,300 vessels became victims of the U-Boats. Organizing ships into large convoys – groups of vessels protected by naval craft – provided some measure of relief, but for a time the German submarines ruled the seas. From 1939-45 10,000 Newfoundlanders and Labradorians volunteered for service in the merchant marine, most being teenaged boys or older men not eligible for service in the armed forces. There were also a number of women at sea, mainly stewardesses on passenger vessels. By war's end about 60,000 Allied merchant mariners were dead, over 300 of these from Newfoundland. Some locals who served as merchant mariners during the war include Joseph L. Pickett, Ned Miller, Harvey Willis and Arthur Oake of Fogo, Leo Dwyer from Tilting, along with Chesley Pelley, William G. Bridger, Ernest Legge and Baxter Rogers from Twillingate.

Merchant mariner Chesley Pelley of Twillingate, and his medals. From the Legion Memorial Wall, NDB Memorial Health Centre

Born in 1921, Ernie Legge served as a merchant mariner after a stint with the Forestry Unit, working on a vessel carrying freight between Newfoundland and Sydney, Nova Scotia. Baxter Rogers served as a merchant mariner for two years carrying cargoes like coal, foodstuffs and fish between Newfoundland, coastal Labrador and Nova Scotia. While neither Legge nor Rogers were involved in the trans-Atlantic convoys, their service was perilous nonetheless. This was proven in 1942 when the 2,222 ton freight and passenger ferry *Caribou* was sent to the bottom by U-69 on her regular run between Newfoundland and Nova Scotia. More than 100 passengers and crew perished. A pair of attacks on shipping at Bell Island saw four other vessels sunk and sixty-nine seamen dead.

At least one Isles merchant mariner *did* fall prey to U-boat attack while travelling the Atlantic in convoy. Arthur William Gillett of Twillingate served as Third-Officer aboard the catapult armed merchant ship *Empire Spring*. The 6,946 ton vessel was built in 1941 by Lithgows Ltd., Port Glasgow. In the Winter of 1942 *Empire Spring* was part of convoy ON-63 which sailed from Manchester to Halifax on 29 January. At about 3:30 am on 14 February

Empire Spring, under Alexander McKechan, had been dispersed from the convoy when it was struck by a torpedo launched from U-576 captained by Hans-Dieter Heinicke. About fifty men went down on *Empire Spring*, including Arthur Gillett – there were no survivors.

Newfoundland postage stamp commemorating SS Caribou

The loss of vessels like the *Empire Spring* very nearly crippled the Allied war effort in both World Wars, but the sacrifice of men like Arthur Gillett and Charles Hart was not in vain. By the end of World War II, in particular, massive shipbuilding programmes and better sub-killing technology made Germany's U-boat campaign untenable. Had it not been for those merchant mariners who saw the Allies through the darkest days of 1917 and 1942 (the worst years for submarine attacks), either conflict could have seen a German victory.

The Newfoundland Foresters. One effect of Germany's World War I U-boat campaign was a severe shortage of timber in the United Kingdom. Even in peacetime Britain was a timber importer, and during hostilities the need for wood was even greater. With food and war materiel taking priority, the British simply could not import enough timber to meet its needs. Fortunately, the country had ample stands of trees, often growing in areas difficult to access. In 1916 a Canadian Forestry Battalion arrived in Britain, and the idea of recruiting a similar unit in Newfoundland was also discussed. Recruiting began with an appeal to all Newfoundland lumbermen and skilled workers who could not serve with the Regiment or NRNR. In all, 500 foresters enlisted. Many had worked for AND at Grand Falls or with Albert E. Reed in Bishop's Falls.

Another 278 volunteers did not meet the minimum physical standards. Officered mainly by men no longer fit for front-line duty, the Newfoundland Forestry Corps, unlike the merchant marine, and the Forestry Unit of World War II, was a military organization.

The first foresters departed on the *Florizel* in May 1917, with other drafts following through to the Spring of 1918. The Newfoundlanders established two camps at Dunkeld, Scotland, erecting a 900 metre log chute to bring timber from the higher reaches of their cutting area. After denuding their initial cutting area of timber the Forestry Corps moved to another location in early 1918. Here the resourceful men proposed to build large scows to float along Loch Tay to railway facilities at Killin. The end of the war prevented this project from being realized. Work continued past the armistice of November 1918, but by January operations were winding down. The efforts of the Newfoundland Forestry Corps earned high praise from British officials. Though they fired no shots in anger, the foresters had certainly done their part to help win the war.

Provincial Archive records give us the names of all Isles residents who served with the Corps.[25] Enlistees from the town of Twillingate were: L. Corp. Hubert Bulgin (Regt. # 3011); RQMS John A. Barrett (Regt. # 8028); Martin R. Sampson (Regt. # 8085); Corp. Melville Colbourne (Regt. # 8150); Clarence S. Lunnen (Regt. # 8171); Beatie Rideout (Regt. # 8203); Archibald C. Pardy (Regt. # 8204), and Herbert Young (Regt. #8365). Walter Harvey (Regt. # 8062); Charles Rideout (Regt. # 8087); Caywood Rideout (Regt. # 8247); Ralph Harvey (Regt. # 8270), and Oliver Osmond (Regt. # 8314) all enlisted from Moreton's Harbour. Fogo residents with the Corps were Sidney Torraville (Regt. # not known); Edgar Simms (Regt. # 8367), and Gilbert Sibley (Regt. # 8508). Three Change Islanders volunteered, namely Stewart Hart (Regt. #8168); William Joseph Rendell (Regt. # 8240), and Stanley Jeans (Regt. # not known). Other Isles recruits were, Walter G. Hoddinott (Regt. # 8094) of Indian Islands; Joseph Gleeson (Regt. # 8157) from Virgin Arm; Alfred E. Pike (Regt. # 8188), Barr'd Islands; Alfred L. Vivian (Regt. # 8269) of Friday's Bay; Pierce Hayse (Regt. # 8382) from Tilting, along with Fred N. Dawe (Regt. # 8410) and Rowland Dawe (Regt. # 8411) of Seldom-Come-Bye.

Twenty years after the Forestry Corps disbanded a new war required the services of another generation of experienced lumbermen. The situation in 1939 was much the same as it had been twenty-five years before. A German submarine campaign resulted in timber shortages. Though Britain still had good supplies of wood, there were too few foresters to harvest the product. Of special concern was a lack of pit props, wooden frames needed to support mining tunnels. The British authorities passed word of this pressing need along to the Newfoundland Commissioners, and in November word went out for experienced volunteers to serve as foresters. As time was of the essence it was decided to constitute the new unit as a civilian force which could be readied more quickly. Thus, the Newfoundland Overseas Forestry Unit, unlike its predecessor, was not a military force. Men signed up for a six month enlistment term, and the first 350 Newfoundland foresters sailed for the UK 13 December 1939.[26]

Newfoundland foresters at their camp in Scotland, 1940. Most of the men are from the Twillingate area. Rear, L-R: Wesley Hynes; Unknown; Unknown; William Lambert; Arthur Froude; Unknown; Albert Mitchell; Peter Troake; Bennett Froude; Stanley Stockley; Lee Adey; Stewart Burton. Front (Seated), L-R: Unknown; Aubrey Stuckless; Allie Elliott; Unknown; Albert Froude; Unknown; Stanley Sharpe

Arriving in Liverpool, the foresters were soon on their way to various base camps. By the early Summer of 1940 permanent logging camps were nearly complete, in forest areas from southern England to northern Scotland, and the men began harvesting in earnest. At this time a problem arose when the mens' six month contracts were up; many opted to enlist in the armed services or to return home. A new recruiting drive saw another 1,000 Newfoundlanders join the unit by the end of the year. By this time some thirty camps were established, housing up to 100 men each. The foresters cut all of their timber by hand with buck saws and axes, manually loading the product onto trucks and trains for transport. Tractors and horses were used for hauling the cut timber. It was a dangerous job, and almost three dozen Newfoundland foresters were killed while serving in Britain. Though far from the front lines, the Forestry Unit was not immune from attack. When interviewed by Erica Greenham in 1998 Twillingate forestry veteran Ernest White (# 196) recalled that his camp was bombed on one occasion, while another Twillingate forester, William R. Warr (# 194), was strafed by German planes as he and his comrades were loading wood for transport to a railway station.

Some of the foresters did additional service by enlisting in the Home Guard, a volunteer organization formed in 1940 against the possibility of a German invasion. Many foresters started out with the local command nearest their camps, but in 1942, with most of the Newfoundland foresters working from the Scottish Highlands, it was proposed to form a battalion of the Guard entirely composed of Forestry Unit members and officers. Their duty would be to defend the remote Scottish coasts from possible German landings. On 30 September 1942 the 3rd Inverness (Newfoundland) Battalion Home Guard was formed with more than 700 men in its ranks. Foresters who served in the Home Guard were eligible for the Defence Medal.

Isles men in the Home Guard ranks included Samuel Burt (# 392) of Hillgrade; James Farewell (# 766) and Arthur Freake (# 764) from Fogo; Charles Gosse (# 2836) of Herring Neck; Bert Hustins (# 800), Cottles Cove, plus Cyril Froude (# 772); Lewis Jenkins (# 158); John Keefe (# 814); Hardy Cooper (# 119); Reginald Reid (# 180); Arthur S. Hamlyn (# 147); Bennett Simms (# 900), and William Vineham (#921), all of Twillingate.

One of the foresters who did service with the Home Guard was John W. Gillard (# 780) of Gillard's Cove (now part of Bayview), Twillingate. Mr. Gillard was interviewed by *Lewisporte Pilot* correspondent Howard Butt in November 2009, at which time he was the last remaining forester who went overseas from Bayview. The second child of Augustus and Lydia Gillard, John was at Roberts Arm cutting wood for the Bowater Mill at Corner Brook when he enlisted in 1939. Aged only seventeen, though soon to turn eighteen, Gillard sailed across the Atlantic on the *Duchess of Richmond.* His elder Brother Pearce (# 134), who later joined the Royal Navy, was part of the first draft of foresters. John told Howard Butt that his service with the Home Guard was the closest he came to the regular forces.

While the foresters had their share of hardship, and even some danger, there were many lighthearted moments. At one point two of the Home

Guardsmen played a prank on another Bayview resident, George Hicks (# 794). Grabbing Hicks, and pretending they thought he was a spy, the pair escorted their struggling comrade to John Gillard for identification. Realizing the joke, Gillard pretended he'd never seen Hicks before, to which Hicks replied, "You listen here, John Gillard, you damn well knows me."[27] At this Hicks was released to the good-natured laughter of his companions. Though war can strain men to the breaking point, it also forms bonds of comradeship and shared experiences that last a lifetime. In this the men of the Newfoundland Overseas Forestry Unit were no exception.

Post War. Sadly, the post war treatment of both the merchant mariners and foresters left little to laugh about. The remaining Newfoundland foresters were released from their contracts when the European war ended in May 1945, though many continued working until British timber imports returned to normal. Neither the Overseas Forestry Unit nor their brethren in the merchant navy received much consideration from the authorities, at least in the short-term. Classed as civilians, both groups were neglected by the Commissioners, and later the Canadian Government. In his work on the unit Tom Curran notes that the foresters, so eagerly sought for their expertise early in the war, appeared like an embarrassment to be sent home and forgotten. They and the merchant mariners were ineligible for many of the programs available to ex-armed forces personnel. The foresters were further disadvantaged by a low rate of pay that prevented them accumulating much in the way of savings.

This sorry state of affairs began to change in 1962 when ex-foresters were finally recognized under the Civilian War Allowances Act. In 1999 the merchant mariners were declared veterans equivalent to those from the armed services, while the following year they and the foresters were made eligible for pensions and benefits. The merchant marine was further honoured in 2003 when 3 September was declared Merchant Navy Veterans' Day. A memorial was unveiled outside St. John's Marine Institute in 1997 to commemorate those Newfoundland and Labrador merchant sailors who helped win the war, and to recognize the more than 300 of their number who died in the fight.[28]

....

Wartime Women

Women at War. Among the names inscribed on the Marine Institute's Merchant Marine Memorial is that of Stewardess Bride Fitzpatrick of Bay Roberts, who was lost when the *Caribou* was sunk. Ms. Fitzpatrick was the only Newfoundland woman to lose her life with the merchant navy in World

War II. Her sacrifice reminds us that, though ineligible for front-line duty in those days, the women of Newfoundland and Labrador did their part in seeing their homeland through two devastating World Wars. Some, like Ms. Fitzpatrick, paid for their devotion with their lives.

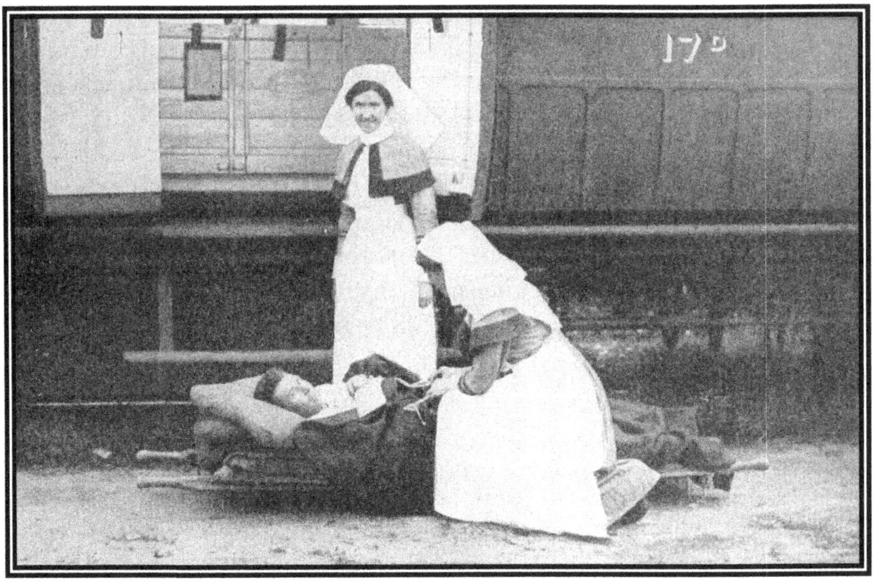

Nurses tending to a patient, World War I

During the Great War a number of Newfoundland and Labrador women served as nurses, either in their professional capacity, or as members of the Volunteer Aid Detachment (VAD). Receiving a short course of training, the VAD nurses were active in hospitals, as ambulance drivers, cooks, maids and clerks. The VAD was formed by the British Red Cross in 1909, and Newfoundland's first VAD nurses went overseas in 1915. By the end of hostilities more than three dozen Newfoundland and Labrador women had enlisted with the VAD, one of the few ways they could actively serve in those days. Despite the long hours, difficult working conditions, and the traumatic events they witnessed, Jenny Higgins points out that the VAD experience gave women a sense of independence and self-reliance they had never known before.

The interwar period saw Newfoundland women relegated to the traditional roles they occupied before 1914, but a new conflict offered renewed opportunities. During World War II many Newfoundlanders and Labradorians served with the Canadian forces, and among this number were more than 200 women. These women served with all three branches of the Canadian forces as members of the RCAF Women's Division, the Canadian Women's Army Corps and the Women's Royal Canadian Navy Service. In an article for the *Newfoundland and Labrador Heritage* website Higgins notes that the main goal behind enlisting the women was to free up men for front-line duty. Although many of their duties involved what was then considered "women's work," and they received lower pay rates than their male counterparts, many women went on to prove their worth in jobs like signalling and intelligence operations.

The Royal Canadian Air Force (RCAF) was first off the mark in its Newfoundland recruiting, and went on to enlist more local women than either the Army or Navy. The original Women's Air Force members left Newfoundland in July 1942, with the Army's and Navy's first women volunteers sailing about a year later. By the end of the war many military jobs were opened to women recruits including transport drivers, telephone operators, lab technicians, photographers, teletype operators and messengers. When the war ended some women wished to remain with the armed forces, but all three women's divisions were disbanded by the Fall of 1946. It was only in 1951, during the Korean War, that women could enlist once more.

Like their male counterparts, Isles women made their own contribution in uniform, through volunteers like Gertrude Layman, Annie Jones, Mary Snow and Lorna Scott, Fogo Island's first female servicepeople. Though not serving in uniform, another Fogo Island resident, Margaret (McKenna) Butt, made her own unique contribution to the war effort. Mrs. Butt's story was recounted to Sonya M. Foley for the book *The Women of Fogo Island: Hear Them Speak*. She recalled being asked to serve as an aircraft spotter, possibly because, as Postmistress, Butt had one of her community's few telephones. Though planes didn't normally land on Fogo Island, there were many passing overhead during the war. It was Mrs. Butt's job to run outside whenever she heard the telltale noise of aircraft engines and note, as best she could, what the plane looked like. Presumably her work was intended to alert the authorities of the presence of enemy planes. Mrs. Butt was not aware of anyone else who performed this duty, for which she was not paid.

<u>The Home Front and the WPA</u>. Though women were more than willing to serve, the era of the World Wars was still male-dominated. Uniformed personnel were overwhelmingly men. This did not mean that the women's part was insignificant, and their presence on the home front was especially strong. This trend did not start with the Second World War. Women, along with

children and non-combatant men, all did their part to see the troops through to victory in two world conflicts.

Unlike Margaret Butt, mentioned above, some women *did* receive a gratuity for their valuable work on the home front, even if it wasn't an official salary. During the First World War Miss S. Foley served as a telegraph operator at Twillingate. At their annual meeting of 6 April 1918 the Directors of the Twillingate Telephone & Electric Company voted that the sum of $10.00 be paid to Foley for her "...very valuable services in reading out the war news to the phone holders."[29] Miss Foley would probably have done so even without such recognition.

The full story of what locals did for their boys overseas will probably never be known, but the *Twillingate Sun* ran numerous stories about the events and fundraisers Isles residents organized in support of the troops. One of the first of these types of events was a patriotic concert staged at Fogo in the Fall of 1914.

> Last Friday week some of the young people of this place held a patriotic concert in the L.O.A. Hall which the society patriotically gave free of charge. It was a doubtful looking morning but the evening turned out fine and the Hall was packed. Everybody seemed pleased with the performance and the performers knowing that they were working for a good cause and being encouraged by the splendid audience to do their best. The gross receipts were $67 and after expenses are paid the Patriotic Fund will benefit by over $60. After the concert the Rev. Father O'Brien gave a very patriotic address and called upon us all to forget our differences and stand shoulder to shoulder to defend or help those who are defending those glorious liberties which we enjoy as British subjects.[30]

Fundraisers of this type were staged through two World Wars, and this community activity was greatly assisted by a number of volunteer organizations, some active in both conflicts. The Newfoundland Patriotic Association (NPA), originally the Men's Patriotic Association, had been formed during World War I and later disbanded. It reformed in 1940 to help with recruiting, and to ensure that programmes like pensions would be available to those returning from military service. The World War II version of the NPA was especially noted for its innovative and successful fundraising efforts. During World War II the Red Cross was active in Newfoundland caring for the survivors of U-boat attacks. Many other organizations like the YMCA and St. John Ambulance played commendable roles in the local war effort.

Women's Patriotic Association founder Lady Margaret Davidson (right), and her Husband, Newfoundland Governor Sir Walter Davidson

The group most associated with Newfoundland and Labrador women was the Women's Patriotic Association (WPA), active on the Isles during 1914-18 and again from 1939-45. The original WPA was founded in 1914, largely through the efforts of Lady Margaret Agnes Davidson (1871-1964), Wife of Newfoundland Governor Sir Walter Edward Davidson (1859-1923). The Daughter of General Hon. Sir Percy Fielding (1827-1904) and his Wife Lady Louisa Thynne (d. 1919), Margaret wed Walter Davidson in 1907. Her voluntary efforts were wide-ranging, and Lady Davidson was made a Dame Commander of the Order of the British Empire for her work with the Red Cross, and her involvement with the Scouting and Girl Guide movements.

By war's end Lady Davison's brainchild, the WPA, had some 200 branches in the Colony, and could boast over 15,000 members, drawn from all walks of life. With the close of hostilities the WPA devoted its attention to child welfare causes, but was Disbanded in 1921. The WPA was revived in 1939 by another Governor's Wife, Lady Eileen Walwyn.[31] During both wars the primary goal of the WPA was to provide comforts like knitted socks to the troops overseas. The WPA also helped prepare bandages and, in World War II, it provided recreation services for servicepeople.

While the main WPA organization was founded at St. John's, the ladies of our rocky isles were by no means backward in their efforts to help. A group similar to the WPA, and later merged with it, was founded at Twillingate in 1914, the Colony's first such aid organization. In 1915, ten months after the group was inaugurated, the *Twillingate Sun* carried a report on the local WPA's activities and origins. Editor Temple recalled that the society,

> ...had its beginning in a meeting of ladies held in the Courthouse on August 20th 1914, Magistrate Scott inaugurated the society and thirteen ladies who were present signed the roll. From these Mrs. L. Earle was elected President, Mrs. Facey Vice-prest. and Mrs. W. B. Temple Sec.-Treas.
>
> A circular was prepared by the secretary and copies mailed throughout the District. The result was a gratifying gift of socks from many parts of the district, while some other places affiliated with the main society and sent their gifts direct to St. John's. As a result of the appeal the society was able to forward last October a bale of socks containing 1144 pairs.
>
> ...Twillingate people contributed out of the first shipment of socks some 360 pairs. During the winter forty two flannel shirts and 57 pairs of socks were shipped, while by first steamer this spring 119 pairs of socks were sent forward...[32]

The Twillingate WPA also worked at producing dayshirts for the troops, and held a social which raised forty-five dollars for Belgian relief. Two other Twillingate branches of the WPA later came into being, the WPA II (Durrell) and the WPA III (Crow Head). The WPA organized many events to benefit soldiers and sailors, including a garden party at the Twillingate Masonic Hall. The party was staged to honour a number of servicemen – Garland Rogers, Fred Randell, Isaac Keefe, Harold Young, George Osmond and Albert Young – home on leave, and to entertain the families of all those serving overseas. In 1917 the WPA III organized a cooked supper fundraiser at Crow Head, while the groups also packed Christmas parcels to send to the front lines. In 1918 the WPA sponsored lectures at Tizzard's Harbour and Twillingate by Rev. Captain Clayton, a veteran of the Western Front.

Perhaps the most appreciated of all the WPA's gifts to the servicemen were the knitted socks and other items of clothing sent to the Front. In some cases women attached a note to the socks containing their name and address, hoping that the recipient would write back. Many letters of gratitude were sent to the donors, and the Sun reprinted a number of these. These short notes say far better than anything else how treasured small comforts from home were to the troops, and how important were the WPA's services to morale in the World Wars. One letter that appeared in the Sun during 1918 read as follows:

On Active Service
Jan. 24th, 1918.
Miss Kate Horwood
Dear Friend: —

I received a pair of socks a couple of days ago with a note enclosed in them from you asking the person that received them to write you. Well here I am and I am very thankful to you for the socks. Its [*sic*] very good of you folk at home sending us out socks and shirts. This is the second time I have had socks from Twillingate with notes in them, the first was from a Mrs. E. G. Linfield maybe you know her. I am quite sure all the boys are very pleased with the socks we get from home especially now we are getting it very muddy and a pair of dry socks are always a welcome guest. I shall have to put my address here as it might be crossed out, it is Pte. Jas. F. Hibbs, No. 299 1st, Newfoundland Regt. B. E. F. France.

I hope my letter reaches you safely and that if you have time you will answer it. So thanking you again I will close.

I remain yours sincerely,
Jas. Hibbs.[33]

In 1939 local chapters of the WPA once again took up the challenge of providing servicemen on the front lines with some comforts from home. Knitted socks were no less valued than they had been in the First World War.

In an interview for *The Women of Fogo Island*, Anora (Cull) Osmond recalled that wool was sent out from St. John's to knit the socks, and the WPA ladies were given a pattern to work from. Mrs. Osmond's Sister was a skilled knitter, though she had less experience. Many years later Osmond was still proud of her first successful effort at knitting the socks on her own.

As it had done twenty-five years earlier, the *Twillingate Sun* continued its coverage of the local WPA's patriotic work. The Twillingate WPA's year-end report for 1942, published in the paper, gives the following:

> On Thursday evening, 7th inst., the Twillingate Branch of the Women's Patriotic Association met at the Court House for their Annual Meeting...The election of officers was as follows: Hon. President, Mrs. A. J. Wood, re-elected. Hon. 1st Vice-Pres., Mrs. E. J. Linfield, re-elected. Hon. 2nd Vice-Pres., Mrs. T. J. Pitt, re-elected. Hon. Secretary, Miss Dorothy Hodder, re-elected. Hon. Asst. Secretary, Miss Eleanor Peyton, re-elected. Hon. Treasurer, Mrs J. C. Loveridge, re-elected.
>
> During the past year 21 meetings were held, 218½ lbs. wool, valued $416.95, were received and the average attendance of membership was 38. Comforts for our fighting forces forwarded to Headquarters, consisted of 162 prs. Socks, 81 prs. Mitts, 56 prs. Gloves, 51 Helmets, and 140 Sweaters.[34]

The full value of the WPA's contribution to the fighting forces overseas cannot be measured by territory gained, or even in purely economic terms. *Twillingate Sun* Editor William Temple may have summed up their importance as well as anyone. Though writing in 1915, his words apply equally to the Women's Patriotic Associations of both World Wars. He proclaimed "[t]hat the cause of Britain must triumph when her women are so interested on her behalf ...and our own boys will fight the better when they know that there are many "Sister Susies" knitting and working and thinking of them."[35]

....

The Sandy Cove (Tilting) Radar Station

Though the World Wars impacted the Isles in many ways, there were few physical reminders of the conflicts on our shores. One of the rare exceptions was the infrastructure established by our American allies. During the Second

World War the US military constructed several major bases in Newfoundland and Labrador, including the Argentia Naval Air Station and Fort Pepperrell, the Americans' Newfoundland headquarters base. Twillingate was home to a US Coast Guard station, which in 1945 was manned by sixteen personnel under commanding officer Richard J. McGuire. Another important American military facility on the Isles was located at Sandy Cove, near Tilting. Mentioned in ENL, the station's story is recounted in detail in John N. Cardoulis' work *A Friendly Invasion. The American Military in Newfoundland: 1940-1990*; it also features in Robert Mellin's architectural/sociological account of Tilting.

Soon after they entered the war in late 1941 the Americans initialized plans to build radar stations in Newfoundland as an early warning measure against enemy activity. As part of a classified mission, members of the US Army Signal Corps 685th Air Warning Company were dispatched to Newfoundland. Sandy Cove was selected as the site for the Americans' first North Atlantic ground radar station.

Construction of the Sandy Cove base began in the Summer of 1942, though no civilians on Fogo Island were sure why it was being built – until 1944 most people knew only that the US was carrying out weather observations. Work on the facility began at once. All supplies were transported to Fogo Island by sea, and the station was ready to receive its permanent staff – fifty-two personnel, including officers and a medical contingent – at the end of Summer 1942. The American facility had a total of ten buildings, including a barracks, headquarters, radar shack and warehouses. The radar shack was off limits to anyone without proper clearance, and the area was guarded by soldiers, attack dogs, and a screen of heavy machine guns. The radar unit was equipped with a twenty-four metre, motor-driven antenna, giving the station a range of about 240 kilometres. As Cardoulis notes, this range was not great when compared to modern tracking facilities, but did allow Fogo Island to provide Gander Airfield and Fort Pepperrell with early waring of enemy activity. In 1943 a new antenna was installed, effectively doubling the station's range.

By 1943 Sandy Cove was one of a series of five Newfoundland radar units operated by American forces. Each of these was assigned a secret code name. Sandy Cove, which Cardoulis asserts was the most active station, was code-named *Quad*. Supplied from St. John's by sea using the vessel *Captain Mitchell*, the Sandy Cove facility saw its personnel numbers reduced in late 1944, as Allied forces were clearly winning the European war. In early 1945 Sandy Cove and its sister stations were closed, and their infrastructure turned over to the Newfoundland Government. Today only fading memories remain of Sandy Cove's own World War II military facility. Still, Mellin notes that echoes of the American presence remain at Tilting, where visiting military personnel struck up friendships and romances with locals that lasted for decades. Like the Fogo Marconi station, the Sandy Cove radar facility saw a good deal of its furniture and building materials recycled into local homes and outbuildings. The station, and the World Wars, were things of the past.

The Sandy Cove radar station

13

Medical Matters

Twillingate Medicine

Early Doctors. The Notre Dame Bay Memorial Health Centre is a venerable institution on Newfoundland's northeast coast. Though it is a familiar symbol of local medicine today, the Memorial Hospital didn't provide Twillingate residents with their first health care – the town had medical services some 100 years before the hospital was built.

The community's first resident doctor was Dr. Robert Tremblett. Probably a native of St. John's, Tremblett practised at Twillingate from 1822 until his death twenty years later. He was appointed as health officer for the community during the cholera scare of 1832.

About 1850 William Stirling Jr. set up practice on Twillingate's North Side. Born in 1813 (or 1818), Stirling received a MD from the University of Edinburgh and a diploma from Edinburgh's College of Surgeons. In his practice Dr. Stirling combined the duties of general practitioner and surgeon. Stirling married Ann Peyton, and the couple had several children, including renowned opera soprano Georgina (See Chapter Nine). Dr. Stirling died at Twillingate on 10 April 1890.

Another Twillingate doctor of the era was named Chandler, and he was followed by Frederick I. R. Stafford. Stafford was born at Montreal on 28 February 1856, and was a graduate of McGill University. He arrived in Newfoundland around 1878, setting up practice at Little Bay Mines. Stafford married Elizabeth, Daughter of Stipendiary Magistrate J. B. Blandford of Little Bay. The couple had four children, Augustus, Bennett, Amy and Lily. Stafford relocated to Twillingate in 1882, remaining there until 1906 when he moved to St. John's. In later years Stafford became known for his pharmaceutical business and medical preparations like Stafford's Phoratone. He died 5 March 1920.

At the turn of the twentieth century Nova Scotian Dr. Owen Van Buskirk Smith spent five years in Twillingate, until appointed medical officer for the Cape Copper Company at Tilt Cove in 1900. Nigel Rusted believes that after Stafford's departure Harvard graduate John Peter Smith may have also practised at Twillingate. Local phone company records from 1916 mention a Dr. Smith, and it appears that he left the town in that year.

Twillingate's last private-practice physicians were Dr. Isaac LeDrew and A. J. "Doccy" Wood. Prior to serving as a doctor LeDrew was the second Principal of the Central Superior (High) School at Twillingate from 1897 to 1900. LeDrew then resigned to take a medical degree in Canada, graduating from the University of Toronto. On his return Doctor LeDrew became a member of the Methodist Educational Board, serving from 1906 to 1912. He practised at Twillingate from 1904 to 1933. He later set up practice in St. John's. LeDrew was also noted for opposing, and then boycotting, Twillingate's Memorial Hospital project.

Albert J. Wood was a 1905 graduate of Tufts University, Boston. Wood started his practice at Herring Neck in 1907, and worked out of Fogo from1908-11. He then settled permanently at Twillingate, where he practised until just prior to his death in 1959. Wood was known for his friendly manner and love of children, whom he always addressed as "my little woman" or "my little man." Unlike LeDrew, Wood was a champion of the Memorial Hospital, from where his general practice was later based.

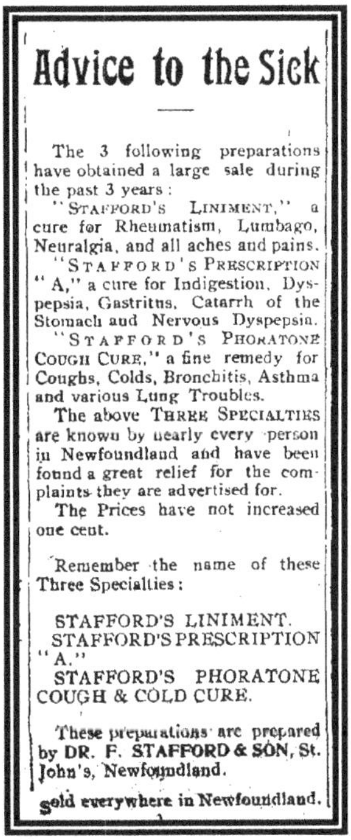

Advice to the Sick

The 3 following preparations have obtained a large sale during the past 3 years:

"Stafford's Liniment," a cure for Rheumatism, Lumbago, Neuralgia, and all aches and pains.

"Stafford's Prescription "A," a cure for Indigestion, Dyspepsia, Gastritus, Catarrh of the Stomach and Nervous Dyspepsia.

"Stafford's Phoratone Cough Cure," a fine remedy for Coughs, Colds, Bronchitis, Asthma and various Lung Troubles.

The above Three Specialties are known by nearly every person in Newfoundland and have been found a great relief for the complaints they are advertised for.

The Prices have not increased one cent.

Remember the name of these Three Specialties:

STAFFORD'S LINIMENT.
STAFFORD'S PRESCRIPTION "A."
STAFFORD'S PHORATONE COUGH & COLD CURE.

These preparations are prepared by DR. F. STAFFORD & SON, St. John's, Newfoundland.

Sold everywhere in Newfoundland.

Twillingate Sun *ad for Stafford's medicines, 1915*

The Wild Cove Hospital. Around the time Doctors Stafford, Smith, LeDrew and Wood were active at Twillingate the town had its own small hospital facility. Located about half a kilometre outside Wild Cove, on North Twillingate Island, the hospital was listed in *McAlpine's 1898 Community*

Gazetteer. At that time its keeper was Lucy Simms, with Selina Roberts assuming the role in 1903. It was noted that in 1912 the matron received $40.00 per annum for her services. A *Twillingate Sun* article from that year reported that the facility was first used to accommodate suspected small pox sufferers off a ship that arrived from Montreal; the vessel's mate died, and was apparently buried on Burnt Island.[1] Following this incident the building was used for housing victims of infectious diseases, though admission required authorization from medical authorities in St. John's.

Evidence suggests that the institution operated into the mid 1920s. Early in 1920 a telephone was installed at the hospital by the Twillingate Telephone and Electric Company "...for the convenience of Wild Cove and Crow Head people..."[2] This was a temporary measure until a phone line was completed to the Long Point Light House. In May of that year Dr. LeDrew petitioned the company for a permanent phone at the hospital, but the Directors felt this could only be done at government request, since the hospital was "...a governmental institution." Apparently some long-term arrangement was made which lasted until 1925. In that year repairman Edwin Colbourne was instructed to "...have [the] phone taken from [the] old Hospital at Wild Cove as soon as possible."[3]

In 1927 the hospital was hauled away across the ice to become a nurses' residence at the new Notre Dame Bay Memorial Hospital, which opened in 1924. The Hospital Association,

> ...decided to have the old hospital building at Wild Cove removed to the site of the Memorial Hospital where it is purposed to be converted into a nurses' home...Messers Jonas Elliott and George Roberts are now making preparations for the launching [of] the Wild Cove Hospital building...to some convenient place near the Hospital. Now that the ice at Wild cove is in good condition it is thought advisable to move the building immediately.[4]

<u>The Notre Dame Bay Memorial Health Centre</u>. Though the Wild Cove Hospital, and doctors like Wood and LeDrew, served their community well, the feeling grew that something more than private practise doctors and a small infectious diseases hospital were needed, not just for Twillingate but for all of Notre Dame Bay. In the mid 1920s NDB had only four physicians outside Twillingate. The nearest hospitals, apart from one that briefly served miners at Pilley's Island, were at St. Anthony, 144 kilometres away by sea, and at St .John's, 400 kilometres away.

At the end of World War One locals started a movement to establish their own full service hospital. The idea had first been proposed in 1913, but the plans were delayed due to the war. A 1919 meeting at Twillingate's Alexandra Hall was presided over by the famous northern doctor Sir Wilfred Grenfell, a longtime advocate of a hospital for the large area of Notre Dame Bay. Despite Grenfell's role in the project, the Twillingate Hospital was not a Grenfell Mission Hospital, as is sometimes assumed.

Twillingate Sun editor William Temple campaigned actively for funds through the paper's columns. Former Sun editor, Magistrate George Roberts, also promoted the hospital project, contributing his own large donation. It was Roberts, along with the local SUF, who originally interested Wilfred Grenfell in the plan. Sadly, Roberts never lived to see the hospital completed. At the Alexandra Hall meeting $1,800 in subscriptions were raised for the hospital project. Grenfell played a key role in securing a large donation – sources say either $25,000 or $50,000 – from the Commonwealth Fund (CF) in New York. $5,000 came from the British Red Cross, and $10,000 from the Newfoundland Government. The Twillingate Hustler's Club, made up mainly of youths, raised $15,000.00 for equipment. Besides plays, for which Georgina Stirling helped them rehearse, the Hustlers sold crafts, put off concerts and held bake sales.

While Twillingate's efforts were impressive, the credit for fundraising cannot go to any one community. A "Statement of Receipts" issued through the *Twillingate Sun* details the contributions made by other Isles towns: Summerford – $176.30; Cottles Island – $60.00; Bridgeport – $101.00; Moreton's Harbour – $443.95; Herring Neck – $938.85; Tizzard's Harbour – $158.50; Fogo – $892.00; Change Islands – $1,085.35.[5] Many other NDB towns collected funds for the new facility, while locales like St. John's and Toronto were also represented as donors. This was truly a case of pulling together, and recognition of the great need the hospital was intended to fill. The hospital was also meant as a tribute to area residents who had been wounded or died in the Great War.

The Notre Dame Bay Memorial Hospital Association was formed under the Companies Act in 1920, with Dr. Grenfell as its only member from outside Twillingate. It was later incorporated and empowered to elect Directors for an annual term, to supervise building of the structure, and to oversee operations when the hospital was ready for patients. Grenfell, along with eight Twillingate residents, including Sun editor Temple, and businessman Arthur Hodge, who Chaired the Hospital's first Board of Director's meeting, signed the articles of association on 23 June 1920. J. W. Minty was named the Association's first business manager, serving until 1938. Arthur Hodge's Wife

Elsie was also prominent in the success of the Memorial Hospital. Arriving at Twillingate with Dr. Grenfell, she worked at the new facility for two years without pay. Mrs. Hodge started off as an operating room nurse, and was later named the hospital's head nurse.

Board of Directors scouting a site for the new hospital. L-R: Elias Young; Arthur Manuel; Arthur H. Hodge; George Blandford; Dr. Charles Parsons; Charles White; Benjamin Roberts; J. W. Minty, and Henry Rideout. Captain James Gillett is believed to be standing partially out of frame at the right of the photograph

With help from Dr. Grenfell, a site was chosen on South Side, near a good source of water. Its plans were drawn up by prominent New York architect William Adams Delano, an admirer of Grenfell. The plans were given to Dr. Charles Parsons, later the hospital's Administrator, once bids for construction were requested. Local mason and builder Henry W. Rideout, who had trained in England and worked with several large New York building firms, was awarded the contract, worth $50,000.00. Rideout began work in mid June 1921. The plans set out a full basement about thirty-six metres by twelve metres, which had to be drilled by hand then blasted from solid rock. The job was largely done manually, using locals trained on the job. Rideout schooled his men in the arts of concrete mixing, masonry and plastering. Concrete blocks used in the building were designed by Rideout, and made by him and his crew. Total expenditure on the initial phase of the project came to about $100,000.00. Building took three years, not counting the Winters. The Notre Dame Bay Memorial Hospital was officially opened by the Governor, Sir William Lamond Allardyce (1861-1930) and Lady Elsie Elizabeth Allardyce

(1878-1962), who arrived on HMS *Wisteria*, on 30 September 1924. It received its first patients on 1 October.

The Notre Dame Bay Memorial Hospital, 1926

The original hospital was kept in good, clean condition and lit by its own water-driven generator. The first floor had x-ray equipment (after 1936), an outpatient department, a darkroom, laboratory and its own pharmacy. Offices, staff dining rooms and doctors' quarters were found in the west wing. Most of the second floor was taken up by patient wards, one for women and one for men. The east section was home to a kitchen, linen room, and bathrooms. There was also a private, and two semi-private rooms. The northwest corner of the hospital was occupied by the operating room, with an outside space for sterilization. On the west end of the building both the first and second floors had a solarium. Staff used the bottom, while the top was reserved for tuberculosis (TB) patients. Besides the two main floors, there was a top floor containing a small medical library. Wood for the rafters and roof came from a schooner wreck. The hospital's main kitchen (which served more than 50,000 meals per year), laundry rooms and food storage area were all in the basement. There were also some bedrooms, plus a dining area for the hospital's maids and nursing assistants. The basement's east end was taken up by steam boilers which heated the building. In 1953 a much needed dental clinic was opened at the Hospital by Premier Smallwood.

Apart from the main hospital, there were a number of outbuildings. Just to the west was the two-storey nurses' residence, which had been hauled from Wild Cove by 600 volunteers. A residence for Administrator Dr. Parsons was also hauled to the site, but not from so far away. There was also a concrete warehouse, a workshop, a barn, and root-cellars to store food. The hospital was almost self-sufficient in meals, making numerous preserves, and having its own livestock. At the time the Hospital opened the property owned by the Association was valued at $103,500.00.

The first Medical Superintendent was Doctor Parsons, Johns Hopkins Medical School class of 1919, who served until his resignation in 1934. Parsons had been working as Medical Officer in charge of Battle Harbour, Labrador. It is a tribute to Grenfell's commitment that he released Parsons from his duties there to go to Twillingate. During his tenure Dr. Parsons normally had a single qualified doctor acting as his assistant. The doctors were usually replaced on an annual basis, and were aided by American medical school students who came to Twillingate at Parsons' invitation during their Summer holidays.

One of these students was Connecticut-born John McKee Olds. Olds had been invited out to Twillingate in the Summer of 1930 and promised a job following his internship, if he wanted it. The young doctor returned in 1932 with his bride, Elizabeth "Betty" Arms, herself a Johns Hopkins School of Nursing graduate. Olds eventually replaced Charles Parsons (who died at Philadelphia in 1940), serving with the hospital in some capacity until the 1980s. Born in 1906, Olds lived mainly in his adopted home town until he passed away in 1985. Though his manner was generally gruff, Olds was well-respected by the patients he served.

Doctor Olds, or "Hose" as his name was often pronounced locally, was also known for introducing one of Newfoundland's first medical insurance schemes, the "contract plan." J. T. H. Connor speculates that one inspiration for the contract plan may have come from the Swiss physician/historian Henry Sigerist, a professor at Old's *alma mater*, and an exponent of socialized medicine. Dr. Olds' plan had two components, one for better-off families, and another portion for communities as a whole. The expensive contract cost ten dollars, but guaranteed a family all medical care free. The blanket contract covered all persons in a community. To make the plan work Olds parcelled the bay into thirty-nine districts; any settlement wishing to join formed a Committee, and families were assessed forty-four cents a head. Amounts raised entitled everyone to basically the same level of care as the expensive contract, excepting a nominal fee for some services like x-rays, lab work and medicine. The contract system remained in place, largely unaltered, until 1958. By 1945 the money generated by the contracts brought in more revenue than the government grant. The contract system was only one of many contributions J. M. Olds made to the life of patients in Notre Dame Bay, and Twillingate's high school is named in his honour. His efforts also garnered Olds the Order of Canada and the Continental Medal.

Doctor and Mrs. Olds, with Twillingate Sun *editor Ernest Clarke at left*

The need for a system of contracts highlights some of the problems faced in funding a hospital in pre Confederation Newfoundland. Unlike the Grenfell Hospital at St. Anthony, which was funded by an endowment, the Memorial Hospital had to meet expenses by payments for services from some of the better off patients, plus government grants, private donations and gifts (this apart from the contract money). On 17 January 1926, for example, churches across Notre Dame Bay held a "Hospital Sunday," donating monies collected to the cause. Two years later a "sacred concert" of music and singing was held at St. Peter's Church to benefit the hospital. With a large crowd in attendance, the concert raised $68.15 in collections from audience members, plus an additional $10.10 pledged by the church. One week later, on 21 March

1928, the successful fund raiser was repeated at Twillingate's South Side United Church. In 1946 Commissioner for Health and Welfare John C. Puddister (1881-1947) wrote that, "I believe the organization there [Twillingate] succeeds in collecting money where a Government Department would find it extremely difficult to do so."[6]

The Loveridge diaries record that about two months after the 1926 Hospital Sunday fund raiser, Charles L. Hodge and Arthur Colbourne travelled to St. John's to arrange an additional grant for the facility.[7] On 15 March word was received that the government had granted an additional $5,000.00 per annum. The grant was eventually set at $28,000.00, allowing the Hospital to operate with only a minor deficit. Apparently the Memorial Hospital was a good bargain for the money. The *Twillingate Sun* reported that in 1927 upkeep costs for the facility stood at $2.70 per patient per day, compared to $5.70 at St. John's General Hospital.

The government's grant provided free care for patients too poor to make payment under the contract system. At the end of its first year the Hospital had provided 7,500 days of patient care, a figure which rose to 17,000 days by 1928. The scale of the Memorial Hospital's operations can be gauged by a report prepared for Secretary of State for Dominion Affairs, Viscount Cranbourne (1893-1972), by Governor Walwyn on 14 October 1943. Walwyn's report gives the following statistics:

	1936-7	**1937-8**	**1938-9**	**1939-40**
Total days of care	25148	28176	28422	31930
Average number of patients per diem	68.89	77.12	77.87	87.4
Number of admissions	593	732	745	835
Number of discharges	593	738	745	825
Mortality rate	1.9%	4.5%	1.7%	2.99%
Number of x-rays	368	642	715	739
Number of operations	402	521	532	633

From: PANL, GN 38, Commission of Government, Public Health & Welfare, Medical Services

By the late 1920s it was found that the Hospital, which many thought would be too big, was too small. The TB problem was most to blame, requiring long term care with little turn-over in beds. *Mycobacteria tuberculosis*, or TB, was a disease prevalent in many Newfoundland communities until about the 1960s. TB infected the bones and internal organs, essentially causing them to rot. It related to Newfoundland's pre Confederation poverty, since malnourished people are more susceptible. Tuberculosis required a long period of convalescence. In some years almost half the beds at the hospital were taken up by long-term tuberculosis patients. Fundraising for expansion began in 1928. The following year a second grant of $50,000.00 was received from the CF. The fund's executive were quite impressed by the efforts of locals in establishing a successful medical facility, serving 50,000 people, in such a remote locale. The CF funds were supplemented by a special government grant, plus private donations in America, Canada and Newfoundland. Henry Rideout set to work making more blocks, and a new wing was added to the hospital in March of 1931. Officially it now had beds for ninety patients, although there were sometimes many more than that.

In the 1930s Parsons and Olds tackled a health issue that was almost as serious in the Isles region as TB. Ironically, this disease could be easily prevented. During the Great Depression many people were out of work, or at least underemployed; there were few who would not work for some kind of wages, or even provisions. Actual starvation was a real fear, and the government issued "dole" rations to those certified as paupers. The dole issue amounted to about six cents daily for adults, providing enough food for about 1,200 calories per day. The problem was the vitamin value of the items allowed for, which stood at zero.

A lack of the vitamin thiamine (vitamin B) causes Beriberi, a condition marked by inflamation or degeneration of the nerves, digestive system and heart. In many cases patients become crippled, but often recover if treated in time. One of the main foods issued to dole recipients was white flour. Parsons knew that brown flour, substituted for white, would provide enough thiamin to prevent Beriberi. He initiated a campaign to have the dole ration of flour switched from white to brown. Dr. Parsons succeeded, though many people still got Beriberi due to the stigma attached to brown flour. Though poor, the people were proud, and eating brown flour was seen as somehow beneath them. Olds had to continue an education campaign after Doctor Parsons left. With Parsons successful in persuading the Commission of Government to substitute brown for white flour, the hospital was once given the flour in lieu of money to pay for infrastructure. As Doctor Robert Ecke later recounted, the commodity was sold to pay for a road on the hospital grounds, and the thoroughfare became known as the "Brown Flour Road." The local distaste for brown flour remained, and it was an unwelcome form of currency.

Floating clinic Bonnie Nell *at Twillingate's Coastal Wharf, with the schooner* Shirley C *at right*

While the Beriberi campaign was underway the hospital began operating a travelling clinic to serve the many bays and towns along the coast. Starting in 1936 the twenty-five ton motor vessel *Bonnie Nell* was chartered from Captain Elias Chaulk of Carmanville. The *Bonnie Nell* would transport medical staff to the smaller communities along the coast, and over sixty ports were visited in the first year. At first many people did not fully understand what the boat's purpose was, but by the second year most had caught on, and the ports of call rose to ninety-six. After two years the Directors voted to buy their own boat, but the first vessel tried was unsatisfactory. In the end the *Bonnie Nell* was purchased from Captain Chaulk. In 1952 a government grant allowed for the building of a larger vessel, the *Bonnie Nell II*, which was over sixty feet in length and boasted an eighty-four hp diesel engine. An undated document held at the Provincial Archives gives an account of one voyage made by the original *Bonnie Nell*:

Twillingate [Travelling] Clinic:

Total ports called at During Trip	28
Total Patients seen	564
Visits ashore by Medical officer	54
Local anaesthetics	218
Minor operations	11
General Anaesthetics	0
Teeth extractions	624
Cash Collected During Trip	$420.40

"Financial outlay and cost of Same Trip of Twillingate Travelling Clinic"

Hire of Boat & Crew 1⅓ months @ $150.00	$200.00
Gasoline & Lubricating oil	121.65
Pilotage	1.25
Doctor (Salary and keep)	420.00
Nurse (Salary and keep)	62.50
Drugs, Medicines and Equipment	110.00
[Total Expenses]	$915.40
Money Collected from patients	$420.40
Deficit	$495.00

Source: PANL. GN 38, Commission of Government,
Public Health and Welfare, General Administration

While the floating clinics were a godsend for isolated outports with few if any medical facilities, the above report makes it clear that the *Bonnie*

Nell was not a paying proposition.

There were other obstacles to overcome as well, since the boats were immobilized by ice for five to six months of the year. This meant that horses and dog teams were needed to reach patients in the Winter months. Snowmobiles came into use for house calls after World War II, until regular snow plowing started in 1960.

Aftermath of the hospital fire, 1943

Not all developments were positive for the hospital – the facility was hit by fire on two occasions. The first blaze, on 28 February 1939, saw the hospital cottage completely destroyed. Doctor Olds lost all his belongings, including a medical library, but luckily he and his family made it out safely. Doctor Ecke was a witness to the fire, which engulfed the upper storey of the cottage in only two minutes. Although Ecke and a number of others were able to save a few items, like the hospital's motorcycle, much was lost, including antique furniture Dr. Olds had bought from the Stirling family.

The second hospital fire was even more serious. On 28 February 1943, exactly four years after the cottage fire, part of the original hospital burned down, luckily with no fatalities. The greatest loss was the staff house and storage space. The *Twillingate Sun* offered this first-hand account of the blaze:

As the hours of darkness were fading away to daylight last Sunday morning, February 28th the startling cry of "fire" sounded down the corridors and throughout the wards of the Notre Dame Bay Memorial Hospital. Immediately the hospital staff rendered herculean and heroic service. Not looking to their own safety or mindful of saving their own personal belongings, many of whom lost practically all they possessed, their first thought was for the hundred and more patients under their care and supervision. Soon after the outbreak dense smoke issued from the source of the fire which appeared to have started on the top flat in or near the library, and poured downstairs and spread throughout the institution. An instant alarm was sounded around Twillingate and citizens were awakened by ringing of the church bell and general telephone calls. There quickly gathered on the spot hundreds of citizens.

Before many people reached the scene of the conflagration, the heroic staff of doctors and nurses and assistant nurses aided by the few who had by then responded to the alarm, had cleared the building of its patients, some of whom escaped by jumping from their beds and through the emergency exit on to the snow outside, clad only in their bed attire. Following the storm of the previous day and with the temperature near zero some patients were seen struggling in the snow in an effort to escape the flames which by then had broken through the centre roof of the main building and reflecting all around the town. Those escaping were at once lodged in surrounding homes and the two hotels nearby. How some of them were enabled to survive the ordeal can hardly be imagined – there were some very sick patients. There was no loss of life or injury, all having escaped safely.

Concurrent with the alarm the electric power cut off plunging the whole building, including the wing, into semi-darkness. This added to the difficulty of escape. An operation in progress at the time was continued and completed; aided by the emergency lighting system, the doctor remaining at his task. A baby was born at the time the alarm was given and together with the mother was rushed to a nearby home.

When evening came, what was once an up-to-date and modern equipped institution was now in reality partly ruins

> and the remainder damaged by smoke and water.
>
> Some of the equipment and patient's belongings were removed to the ground outside; but much was lost, as well as a large quantity of essential supplies stored for the winter months and reserve equipment. The L.O.A. and S.U.F. halls were immediately placed at the disposal of Dr. Olds, the Medical Superintendent, and some of the beds which were saved were moved to these buildings where a temporary hospital is being established...[8]

A great gloom fell over those connected to the hospital, but this was lessened when businessman Gerald S. Doyle pledged $1,000.00 towards reconstruction costs. A Rebuilding Committee began soliciting other donations. The Department of Health pledged it would match, dollar for dollar, any donations up to $90,000.00. In the end the Committee received $186,000.00 from various sources. St. John's architect William D. McCarter was commissioned to do the rebuilding, which took three years owing to wartime shortages.

Since the fire the Hospital has had its share of ups and downs. While the facility's books were sometimes in the red, expansion continued. On 25 March 1946, hospital Secretary Malcolm G. Loveridge reported to Puddister that "...an additional thirty (30) beds have been installed...which addition increases the bed capacity of the Hospital by 30%."[9]

The War prevented Olds from recruiting new doctors, and for several years he worked with little assistance. Following the War Dalhousie alumnus Doctor Louis E. Lawton of St. John's was recruited for the Memorial Hospital. After 1954 a number of doctors arrived from mainland Canada and England. In 1958, with the federalization of hospitals, doctor turn-over slowed down considerably. Three long-serving physicians who joined the staff in this era were Liborio "Bob" Garcia (1958) of the Philippines, along with Alfred H. Dennison (1962) and Fred W.Woodruff (1964) from England.

Their legacy is carried on by Mohamed Iqbal Ravalia. "Ravs," as he is familiarly known, has been a doctor at Twillingate since 1984. Originally from Zimbabwe, Ravalia was named Newfoundland and Labrador's Family Physician of the Year for 2004. He is also a winner of the Canadian Family Physician Award, and a two-time recipient of Memorial University's Community Teaching Award. Recently, Ravs has been the subject of a CBC radio documentary detailing his experiences as a "come from away" physician on Newfoundland's northeast coast.

Like doctors, nurses could also be a problem to recruit, especially during the war years, when the hospital could sometimes call on the services of only a single graduate nurse, along with a few nursing aides. In the beginning Dr. Parsons recruited nurses from the US, while a number of locals served as aides. The hospital's first staff nurses were E. McArthur and Olive Crowe. The first Head Nurse was Ethel Gordon Graham. Another well known Head Nurse was Stella Manuel, Daughter of merchant Arthur Manuel. During 1930-1, when Dr. Olds was interning at NDB Memorial, the nurses included Dorothy Blackman, Betty Arms, E. Robertson, Ethel Graham, Elinor Cooke and Joyce Scammell. After the war a number of English nurses were recruited by an employment agency, and from 1955-64 the hospital was served by several Mennonite nurses. Thereafter, nursing graduates from the Philippines helped fill gaps in the staff roster, and many Bay residents can recall the care provided by the Mennonite and Filipino nurses. The dedication of these professionals was demonstrated in 1969 when more than fifty of the hospital's nurses and aides, under Director of Nursing Goldie White, organized a twenty-four kilometre walk around the Twillingate Islands to raise money for training equipment.

NDB Memorial Health Centre at Twilight, 2011

Medical services in Notre Dame Bay greatly improved after World War II. Doctor Olds had long been advocating a replacement for the aging hospital, and the current Memorial Health Centre opened near the site of the original hospital on 24 September 1976. The new facility was built adjacent to the original structure, and the two were linked by an above-ground walkway. The old hospital has since been torn down, and the Twillingate war memorial stands on its site. Built at a cost of nine million dollars, the Memorial Health Centre was a sixty-five bed facility with nine examining rooms, compared to three in the old hospital. The hospital contained the Twillingate islands' first elevators, plus patient lounges and a physiotherapy department. The St. John's-based Newfoundland Engineering Company did the building's architectural work, while William Tiller & Company were responsible for electrical installation. The centre is now of less importance to locals as many procedures are performed regionally in St. John's, Gander and Grand Falls. While still a source of great pride in the community, the NDB Memorial Health Centre's main role today is as a primary health care site.

....

Fogo Island Healthcare

Private Physicians. Like Twillingate, long-settled Fogo Island has its own august tradition of medical services, often focussed on, or based in, the town of Fogo. We often think of early Newfoundland outports as having little or no health care. Research conducted by historian Jerry Bannister suggests otherwise. Starting in the late seventeenth century, English merchants would often engage the services of a medical practitioner called a "surgeon" – in those days a separate profession from a "physician" – to look after the welfare of his workers. All servants in the migratory fishery were required to sign on to the surgeon's books, paying a flat fee at the end of the fishing season. In case of injury or prolonged illness, the servant paid the "Doctor," as he was known, an extra fee.

Bannister found evidence of numerous surgeons, who sometimes doubled as Justices of the Peace or Magistrates, in early outport Newfoundland. Given this fact, it would be surprising if larger outports like Fogo and Twillingate did not have their own surgeons, at least during the fishing season. In this era Fogo was visited by George Cartwright. On Thursday, 8 August 1771 Cartwright and some associates made anchor in Fogo Harbour, where they proceeded to unload a cargo. Three days later Cartwright recorded that he sailed for Charles Harbour, accompanied by Mr. Bell, "the surgeon of this place." Assuming Cartwright sailed to Charles Harbour directly from Fogo, then this Mr. Bell would have been based at that port, though Cartwright does not make the point clearly.

Another commonality between Fogo Island's and Twillingate's medical history was the appearance of private-practise physicians long before the construction of a hospital. Conditions for these early doctors was not easy. Aside from covering the whole of Fogo Island in an era when transportation was primitive and roads few, the doctor was always "on call," even in the worst of weathers.

A doctor named Power may have practised at Fogo around 1825. It is possible that this man was Nicholas Power. Educated at Edinburgh, Power may have been the first native-born Newfoundlander to study medicine. He started a medical practice at St. John's in 1810 along with William Carson. In 1814 Power became one of the first two visiting physicians at the city's civilian hospital. Another doctor, Lambert Bryand, and his family were listed as Fogo residents in an 1836 census. Documents held by the Provincial Registry of Deeds indicate that St. John's medical doctor John Winter owned land at Fogo from 1848 to 1878, but whether he had a practice in the community is unknown.[10]

The first doctor who can be firmly established with a permanent practice at Fogo was Hay Findlater (1814-89). A Perth native, Findlater arrived at Fogo sometime before 1846. He married Susanna Winter of St. John's, and family tradition asserts that the couple met at a Government House dance. Apart from treating illness, Findlater served as a Justice of the Peace, Fogo's Foreign Consul to Spain, and on the local Road Board. According to Nigel Rusted, Findlater once carried out emergency surgery while suffering from a paralysed arm. The regard in which Findlater was held by his patients was reflected in his obituary:

> The death of the late Hay Findlater, Esq., M.D. of Fogo, was announced in last week's paper...For nearly fifty years he resided at Fogo and during that long period, was very successful in his profession; especially was he most skilful in that dreaded disease diphtheria which has made such ravages in St. John's during the past several months, but in treating the many patients that had come before him during his long professional career, very few fatal cases occurred, which is sufficient evidence of the skill he possessed in treating them. For some years past he had been somewhat an invalid, but notwithstanding he continued his practice, and many in need of his professional services, even from distant places, were glad enough to convey him to their homes and back to his own residence after being in attendance on the sick. Dr.

> Findlater was much beloved and respected by a large circle of acquaintances, and his death will be lamented in the community where he has so long resided, as well as in the adjacent localities where he has so many times administered ease to the suffering. He passed calmly to rest after a long and useful career, on the 23rd ult, at the ripe age of 73 years, and to the bereaved we tender our sympathy.[11]

Findlater was succeeded at Fogo by another Scot, Thomas Malcolm (1853-1907), who had previously practised in Nova Scotia. Malcolm arrived in the 1880s. Like Dr. Findlater, Malcolm provided his adopted home with much more than medical services. During his first years at Fogo Malcolm served with Findlater on the Road Board; the evidence suggests that both doctors had unpleasant experiences trying to reach patients on the ill-kept Fogo to Seldom road. Malcolm was also a figure of first-rank importance on the local judicial scene, serving as the town's Stipendiary Magistrate from 1898 until he died. Doctor Malcolm acted as a Commissioner of Pilots for Fogo, along with merchants Henry Earle and John Hodge. His medical clinic and residence, Lowland House, stood on the corner of Parson's Hill. It was purchased in 1884 from the family of English merchant Joseph B. Highmore Sr. Malcolm remained in practice for as long as he lived – he was reported to have delivered a baby on Fogo Island the same day he died.

Dr. Hugh F. Donahue and Daughter Margaret at Fogo, c.1914 (left). His Fogo dispensary is pictured at right

Shortly after the passing of Thomas Malcolm, Dr. Wood arrived from Herring Neck, remaining at Fogo until 1911. About the time Wood left for

Twillingate Dr. Hugh F. Donahue (1880-1956) came to Fogo. Donahue was born at Brooklyn, New York and earned his medical degree from McGill University, Montreal. Donahue and his Wife Ethel (McConniff) had several children, two of whom, James and Margaret, were born at Fogo. Sometime after 1914 the family moved to Torbay, where Donahue practised for several years before relocating to St. John's.

Other doctors at Fogo during the Great War era were Stephen Reginald Johnston and J. P. Sweeney. In the 1920s Queen's University alumnus Dr. John MacKenzie was practising in the community. During the late 1930s and early 1940s New York Medical College graduate S. A. Beckwith, and Jefferson University MD W. A. Swanker were the local doctors. Documents from a Magisterial inquiry held at Fogo record that in November 1938 Beckwith had been present during a tragic fire at Eastern Tickle that claimed the life of a small boy. He stated that "[w]hen I arrived to the scene of the fire the house was practically burnt down. I remained until it was possible to remove what remained of the body of a child that had been entrapped in the house."[12]

An interesting Fogo physician was Dr. Eric Wermuth, who worked in the community during 1943. Born in 1914, Wermuth was an Austrian national who graduated from the University of Vienna in 1937. When Austria became part of Nazi Germany the following year the young doctor fled his homeland. In 1939 Wermuth was living in Britain when he was among a small group of physicians recruited to work in Newfoundland. From 1940-8 Dr. Wermuth practised in several Newfoundland communities, including the capital, St. John's. In 1941 he married Madeline Martin of St. John's, and following her death wed another Newfoundlander, Evelyn (Ash) Rossiter. In 1948 Wermuth moved to London, Ontario where he carried on a successful practice for thirty years. He retired to British Columbia, and died in 1986.

Though recruited by the Newfoundland authorities, Wermuth's origins always made him the target of official suspicion during the war years. As Malcolm MacLeod notes, with every new posting in Newfoundland, concerns were raised that Wermuth was an enemy spy. He was kept under surveillance and his mail was censored. When it was proposed that Wermuth go to Fogo in 1943 the General commanding US forces in Newfoundland wondered wether he could be trusted in a community so close to the Sandy Cove radar station, Gander Airport, and large oil storage facilities. In the context of wartime fears the surveillance maintained on Wermuth may have been justified. Still, there was little evidence implicating the doctor in spying, and his treatment marks a shameful chapter in Newfoundland medical history.

Though many of the doctors who practised on Fogo Island prior to the twenty-first century lived in Fogo, there were some exceptions. A doctor was noted at Joe Batt's Arm in the 1870s, and the 15 August 1908 issue of the *Twillingate Sun* carried the story of an operation carried out jointly by three local physicians, one of whom was a Dr. Anderson of Joe Batt's Arm. A Provincial Archive document mentions a doctor named McLean who was living at Joe Batt's Arm around 1912.[13] Likewise, after spending several years at Fogo, Dr. McKenzie relocated to Joe Batt's Arm in 1930, and stayed there until around 1938. During this period it appears that Fogo had no doctor of its own, a situation that only changed with Dr. Beckwith's arrival.

Nurses and Midwives. Newfoundland's first nurses were noted at St. John's in 1814, though they had no formal medical training. Two notable early nurses at St. John's were the Cowan Sisters, Janet and Agnes. Like their predecessors, the Cowans were not formally trained as nurses. Other important caregivers in the nineteenth century were nuns like the Irish Sisters of Mercy. In 1893 the first two qualified nurses arrived to work in Newfoundland. A major development in the nursing profession occurred in 1903 when Mary Southcott (1862-1943) founded the General Hospital School of Nursing, though it would be many years before Newfoundland and Labrador nurses were accorded full professional training and status. In 1920 the Governor's Wife, Lady Constance Harris (d. 1941), formed the Outport Nursing Committee, which later evolved into the Newfoundland Outport Nursing and Industrial Association (NONIA). The Outport Nursing Committee recruited British nurses to work in a number of rural Newfoundland communities. One of those outports chosen to receive a nurse was Joe Batt's Arm.

Though Fogo usually had a resident doctor, it was not easy for a physician to make the journey to the island's other towns in inclement weather. A Committee was formed to lobby government for the stationing of a nurse in the area. In the end the efforts paid off. Nurse Harvey arrived on Fogo Island in 1921. Her appearance was greatly appreciated by the residents of towns like Joe Batt's Arm, Barr'd Islands, Shoal Bay and Tilting. Harvey stayed on through 1922 when a lack of funds saw nurses' salaries cut, though a new grant finally reinstated her pay. Sonya Foley notes that Harvey was impressed by Fogo Islanders, and remained until 1924, when she returned to England. It was reported that Harvey died of TB soon after her homecoming. In September 1924 Harvey was replaced by another English nurse, E. M. Davies, who worked at Joe Batt's Arm until 1929. Nurse Robinson arrived in 1930, and lived on Fogo Island for about a year. In the 1930s nursing came under the direct control of government, and Robinson was the island's last NONIA nurse.

Another nurse, Margaret Parsons, came to Fogo Island in 1942. Born at Carbonear in 1919, Parsons was the Daughter of a merchant. Training at the Grace General Hospital, she graduated in 1941. After a stint at Grand Bank she went to Joe Batt's Arm, and worked there until 1946 when she married local Harvey Cobb (Cobb's contribution to Fogo Island medicine has been honoured through the Margaret Cobb Lounge on the ferry MV *Veteran*).

Other nurses recalled by Foley's informants include Charlotte Cluett, Lydia Baldwin and Mercedes St. John. The conditions for all these women were hard. Parsons recalled arriving at Fogo by the steamer *Glenco* to find that, unlike St. John's, her new home had no electricity or running water. The nurses' territory covered Joe Batt's Arm, Barr'd Islands and Shoal Bay. Though Parsons held clinics from nine to ten am and then from two to three pm, Monday to Saturday, she also made house calls and dealt with maternity cases. In effect, Fogo Island's pre Confederation nurses were on duty twenty-four hours a day.

Another well-known Fogo Island nurse was Christina (MacLennan) Cole. She first saw the island's rocky outlines in July 1946. As the passenger boat from Lewisporte docked at Fogo that day it was greeted by members of the Cole family, eagerly awaiting the homecoming of Gregory Cole. Departing on the steamer *Duchess of Richmond* in January 1940, aged only nineteen, Greg served with the Newfoundland Forestry Unit in Scotland for six years. Accompanying Gregory home was his bride Christina. Born in 1921, she was a native of Kinlochewe in the Scottish highlands, and had completed a four-year nursing program at Glasgow's Stobhill Hospital. Hired by the local Medical Committee, Christina Cole spent much of her first five years at Fogo providing medical care on her own, as the closest doctors were sometimes at Twillingate and Lewisporte. Nurse Cole learned how to pull teeth from Dr. Wood at Twillingate. As Fogo Island lacked a pharmacy of any kind, she arranged for medical supplies to be brought in from the larger towns. Among the many important services Nurse Cole provided to Fogo Islanders was delivering babies. Although the small settlements had midwives, Mrs. Cole assisted with numerous births over the years. Christina Cole's contributions to Fogo Island went beyond even this; she was sometimes called upon to act as a veterinarian or undertaker. Over the course of her long career Fogo's resident nurse covered many miles by dog team, boat, and later a snowmobile provided by the Department of Health. In 1949 weekly clinics were set up which Nurse Cole, sometimes accompanied by a doctor, manned on Tuesdays at Seldom and on Thursdays at Joe Batt's Arm. As Cole explained to Sonya Foley, travelling was so difficult in those days that it was easier for her to have the weekly clinics than for patients to journey to Fogo. In all, Nurse Cole cared for some

5,000 people on Fogo Island.

In 1983 she retired from the Fogo Island Hospital, where she had been based for the previous twenty-nine years. Even at this stage in her life Christina Cole was dedicated to helping others, continuing to perform volunteer work. In January 1991 her commitment was recognized with the presentation of the Order of the Red Cross. In a ceremony at Ottawa later that year Nurse Cole received Canada's highest civilian award, the Order of Canada, from Governor General Ramon Hnatyshyn (1934-2002). A special dinner was given in grateful recognition of her nearly forty years service. Nurse Cole passed away in 2010, but is still held in great esteem on Fogo Island where, following a spirited campaign, the local Health Centre's long-term care facility was renamed "The Christina Cole Memorial Residence."

Nurse Christina Cole (right), with a doctor, possibly Patrick J. Solan

Before Confederation outport nurses like Christina Cole had very little assistance. Nurse Parsons noted that about the only medical help they received came from local midwives. The lack of a doctor, and even nurses, in many small Newfoundland communities was partially offset by the presence of these midwives. All communities on the Isles would have had a midwife, sometimes more than one. Stephen Nolan points out that the modern perception of midwives was not how they were viewed in pre Confederation outport Newfoundland. Today midwives are associated only with assisting in childbirth, but in old Newfoundland they might be called on to treat all kinds of medical conditions and ailments. Though many had no formal medical training, Nolan believes they were often the only source of relief for communities with no other source of medical knowledge.

In Sonya Foley's work Ella (Combden) Cobb recalled the services of one Fogo Island midwife, Mrs. Annie Head. Though a widow with ailing children of her own to care for, Mrs. Head also tended to the sick, and delivered babies. After a birth Mrs. Head would make regular trips back to the Mother's home for over a week, washing Mother and child, and changing their clothes. She was respected by both men and women, and the menfolk would often come to Mrs. Head to apply a poultice if they injured their fingers. Mrs. Head may have been one of those midwives with some form of training, as Mrs. Cobb heard that she had done some studying under one of the doctors stationed at Fogo.

With the large families women often had in those days the rural midwife was always busy, and they sometimes had other women who assisted them as helpers. In other cases the midwives worked with local nurses. Nurse Cole told Foley that in one case she had been caring for four expectant Mothers at the same time. By the time she made it around to one house the midwife, Dorothy Hoven, had already delivered the infant.

<u>The Fogo Island Hospital</u>. By the twentieth century Fogo Island had dedicated medical professionals in nurses Harvey and Cole, plus doctors like Malcolm, Wood and Donahue, not to mention the many midwives. In terms of an actual hospital, however, the island had nothing until the 1940s. Since the 1920s islanders could avail of the NDB Memorial Hospital, but the journey to Twillingate in those days was a daunting prospect, especially for the sick or injured, involving a three to four hour boat trip when the bay was free of ice. Clearly, a better solution was needed for Fogo Island residents. In 1943 the island received its first hospital, which was part of the infrastructure of the American base at Sandy Cove. Serving the US military personnel stationed at the base, its hospital also provided free medical care for locals. Following the war and the American departure, the base was closed and its facilities, including the hospital, were taken over by Canadian authorities and dismantled.

Soon after, the island received a new health care facility, located at

Fogo. The idea was not a new one; in the 1930s an organization was formed dedicated to the establishment of a hospital in the town. In the Fall of 1937 Mr. B. Bennett, Secretary of the Fogo Hospital Committee, wrote the Assistant Secretary of Justice to ask if the Committee might use the local court house for one or two meetings in the Fall. The request was granted, provided that the building was used "...solely for the purpose of the business of the Committee and [it] must be left in a clean and tidy condition."[14]

In the Summer of 1943 Dr. Olds at Twillingate compiled statistics on the number of Fogo and Change Islands patients using the NDB Memorial Hospital. The stats were prepared at the request of Health Commissioner Puddister. It is clear that the Commissioners were mulling over the idea of a cottage hospital for Fogo Island, perhaps at the prodding of the Fogo Hospital Committee. Olds tabled the following information for Puddister:

"Admissions to the Notre Dame Bay Memorial Hospital...which Could be Served by a Cottage Hospital at Fogo, from July 1st, 1940 to June 30th 1943"

[Town]	*Population*	*July-June 1940-1*	*July-June 1941-2*	*July-June 1942-3*	*TOTAL*
Fogo	1500	26	25	36	87
[JBA]/ Barr'd Is.	1400	4	23	7	34
Tilting	490	1	1	16	18
Seldom	384	4	11	21	36
Indian Islands	256	9	6	8	23
Stag Harbour	200	2	5	15	22
Change Islands	967	38	33	49	120

From: PANL, GN 38, Commission of Government, Public Health & Welfare.

Olds' table had the following note written in red ink, referring to Change Islands: "[Patients] cannot use Fogo any better than Twillingate in Winter. The average number of patients per year, excluding Change Islands –

seventy-three"[15] When Dr. Olds prepared his report to Puddister William McCarter was on his way to Twillingate to discuss hospital rebuilding. In the wake of their meeting Olds penned another letter to Puddister. His opinion on the proposed cottage hospital for Fogo Island was clear:

> Cottage hospitals at Fogo and Little Bay Islands were discussed [with McCarter, and]...you know my feelings on this point. I believe that a large institution where enough doctors can be employed so that there is a chance for specialization in various fields can give a much better service to the Bay than three small hospitals and it is much easier to staff the larger institution. To make this feasible transportation must be improved and this can and will be done by air as soon as the war is over. We already have on order a helicopter type of plane which should be ideal for our purpose, distances being so short and the ease with which they can be landed.
>
> I would hope that you would let us try out this project before committing yourself to building the Cottage Hospitals. It seems to me far cheaper to maintain two small planes and several nursing stations over the Bay than two cottage hospitals, and also the large institution offers many advantages that smaller ones cannot.[16]

Olds was certainly not intending that Fogo Island (or Little Bay Islands) be short-changed in the provision of health care. He apparently believed that Notre Dame Bay would be best served by the one world-class hospital, offering as great a range of surgical and treatment options as might be available in larger centres like St. John's. Fogo Islanders in distress would be rushed to treatment at Twillingate via air ambulance, and could avail of the services of their nursing station for more minor problems, or when inclement weather made air travel impossible. Olds' dream of a fully-serviced hospital for the Bay was never quite realized; today people from all Isles communities travel long distances for many medical procedures, or to see a specialist.

Happily for the people of Fogo Island, the hospital *did* become a reality, though not until after Confederation with Canada. Construction of the Fogo Island Hospital began in the town of Fogo in 1952, on land donated by merchant Harry Earle. The hospital was officially opened in August 1953, then having six beds and a pair of cots for patients. Staff in those days consisted of one doctor, two nurses and an equal number of nursing assistants, along with a half dozen other personnel, who did everything from x-ray and lab work to cooking the meals. The facility received an extension in 1957 and again in 1972. In 1986 an outpatient facility was added, dedicated to public health and home care nurses. Run by the Province until 1973, its operations were then taken over by a Board of Management. By the 1990s the hospital could boast forty-five full time staff, of which three were doctors and seven nurses. Having seventeen beds, the fully accredited facility had both x-ray and laboratory capabilities, serving some 16,000 outpatients and another 500 inpatients each year. Affiliated with Memorial University's School of Medicine, the Fogo Island Hospital was also a teaching hospital for medical students, interns and residents.

Grand opening of the Fogo Island Hospital, 1953

Like the hospital at Twillingate, the Fogo facility owed a tremendous debt to those dedicated individuals who worked there over the years. Apart from the many nurses, nursing assistants, and other staff who kept the hospital running, there were of course the physicians. The first doctors based at the Fogo Island Hospital were Cyril J. Walsh, Alfred H. Bartley, George W. Cruickshank, William Jack, and Hedley C. Rolfe. One of the hospital's longest-serving doctors, with seventeen years at Fogo, was Conleith O'Maonaigh. Serving as the hospital's Chief Medical Officer, O'Maonaigh, like Dr. Olds in Twillingate, was given a unique twist on his surname by locals who called him "Dr. Mooney." Dr. O'Maonaigh left Fogo in 1999, having served the community not only as a physician, but also as an organizer and supporter of the Brimstone Head Festival. The old hospital's last Chief Medical Officer was Dr. Kehinde.

Not all those who dedicated themselves to the Fogo Island Hospital were themselves health care professionals, and no account of the facility would be complete without mentioning the career of Mr. Raymond Oake. On his retirement in 1996 Mr. Oake had served a full thirty years at the hospital, all but two of them as its Administrator. With his departure administrative duties were taken over by a Nurse Manager and a corporate team from the Board at Gander's James Peyton Memorial Hospital.

Perhaps this shift reflected the "writing on the wall" for Fogo's old hospital. A year after Ray Oake retired a second edition of Patrick Pickett's history of Fogo appeared. In it the author noted that a growing number of people were using the hospital's outpatient facilities, and that many babies were still being born at the facility. Yet by 1998 Fogo Island Hospital's obstetrics role had been transferred to James Peyton in Gander. In the same period growing numbers of people were being transferred off Fogo Island for anything other than routine procedures. By 2004 the hospital stood vacant, and was demolished beginning in January 2007.

This is not to say that Fogo Islanders have returned to the days of having no on-island health care facility. A new hospital – the Fogo Island Health Centre – began operation in 2004. There was some controversy surrounding the location of the new facility. In 1999 it was decided that the nine million dollar facility would be built at Fogo Island Centre, rather than in the town of Fogo. The decision created considerable enmity, and led indirectly to the resignation of Dr. O'Maonaigh. Nevertheless, the hard feelings have mostly subsided, and the centre is a fine successor to the old hospital. Serving about 2,600 people, the centre is home to five acute care beds, along with eight long-term care beds and a single respite bed. A variety of medical services including public health, x-ray, a lab, and diagnostic imaging are offered, with three doctors on staff. Like Twillingate residents, Fogo Islanders must still travel away for certain medical services, but the days of a single doctor, or nurse, serving the entire island are long in the past.

....

More Isles Medicine

New World Island. Unlike Twillingate and Fogo Island, neither New World Island nor Change Islands have been home to their own hospital. This does not mean that residents have had no medical services close at hand, at least since the late 1800s. From 1899 to 1902 the *Year Book and Almanac of Newfoundland* listed G. S. Chamberlain as practising at Herring Neck. Nigel Rusted records him at Herring Neck as early as 1897. Chamberlain was not an MD but an Anglican clergyman. Rusted notes that in time of crisis it was common for people to call first on their local missionary or priest. It was only a short step from there to being considered the community doctor; Rusted's own clergyman Father kept medicines at home for his parishioners. In 1893 a Newfoundland Medical Act was passed making it unlawful for unlicenced persons to practice medicine. Recognizing that many unlicenced "doctors" in the Colony had considerable experience, section 37 of the Act allowed those in practice more than five years to be registered. Chamberlain was among this group. He later moved to Brigus, and Herring Neck appears to have had no doctor from 1903-7. A. J. Wood set up practice in the community in 1907, although his tenure was a short one. Around 1910 University of Toronto graduate (1908) William Gordon Sheppard arrived, serving New World Island until the First World War era.

House call, 1940. Doctor Hardy on dog team at Twillingate

Upon Sheppard's departure New World Islanders had to make their way to Twillingate to avail of professional medical services. Since no causeways or roads then connected the islands, patients would face a journey to Twillingate by boat, or over the ice in Winter, using dog teams or horse-drawn sleds. As the Cottlesville town history notes, even getting from one's community to embark for Twillingate wasn't an easy task. Residents might leave Cottles Island and Luke's Arm by boat for Wiseman's Cove in Dildo Run, then take a rail trolley overland to Virgin Arm, and from there catch a boat for Twillingate. Sometimes doctors made house calls, but in such cases a fee was involved, often beyond the means of ordinary fishing families. As was the case on Fogo Island, most births in this era were overseen by midwives rather than doctors or nurses.

The inauguration of the Twillingate Telephone and Electric Company made things a little easier for some residents of New World Island. By 1916 the post office at Little Harbour, one of the closest Twillingate communities to New World Island, was connected by phone. As company secretary Arthur Manuel explained to MHA James A. Clift (1857-1923), there was,

> "...no Doctor at Herring Neck and all that vicinity, and the calls from the Little Hbr installation for doctors are very numerous and...many men will prefer to use the telephone for call[ing] for a doctor than to walking the 3 miles up & 3 back to Little Hbr. Any record of calls from Little Hbr for the year to middle of April shows over 80 calls for one or other of the doctors from that place nearly all by Herring Neck Merrits Hbr or Fridays Bay people...[T]he Little Hbr phone serves a great many more people than the sixty at Little Hbr..."[17]

Another boon for New World Islanders came in the 1930s with the inauguration of the floating clinic *Bonnie Nell* and her successor the *Bonnie Nell II* (See above). During the Winter months the *Bonnie Nell* was berthed at Herring Neck. In the Winter of 1958-9 Nurse Irene (Young) Pardy was stationed at Carter's establishment, and used the vessel for clinics. Later, Nurse Molly King was stationed at Herring Neck. In 1958 Pat Wylie, RN served at Bridgeport. By the 1960s the roads and ferry made access to the Twillingate hospital, and those in places like Gander, much more accessible. Still, a solution closer to home was needed.

Following a year and a half of meetings, the New World Island Medical Committee was formed at Summerford 10 May 1960, with the goal of finding a doctor for the island. After meeting with the NDB Memorial Hospital's Board it was agreed to meet the expense of such by a small increase in the annual family medical fee. The first doctors engaged were Eduard Koch and Terence Richards, based at Twillingate. In an article he wrote for the hospital's fiftieth anniversary, Doctor John Sheldon noted that the arrangement proved to be a failure, as travelling was a problem, and both doctors departed after short tenures.

It was then decided to collect funds locally to build a doctor's house. After islanders raised almost $7,000.00 they approached the Provincial Government in 1961. As a result of their meeting the Smallwood Administration pledged additional funds to construct a residence and clinic for New World Island. The doctor's home took shape over the Winter of 1962, and in the Fall of 1963 Dr. Emeric J. Ballard arrived. A medical graduate of the University of Bologna, Ballard was also a qualified dentist. Assisted by his spouse, a trained midwife, Ballard practised on New World Island for about a year. With his departure in the Fall of 1964 the island was once again without a physician.

The situation was soon remedied by the arrival of English doctor John H. Sheldon, a University of Cambridge alumnus. In 1965 an extension was built to the doctor's residence, which acted as a waiting room and dispensary. With the help of nursing aide Frances Flynn, and teams of nurses from the Twillingate hospital, regular immunization clinics were held at local schools. Dr. Jeremy Brown replaced Sheldon for one year in 1969, and for a time Helen Butt was the nursing aide. Sharyn Noel became Public Health Nurse in 1972.

New World Island Medical Clinic

As Sheldon points out, improved transportation meant that the house/clinic served patients as far away as Gander Bay. With patient numbers on the rise it was decided to seek the construction of a new clinic. In 1972 the New World Island Lion's Club compiled a petition of residents who supported a new health clinic and the building of a residence for a second doctor. Minister of Health Hon. Edward Roberts gave his approval for the venture, and construction was started by Raymond Farr & Sons. An extension of the NDB Memorial Hospital, the New World Island Medical Clinic opened on 1 July 1973 at a cost of $89,000.00. With the clinic's opening Doctor Paul Patey arrived, and Norma Jennings joined the staff as Secretary-Dispenser.

Like all Isles residents today, New World Islanders rely on large hospitals in regional centres like Gander, Grand Falls and St. John's for their most serious medical needs, but almost forty years after it first opened, the clinic still provides the island with primary health care, a far cry from the days of travelling by boat to Twillingate!

Change Islands. The story of medical care on Change Islands is not very different than that of New World Island, and Change Islands had its own private-practice doctors by the early 1900s. Around 1904 locals held a public meeting to consider getting their own resident doctor. A Committee was established to engage the services of a physician, and Dr. Leslie was hired. He departed after only a year or two on Change Islands, to be followed by Dr. Campbell. A Canadian, Campbell was described in glowing terms by *Twillingate Sun* correspondent William E. Sheppard of Indian Islands. Sheppard declared that Campbell was "...a credit to his country...and I am sure he is as much to Change Islands and well might the people of that place be pleased to have such a physician in their midst...I can say that he is in all points a gentleman...God blesses the work of his hands."[18] Campbell left after three years, and with his departure a controversy arose.

Dr. Eacrett arrived and set up practice on Change Islands on 1 July 1909. He was not directly engaged by the local Committee, but was accepted by them. Within three years Eacrett was in Magistrate's court at Fogo trying to recover fees he felt were owed him by certain residents. During this era outport physicians carried on what was known as a "book practice." This operated in much the same way as the old surgeon's books had in the seventeenth and eighteenth centuries. Families would have their names entered on their doctor's book, paying a set fee. This lump sum entitled all family members to a year's worth of office visits and house calls. Some services, like pulling teeth and delivering babies carried an extra charge, as did medications. Eacrett claimed to have taken over Campbell's books, and was thus owed the annual fee by those persons listed. The defendants argued that they had never signed on to Eacrett's books. Eacrett had put up notices saying that he would be taking over Campbell's books, and would consider any clients on them his own unless they indicated otherwise. The defendants said they had not seen the notices, and felt this did not apply to them in any case. Magistrate Andrew Cook asked the Deputy Minister of Justice his opinion on the case, to which the Deputy Minister replied,

> [that]...unless Dr. Eacrett can establish the fact that the Committee, which I understand accepted him as medical advisor of the locality in place of Dr. Campbell, had authority from the defendant to represent he cannot now recover [the fees]. In fact it is also doubtful if the Committee sufficiently recognized his services or if they did did so in compliance with the wishes or instructions of those who authorized them in the first instance. The publication of the notices referred to by Dr. Eacrett in his evidence has absolutely no bearing on the case whatever. He must establish privity of contract between himself and the defendant either directly or indirectly through the Committee.[19]

The records do not show how long Dr. Eacrett remained at Change Islands after the case, but in 1919 the *Twillingate Sun* noted that "Change Islands now has a new doctor in the person of Dr. O'Connel who is claimed to be a most painstaking and competent young man."[20] Likewise, the *Newfoundland Medical Register* reported University of Edinburgh and Glasgow graduate H. A. Newton at Change Islands in 1930.

In later years the services of private-practice doctors like O'Connel and Newton were replaced by a small nursing clinic. An account of the original clinic was provided for the town's 50th anniversary book by Nurse Elizabeth (Krauss) Chaffey. A native of Saskatchewan, Chaffey worked at Change Islands for nearly thirty years, and made the community her home for even longer. The community's first Winter clinic, located where the town fire hall (then a post office) now stands, opened in January 1960. The building was not heated except when nurse Chaffey was working, so supplies were kept at another location. Nurse Chaffey left Change Islands for two years and was replaced by Molly King, RN, but returned in 1964. In the beginning Nurse Chaffey had set up a clinic at her own home, always finding the house full when doctors came in for clinic days. The coming of electricity in 1965 allowed refrigeration of insulin and vaccines, which Mrs. Chaffey says was "a great help." Medical students were sometimes stationed at Change Islands in the Summers, and in the 1970s a dentist and optician made calls at the clinic. Still, conditions were not ideal by any means. Before the ferry service was established at the South End in 1979 it was often hard to get patients out, and many went to Gander by helicopter in the Winter and Spring. Even with this difficulty, Nurse Chaffey says that only one patient died during her tenure at the clinic due to weather conditions.

Today Change Islands has a more up to date clinic, located on Tickle Point Road near the modern post office. There is also a First Responder's crew, and an ambulance to transport patients off the island for emergency treatment. Since Nurse Chaffey retired in 1993 Change Islands has been served by a number of health care professionals like Nurse Practitioners Medina Foley, Elizabeth Jenkins, and Mrs. Goldie White, formerly with NDB Memorial Hospital, and later based at Makkovik, Labrador.[21]

....

The experience of Isles' communities should remind us that, while we often look upon the past as a "golden age" when times were simpler, we should not forget that our ancestors had a very harsh existence in many ways; the lack of medical care was by no means the least of their problems. It would be hard to imagine the days before the foundations of proper health care in the region were laid by people like Hay Findlater, Christina Cole, Charles Parsons, John Olds, John Sheldon, Elizabeth Chaffey and many other medical professionals, administrators, volunteers and staff. If our history teaches us nothing else, it should at least remind us of the gratitude we owe to those who have kept us well, and ministered to us in sickness, over the years.

14

Facts from the Past – Isles Historical Vignettes

Here are some interesting historical tidbits that you may not have known about central NDB's historic Isles and their history:

The Sabbath

For many years after it was first settled Twillingate did not have its own churches. This did not mean the early settlers lacked any strong religious feeling. The evidence is quite to the contrary, especially as concerns keeping the Sabbath. Documents held by the Library and Archives Canada at Ottawa detail an early religious controversy at Twillingate. In June 1770 a number of prominent citizens of the port, including merchant J. W. Slade, addressed a petition to a French captain named De La Rue. The petitioners asked the captain to desist from fishing on Sunday in contravention both of the laws of God and of their nation (i.e. England). This minor tempest brought forth a proclamation from Governor Byron stating that, as French fishing rights were protected by treaty, settlers should refrain from interfering with any French vessels wishing to fish on Sunday. Governor Byron then had the proclamation posted at various points around the harbour to dissuade any would be religious enforcers. A similar situation arose nearly fifty years later, though the official response this time was very different. In 1817 Twillingate residents petitioned Governor Francis Pickmore (c.1756-1818), complaining that some of their neighbours were working on Sundays. Pickmore's reply affirmed the Governor's desire that the Sabbath not be profaned by toil.

....

Musical History

The Beothuk woman Shanawdithit has found renewed life at Twillingate in recent years as the subject of a musical. *Shanadithit* was first performed in 1999, and was written by local music teacher Eleanor Cameron-Stockley. Cameron-Stockley, a native of Nova Scotia and graduate of Dalhousie University, researched and wrote all the dialogue and music for the play. Mrs. Cameron-Stockley's Toulinguet Players later staged the musical at the Holy Heart of Mary School Theatre in St. John's. Another famous Twillingate resident immortalised by Cameron-Stockley is Georgina Stirling (*Georgie*). She has also produced musicals about the NDB Memorial Hospital, and Newfoundland's first Premier, J. R. Smallwood. In 2011 Cameron-Stockley was the recipient of the Newfoundland and Labrador Teachers' Association Special Recognition Award, in honour of her contributions to the Province's culture. Since 2003 her plays have been performed by the Twillingate Theatre Company at Cameron Hall on South Side. The Hall is also part of Twillingate history. Built in 1930, it served as a family home for Herbert and Floss Pardy, who operated a restaurant in the building.

....

A Twillingate Royal?

Around the year 1800 a baby christened Solomon – surname Beadon or Beadle – was born to a Twillingate resident named Susannah. It was long rumoured that Beadon was a relation of Queen Victoria, perhaps even her Half-Brother. Both Victoria's Father Edward, the Duke of Kent and Strathearn (1767-1820), and her Uncle, the future King William IV (1765-1837), spent time in Newfoundland. Perhaps Susannah was a royal mistress? She may even have given birth to Solomon in England, the illegitimate child being raised in his Mother's home Colony to avoid potential embarrassment. A trunk inherited by Solomon's descendants was rumoured to be full of gold sovereigns, sent to take care of the royal offspring's needs. Whether or not he was truly of royal parentage, Beadon appears to have had some standing in Twillingate, being one of a number of prominent citizens who made up an anti-cholera Committee in 1832.

Solomon and Wife Deborah had one Daughter named Susan, born that same year. Solomon died in 1833, his estate worth the sizeable sum of £3,000. Susan Beadon married Josiah Colbourne, and their descendants lived at Twillingate for many years. Susan was said to have closely resembled the young British Queen, and was sometimes called "Little Queen Victoria." A later male relative supposedly looked like King Edward VIII (1894-1972).

....

Peyton

One of the names most closely linked with Demasduit, Shanawdithit, and their people is John Peyton Jr. Peyton had a remarkable career apart from his involvement with the Beothuk. Attending school at Christchurch, near his home of Wimbourne, the young Peyton worked at London's Navy Pay Office before travelling to Newfoundland in 1812. Early on Peyton helped protect the family's claims at Upper Sandy Point, and worked as a trapper. During 1815-16 he assumed the reigns of his Father's business, expanding the enterprise with two shipyards at Exploits Islands and Indian Point.

In 1818 Peyton, Jr. became Twillingate District's first Justice of the Peace, and fourteen years later completed one of the region's first censuses. He was named the area's first Stipendiary Magistrate in 1836, retaining the position into his eighty-seventh year. In 1823 Peyton had married Eleanor Mahaney of Carbonear, and took his family to live at Twillingate the year he was appointed Magistrate. Eventually the couple had eight children, the eldest Son lost in a shipwreck while returning from school in England. Peyton had a two storey house built at Back Harbour shortly after relocating to Twilingate. The woods which stood at the rear of the dwelling are still called Peyton's Woods, and today are the site of a fine serviced trailer park. Peyton died on 25 July 1879, and was buried alongside his Father in the graveyard on Burnt Island, adjacent to Exploits Island (Not to be confused with Burnt Island off Twillingate).

John Peyton Jr. also contributed to Twillingate's heritage through his writings. Between his diary and other manuscripts he left an invaluable record of nineteenth century Twillingate. A number of items belonging to Peyton Jr. are on display at the Twillingate Museum, including a travel trunk inscribed "G. Mundon Saddler Collar, Harness and Trunk Maker Poole, England." John Peyton Jr. is honoured in Newfoundland and Labrador in having a number of geographical features named after him. Peyton's Son Thomas also became a JP and Magistrate, and served as a member of Newfoundland's House of Assembly (1889-93).

Exploits, c.1900

....

Historic Home – The Loveridge House

One of the oldest structures still used as a residence at Twillingate is now known as the Loveridge House. It stands on North Side near the modern Post Office. No one is sure when it was built, but it was certainly standing by 1880, perhaps as early as 1845. The house was first mentioned in written records in 1907 when then-owner Peter Samways sold it to the family of Head Constable Nathaniel Patten. According to the Loveridge diaries, Samways was the original owner; he may have been quite elderly when he sold the property. Originally from Poole, Samways was known for his involvement with the Methodist Church.

Peter Samways

His old homestead has some interesting architectural features. Donald Loveridge believes that Samways may have built the five distinctive dormer windows – three in front, two at back – which now grace the house. Loveridge family photographs, taken from Twillingate's old court building, show the house in the 1890s and again in the 1960s. The dormers can be clearly seen in the more recent picture, but are absent from the first. Peter Samways is thought to have removed a large chimney on the right side of the dwelling, replacing it with one in the centre of the house. The interior preserves evidence of an old trap door on the second floor above the kitchen, which would have led down to where a stove was later placed. Indentations on the upstairs floor suggest something heavy like a bed was once placed there, but a wall now runs right through these. A Twillingate Museum display notes that the house features a "symmetrical three bay facade." The dwelling's main entrance is not located on this facade, but on the back porch or "linhay," a common feature of contemporary Newfoundland homes.

After the Pattens sold the dwelling it was operated for a time as the Ford Hotel, and was then purchased by Merchant Arthur Ashbourne. As of 1931 it was being used as the Bank Manager's residence. Ashbourne sold the house to Malcolm G. Loveridge in 1938. Malcolm served on the local hospital's Board of Directors, while Wife Agnes was a nurse. Both of the Loveridges were actively involved in community life. The old residence passed to Malcolm's Son Donald in 1980. Now having new owners, the Loveridge House became a Registered Heritage Structure in May 1993, and was added to the Canadian Register.

....

The Great Seal Haul

St. Peter's Anglican Church contains a relic of one of the most famous events in Twillingate's early history, the Great Seal Haul of 1862. The town was once an important centre of the sealing industry, as the ice flows on which seal herds travel often strike the land here. In 1862 a seal catch unheard of even in Twillingate blessed island residents. The seals first struck on 10 March, but the ice drifted offshore and five men were lost. Four days later the winds turned around strongly from the northeast, pushing the seals on their ice pans back within reach of Twillingate sealers. One lucky man even retrieved a batch of seal pelts he marked from the earlier strike. It is said that many men made in the range of £100. About 30,000 seals were taken, including some caught by a woman who struck out to feed her family, her Husband being too ill for the work. This was Twillingate's largest seal harvest up to that time. In thanks residents commissioned a bell in England to place in the tower of St. Peters Church, where it remains to this day. On the bell are inscribed the words, "In memory of the great haul of seals 1862." The bell was paid for with profits from the Great Haul, and it rang for the first time on Christmas day, 1863.In later years profits from another bountiful seal harvest were partially responsible for the town's, and Colony's, recovery in the wake of 1894's bank crash; Newfoundland vessels took almost 300,000 seals in the Spring of 1895.

....

The Queen of Swansea *Tragedy*

A trunk found near Back Harbour, Twillingate at the end of 1867 pointed to one of the most heartbreaking marine tragedies in Newfoundland history. The trunk belonged to Captain Patrick Duggan of LaScie, pilot of the 360 ton Welsh brigantine *Queen of Swansea*, bound for the copper mining town of Tilt Cove. Wreckage was discovered along with the trunk, leading to fears for the vessel's safety. Searches failed to locate any trace of the *Queen*, but as J. P. Andrieux relates, the grim fate of its survivors was learned four months later.

On NDB's desolate Cape John Gull Island sealers discovered a pair of skeletons, plus a number of frozen bodies under a sheet of sail canvas. Notes left by some of the victims revealed that a number of the *Queen*'s passengers and crew made it ashore after the vessel stranded on the island during a gale on 12 December. Able to salvage few supplies, the survivors gradually perished from exposure and lack of food but not before, in their final miseries, being forced to resort to cannibalism. One of the notes, found with the remains of passenger William Hoskins, gave some of the grizzly details:

> We struck the Gull Island in the morning before daylight and the ship was wedged into a narrow gulch. A line was got on shore and the ship made fast.
> We all landed inside of 20 minutes. Captain Duggan who is pilot with [John] Power a passenger, the ship's boatswain, and a sailor returned to the ship and got some food and while on board the line broke and the ship drifted out to sea. God help us.
> We are frozen and starving and must draw lots so that some may keep longer alive should help come.
> We have drawn, the lot fell on my poor sister. I have offered myself and am taking her place. The horror of it all. W. H.[1]

As a result of this disaster a lighthouse was established on Gull Island in 1884. The station's first keeper was Captain Mark Rowsell, the man who'd found the bodies of the *Queen of Swansea*'s passengers and crew in the Spring of 1868!

....

Another Musical Hero

Most Twillingate residents, and many tourists, are well aware of the part opera diva Georgina Stirling played in her era's music scene. On the other hand, John Edward "J. E." Brewster, is all but forgotten. Brewster travelled to England around 1872, setting up a successful banjo teaching school. He was also known as a banjo performer, and made a number of contributions to the instrument's development. Brewster's long-time collaborator was John E. Dallas. The pair set up a workshop at Oxford street in 1873. Although Brewster (along with one Richard Langham) was awarded an 1896 patent relating to the construction of zither-banjos, all the instruments produced bearing his name were actually made by Dallas. Brewster was probably best-known for his series of banjo "tutors," including the *Brewster Banjoist*. "Containing a fine selection of solos, intended for the amusement and advancement of Young Banjoists," the work sold for two shillings and sixpence; it was published by John Dallas. Brewster died at Paris, France in 1912. His career would have little connection to the Isles except that Brewster was born at Twillingate in 1853, Son of Rev. John Brewster and Wife Emma (Billing)! Like Georgina Stirling, J. E. Brewster can be claimed with pride as a native.

....

Twillingate Counterfeiter?

It is said that Twillingate once had its own counterfeiter. In the early 1880s Thomas Every (or Avery), who may have come from Black Duck Cove, settled near Shoal Tickle Bridge. A trader, Every sailed a small schooner around the coast alone, steering the vessel and setting its sails using controls he invented. Every was a member of Twillingate's Sons of Temperance Society but was more than once accused of breaking its rules by drinking alcohol, charges that were never proven. Every was also charged with counterfeiting money. These allegations did not stick, but it was reported that when he died in 1897, aged almost eighty, Every confessed to the crime. He handed over a quantity of counterfeit coins dated 1882 and 1885, along with the dies for making them. Despite these alleged activities, Every was a church goer, and involved with Twillingate's Congregationalist movement. Later, he seems to have joined the local Anglican congregation. Probably the most surprising thing about Every, as Howard Butt reports in the new *Twillingate Sun*, was that he supposedly made a pact with Satan! As part of this agreement Every said that the Devil could take him once his house was finished. With this in mind, Every's large, rambling home near Tickle Bridge was always under construction, and was still not finished when he died! This is certainly just a rumour, but it does nothing to lessen Thomas Every's status as a local character.

....

The Curtis Family and its Twillingate Connections

ENL notes that the Reverend Dr. Levi Curtis can be rightly claimed as a founder of Memorial University of Newfoundland, and this is but one of many accomplishments! Likewise, Rev. Curtis' Son Leslie had his own distinguished public career. Both Father and Son had connections to the Isles, Twillingate in particular.

Reverend Dr. Levi Curtis

Reverend Curtis was born at Blackhead, Conception Bay in 1858, and received an extensive education, including a Bachelor of Arts degree from Mount Allison University, where he was class valedictorian, in 1889. Upon his ordination as a Methodist minister Curtis was posted to Bay Roberts. He served two (non-consecutive) terms as President of the Newfoundland Methodist Conference, and in 1899 was named Superintendent of Newfoundland's Methodist schools, a position he held until 1935. Curtis also acted as Inspector of Schools and Examiner of Teachers, from which vantage point the Reverend worked diligently for many years to address deficiencies in the Colony's education system, and to persuade government to open a training college for teachers. Partly through Curtis' efforts, the Normal School for Teachers was founded in 1921, a development that in 1925 led to the establishment of Memorial University College in St. John's. The ten years Curtis spent as a member of the institution's governing body lead many to consider him a founder of MUN. Curtis made another important contribution when he proposed distinguished English educator John Lewis Paton (1863-1946) as the first President of Memorial University College, a post Paton held until 1933.

Apart from all this, Curtis was Chair of the St. John's District of the Methodist Conference, and for a quarter century edited *The Methodist Monthly Greeting*. Curtis' accomplishments were recognized with a number of honours, including the award of a honorary Doctorate of Divinity from Toronto's Victoria University in 1900. He was later made a Member of the Order of the British Empire, mainly for his recruiting work in Newfoundland during the Great War. He passed away in 1942.

Reverend Curtis' connection with Twillingate stems from his posting in the community during the 1890s. It was here in 1895 that his Son, Leslie Roy, was born. Leslie Curtis received an education at St. John's Methodist College, and read law with future Newfoundland Prime Minister Richard Squires. The younger Curtis was called to the bar in 1920, and was created K.C. (King's Counsel) in 1931. Curtis practised law through the 1940s, founding his own firm, Curtis and Dawe, later Curtis, Dawe, Fagan and Mahoney, in 1939. Upon Confederation in 1949 Curtis became part of Newfoundland's first provincial cabinet as Minister of Justice and Attorney General. Curtis remained in the portfolio until 1966, when he took up the post of President of the Council. He was the Province's Justice Minister longer than any other politician, and served as Deputy Premier. Throughout his time in politics Leslie Curtis sat as the member for Twillingate District, a seat he twice won by acclamation. Curtis was honoured by having a causeway in his district named after him. Aside from his careers in the law and politics, Curtis was a Director of numerous corporations, and like his Father, was active with church and organizational groups.

....

The Bevington Organ

Twillingate's old South Side United Church – now the Notheast Church Museum – has a rare piece of history contained within its walls. Among the items on display is a Bevington Model pipe organ. The Bevington firm originated with Henry Bevington in 1794. Located in London's Soho District, the company produced more than 2,000 organs during its existence, and won a number of medals at exhibitions. Bevington's facilities were severely damaged during the Blitz in 1941, and the company was later bought out by the firm of Hill, Norman and Beard – One source says in 1944, another 1950.

Twillingate's Bevington was built in 1903, and installed at the church in 1906. It was last played for a church service on 26 November 1972. Newfoundland and Labrador has only four other Bevingtons still in working order. The organ was serviced in the 1960s, and again in 2006, by retired music teacher Lester Golding, the only Newfoundland-based technician with the skills needed to carry out such work. Originally from Grand Falls-Windsor, Mr. Golding once worked at Quebec's Casavant Pipe Organ Factory (The Casavant Company was also involved in the 2006 Bevington restoration). In an interview with *Lewisporte Pilot* correspondent Howard Butt, Golding indicated that Twillingate's organ is of a relatively simple design. It has about 250 pipes of different sizes, compared to some 4,000 pipes in one of the organs used at St. John's Roman Catholic Basilica.

....

Distinctive Dwelling – the Ashbourne House

Twillingate is known for a number of historic buildings like the Loveridge House, many of which date back over a century. The oldest of these – the only one that may have been built in the 1700s – is the Ashbourne Longhouse. This is not the only venerable residence at Twillingate with ties to the Ashbourne family. Near the Longhouse stands another dwelling, about 100 years old, whose architecture is unique enough for it to feature in two works on Newfoundland historic buildings. It is also the subject of a souvenir miniature, as is St. Peter's Church.

The Ashbourne House was built on land once owned by Edwin Duder, and later sold to Dr. Stafford. According to one version of its history, an older dwelling that once stood on the site was consumed by fire in 1911, the same year the new house was built. Its builders were the Skinners, who constructed the new house for Cupids native Doctor Isaac LeDrew and his Wife Laura (Ashbourne). The house's current owners, Chet Caruthers and Gaye Anne Flyer, have heard a different account. According to Mr. Caruthers and Ms. Flyer, the Ashbourne House was actually built in 1905. While it *did* catch fire about 1911, only the front of the residence was burnt, and this damage was then repaired. In fact, scorch marks can still be seen on the house's original bannisters and some of its period furniture. In 1947 the house was acquired by Laura's Nephew, Bill Ashbourne, and his Wife Helen (Moore), who originally came to Twillingate to work as a nurse.

The book *Ten Historic Towns* described the Ashbourne House as basically a large mercantile outport home, made unique by the later addition of an elaborate porch and a distinctive turret done in the Queen Anne style. The house is now smaller than in years past, with about three metres missing from the rear. With four bedrooms upstairs, the house has a dining room with its own marble fireplace, one of several still remaining in the dwelling. Like the Longhouse, the Ashbourne House has pine floors, plus doors framed with wide pine moldings. As author Jean Edwards Stacey notes, the Ashbourne house is solid and substantial, its only "whimsical" touch being the turret. While not a designated heritage structure, the Ashbourne House is certainly one of the most recognizable pieces of architecture on the Twillingate islands.

....

Anauta

Before the Loveridge House was purchased by Arthur Ashbourne it was owned by photographer Henry T. Ford. Ford operated a photo studio and an inn in the house, which he named the Ford Hotel. The hotel was known as a popular stop-over for mariners and Hudson's Bay Company (HBC) agents heading north. The family had a long connection to the HBC, with generations of Fords working for the company.

For a number of years the Ford Hotel was run by Henry's relative, Sarah Elizabeth Ford. Anauta (1888-1965), as she was also known, was the Daughter of George "Yorgke" Ford and an Inuit woman named Alea. Not unlike Lady Pamela, some mystery surrounds Anauta's life. She's been described both as Henry Ford's Sister and as his Niece, though it appears that the former is correct. Likewise, Anauta's birthplace has been given as Ford Harbour, Labrador, and as Chekettauk (Pond Inlet), Baffin Island.

Anauta married twice, her first Husband being William "Uille" Ford. Born at Rigolet, Labrador in 1883, Uille was a distant Cousin of Anauta's. He drowned at Wolstenholme, Hudson Strait in 1913. Anauta wed for the second time in 1920, while living in the United States. This (unsuccessful) marriage was to Harry John Blackmore, the Son of a woman she met at Twillingate. According to ENL, it is not certain whether Blackmore was a Newfoundlander or an American. Family records confirm that he was, in fact, born at Twillingate in 1880, the Son of Reuban and Isabella Blackmore of Old House Cove.

Anauta arrived at Twillingate prior to 1915, information provided by her Granddaughter, Sylvia Ewer Koening, suggesting this may have been as early as 1913. Anauta's co-written autobiography, *Land of the Good Shadows*, devotes several pages to Anauta and her children's stay in the community, "...the prettiest place they had found in their wanderings..."[2] The biography is silent concerning Anauta's role as a hotel proprietor, though it does refer to her living in a hotel at Twillingate. Likewise, newspaper items from 1917 and 1918 give "Mrs. W. Ford," as the proprietor of the Ford Hotel.

Anauta

Another minor puzzle of Anauta's life concerns the length of time she spent at Twillingate. By some accounts, Anauta and her two oldest Daughters lived in the town from around 1913 to 1920, while ENL asserts that she left Newfoundland in 1917. She was certainly living at Twillingate until at least late 1918. At this time Yorgke travelled south from Labrador to settle some of his business affairs in St. John's. The 19 October issue of the *Twillingate Sun* reported that Anauta intended to close her hotel for the Winter to stay with her Father in the capital, and then return to Twillingate in the Spring. Before she could reach him, Yorgke died. Arriving in October on the steamer *Nascopie*, he became a victim of the Spanish influenza then raging in St. John's (Anauta's Mother had passed away some years before).

However long she stayed at Twillingate, it seems that with her Father's passing the Inuit woman became restless, spending a year or two moving between Twillingate, St. John's, Labrador, and other locales. Along with Daughters Harriet and Dorothy, Anauta finally left Twillingate for good. She eventually settled in Indianapolis. While living in the United States Anauta became a recognized author, although her first published work appeared during her years at Twillingate. The 1915 Christmas edition of the *Twillingate Sun* featured her article "In the Lonely Arctic," which told of how a mysterious White stranger came to live with Anauta's family in the North when she was a child. A version of the tale was included in Anauta's autobiography.

She penned *Land of the Good Shadows. The Life Story of Anauta, an Eskimo Woman* in 1940 with collaborator Heliuz Chandler Washburne (b. 1892). Anauta is remembered in the literary world for two other works, *Children of the Blizzard* and *Wild Like the Foxes*, the latter based on her Mother Alea's life story. Lauded as a writer, Anauta also became an accomplished lecturer, enthralling American audiences with tales of her early life in Labrador. Thus, a woman who once ran an inn at Twillingate can rightly be considered one of the world's first Inuit celebrities.

....

The Accomplishments of Edith Manuel

Mrs. Elsie B. Hodge, mentioned in Chapter Three, wasn't the only distinguished Twillingate resident with close connections to both a merchant family and the Girl Guide movement. Edith Mary Manuel was born in 1902, the Daughter of merchant Arthur Manuel and his Wife Georgina (Maidment). Despite a life-long ailment that made walking difficult, she became an accomplished educator. ENL describes her as one of the Province's most influential teachers.

Ms. Manuel began her long teaching career at Twillingate in 1917, straight out of grade ten. She later moved to St. John's, finishing grade eleven, and then taught in several communities including Fogo. She was a teacher at Bishop Spencer College for more than thirty years, starting there in 1929. While working at Bishop Spencer Ms. Manuel completed a Bachelor of Geography, and later a Master of Education at Columbia University. She finished her tenure at Bishop Spencer in 1963, but returned to the profession in 1969, spending four years at St. John's Cerebral Palsy School.

In 1929 Ms. Manuel founded Newfoundland's first Brownie Pack. Edith Manuel was active with the Brownies and Girl Guides in several communities, and founded a number of Troops. She was awarded the Guiding Medal of Merit, along with the Beaver Award, and was made a lifetime member of the Guides.

Ms. Manuel was involved in other organizations, including the Local Council of Women, and was a charter member of the Canadian Federation of University Women. Edith Manuel was twice named St. John's Citizen of the Year. In 1978 she was awarded a honourary Doctorate of Law degree at Memorial University. The following year Ms. Manuel was named the Year of the Child patron for Newfoundland and Labrador. Aside from her other interests and accomplishments, Ms. Manuel was a published author. She wrote three geography texts for Newfoundland schools and penned a history of St. Peter's Church. She was working on a history of Twillingate when she passed away in 1984.

....

Twillingate's own Rhodes Scholar

Since 1904 one Newfoundlander per year – none from 1941-6, two in 1948 – is chosen for the prestigious Rhodes Scholarship. Among this elite group is a Twillingate native, Elmo Linfield Ashbourne, born 1897, scholarship 1920. Ashbourne served in the Royal Canadian Navy Volunteer Reserve from 1917 to 1919 and witnessed the great Halifax explosion of 1917 first-hand. His vessel was docked in the port, and luckily the young man was below deck or he may not have survived the biggest man-made explosion before Hiroshima. The *Twillingate Sun* reported that:

> It is probably not generally known that Mr. Elmo Ashbourne, who is serving in the Canadian Patrol, was at Halifax at the time of the disaster. He was on a ship only 350 yards from the Mont Blanc when she blew up, but fortunately escaped uninjured, though some of his comrades lost their lives. During the winter he has been doing duty on the Pacific Coast from the Naval base at Esquimault; but had a few days leave to visit his parents before they left Toronto.[3]

Following his wartime service Ashbourne practised law in Toronto for a number of years, then worked for the Federal Government before returning to his legal practice. Married in 1923, Ashbourne had two Sons. He passed away in 1979.

As a Rhodes Scholar Elmo Ashbourne is in good company. Former Premier Danny Williams (1969), journalist Rex Murphy (1968), politician/journalist Bill Rowe (1964), and renowned educator Moses Morgan (1938) also share the honour. Biographies of all ninety-two of the Province's recipients up to the year 2000 are profiled by Doug Cole, in *Rhodes Scholars of Newfoundland.*

Elmo Linfield Ashbourne

....

On the Rocks

One of the many interesting craft owned by the Ashbourne business was the *Ariceen.* Seafaring lore tells of jinxed ships, whose careers are riddled with misfortune – it is no stretch of the imagination to picture the *Ariceen* as one such vessel. The 416 ton, three-masted schooner was built at Liverpool, Nova Scotia for one J. O. Williams in 1917. It was bought at auction by William Ashbourne in December of that year (or possibly 1918), at a reported price of about $80,000.00. In October 1918 the *Daily News* reported that two members of the *Ariceen*'s crew were admitted to hospital after contracting the deadly Spanish Influenza. The vessel's mate, Walter Hyson, died the following day. A year later the vessel found itself in danger when a cargo of hay came loose off the Funks. Fearing the bundles would smash in *Ariceen*'s hatches, her crew was forced to jettison fourteen tons of a fifteen ton cargo before making it to port at Twillingate. After this inauspicious beginning the Ashbournes mainly used the *Ariceen* for carrying fish cargoes to the Mediterranean. In October 1921, during one of Twillingate's infamous gales, the craft broke anchor and was driven up on a marine feature known locally as "Harbour Rock." The vessel rested there for a number of years, as if at anchor, until it finally broke up and sank.

Schooner Ariceen

In 1935 Stephen Loveridge recorded that another old Ashbourne vessel, the *Sordello*, which he described as a "hulk," was broken up for fuel at Harbour Rock by a crew of five or six men. The work began in February, when Twillingate harbour was frozen over, and was still continuing in March when Stephen and his Wife visited to observe its progress.

....

Albert Dekker, Film Star

An American movie actor, and Democratic member of the California legislature, who went by the stage name Albert Dekker, had a familial connection to Twillingate. His Brother was Dr. Robert Ecke who served on the staff of NDB Memorial Hospital in the 1930s and 1940s. Dekker, who used his Mother's maiden name on stage, had a fairly distinguished and long-lasting career in entertainment. He appeared on Broadway starting in the 1920s, acting in stage productions of such famous plays as *Death of a Salesman*. Dekker acted in seventy motion pictures, among them 1969's *The Wild Bunch*. Albert Dekker was found dead at his Los Angeles home the year before *The Wild Bunch* was released. His personal papers are held at the University of Wyoming. Incidently, Dekker's Brother outlived his sibling by many years: Dr. Ecke passed away in 2001 at the age of ninety-one.

....

Minty's Farm

The Twillingate-area once had its own dairy. It was started in 1945 on fifty acres of land by the late Marvin Minty. Minty brought four gurnseys to Twillingate, and operated his farm from 1945-7, even selling milk to the hospital. After closing his business and working in Toronto for sixteen years, Minty returned to Twillingate in 1964 and reopened the dairy. Minty sold his milk from door to door. At the time it was one of the few places customers could get unpasteurised milk, enjoyed for its texture and taste. The dairy operated until 1978 when rising hay prices forced Minty to close down. For a number of years Mr. Minty maintained a walking trail on the grounds of his old dairy.

....

Captain Peter

Peter Troake of Twillingate (1908-97) captained the floating tuberculosis clinic, MV *Christmas Seal*, for twenty years. Captain Troake's role in persuading reluctant Bay residents to get tested for TB earned him the Order of Canada in 1987. According to J. K. Crellin, who compiled and edited a collection of Troake's reminiscences, the captain's ability to put people at ease and coax them to have the test earned him the nickname "the Pied Piper of Newfoundland." Still, not everyone was convinced. In at least one case the residents of a Placentia Bay community refused the TB scratch test on the grounds that it was "God's will" whether or not they got tuberculosis. In 1992

Captain Troake was awarded a honourary Doctorate from Memorial University, and the Commemorative Medal on the 125th anniversary of the Canadian Union. That same year he was recognized by the town of Twillingate. In 1993 he received the Newfoundland Volunteer War Service Medal, and the next year a Life Achievement Award from the Lung Association of Newfoundland and Labrador. Peter Troake was also the first President of the Newfoundland branch of the Canadian Rescue Auxiliary.

Captain Peter Troake

Captain Troake was a lifelong seaman who started fishing at Twillingate with his Father Lewis when he was only six years old. He made his first trip to Labrador as a fisher in his teens. Troake served with the Newfoundland Forestry Corps from 1940-2, and later skippered the famous SS *Kyle* at the seal hunt. After his tenure on the *Christmas Seal* he captained the Grenfell Association's vessel *Strathcona* from 1971-9. Retiring just shy of age seventy-nine, Captain Troake was the oldest man to skipper a vessel in Canada. Marrying Hilda Primmer, Captain Troake was the Father of one Son and two Daughters.

....

The Christmas Seal

Captain Peter Troake's old vessel, the *Christmas Seal*, was first known as PT 107 – a sister ship to American President Kennedy's famous PT 109. A reader of *Downhome* magazine gives the vessel's wartime name as FP 102, information related to him by a man who served on her from 1943 to 1945. The vessel was bought from the US government by the Newfoundland Tuberculosis Association on 10 September 1947. The Americans apparently sold the craft for less than a tenth of its original cost after learning of its intended use.

The *Christmas Seal* was lost to fire, and a resulting explosion in its engine room, in May 1976 *en route* from Dartmouth, Nova Scotia to Souris, PI. Luckily her skipper, Captain Chaffey, got everyone off safely. At the time of the fire the vessel was under charter to the Bedford, Nova Scotia Institute of Oceanography.

....

The Whites & their Vessels

The schooner *Shirley C* was featured in the 1952 Hollywood movie *World in His Arms* starring Gregory Peck and Anthony Quinn. For the picture she was renamed *Pilgrim*. The *Shirley C* was once owned by Twillingate resident "Skipper" Jack White. The vessel was American, and built of white oak. White bought the vessel from Stanley Barbour of Salvage in 1943. One of Skipper Jack's first voyages in the *Shirley C* was a stormy passage from St. John's to Twillingate with provisions. The schooner suffered some damage during the trip, but was repaired. In the Spring of 1944 she set out for the Labrador fishery under Skipper Jack, with his Brother Fred as second hand (mate). In 1948 Skipper Jack's teenage Son Harry made a Labrador voyage on the *Shirley C*, but 1950 proved to be her last in the northern fishery, as foreign markets for Labrador fish had collapsed. In 1951 the schooner was sold to Captain Bill Hancock, and from there went on to big-screen fame. After production wrapped on the movie Captain Hancock used the *Shirley C* to transport a load of coal from Sydney, Nova Scotia to Newfoundland. As Harry White relates, Hancock stopped off at the French-owned island of St. Pierre for the night, where the vessel dragged her anchor. Hitting a shoal, the *Shirley C* sank.

Though his old schooner was gone, Jack White's nautical career continued for many years. After Confederation he became one of Newfoundland's first Fishery Patrol skippers with the Department of Fisheries. In 1960 he transferred to the Ministry of Transport as a marine pilot at Goose Bay, Labrador. Skipper Jack retired in 1966, but was soon back at sea, working for Imperial Oil as an Arctic ice pilot. White reluctantly gave up life at sea at age seventy-five, though not before making one last trip on board a local freighter. He passed away in 1986.

The *Shirley C* wasn't the only interesting vessel associated with Twillingate's White family. A "co-star" in *World in His Arms* was another Newfoundland schooner, the *Margaret B. Tanner.* This vessel was once captained in the coasting trade by another member of the White clan, Saul "Brud" White Jr. Another White schooner was the *Marina.* According to one source, Jack and his Father, Saul Sr., were paid £400 by Britain's Royal family for the rights to the name, and the vessel was renamed *White and Sons.*[4]

Gus Young, with Captain Saul White, in his Model T Ford on Twillingate's harbour ice

....

The Last "Tin Lizzie"

Until 1955 Twillingate resident Gus Young owned the last Model T Ford automobile in Twillingate, and probably for many kilometres around! It was a 1924 model, originally brought to Twillingate by Dr. Wood. Mr. Young bought the car from Paul Moores for $75.00 in 1944. "Uncle" Gus would sometimes take local children on Sunday school outings to Long Point, or all around Twillingate. The car could not always make the steep Long Point Hill with its load of passengers, who then had to walk for that part of their outing.

After many years in use the car's fabric top wore out, and Mr. Young replaced it with his own creation made of plywood with plastic windows. The Model T originally had solid rubber tires, one of which came off while Uncle Gus was driving down Yates' Hill. He fixed the problem by bolting all the tires onto their rims, a solution that lasted until Gus replaced the solid tires with inner tube models.

The auto was so well-known in Twillingate that Margaret Burton, a friend of Gus and his Wife Nellie, composed a humorous poem about it that she recited at concerts ("Aunt Maggie" Burton was a Scottish war bride, locally-renowned as an entertainer). Gus Young eventually sold the Model T to a resident of Bay Roberts.

....

Lost in the Arctic

Donald Baird, Son of Harold and Louise Baird of Twillingate, was once lost and presumed dead in the Arctic. Baird was hired by the Hudson's Bay Company in 1949. In 1955 he and an Inuit guide set out from Cape Dorset, North West Territories *en route* to Frobisher, about 480 kilometres away. Not long after their departure a fierce blizzard set in. The men became stranded and survived by eating five of their eleven sled dogs, and later by killing a pair of caribou. After air searches failed to find the men they were considered lost. Soon, though, the two arrived back at the Cape Dorset trading post a little worse for wear, but with no permanent injuries. Don Baird lived until August 2000.

....

Loss of the Winnifred Lee

On 6 September 1955 the MV *Winnifred Lee*, used for the carriage of gas and fuel products to northern communities, caught fire while docked at Twillingate's Coastal Wharf. The vessel had narrowly escaped destruction from a fire in June 1949, but this time she was not so lucky. Carrying a full cargo of combustibles such as gasoline, naphtha, and kerosene, the *Winnifred Lee* could easily have exploded, causing great damage and loss of life. Her skipper, Les Andrews, and seaman Leo Kane, helped by two other mariners, Captain Douglas Manuel of the MV *Shirley Louise*, and Christopher Sturge, tied ropes to the vessel, hauling it to the middle of the harbour. Soon the *Winifred Lee* starting drifting back toward the shore. The four men then reboarded the craft, dropping its anchors as oil drums began exploding. Soon after they left the vessel, it erupted in a ball of flame. The burned out remains of its hull were still afloat and smouldering the next day, but soon sank, perhaps scuttled as a hazard to navigation. Andrews, Kane, Manuel and Sturge were all presented with awards for their heroism by the Department of Transport.

MV Winnifred Lee. *At Twillingate Coastal Wharf (left), and on fire, 1955 (right)*

....

The Veslekart

In 1961 a Norwegian sealing ship named *Veslekart* was trapped in the ice off Twillingate. *Veslekart* was only one of many vessels caught by Notre Dame Bay's pack ice that Spring, some being stuck for fifty-five days! As Barry Vineham reports, Twillingate resident Ralph Horwood made two trips to the ice seal hunting near the Norwegian vessel. On the second of these Ralph, accompanied by a Cousin, was asked aboard for dinner with the crew. Afterwards Horwood and his Cousin left, taking off mail for the stranded mariners. The next day the Norwegians, running low on food, struck out for shore across the rough ice pack. After the crew landed safely they were cared for by the local Red Cross. In later years crew members sent a vase inscribed with their names to Twillingate as an expression of thanks. The beautiful vase is now housed at the Twillingate Museum.

....

Lobster Factories

A typical feature of some Isles communities at the turn of the twentieth century, especially those on New World Island, along with Seldom-Come-By and Island Harbour (Fogo Island), was a lobster "factory." In his famous history of Newfoundland, Judge Prowse gave a detailed account of such factories as they existed on the Island's west coast in 1895. Lobster canning was apparently introduced to Newfoundland sometime in the 1860s. The factories generally had a boiling room, bath room, a packing room and a cookhouse. Lobsters were boiled for about thirty minutes then taken to a smasher to break the shells and take out the meat. The meat was washed and packed in tins which were then dried for soldering. The tins would next be closed up and bathed for one and a half hours. They were then punctured to let vapour escape, and bathed again for the same amount of time. Resealed, and packed in cases of about four dozen tins, the canned lobster was then sent to buyers, usually in Halifax and St. John's. In 1895 each case of lobster was worth about $6.25, with a profit of around $2.00. While these details may not apply exactly to NWI's lobster factories, they do give some idea of the business as it was carried on at the time.

....

"Uncle" Fred at the Ice

In his 1986 work on the Newfoundland seal fishery Michael Harrington recounts a story about Frederick "Uncle Fred" Knight of Moreton's Harbour. Born in 1853, Uncle Fred was renowned for his fishing abilities. In 1946, aged ninety-three, he recounted his first sealing trip aboard a steamer, the 505 ton *Eagle*. Knight and two friends from Moreton's Harbour secured berths (sealing jobs) on the steamer in 1878. The men had to find their own way to Pool's Island, Bonavista Bay, from where the *Eagle* was due to sail, or lose their coveted berths. With forty pounds of clothes and gear on their backs, the trio first headed to Twillingate and met up with another group of sealers bound for the *Eagle*. Travelling by bay ice or sometimes by land, the group made their way to Musgrave Harbour, then Cat Harbour (Lumsden), and finally Pool's Island itself. In all, Knight and his companions probably covered more than 160 Kilometres just to reach their vessel. With all that, their sealing season was only just beginning!

On this trip Uncle Fred served with a number of men who became celebrated sealing skippers, including George Barbour and Abe Kean. After encountering a party searching for men lost in a gale, and blowing the *Eagle* out of pack ice with gunpowder, Knight and his crewmates, under Captain Billy Knee, put into Green Bay with 18,000 seal pelts. As remarkable as this story seems today, it was typical of what many Newfoundlanders did, and risked, to earn a living in the nineteenth and early twentieth centuries.

....

Babie

In November 1929 Tom White of Hayward's Cove, near Valley Pond, NWI, shot himself a bird, probably for supper. White only wounded the creature, which was heavily banded and must have been domesticated. He took the bird to Sandy Knight and his family in Moreton's Harbour. Using her bands, Knight located the bird's owner across the Atlantic in England. The bird was a homing pigeon named "Babie" who strayed off course while on a flight to France. Babie must have landed on a west-bound ship, finding her way to Newfoundland. After keeping her for the Winter of 1929-30 the Knights returned Babie to her owner, who paid to have the valuable pigeon shipped home. The story, retold by Sandy Knight's Son Gerald in 1989, can be seen at the Moreton's Harbour Museum, along with a picture of Babie.

Homing pigeons, from Harper's New Monthly Magazine, *April 1873*

....

Pirate Treasure

One of the many popular legends associated with Newfoundland concerns the pirates' treasure that many children growing up by the seashore have dug for. Most experts dismiss the idea that the old-time pirates really buried treasure, but almost every maritime locale has its tales about hidden chests of gold.

Pirates burying treasure, by Howard Pyle

Ms. Elaine Woodford recounted a New World Island treasure story to Eileen Smith for the book, *From Me...to You*. As the story goes, sometime during England's many wars with France pirates robbed a British vessel, and the pirate captain allegedly buried his booty near the modern community of Too Good Arm. Like many of these stories, the legend would have little foundation, except Ms. Woodford relates that a local gentleman found a number of old coins in the area around a grey-coloured rock in Burton's Cove. Perhaps there is something to the treasure of Too Good Arm after all!

....

A Cobb's Arm Ghost Story

A traditional Newfoundland celebration has a supernatural connection in the community of Cobb's Arm, a story detailed by ghost researcher Dale Jarvis in his book *Haunted Shores*. Traditionally, 2 February was celebrated as Candlemas or "Calmus" Day. Commemorating Jesus' first visit to the Temple of Jerusalem with his Mother Mary, it was a time when the yearly supply of church candles was blessed. The day was celebrated with a sweet bread called a Candlemas cake, or a party of the same name, with plenty of singing, dancing, food and drink. Folklore holds that the weather on Candlemas day, good or bad, predicts the trend for the rest of the Winter. In North America Candlemas Day evolved into Groundhog Day.

On one especially severe Candlemas Day Cobb's Arm residents held a party at their local lodge hall. With a blizzard raging outside most partygoers stayed put for the night, except for one determined soul who decided to make his way home come what may. Taking up his lantern, the man set off into the white squall. He was found the next day frozen to death in a bog, lantern still in hand. Since then many people have reported a mysterious light hovering over this Cobb's Arm bog, supposedly the spirit of the lost partygoer still trying to find his way home by the glow of his lantern.

....

Fogo Island Journalism

The *Twillingate Sun* is a well-known part of Isles history. Less appreciated is the fact that over the past forty years or so Fogo Island has had a number of its own periodicals. Since the late 1960s the island has been home to several local newspapers, including the *Fogo Star* which ran from 1968-9. The Star was produced by the Fogo Island Improvement Committee, which launched a new magazine, the *Fogo Islander*, in 1972. This paper only ran for about a year, folding on the departure of editor Patrick Mooney. About the same time Reverend Ivan Jesperson published the *Fogo Island Profile* (June 1969-December 1971). Another local paper was the *Fogo Island Flyer*, which had a run of around five years. The Flyer was produced by volunteers, and edited by Cheryl Penton. One of Ms. Penton's staff was Carol Penton, a former freelance writer for the *Lewisporte Pilot.* In 2005 Carol Penton launched her own community interest paper, the *Fogo Island Flame*, which provided monthly insight into the Fogo Island scene, especially its human interest stories.[5]

....

Jeffrey and Street

Though not well-known today, John Jeffrey and Thomas Street were important players in the contemporary Newfoundland fishery. Both partners hailed from Poole, and had close connections with the city's influential Quaker family, the Whites. Thomas Street (1724-1805) captained Joseph White's vessels *Mermaid* and *Speedwell* in the years 1764-71. John Jeffrey was Joseph White's Nephew, and a major beneficiary in his will. As one of White's Newfoundland agents, Street also received a considerable bequest from his late employer. By 1775 Jeffery and Street were partners, a business relationship that lasted until 1789. With premises at Fogo, Trinity, Bonavista, Greenspond and other Newfoundland locales, Jeffrey and Street were heavily involved with the cod fishery. They also participated in Gander River salmon fishing, sealing, the import of supplies, and shipbuilding. Like many Newfoundland merchants of the era, Jeffrey and Street suffered at the hands of American privateers, but soldiered on. One of the firm's best years was 1786, when they exported 50,000 quintals of Newfoundland salt cod, second only to Benjamin Lester.

In the wake of a declining fishery, Jeffrey and Street's partnership dissolved. Street left the running of his own company to his two Sons and retired to England. The business outlasted him by a mere four years, when Street's last surviving Son was lost at sea *en route* to Poole.[6]

....

John August

Jeffrey and Street not only have a connection to Fogo, but to the Beothuk as well. In 1768 a Beothuk boy about four years old was captured near Red Indian Lake by two Trinity fishers (or furriers), who killed the youngster's Mother in the process. It was one of these men who approached John Cartwright in hopes of a reward for bringing in the boy. This killing and abduction was an unintended result of Governor Palliser's plans to establish relations with the Beothuk. Due to his youth the boy, called John August by his captors, could give authorities little information on his people's customs and language; he was certainly too young to act as an ambassador. After being put on display in England, possibly by Thomas Street himself, August was returned to Newfoundland and raised in an outport community. By 1785 August was working for Jeffrey and Street's agent at Catalina, Trinity Bay. Soon afterwards, August went to work for Street at Trinity, and was reportedly master of a fishing vessel. Acquaintances said that August always wished to meet his Mother's murderer and avenge the crime. Much like Tom June, John August reportedly left Trinity for a period of time each year to visit Beothuk kin in the interior. August died in October 1788 at the young age of twenty-four. Trinity church records note him as a Native Indian and servant of Jeffery and Street.

....

Father Lundrigan

The Isles have been home to many interesting characters over the years, and Father Thomas Patrick Lundrigan surely qualifies. Lundrigan (also spelled Londrigan, Lonergan and Landergan) was a priest who began ministering to Newfoundland's Catholic population in 1782, when their religion was not officially tolerated in the Colony. Lundrigan was reportedly the first Roman Catholic priest to visit Fogo Island, where he died on 25 October 1787. This merits distinction for Lundrigan, who was honoured with a new grave marker erected by the Grand Falls Knights of Columbus in 1959.

Evidence presented by Mike McCarthy in his examination of the Newfoundland Irish, and in Cyril Byrne's volume of correspondence from the Island's early Roman Catholic missionaries, suggests that Lundrigan was a controversial figure in his day, even with the Catholic establishment. Born in Ireland circa 1749 – Byrne gives the date as 1752 – Lundrigan was a Dominican friar who ministered at St. John's before moving on to the Colony's old French capital, Placentia. It was said that Lundrigan's behaviour while at Placentia caused great outrage with the Catholic authorities in Newfoundland.

Upon formal recognition of the Roman Catholic religion by Newfoundland's Colonial authorities in 1784, James Louis O'Donel, later Bishop O'Donel, was appointed the Island's first Vicar Apostolic. O'Donel then sent one Fr. Burke to Placentia, charging him with the task of establishing a parish there. It seems that Burke and Lundrigan were soon at loggerheads with one another, and complaints about Lundrigan's behaviour quickly reached Governor John Campbell (c.1720-90), who promptly instructed the Magistrate at Placentia to deport the troublesome priest. It should be said that Campbell had no reason for vindictiveness toward Lundrigan by dint of his faith; it was Campbell who issued the proclamation of religious toleration, and the Governor seems to have been friendly with the Colony's official Catholic hierarchy.

In any case, it seems that Lundrigan escaped the authorities' net and headed to Newfoundland's southern shore. O'Donel branded Lundrigan an apostate, having excommunicated him as soon as he landed at Placentia. In letters of 1786 and 1787 O'Donel went so far as to call Lundrigan "...the worse [*sic*] man I ever heard of...an utterly lost outlaw, abandoned by God and man..."[7] Lundrigan nevertheless continued to carry out priestly duties, though he was accused of everything from drunkenness, to violating the sanctity of the confessional, to living in sin with the Wife of a Protestant doctor named Dutton. Not satisfied with the Placentia excommunication, O'Donel followed the wayward Father, repeating the ritual in every village along the southern shore.

O'Donel asserted that his first official act upon meeting Lundrigan would probably be administering last rites at the gallows. Given his past behaviour, the Vicar Apostolic was sure the wayward priest would eventually commit a murder! In the end, the renegade escaped this fate. After spending some time at St. Mary's Fr. Lundrigan finally travelled to Fogo Harbour, where he died. Even here controversy dogged him. O'Donel reported that Lundrigan passed away at a local planter's house, lying in a drunken stupor, on a bench in front of the fire.

These reports paint a very black picture of Fogo's first, if unofficial, Roman Catholic priest. Still, there are two sides to every story, and Fr. Lundrigan never had the chance to tell his. It may be that the reports of his behaviour were exaggerated by church and civil officials unhappy about his popularity with Newfoundland's common folk, compared to the officially sanctioned priests. Whatever his true nature, Father Thomas Lundrigan deserves to be remembered for his place in Isles' history.

....

The Last Great Auk?

The Isles are home to many mysteries. One of the most fascinating is the possibility that the world's last great auk may have been captured and eaten in Fogo. The great auk (*Pinguinus impennis*) was the largest modern member of the Alcidae family of birds. Standing about 80 cm tall and weighing around 5 kg, the great auk was distinguished by its black top plumage and white underbelly – it was also the only flightless auk. The great auk, like its cousins, was a powerful swimmer and diver, feeding mainly on fish. Laying a single egg, great auks bred in large colonies on a number of low-lying offshore islands in the North Atlantic. The species ranged as far north as Greenland and as far south as Florida. They were noted as being especially numerous on Newfoundland's Funk Island.

A food source for the Native Beothuk, the great auk was once numerous enough to guide mariners on the Grand Banks. The species soon came under threat from Europeans who harvested the birds in large numbers for their feathers, oil and meat. By the late seventeenth century the great auk population was in serious decline. This trend was noted by George Cartwright in his journal for 1785. Cartwright observed that the birds were an important food source for the inhabitants of Fogo, who travelled to the Funks to harvest the auks and their eggs. It was common for Fogo islanders to salt the meat in place of salt pork. However, the practise of taking large numbers of the birds simply for their feathers put serious pressure on the auk population. Cartwright believed, correctly as it turned out, that over-hunting would soon do the species irreparable harm.

Great auks, by John James Audubon (1785-1851)

Besides the human threat, the naturally cold conditions of the period, called the "Little Ice Age," may have made the auks' islands more accessible to predators like polar bears. For the most part, though, over hunting was to blame for reduced auk numbers; by 1800 the Funk Island population was destroyed. Smaller colonies hung on elsewhere, but these were eventually wiped out. The last known great auk in the British Isles was killed in 1840, by which time the species was nearly extinct, a remnant population residing on the small island of Eldey, off Iceland. The colony moved there after their original breeding island, *Geirfuglasker*, or Great Auk Rock, submerged in 1830. Unlike the birds' former home, Eldey was accessible to humans. On 3 July 1844 the last nesting pair was killed by locals and its single egg smashed. The bird was officially declared extinct and its story was over.

Perhaps not. In 1852 a single great auk was reportedly sighted on the Grand Banks. This footnote in natural history would have no direct bearing on the Isles were it not for an 1888 *Twillingate Sun* article. According to the Sun, two residents of Fogo, a Father and Son, found a large bird alive but floating exhausted among slob ice in the harbour. They'd never seen a bird of its kind before but, unwilling to turn down the prospect of a good dinner, the two killed the bird and took it home to cook – the strange creature made three meals for the family!

Neither Father nor Son made much of the incident, but the story soon spread through the town of Fogo and eventually to the capital city, St. John's. Fogo Magistrate James Fitzgerald even received a telegram from Governor Sir Henry Arthur Blake (1840-1918) enquiring about the bird, which was reported as a great auk or "penguin" (not related to the flightless southern bird which now bears the name). Having received a drawing of a great auk, Fitzgerald proceeded to interview the fishermen who caught the mysterious bird. Although only the head, feet and wings of the bird remained, these were duly sent to Governor Blake. According to the Sun there was "no doubt of its being a penguin, but where it came from [was] certainly a mystery."[8]

If the tale is true, Fogo may be the last place where a living great auk was encountered (and eaten!). It also begs the question, raised by the *Twillingate Sun*, of where exactly the bird originated. Forty-four years after the species was declared extinct, and well over thirty years after the Grand Banks' sighting, how could a great auk have made it to Fogo Island? Was there a viable breeding colony on some island off Newfoundland's rocky shores? If so, what eventually happened to it? Perhaps we'll never know, but the incident still generates interest. Fogo's great auk was the subject of historical signage in the town, and appeared as a topic in Benson Hewitt's newspaper column. Like our ancestors, we enjoy a good mystery.

....

Thomas C. Duder

For Thomas C. Duder, acting as his family's business agent at Fogo, and starting his own firm in the community, was only the beginning of a successful career. Not just an entrepreneur, Duder was appointed Justice of the Peace for Newfoundland's Northern District in 1875. Elected MHA for Fogo District in 1893, the following year he served as the government's Financial Secretary, a post he soon resigned to become Chairman of the Board of Works. Duder was re-elected to the legislature in 1897, and appointed Minister of Agriculture and Mines. In 1900 Thomas Duder became a Magistrate at Bonne Bay, a position he retained until his death twelve years later. Duder was also known for his active role in the Methodist Church, and was a member of the Freemasons for many years.

Thomas C. Duder

....

The Remarkable Earle Family

Thomas Duder wasn't the only Fogo merchant with outside interests. Although best known for their business activities, the Earles were a multi-talented family. We might recall that Henry Earle Senior was a tailor, and his Son Henry John started out as a piano teacher. This musical gift was by no means rare in the Earle family. Henry John's Brother, Samuel, was the long-time organist at the Anglican Cathedral in Charlottetown, PI, while two Earles of the next generation, Ralph and June, also served as church organists.

Bleak House, Fogo, c.1900. The people in front are believed to be members of the Earle family

Music was but one strand of the family's interests. Patriarch Henry Earle served St. Andrew's Church as a lay reader, organist and church warden, and was lay delegate for Fogo at the Diocesan Synod. He was also a member of the local SUF, a Justice of the Peace, and Portuguese Vice-Consul.

Henry Earle started a longstanding family tradition of public service, representing Fogo District in the House of Assembly from 1900 to 1913. Henry's Son Harold was active on school, road, and medical service boards. He followed in his Father's footsteps when, in the last election held under Representative Government (1932), Harold became the member for Fogo District. According to Patrick Pickett, Earle felt that his successful lobby for the government provision of free potatoes in the midst of the Great Depression was his greatest accomplishment as a MHA. Harold Earle is also fondly recalled for his donation of land for the construction of the old Fogo hospital.

Henry and Harold's energy was reflected in other members of the clan. One particularly accomplished member of the family was Henry Robert Valence Earle (1911-96), familiarly known as "Val" or "H. R. V." Val Earle's business titles – President of Earle Sons & Company, Chair of Newfoundland Associated Fish Exporters Ltd., and President of Val Earle Ltd. – reflect his drive, but his other accomplishments are just as impressive. Earle served as Director of the Fisheries Council of Canada, Commissioner of the North West

Atlantic Fisheries Organization, Canadian Observer of the United Nation's Educational, Scientific and Cultural Organization (UNESCO), President of the St. John's Rotary Club, President of the Newfoundland Board of Trade, executive member of the Diocesan Synod of Newfoundland, and Chairman of the Anglican School Board of St. John's. Of all the family Val Earle was the most successful politician, being elected to Newfoundland's House of Assembly on three occasions. Having served as a cabinet minister under the Smallwood Administration, Earle crossed the floor in 1969 to sit with the Progressive Conservatives. Though defeated for re-election in the 1971 general election, Earle returned to the House the following year, and was appointed to cabinet by Premier Frank Moores. As a minister (under Smallwood and Moores) Earle held a variety of portfolios including Economic Development, Education, Finance, Municipal Affairs and Housing, Public Welfare and Public Works.

....

"Mayo" Lind

Of all the Isles' Blue Putties, the most famous was Francis Lind. Although not as well-known today as Victoria Cross recipient "Tommy" Ricketts, Francis T. "Frank" Lind was probably the most famous Newfoundland serviceman of his day. Lind was born in the now-resettled community of Bett's Cove, Notre Dame Bay on 9 March 1879. His paternal Grandparents, Henry and Caroline Lind, came to Newfoundland as school teachers in 1829. Maternal Grandfather John Walker was a ships' carpenter who moved from Scotland to set up shop in St. John's. Frank's parents, Henry and Elizabeth, were married in 1865, moving to the mining town of Betts Cove. The family moved to Little Bay in 1885, where young Frank attended school. At the age of fourteen Frank moved to Fogo, and was employed by J. W. Hodge for several years. After working in St. John's and Nova Scotia, Frank returned to Fogo, taking a job with Earle, Sons & Company. Still working at Fogo, and old enough to avoid active service, Lind selflessly enlisted with the Royal Newfoundland Regiment on 16 September 1914. Assigned Regimental No. 541, Lind signed up along with his friend Jonathan Brett and Fogo residents, Bertram Oake, Arthur Purchase and William Shave.

During his service Lind sent a series of thirty-two letters to the St. John's *Daily News*, the first of which was written on Boxing Day, 1914. These were meant to acquaint Newfoundlanders on the home front with their Sons' daily lives in the trenches. Archivist Bert Riggs notes that, starting with the Gallipoli campaign of 1915-16 Lind often suffered from ill-health, but his letters were renowned for their friendly and cheerful tone.

Francis "Mayo" Lind. Enlisted at Fogo, 1914

In a letter penned at Stob's Camp, Scotland in May 1915 Lind asked his readers to send along tobacco to cheer the troops, especially Imperial Tobacco's Mayo Brand. Thereafter Frank was known to all as "Mayo" Lind. His efforts resulted in the Mayo-Lind Tobacco Drives. These appeals sent tobacco for smokers among the troops, and allowed non-smokers to trade their Mayos for other comforts. In only a month the first Mayo-Lind appeal saw a generous supply of tobacco and cigarettes sent to Newfoundlanders serving overseas. In all, six Mayo-Lind campaigns from 1915-18 raised over $8,000.00 that purchased thousands of pounds of tobacco and hundreds of thousands of cigarettes.

Frank Lind didn't see the last of these campaigns. Mayo's final letter was dated 29 June 1916. In it Lind said that he would not even try to describe the tremendous noise produced by artillery bombardments along the Western Front. He felt that only those who were there could appreciate the din. Even under these conditions, Lind found amusing happenings to report, and expected to send off many interesting letters in the days to come. He never did. Two days later Mayo Lind was among those killed storming the German lines at Beaumont-Hamel.

....

Story of Sacrifice – the Mahaney Brothers

The World Wars have produced countless tales of bravery and sacrifice like that of Mayo Lind. An especially poignant wartime story from Fogo concerns the Mahaney Brothers, James ("Jim") and Stanley. The tale spans both world conflicts, and was recounted to me by Jim and Stanley's Niece, Elsie (Mahaney) King, and has been rounded out with information from other sources.[9]

The Mahaney Brothers both served with Britain's Royal Navy. As a member of the Newfoundland Royal Naval Reserve, Jim (# 2216X) was a crewman on HM Trawler *Lord Durham* in the First World War. In October 1918, only a few weeks before the war ended, Jim passed away in hospital, by some accounts mortally wounded, in others dying from an illness. He was buried in Ireland at County Cork's Cobh Old Church Cemetery.

Jim's younger Brother Stanley was born in 1909, and was too young for service in the Great War. When World War II erupted in 1939 Stanley Mahaney was given *his* chance to enlist. Assigned service number JX217858, Stanley served on HMS *Rosabelle*, a 515 ton steam yacht bought by the Royal Navy for use as an armed boarding vessel, and later as a patrol yacht. On 11 December 1941 *Rosabelle*, under Lieutenant Hercules S. Findlay, was pursuing U-374. Commanded by Unno Von Fischel (1915-42), U-374 had just torpedoed another vessel, HMS *Lady Shirley*. The submarine turned the tables on its pursuer, torpedoing *Rosabelle* as well. *Rosabelle* went down in the Straights of Gibralter with most of its crew, including Stanley Mahaney. Only three officers and nine ratings survived. Unlike his elder Brother, Stanley was not buried ashore. Like so many seaman through the ages, his final resting place is the sea. The sacrifice of two Sons in two World Wars may be unique in the town of Fogo, and perhaps on the Isles in general.

....

Wreck of the Francis P. Duke

For centuries the sea has provided a rich bounty to the people of the Isles. Sadly, this boon has always come with a price. Even today fishing the North Atlantic is considered one of the world's most dangerous occupations. Some of the earliest written reports from towns like Fogo tell of ships and men lost at sea, and local mariners have perished right up to the present day.

A maritime disaster that is still remembered by some of the older residents of Fogo Island concerns the loss of the *Francis P Duke*. The forty-two ton auxiliary schooner was owned by Captain Patrick Miller of Fogo (See Chapter Four). During the Spring of 1947 the vessel helped avert a near-tragedy when she rescued Christopher Cobb of Barr'd Islands, who had been drifting on an ice pan for several days. The man had been spotted by an aircraft and his position relayed to Fogo.

On 16 December of that year the *Francis P Duke* was unable to avoid her own date with disaster. That night the vessel was en route from Fogo to St. John's with a load of fish. As Benson Hewitt reports, the weather forecast had not been promising, and it was thought that the vessel would take shelter at Seldom. For some reason her captain elected to cross Bonavista Bay for Catalina. At this point the schooner was overtaken by a powerful Winter storm, and may have tried to run for the safety of Valleyfield. Instead, the vessel struck squarely on the Shag Rock in the tickle between Pool's Island and Badger's Quay, the vicious waves soon pounding the hapless craft to pieces.

The next day locals found the wreckage of the *Francis P Duke* but, perhaps because of the severity of the previous night's weather, there were no witnesses to the disaster.

On board the schooner were Captain William and Ignatius Miller, Sons of the vessel owner, Royal Navy veteran Augustus Pickett, and Maxwell Payne, both of Fogo, Stewart Keefe, formerly of Twillingate, Alfred Mullin of Recontre East, and Donovan Bryan.

Marine authorities were alerted to the disaster, and a search for bodies was begun as soon as the weather permitted. The remains of William Miller, Pickett and Payne were recovered and brought to Fogo for burial by the steamer *Glenco*. Although Patrick Miller posted a reward of 500 dollars for the recovery of Ignatius' body, the other four men were never found.

....

Lem's Forge

During the first half of the twentieth century blacksmithing in the town of Fogo was dominated by one family, the Anthonys. The founder of their local forge, Abraham Anthony, was apprenticed as a blacksmith at Harbour Grace. He moved to Barr'd Islands, where he married, in 1888. Anthony and his bride Francis (Reid) soon moved to Fogo where he set up a smithy on Fogo "Neck." About twelve years later Abraham's young Son Lemuel or "Lem" (d. 1952) left school to learn the blacksmithing trade.

Because of the heavy fishery traffic in those days the Father and Son operated two forges to keep up with the demand for repairs and iron work. The dependence of Fogo on their blacksmiths is brought out by the fact that residents had to travel all the way to Twillingate to get such work done before the Anthonys set up shop.

Lemuel "Lem" Anthony

With Abraham in poor health, Lem took over the business when he turned eighteen, operating the forge until 1923. He then moved to New York but returned to Fogo in 1932 at the height of the Great Depression. Lemuel ran the smithy until he retired in 1950, when it was taken over by his Son Donald, who ran the forge as part of a garage until 1965.

In Lem's day the forge was a favourite stop for young children heading off to St. Andrew's School at Riverhead. Children were impressed by Lem's kindly nature, and would often stop to watch him making everything from small anchors to horseshoes.

Lem was also a churchgoing man, and a stalwart of Fogo's old United Church (Two of his Brothers were ministers). With the passing of "Lem's Forge," another important chapter closed in the book of Fogo history

....

Lost on the Ice

All Isles communities have their tales of maritime tragedy. One such incident, associated with Barr'd Islands and Joe Batt's Arm, occurred in 1917. Like the better-known *Newfoundland* disaster, this mishap was connected with the hazardous Spring seal fishery. The melancholy event is recounted in Eric Witcher's work on Barr'd Islands, and involved six men from the area: Brothers Joseph, Stephen, and Walter Jacobs, along with Francis Pomeroy (whose Mother had remarried to a Jacobs), and siblings William and Hubert Freake. Only three years after the *Newfoundland*'s crew met their fate on the ice, and the *Southern Cross* was lost with all hands, these six men set out to hunt seals on the Spring pack ice near their homes. While they were at the flows the weather took a turn for the worse, with heavy seas, wind and rain. Witcher speculates that the men may have become disoriented, walking out to the edge of the ice, where they drifted away. The *Twillingate Sun* reported the story as follows:

> Last Saturday morning six men from Joe Batts Arm went sealing, and up to the present no trace of them has been found though the Diana and Bloodhound are searching for them. The men were three brothers named Jacobs and an adopted brother Pomeroy, and two others named Freake...Apparently they had no boat as none is spoken of.
>
> Mr. Fred House Jr. had a wire from Joe Batt's Arm Sunday to look after the men if they landed here, but so far nothing has been seen or heard of them. The Diana Tuesday reported herself as 15 miles off the Wadams [*sic*] with no ice, and no sign of the missing men.[10]

For several months it was as though Francis Pomeroy, along with the Jacobs and Freake Brothers, had vanished, their fate a complete mystery. Then an object was found that shed a small ray of light on their end. On 11 June

Joseph Adey of Twillingate was travelling past Western Head in his motorboat when he noticed a gaff floating in the water. Adey retrieved the object, which was covered in seaweed. The gaff lay in Adey's stage until 27 July, when he packed it onto his schooner for use at the French Shore fishery. That night one of his crew noticed that the gaff had writing carved onto it. As the Sun noted:

> ...The only record ever found of [the men missing since 7 April] is a gaff which was picked up by Mr. Jos. Eddy [Adey] this spring and lay unnoticed for some time until a visitor [*sic*] examining it discovered cut or scratched on the gaff these words "Lay down to perish April 11th. J. J."
>
> J. J. Evidently stands for the initials of one of the men named Jacobs, and apparently the unfortunate men managed to exist from Saturday till Wednesday, and there seems no doubt that had things been properly arranged here and motor boats gone off the men might have been discovered alive...[11]

Sealers hauling pelts over pack ice, early 1900s

The men of Barr'd Islands/Joe Batt's Arm had indeed been carried off on the ice flows, where they probably perished from exposure. The six deaths inspired the local SUF, who delayed the grand opening of their hall out of respect, to rally around the dead mens' families, helping in any way they could.

Upon his return from the French Shore Joseph Adey handed the gaff to *Twillingate Sun* staff, who turned it over to the Jacobs family, and for many years the gaff was displayed in the local Anglican church. Witcher notes that the tragedy had such a profound impact on the communities of Barr'd Islands/Joe Batt's Arm that it is still re-told to the younger generation.

....

The Wreck of the SS Ethie

Chapter Eleven recounted the role played by Fogo's wireless station in two of Newfoundland and Labrador's most infamous marine disasters, the loss of the *Newfoundland*'s sealers at the ice, and the *Viking* explosion. One of Newfoundland's other great maritime tragedies, the wreck of the *Ethie*, occurred in 1919, and has an interesting connection to Fogo Island in the person of its youngest survivor.

Part of Reid's Alphabet Fleet (see Chapter Two), the SS *Ethie* was used to transport passengers and freight. Built in Glasgow, like most of the Alphabet fleet, the *Ethie* was 439 gross tons and measured 155 feet. The ship was launched in 1900, and served the people of Newfoundland and Labrador for the best part of two decades. On 10 December 1919 the vessel was making its run between coastal Labrador and St. Barbe, Newfoundland when it ran into unusually heavy weather north of Bonne Bay. The crew tried beaching their struggling vessel on Martin's Point in an attempt to get passengers to safety ashore. Unfortunately, the effort rent open the *Ethie*'s bottom, and the now-stranded vessel was in imminent danger of foundering. With their charges in peril Captain Edward English and his crew, aided by locals ashore, managed to rig up a "boatswain's chair" to transport survivors to safety by means of ropes and pulleys. Even with heavy seas surging around them, all passengers and crew of the *Ethie* were rescued, including an infant named Hilda Batten. Little Hilda couldn't hold onto the boatswain's chair herself, and there was no room for her Mother or another adult to accompany her. To save the child's life she was wrapped in a blanket and placed in a mailbag that was then strapped to the chair for the "ride" to the shore. Over time the wreck of the *Ethie* became part of the Province's maritime lore, acquiring the legend – discounted today – that a Newfoundland dog played a major role in the rescue.

The connection of the disaster to Fogo Island was made more than thirty years after the *Ethie* "drove ashore" on Martin's Point. In that era the island was experiencing a shortage of teachers. To help fill the educational gap, Mr. Martin Menchions arrived as the first Principal of a multi-grade school serving Joe Batt's Arm and Barr'd Islands. Menchion's Wife also came to stay on Fogo Island, becoming the school's grade eight teacher. Mrs. Menchions' first name was Hilda, her maiden name Batten – the very same person rescued in a mailbag so many years before. Mrs. Menchions passed away in 2007, aged 89. Benson Hewitt records that Hilda's Mother kept the bag for as long as she lived, even giving it an annual wash. Hilda Menchions later donated the mailbag to Gros Morne National Park, where pieces of the *Ethie*'s wreckage can still be seen.

SS Ethie, *in drydock, St. John's, c.1910*

....

The Mystery Box

In his 1974 work *Fogo Island*, educator Clive Marin recounts a mysterious happening at Joe Batt's Arm. On 1 November 1942, workers at the site of a new fish plant found a box just over a metre in length. Although not large, it was very heavy, and nine men were needed to lift it. The local priest and constable decided to have the box buried in the Catholic cemetery. Curious as to its contents, one of the men who had first located the box returned to the graveyard and unearthed it, finding nothing but an old boot! According to

Marin, the man noticed two figures leaving the cemetery, perhaps others who had beaten him to whatever the box had contained.

....

Brother Rangers

Established by the Commission of Government in 1935 to police rural Newfoundland and Labrador, and to provide many other government services, the Newfoundland Ranger Force holds a revered place in the hearts of many locals. Through to the Force's disbandment in 1950, a number of Isles residents served with the Rangers, including Roy Manuel and Ernest Clarke of Twillingate.

The community of Joe Batt's Arm produced no less than three Rangers, two of whom were Brothers. These Brother Rangers were the Sons of shopkeeper Zebedee Ford and his Wife Janet (Hodder). The elder of the two boys was James or "Jim," born 9 November 1919. Younger Brother Donald entered the World on 1 October 1923. Both men joined the Rangers in mid 1943, Donald just out of school, and Jim following a spell working at the St. John's Dockyard. Donald only remained with the Rangers a few months before leaving to join the Royal Navy. Donald served in the Navy as a submariner, one of the only Fogo Island natives in the "silent service." Donald's war came to an end when his hand was injured by a torpedo that fell out of place and landed on him. Jim served a full five year term with the Rangers, posted to Hopedale, Hebron and Rose Blanche. Leaving the force in 1948, Jim soon married. Both Brothers became mechanics, Donald's specialty being diesel engines, and settled in Ontario.

Joe Batt's Arm's third Ranger was Jack Hewitt, Son of fisherman John and Wife Lavenia. Born about a month before Jim Ford, Hewitt finished his schooling in his hometown before entering the Royal Navy, where he served for six years. Hewitt enlisted with the Rangers in June 1947, but took a discharge soon after. In December Jack Hewitt married Emily Hancock. The couple raised a large family, whom Jack supported through a career with the Newfoundland Customs Service, based at Gander. The former Ranger retired in 1980.

....

The Death of Reverend Mercer

Driving into Fogo motorists will see a sign bearing the inscription "Mercer Memorial Drive." This signage recalls United Church Pastor William Seeley Mercer, who died on the spot. Reverend Mercer arrived at the Fogo mission in 1922. On Sunday, 3February 1924 he was ministering to the flock at Seldom-Come-By. Despite a raging snowstorm, and against the wishes of his parishioners, Mercer decided to make the journey back to Fogo the next day. Mercer set out at 10 am, covering a distance of almost thirteen kilometres before he was overtaken by the tempest. Reverend Mercer died only a kilometre and a half from his home. Patrick Pickett reports that those who remembered the tragedy said that Mercer was found with his arm around a spruce stump, his hand clutching a bunch of raisins. Mercer Memorial Drive wasn't the only tribute Fogo Islanders paid to the unfortunate minister, as a fine stone church at Barr'd Islands was dedicated to his memory. It has since closed following the erection of a new, multi-community United Church on Fogo Island.

....

Isles Fast Facts

An underwater shoal about three kilometres off Long Point, Crow Head is called "Old Harry" after a white chalk outcrop at the edge of Poole Bay.

On 10 June 1881 carpenters from the Royal Navy warship HMS *Druid*, then visiting Twillingate, went ashore to help rebuild houses destroyed in a terrible fire.

Joseph Ings of Purcell's Harbour, South Twillingate Island, was the sole survivor of the wreck of the schooner *Blossom* off Gull Island Cove, Bay of Exploits on 15 September 1891.

In 1911 Sidney Bond Young of Twillingate survived the grounding of the Gulf ferry SS *Bruce* and went on to become a Metro Toronto Police Sergeant.

Pearson V. Curtis, eldest son of Reverend Leslie Curtis, was a Rhodes scholar, and served with the British forces in the Great War.

While attending college, one of Twillingater Thomas G. W. Ashbourne's fellow students was future Canadian Prime Minister Lester Pearson.

E. D. Scanlon, chief accountant with AAT at St. John's, and Son of the man who discovered the story of Twillingate's first settlers, died on 23 August 1916, due to head injuries sustained in a car crash, one of the first automobile fatalities in Newfoundland.

As a youth the *Twillingate Sun*'s last editor, Ernest Clarke, was awarded the Boy Scout medal for bravery after saving young Gwen Cook from drowning in Twillingate Harbour.

Royal Navy veteran John Clarke Senior of Twillingate was Newfoundland's longest serving wharf master or wharfinger, holding the job from 1948-86.

Bernard J. W. Hynes of Bayview, Twillingate, born at NDB Memorial Hospital 30 July 1965, was Newfoundland's "half-millionth citizen"

In September 1975 former Liberal Premier Joey Smallwood won election to Twillingate District as leader of the short-lived Liberal-Reform Party.

As of today (2016), John Hamlyn of Crow Head is Canada's longest serving Mayor, having first been elected to the position, which he's held ever since, in 1962 – the town's community centre is named in his honour!

The Baxter Fudge Memorial Hall at Cobb's Arm was once a two-room school, and later became the town's United Church.

Walter Baine Jennings (b. 1864) founded a local Council of the FPU at Moreton's Harbour in 1909, and in 1919 became the first member of the Salvation Army to sit in the House of Assembly, as MHA for Twillingate District.

On 5 August 1952, during the Korean Conflict, Able Seaman 1st Class Ian Torraville of Change Islands died while serving aboard HMCS *Iroquois*, and is buried in the United Nations Cemetery at Yokohama, Japan.

In 1816, while on his way to take up ecclesiastical duties at Twillingate, Rev. John Leigh conducted the first Church of England service at Fogo.

Author George Allan England (1877-1936), best known for his work *Vikings of the Ice* (1924, reprinted 1969 as *The Greatest Hunt in the World*), featured the Fogo wireless station as a plot device in his 1920s serial "The White Wilderness."

The former congregation of St. John the Evangelist – Joe Batt's Arm/Barr'd Islands – has produced a bishop, two arch-deacons, three canons, two priests and one permanent deacon.

END

Endnotes

Notes to Chapter One

1 For a number of years prior to 2015 the communities of Twillingate, New World Island, Fogo Island and Change Islands comprised a single Newfoundland & Labrador Provincial electoral District. In that year Twillingate and New World Island became part of a new Lewisporte-Twillingate District, while Fogo Island and Change Islands were incorporated into Fogo-Cape Freels District. Given the traditionally close historic, cultural, economic and family ties between these towns, I feel that viewing them together remains a viable approach, despite the change in District status. For me, they remain "The Isles" (Incidentally, Route 340, leading into the area, is still known as "The Road to the Isles").

2 Provincial Archives of Newfoundland and Labrador (PANL), MG 200, John Guy.

3 Joseph R. Smallwood and Cyril F. Poole (editors-in-chief), *The Encyclopedia of Newfoundland and Labrador (ENL)*, 5 volumes, CD-ROM Edition, version 1.8 (St. John's, Harry Cuff Publications, 1997).

4 *Decks Awash* (August, 1980), 4.

5 Edmund M. Blunt, *The American Coast Pilot: Containing Directions for the Principal Harbors, Capes and Headlands, on the Coasts of North and South America* (New York, Edmund and George W. Blunt, 1847), 30.

6 The toponym "Durrell" may originate from the surname of a prominent Dorset family that provided Poole with several mayors. Likewise, there was a merchant partnership operating at Fogo in the 1700s under the name Pain and Durrell.

7 Blunt, *American Coast Pilot*, 29-30.

8 Modern Fogo Island includes Fogo Island Centre. The area has a number of residences, but is more of a service centre than a town, *per se*, being home to the island's health centre, schools, stadium, and police detachment.

9 Letter, "Bishop Edward Feild to Rev. E. Coleridge" (2 September, 1846).

10 *A Year Book and Almanac of Newfoundland* (St. John's, J. W. Wither's, King's Printer, 1910), 87.

11 PANL, MG 458, Cox & Company.

12 When Carter first won his seat in Twillingate and Fogo District (1873), local electors also returned two of his political opponents, Charles Duder and Smith McKay (Duder later crossed the floor, joining Carter's Administration).

In that era a number of Newfoundland districts were represented by more than one member – Twillingate and Fogo had three. The district was split in 1885, Twillingate retaining three members, with one MHA for Fogo Dsitrict. By 1932 Twillingate was further divided into four districts, each with a single MHA.

13 *Twillingate Sun* (26 February, 1949), 4.

14 Progressive Conservative Derrick Dalley of Twillingate was twice elected to represent The Isles of Notre Dame. He served in several portfolios as a Provincial Cabinet Minister before his 2015 defeat by Liberal Derek Bennett in the new Lewisporte-Twillingate District.

Notes to Chapter Two

1 A. A. Parsons, "First Settlers at Twillingate and Their Conflicts with the Red Indians," *Newfoundland Quarterly* (December, 1905), 16.

2 Cyril R. Chaulk, "Growth and Development of Fogo, Twillingate & Dependencies. A Paper Presented to the History Department of Memorial University of Newfoundland as Partial Requirements for History 429," Prof. Dr. K. Matthews (10 April, 1969), 8. It has been said that former Premier Smallwood once had the cannister and Peyton diary in his collection of historical material, though this has not been verified.

3 The original Davis letter is held at the National Maritime Museum, Greenwich, UK, GRV/106. See also: George Davis, "Davis Letter. 1764 to Capt. J. Cook, Re First Settler in Twillingate," *Newfoundland Ancestor* (Summer, 1989), 89.

My discussions with genealogical researcher Milt Anstey lend credence to Tizzard's claim to have been Twillingate's first settler. Anstey's research indicates that Tizzard, born at Dorsetshire in 1705, returned to England in his later years, preparing his will in 1779. By the 1760s Twillingate was home to a number of families including the Peytons, Moors, Smiths, Rideouts, Rowsells and others.

4 Quintal = "hundredweight," 112 lbs or fifty kilograms.

5 This figure is from Prowse's classic history of Newfoundland; other sources give the number overwintering as 143.

6 PANL, MG 922, J & W Fryer.

7 PANL, GN 2/2, Colonial Secretary, Incoming Correspondence 1832.

8 *Ibid.*

9 *Ibid.*

10 Though a temporary measure, the Act was a precursor to permanent legislation in 1843.

11 PANL, GN 2/2.

12 *Ibid.*

13 Another source gives the date as 1831.

14 *Twillingate Sun* (30 January, 1915), 1.

15 It seems that the enmity some locals felt toward the Methodists had not gone away by 1843. According to D. W. Johnson, during construction of the new chapel several men concocted a scheme to blow up the structure before it could be completed. A keg of gunpowder was hidden under the building, and it was only the fear of injuring themselves that prevented the conspirators from carrying out the plan. Ironically, the plot was later revealed by one of the guilty party, who by this time had converted to Methodism.

16 It seems that Twillingate's pre-1831 Wesleyan congregation was not counted when calculating the local church's date of origin.

17 See: PANL, GN 2/2 and MG 40, The Rice Collection.

18 Twillingate Museum & Craft Shop, Peyton Collection.

19 *Ibid.*

20 Twillingate Public Library, "Letter books of the Twillingate Telephone & Electric Company, 1915-20, 1924-8."

21 In common with many topics from the Isles' early history, John Slade's life story has more than one version. W. Gordon Handcock, writing in the *Dictionary of Canadian Biography*, gives one John Slade, a mason of Poole, and his Wife Ann, as Slade's parents, noting that the younger Slade was born in 1719. According to Handcock's account, the mason John Slade died in 1727, leaving John and another two Sons, Robert and Thomas, a modest bequest of £10.

Extensive archival research conducted by Milt Anstey strongly suggests that such was not the case, although the Father of John Slade the merchant *was* another man named John Slade. Anstey's research indicates that the mason John Slade of Poole prepared his will on 30 November 1715, naming his Wife, along with Sons John, Robert, William and Thomas, and Daughter Anne, as the beneficiaries. Archival records located by Anstey note that this same John Slade died shortly after preparing his will. He was buried at St. James' in Poole on 4 December 1715, two and a half years *before* future merchant John Slade was baptised, and some four years before the birth date Handcock gives for him. Thus John Slade the mason and John Slade the merchant cannot be Father and Son.

22 PANL, MG 464, Earle Sons & Co.

23 All men in the Slade family were given one of five Christian names: John, James, Robert, Thomas and David. This can be quite confusing for researchers. The firm's founder is often called John Slade the Elder to distinguish him from the many other John Slades in the family.

24 Henry Youmans Mott (ed.), *Newfoundland Men. A Collection of Biographical Sketches With Portraits, of Sons and Residents of the Island Who Have Become Known in Commercial, Professional and Political Life* (Concord, NH, USA, T. W. & J. F. Cragg, 1894), 171.

25 Margaret Duder was widely respected in her own right, celebrated for her charitable and philanthropic works.

26 Government of Newfoundland and Labrador, Registry of Deeds, Volume 21, Northern District, 373.

27 Registry of Deeds, Volume 57, 437-47. Document dated 2 March 1915.

28 *Ibid.*

29 Another Ashbourne competitor on South Island was the Gillett family, who operated premises at Durrell.

30 *Twillingate Sun* (3 February, 1917), 2.

31 When Thomas assumed control of the business he was assisted by his Uncle, Arthur George Ashbourne, who held a minority share in the operation. Arthur's involvement with the enterprise continued until he passed away in 1932. Like their Cousin Thomas, Arthur's Sons played an active role in the family business.

32 *Twillingate Sun* (15 December, 1917), 5.

33 Author Frank Gogos notes that Gibralter was only a paper destination for wartime vessels like the *Sydney Smith* and *Ada D. Bishop.* Had they arrived safely at the British base, the schooners would have been given their true ports of call, perhaps Portugal, Spain, Italy or Greece.

34 See: PANL, MG 464.

35 *Twillingate Sun* (11 April, 1891), 2.

36 PANL, GN 1/3/A, Governor's Office, Local and Miscellaneous Correspondence.

37 *Year Book and Almanac* (1908), 190.

38 PANL, MG 464.

39 *Ibid.*

40 PANL, GN 1/3/A.

41 *Twillingate Sun* (12 December, 1902), 4.

42 *Ibid* (24 March, 1917), 3. There is at least one different account of how much copper was shipped out of Sleepy Cove. According to this source, three cargoes of ore were sent to the United States from 1908-12, two by steamer and one by schooner. The next shipment was not made until 1916, when the steamer *Clothilde Cuneo* loaded a partial cargo of copper, which brought $1,800.00 at the smelters. See: *Twillingate Sun* (7 October, 1944), 4.

43 According to his Daughter, Christine Caskey, Thomas Ashbourne sold the land on which his family's "Upper Room" had stood, for one dollar, to ensure that the fish plant would be built at Twillingate.

44 Bayview was incorporated in 1981, with Gerald Hynes as its first Mayor. Its last Mayor, upon amalgamation with Twillingate in 1992, was Oliver Hynes. Durrell's first municipal council was installed in August 1971, with Ralph Smith as its first Mayor, a position last held by Maxwell Bussey.

45 In December 2010 the communities of Fogo Island signed a historic amalgamation agreement, and are now a single municipality. Since they have so recently been separate entities, the towns of Fogo Island are detailed individually in Chapter Four.

Notes to Chapter Three

1 ENL presents a different time line for the name change, giving the date as 1972.

2 *Twillingate Sun* (15 August, 1908), 4.

3 *Ibid* (17 December, 1949), 4.

4 At the time of writing this infrastructure is somewhat neglected, though the boardwalk and swimming platform have been partly repaired.

5 See: PANL, GN 13/1/B, Justice Department, General Administration.

6 See: George Hamilton May, "Development of Moreton's Harbour Notre Dame Bay, Newfoundland" (Unpublished, 1991).

7 PANL, MG 411, Helen Mackay.

8 By 1921 Alcock was already dead, having perished in a plane crash the same year he and Brown made the first successful trans-Atlantic flight.

9 Today Strong's Island is connected to the rest of Summerford by a bridge. A huge aluminum culvert allows small boat traffic to pass.

10 *Twillingate Sun* (11 June, 1887), 3. Unfortunately, the factories made no significant, long-term contribution to the economies of Tizzard's Harbour or Twillingate.

11 Refer to, PANL, MG 458.

Notes to Chapter Four

1 See: Donald Holly, "An Archaeological Survey of Fogo Island, Newfoundland 1997," www.nfmuseum.com/977Ho.htm

2 *Twillingate Sun* (16 September, 1880), 2.

3 Henry Earle was Rolls' Son-in-law. Hewitt states that Earle assumed control of the Rolls business in 1881, not 1883.

4 Apart from the Anglicans and Methodists/United, a small Pentecostal congregation, now worshipping at Seldom, also called Barr'd Islands home.

5 Some sources contend that settlers with the surnames Brown and Etheridge were present in the Joe Batt's Arm area as early as 1685.

6 Letter, "Feild to Coleridge" (2 September, 1846).

7 The date of 1680 has been given for the first settling of Fogo by Europeans, though it is unlikely that settlers were overwintering there prior to the eighteenth century.

8 PANL, MG 464. Dated 30 April 1870.

9 Mott, *Newfoundland Men*, 73.

10 Refer to: PANL, MG 458.

11 Quoted in, Rev. Charles Pedley, *The History of Newfoundland From the Earliest Times to the year 1860* (London, Longman, Green, Longman, Roberts and Green, 1863), 237.

12 *Ibid*, 238.

13 PANL, MG 458.

14 *Ibid*.

15 *Ibid*.

16 *Ibid*.

17 PANL, GN 5/3/B/19, Magistrate's Court Northern Circuit.

18 *Ibid*.

19 In their work on the Newfoundland Royal Naval Reserve (NRNR) W. David Parsons and Ean Parsons mention a Reservist "...of Stag Harbour, Fogo...," suggesting that some people considered the community home prior to 1918.

20 Sandy Cove boasts Fogo Island's only large, sandy beach, and the area once had a number of dwellings.

21 Drawn from the *Colonial Letterbook*s of 1759 and 1762.

22 Some of the background to the Manning Award presentation can be found in the book, *Old Harbours: A Strange Twilight*, by TRACS member Roy Dwyer, who was involved with the Dwyer Premises project. See: Roy Dwyer, *Old Harbours: A Strange Twilight – Tilting Harbour et al. Essays and Short Stories* (St. John's, Transcontinental Printing, 2007).

23 To supplement the films, MUN's Extension Service held workshops teaching organizational and communication skills.

Notes to Chapter Five

1 At the time of writing (2016), the Change Islands' plant is operating during the Summer months processing sea cumber. Still, the facility's future is uncertain. According to reporter James McLeod of the *Telegram*, workers now struggle to get enough weeks of work at the plant to qualify for Employment Insurance over the Winters. On a Change Islands stop during the 2011 Provincial election campaign then-Premier Kathy Dunderdale said she could not guarantee the future of the facility.

Notes to Chapter Six

1 In a personal communication with the author, Ken Reynolds of the Provincial Archaeology Office noted that the later sites are marked by a lack of objects of *any* kind, a sad reminder of the struggle the Beothuk faced to survive once their access to coastal resources was curtailed.

2 *Twillingate Sun* (5 November, 1887), 2.

3 PANL, MG 323, Thomas Peyton.

4 The Slade merchant family had at least four nets taken by the Natives, while one of their young clerks was killed when berry picking.

5 McCarthy's version also has Turpin's companions saved by the quick-thinking old lady.

6 PANL, MG 323. Yet another version of the Turpin story was recounted by Clive Marin in his account of life on Fogo Island in the early 1970s. In Marin's version Turpin's companion was named William Murray, and that when the Natives beheaded Turpin they mounted the head on a pole at Wigwam Point, "up from Exploits." See: Clive Marin, *Fogo Island* (Philadelphia, Dorrance & Company, 1974), 14-15.

7 PANL, MG 323.

8 *Ibid.*

9 Another take on Peyton's excursion to the Beothuk avers that he was actually seeking revenge, but this has never been proven.

10 See: PANL, MG 257, Rev. John Leigh.

11 *The Star and Conception Bay Journal*, 17 September 1834, 2.

Notes to Chapter Seven

1 Henry Simms had gleaned this information from his Father, to whom Henry's Aunt Nancy often wrote.

Notes to Chapter Eight

1 A verse about newspaper journalism which appeared in various issues of the Sun during 1917.

2 *Twillingate Sun* (2 July, 1887), 2.

3 Yvonne Stuckless and Norma Jennings, "The Twillingate Sun," *Twillingate Sun*, new series (26 July, 1991), 35 and 39.

4 PANL, GN 1/3/A.

5 *Twillingate Sun* (27 October, 1917), 1.

6 John C. Loveridge, "Newspapers of Newfoundland – The Twillingate Sun," *Atlantic Guardian* (June, 1948), 27.

7 *Twillingate Sun* (29 June, 1889), 2.

Notes to Chapter Nine

1 *Twillingate Sun* (11 June, 1892), 2 and (25 June, 1892), 2.

2 A conversation with the late Reverend Raymond Brett suggests that recordings of Georgina Stirling, other than that held by the Twillingate Museum, *do* exist, but have never been released to the public.

3 A good account of the project to provide the "Nightingale of the North" with a suitable memorial is found in Reverend Brett's autobiography. See: Reverend Raymond Brett, *From the Punt to the Pulpit. A Walk Through My Life* (St. John's, HUB Printers, n.d.), 128.

4 Nigel Rusted, *Medicine in Newfoundland c.1497 to the Early 20th Century. The Physicians and Surgeons. Biographical Gleanings* (St. John's, Memorial University of Newfoundland Faculty of Medicine, 1994), 100. In Rusted's version of events Downey was not re-hung on the gallows, but simply cut down by supporters and taken to Stirling's home.

5 Mrs. Peyton is related to Miss Georgie through her Husband, the late Ernest Peyton, whom she met while he was serving with the RAF in World War II. Like her ancestor by marriage, Mrs. Peyton sang soprano, with the Gander Arts Centre Chorale.

Notes to Chapter Ten

1 Prior to his becoming a nationally-known labour leader and politician, this was the only time William Coaker travelled outside Newfoundland. During his years at Coakerville he married Jessie Crosbie Cook at Fogo. The union produced a Daughter, Camilla, though it appears that theirs was not a happy partnership.

2 According to Maritime History Archive (MUN) records, FPU locals on the Isles were founded as follows: 1908: Herring Neck, Pike's Arm, Change Islands; 1909: Moreton's Harbour, Tizzard's Harbour, Twillingate, Fogo, Seldom, Tilting, Joe Batt's Arm, Indian Islands.

3 Bonavista District. In 1914 Coaker gave up his seat in favour of Alfred Morine. He won Twillingate District by acclamation in a November by-election.

Notes to Chapter Eleven

1 PANL, GN 2/15/A, Colonial Secretary's Office – Non-Series Records – Misc.

2 D. W. Prowse, *A History of Newfoundland. From the English, Colonial and Foreign Records* (London, Macmillan & Co, 1895), 639.

3 *Twillingate Sun* (11 June, 1887), 2.

4 Given his interest in Newfoundland history, and his connection to telegraphy, it is probable that this man was Thomas D. Scanlon, who supposedly found the story of Twillingate's first settlers.

5 *Twillingate Sun* (5 November, 1887), 2.

6 PANL, GN 2/15/A.

7 PANL, GN 2/5, Colonial Secretary's Office – Special Files.

8 *Ibid.*

9 *Ibid.*

10 *Ibid.*

11 *Ibid.*

12 *Ibid.*

13 *Ibid.*

14 *Ibid.*

15 *Ibid.* On 9 February 1917 J. M. Vitch of Newfoundland Postal Telegraphs reported that, "[t]he net receipts for traffic through Fogo wireless station for 1916 were $1208.70, as follows: January $23.64; February $21.86; March $116.51; April $31.54; May $24.30; June $64.20; July $154.86; August $232.63; September $282.67; October $179.53; November $39.98; December $36.98. " Evidently, this was not enough to offset expenses. PANL, GN 2/5.

16 An old school book on display at Fogo's Wireless Interpretation Centre contains a number of scribbled notes relating to the *Viking* disaster, obviously jotted by one of the wireless operators as he received information from the rescue vessels.

Notes to Chapter Twelve

1 Quote adapted from Francis T. Lind, *The Letters of Mayo Lind. Newfoundland's Unofficial War Correspondent 1914-1916* (St. John's, Creative Book Publishing, 2001), 137. Lind actually says to "...tell all friends that the 1st Newfoundland are O.K., and never feel downhearted. We will make you all proud of us some day." They certainly did.

2 *Twillingate Sun* (1 December, 1917), 2.

3 Kaiser Wilhelm II (1859-1941). Third Emperor of Germany, from 1888-1918. With the defeat of his nation's armies in 1918 Wilhelm abdicated and fled to Holland.

4 *Twillingate Sun* (19 December, 1914), 2.

5 PANL, GN 19, Royal Newfoundland Regiment. Interestingly, there were *Two* Private Edward Whites from Twillingate serving at Gallipoli. The other was Regt. # 1084. "Ned" White was the Son of Captain E. White of Durrell, and enlisted in February 1915.

This Edward White was also a casualty at Gallipoli, having his shin bone shattered by a Turkish bullet on 23 October 1915. His leg was later amputated below the knee, a procedure that required several more minor operations. He was repatriated in 1917, returning home to a hero's welcome in August of that year.

6 *Ibid.*

7 *Twillingate Sun* (21 October, 1916), 2.

8 PANL, GN 19.

9 *Ibid.*

10 *Ibid.*

11 *Ibid.*

12 *Ibid.*

13 *Ibid.*

14 *Twillingate Sun* (11 May, 1918), 3.

15 PANL, GN 19.

16 Richard Cramm, *The First Five Hundred. Being a Historical Sketch of the Military Operations of the Royal Newfoundland Regiment in Gallipoli and On the Western Front During the Great War 1914-1918* (Albany, NY, C. F. Williams & Son, n.d.), 38, 40.

17 PANL, GN 19.

18 The remains of *Viknor* were finally located in 2006, on the perimeter of an area where the German vessel SMS *Berlin* had lain a minefield some ninety years earlier.

19 The Parsons give Keats' hometown as Twillingate.

20 *Twillingate Sun* (3 February, 1917), 2.

21 See: PANL, GN 1/3, Newfoundland Naval Reserve.

22 The loss of HMS *Avenger* wasn't the only wartime tragedy involving a British carrier which had an Isles connection. Built in the United States, HMS *Dasher* was commissioned into the Royal Navy on 2 July 1942. On 27 March

1943, while in the Firth of Clyde, the carrier was rocked by a tremendous explosion – the true cause never ascertained – which left some 379 of her crew dead. The loss was covered up until 1945, and there is still a great deal of mystery surrounding the event. Among those who perished that fateful night was Able Seaman William Stephen Lloyd Linfield (# 247986) of Twillingate, who had sailed with the thirteenth contingent.

23 Erica Greenham, *Fighting for Freedom. Our Twillingate, New World Island and Change Islands Men Overseas* (Twillingate, Twillingate Public Library, 1998), 45.

24 See: PANL, GN 13/1/B, Justice Department, General Administration.

25 See: PANL, GN 19/2, Newfoundland Forestry Companies, Service Records, 1914-1918.

26 The author's maternal Grandfather, Stewart Burton (# 729), embarked with one of the early drafts for overseas on the liner *Duchess of Richmond.*

27 Howard Butt, "Headline: Veteran Recalls Overseas Experiences," *Lewisporte Pilot* (11 November, 2009), 1B.

28 The neglect of merchant mariners was not only on the part of government. In his *Lewisporte Pilot* column Benson Hewitt details the efforts of Fogo' s St. Andrews congregation to construct a memorial to their fallen Sons following the Great War. Hewitt reminds us that in those days the merchant marine was not accorded the same status as the armed services. Though he lost his life serving with the merchant navy, Hewitt notes that Charles Hart might never have been honoured were it not for the intervention of school principal Wilfred Verge. At a meeting held in Fogo on 20 April 1920, Verge noted that Hart had volunteered for the regular forces, but had been rejected. This fact was enough to sway those assembled to include Hart's name on the memorial.

29 Twillingate Library, Letter Books of the Twillingate Telephone & Electric Company.

30 *Twillingate Sun* (8 December, 1914), 3.

31 Like Lady Davidson, Lady Walwyn was created a Dame Commander of the Order of the British Empire (1947).

32 *Twillingate Sun* (26 June, 1915), 2.

33 *Ibid* (9 March, 1918), 2.

34 *Ibid* (16 January, 1943), 4.

35 *Ibid* (26 June, 1915), 2.

Notes to Chapter Thirteen

1 See: *Twillingate Sun* (4 May, 1912), 2. There are reportedly a number of graves of infectious disease victims on Burnt Island, including at least one child.

2 Twillingate Library, Letter Books of the Twillingate Telephone & Electric Company.

3 See: Twillingate Library, Letter Books of the Twillingate Telephone & Electric Company.

4 *Twillingate Sun* (26 February, 1927), 4.

5 *Ibid* (18 October, 1919), 1.

6 PANL, GN 38, Commission of Government Public Health and Welfare, General Administration.

7 Loveridge later gives the name of Hodge's travelling companion as Arthur *Ashbourne*.

8 *Twillingate Sun* (6 March, 1943), 4.

9 PANL, GN 38.

10 See: Government of Newfoundland and Labrador, Registry of Deeds, Volume 11, Northern District, 389 and Volume 20, Northern District, 233.

11 *Twillingate Sun* (3 August, 1889), 2.

12 PANL, GN 13/1/B.

13 See: PANL, GN 13/1/B.

14 PANL, GN 13/1/B.

15 PANL, GN 38, Commission of Government, Public Health & Welfare, Medical Services.

16 *Ibid.*

17 Twillingate Library, Letter Books of the Twillingate Telephone & Electric Company.

18 *Twillingate Sun* (15 August, 1908), 4.

19 PANL, GN 13/1/B.

20 *Twillingate Sun* (18 October, 1919), 3.

21 In 2008 Nurse Practitioner White received the Canadian Nurses Association Centennial Award for her outstanding contributions to the profession, and was featured in the September issue of *Canadian Nurse*. In 2011 she was a recipient of the prestigious Award of Excellence in Nursing. Nurses are nominated by their peers for this distinction, presented annually during National Nursing Week to honour members of the profession for their contributions to First Nations and Inuit communities.

Among her many accomplishments, Mrs. White became one of the first rural Newfoundlanders to serve as President of the Association of Registered Nurses of Newfoundland and Labrador (ARNNL), and was President of her local chapter for more than fifteen years. For Mrs. White nursing is a family affair – all three of her Sons have entered the profession.

Notes to Chapter Fourteen

1 *The Family Fireside* (January, 1938), 1. As quoted on the *Genealogy. Rowsell-Anstey Field-Taylor-Pike ElliottMcDemid*, website, http://norma.fritzy.ca/Genealogy/ClippingQueenofSwansea.html

2 Heluiz Chandler Washburne and Anauta Ford Blackmore, *Land of the Good Shadows; The Life Story of Anauta, an Eskimo Woman* (New York, John Day Co., 1940). 261.

3 *Twillingate Sun* (6 July, 1918), 2. During the First World War Halifax was a bustling port city, with its waterfront full of civilian and military vessels. On Thursday, 6 December 1917 the Norwegian steamer *Imo*, heading out to sea, collided with the SS *Mont Blanc*, loaded with ammunition and explosive materials. The crew of *Mont Blanc* abandoned ship after their vessel caught fire. Unfortunately, no one in the busy port heard or heeded their shouted warnings; at 9:05 am the vessel erupted in a tremendous explosion. In an instant Halifax was left in ruins. Almost 2,000 people were killed outright by the tremendous blast, with another 9,000 wounded.

4 An account published in the *Twillingate Sun* stated that it was a British shipping line, Kayae & Sons (Whose vessel names all started with the letters "Mar"), which requested that the Whites change the name of their schooner. The Sun noted that the rules then governing the British registry did not allow two vessels to have the same name concurrently. This obliged Kayae & Sons to ask the White family for rights to the name Marina, which they wanted for one of their ships. See: *Twillingate Sun* (16 March, 1935), 4.

Harry White recalls that his Grandfather, Saul, skippered one of the few vessels to transport a load of copper ore from the Sleepy Cove mine.

5 As Chapter Five illustrates, nearby Change Islands had its own journalistic tradition in recent years, with the Summer publication of *The Main Tickle* newspaper by Stages and Stores Inc.

6 This time-line is at odds with records suggesting that the pair bought Pain's and Durrell's Room at Fogo sometime before 1760. Still, the tradition that they were established at what later became the Earle Premises, in the late eighteenth century, is quite strong.

7 Quoted in: Cyril J. Byrne, *Gentlemen-Bishops and Faction Fighters. The Letters of Bishops O Donel, Lambert, Scallan and Other Irish Missionaries* (St. John's, Jesperson Press, 1984), 60.

8 *Twillingate Sun* (10 March, 1888), 2.

9 I am grateful to both Mrs. King and Husband Hayward for sharing this touching story.

10 *Twillingate Sun* (14 April, 1917), 4. By some accounts, the Freake Brothers were not with the Jacobs and Francis Pomeroy, perishing in a separate tragedy at the ice. The Sun reported them as being together in its initial story on the disaster, but in later reports only mentioned the Jacobs Brothers and Pomeroy. Information provided by the late William Keats, who grew up in the Barr'd Islands-Joe Batt's Arm area, suggest the six were lost together. Reports of the event also differ as to exactly where the victims hailed from; some accounts say Barr'd Islands, others Joe Batt's Arm.

11 *Twillingate Sun* (4 August, 1917), 2. The writing on the gaff was discovered on a Saturday evening. Since he left for the French Shore the following Monday morning, Adey was unable to return the gaff (which he did not use) to the victims' relatives until his return.

Photo and Illustration Credits

ARCHIVAL

Memorial University of Newfoundland. Centre for Newfoundland Studies.
Geography Collection. Coll-137.

03.02.003	St. John's Warehouse with Salt Cod...
04.04.009	Newfoundland Constabulary...1937.
05.04.001	Alcock and Brown.
05.04.004	Alcock and Brown's Vicker's Vimy.
05.06.003	Cast and Crew of the *Viking*.
12.01.001	Methodist Church at Greenspond.
13.09.001	North Side Methodist Church, c.1900.
13.12.001	Fogo. View of the Community, c.1900.
13.12.002	Fogo. View of the Community, c.1900.
13.12.003	Fogo. "Lion's Den"...c.1900.
13.12.004	Fogo. "Eastern Tickle," c.1900.
13.12.005	Fogo. "Wigwam Point," Little Harbour, pre 1905.
13.12.006	Fogo. Bleak House with...the Earle family in front.
13.12.007	North Side of Fogo.
24.02.001	Crew Hauling Cod Trap.
24.02.022	Schooners and Dories.
25.01.016	Sealers with Pelts.

________. Digital Archives Initiative (DAI). Maritime History Archive.
Twillingate Sun.
Dr. Stafford Ad. 16 January, 1915 (1).
Cover Page. 31 January 1953 (1).

_______. Maritime History Archive.
PF-306.281 Sandy Cove Radar Station.

Twillingate Museum and Craft Shop.
Georgina Stirling Portrait.
Schooner Wreckage, 1907.

Twillingate Public Library. Twillingate History Collection.
Durrell Academy School, 1908.
Seal of the Twillingate Telephone...Company.
Sleepy Cove Copper Mine.
Sleepy Cove Miners.
Stirling Residence, c.1905.

Photo and Illustration Credits

BOOKS

Campbell, Gerald. *Edward and Pamela Fitzgerald. Being an Account of Their Lives Compiled From the Letters of Those Who Knew Them*. London: Edward Arnold, 1904.
Pamela Fitzgerald and her Daughter (150).
Lord Edward (Facing page 60).

Cartwright, Frances D. (ed.). *Life and Correspondence of Major Cartwright*. Vol. 1. London: Henry Colburn, 1826.
Cartwright Map of Lieutenant's (Red Indian) Lake (33).

Coaker, William Ford (ed.). *Twenty Years of the Fishermman's Protective Union of Newfoundland*. St. John's: Advocate Publishing, 1930.
LOA Lodge, Herring Neck (2).

Cramm, Richard. *The First Five Hundred. Being a Historical Sketch of the Military Operations of the Royal Newfoundland Regiment in Gallipoli and On the Western Front During the Great War 1914-1918*. New York: C. F. Williams & Son. n.d.
Blue Puttees (various pages).
Florizel, with Blue Puttees on Board (25).
Gallipoli Beach (35).
Gallipoli Map, with "Caribou Hill" (39).
William Ford Coaker (16).

Duncan-Clark, S. J., Plewman, W. R. And W. S. Wallace. *Pictorial History of the Great War. Canada in the Great War*. Toronto: J. L. Nichols Co., 1919.
Allied Troops Advancing (249).
British Tank Advancing (131).
First Aid Station (4).
Q-ship Gunners (47).

Holloway, Robert E. *Through Newfoundland With the Camera*. London: Sach & Co., 1910.
Exploits (64).
Herring Neck, with Carter's Premises, c.1900 (66).
Herring Neck and Goshen's Arm, c.1900 (67).
Moreton's Harbour, c.1900 (58).

Squid Jigging, c.1910 (30).
SS *Ethie* in Drydock (34).
SS *Virginia Lake* at Moreton's Harbour (61).
Twillingate South, c.1900 (69).

Howley, James P. *The Beothucks or Red Indians: The Aboriginal Inhabitants of Newfoundland*. Cambridge: Cambridge University Press, 1915.
Beothuk Implements, with Bow and Arrow Pieces (Plate XXXIII).
Beothuk Pendants (Plate XXVI).
Cartwright Sketch of Beothuk Camp (Plate II).
John Cartwright (Plate I).
John Peyton (Plate VII).
Shanawdithit (Plate IX).

McLay, Edgar Stanton. *A History of American Privateers*. New York: D. Appleton & Company, 1899.
American Privateer (335).

Mercer, W. Edgar. *A Century of Methodism in Twillingate and Notre Dame Bay*. Twillingate: Twillingate Sun Printers, 1932.
J. P. Thompson (Facing page 112).
Peter Samways (61).
Stewart Roberts (Facing page 112).

Mowbray, Jay Henry. *Sinking of the "Titanic." Most Appalling Ocean Horror*. Harrisburg, PA, USA: The Minter Company, 1912.
Sinking of the *Titanic* (XXX).

Moreton, Julian. *Life and Work in Newfoundland. Reminiscences of Thirteen Years Spent There*. London: Gilbert and Rivington, 1863.
Winter Tilt (82).

Mott, Henry Y. *Newfoundland Men. A Collection of Biographical Sketches With Portraits, of Sons and Residents of the Island Who Have Become Known in Commercial, Professional and Political Life*. Concord, NH, USA: T. W. & J. F. Cragg, 1894.
Edwin J. Duder (171).
Thomas C. Duder (73).

Prowse, D. W. *A History of Newfoundland. From the English, Colonial and Foreign Records*. London: MacMillan & Co., 1895.
Alexander M. Mackay (641).
Battle Harbour, Labrador, 1857 (608).
Cyrus W. Field (637).
English Fishers, c.1710, from Moll (22).

_____. (ed.). *A History of the Churches in Newfoundland by Various Writers*. London: Macmillan & Co., 1895.
Bishop Feild (6).

Rowley, Owsley Robert. *The Anglican Episcopate of Canada and Newfoundland*. London: A. R. Mowbray & Co., 1928.
Bishop Inglis (16).

Scammell, A. R. *Squid Jiggin' Ground*. St. John's: A. R. Scammell, 1944.
A. R. Scammell (1).

Sydenham, John. *The History of the Town and County of Poole*. London: Whittaker & Co., 1839.
Sketch of Poole Harbour (7).

Townsend, Charles Wendell, M.D. (ed.). *Captain Cartwright and His Labrador Journal*. Boston: Dana Estes & Co., 1911.
George Cartwright Portrait (Frontispiece).

Speck, Frank G. *Beothuk and Micmac*. New York: Museum of the American Indian Heye Foundation, 1922.
Santu (60).

Washburne, Heluiz Chandler and Anauta Ford Blackmore. *Land of the Good Shadows; The Life Story of Anauta, an Eskimo Woman*. New York: John Day Co., 1940.
Anauta (Frontispiece).

PERIODICALS

International Grenfell Association. *Among the Deep Sea Fishers.* January, 1924.
NDB Memorial Hospital Board of Directors (116).

_____. _____. April, 1926.
NDB Memorial Hospital (27).

Newfoundland Quarterly. March, 1903.
Marconi (7).

_____. October, 1904.
Rev. William Pilot (12).

_____. March, 1906.
Royal Newfoundland Naval Reservists (17).

_____. July, 1906.
Fogo North Side c.1906 (18).
George Roberts (16).
Henry J. Earle. (17).
Robert Bond (15).

_____. October, 1912.
Rev. Levi Curtis (12).

_____. April, 1913.
Governor and Lady Davidson (1).

_____. October, 1913.
SS *Kyle* (3).

_____. July, 1914.
Wes Kean and SS *Newfoundland* (2).

_____. July, 1917.
Francis "Mayo" Lind (17).

INTERNET

Maritime Quest. www.maritimequest.com

SS *Atrato*/HMS *Viknor*. Used with permission.

Wikimedia Commons. www.commons.wikimedia.org.

De Havilland Mosquito XVIII (This artistic work created by the United Kingdom Government is in the public domain. HMSO has declared that the expiry of Crown Copyrights applies worldwide).

Great Auk (This image is in the public domain because its copyright has expired).

Demasduit (This image is in the public domain because its copyright has expired. This applies to Australia, the European Union and those countries with a copyright term of life of the author plus seventy years).

HMS *Laurentic* (This image is in the public domain because its copyright has expired).

Homing Pigeons from *Harper's*, 1873 (This media file is in the public domain in the United States. This applies to US works where the copyright has expired, often because its first publication occurred prior to January 1, 1923).

King Louis-Philippe (This work is in the public domain in the United States, and those countries with a copyright term of life of the author plus 100 years or fewer).

La Scala Opera House, Milan (File licensed under the Creative Commons Attribution-Share Alike 2.5 Italy license).

Madame de Genlis (This image is in the public domain because its copyright has expired).

Newfoundland Map. Modified, 2011 by David Clarke (This file is licensed under the Creative Commons Attribution-Share Alike 3.0 Unported license.)

Operation Torch Map (This image is a work of a US Army soldier or employee, taken or made during the course of the person's official duties. As a work of the US Federal Government, the image is in the public domain).

Pirates Burying Treasure, by Howard Pyle (This media file is in the public domain in the United States. This applies to US works where the copyright has expired, often because its first publication occurred prior to 1 January 1923).

INDIVIDUALS AND ORGANIZATIONS

Ashbourne, Ross.
    Schooner *Ariceen*.

Burton, Barbara.
    Howlett Premises.
    Newfoundland Foresters, 1940.

Donahue, Madeline.
    Dr. Donahue and Daughter at Fogo.
    Dr. Donahue's Dispensary, Fogo.

Gianou, Betty (Cook), via Irene Pardy.
    Twillingate Sun Office, 1950s.

Harbin, Vaughn.
    Elmo Linfield Ashbourne..

Jenkins, Elizabeth.
    Long Point Light Tower.

Loveridge, Donald.
    Bay Boat *Clyde* at Twillingate.
    Bessie Marie in the Ice.
    Bonnie Nell and *Shirley C.*
    Court House, Twillingate, 1935.
    Crow Head, c.1950.
    Doctor and Mrs. Olds, with Ern Clarke.
    Doctor Hardy and Dog Team.
    Fish Plant, Twillingate, 1963.
    Gus Young, Saul White and Model T Ford.
    Hauling *Twillingate Sun* Office.
    Hodge's Cove, Twillingate, 1957.
    Hospital Fire.
    Linfield's Shop, Early 1950s.
    Manuel's Store, Bank of Nova Scotia and Arthur Manuel.
    MV *John Peyton* Being Repaired.
    SUF, Twillingate Parade.
    Thomas Ashbourne and Jack Roberts at Long Point.

Tickle Bridge, c.1950.
Winnifred Lee at Twillingate Coastal Wharf, and on Fire.

Pearce, Frederick and Elsie.
James Rolls.

Pittman, Pearl.
Thomas A. Ginn.

Rogers, Becky (Clarke), and Benjamin Clarke Jr.
Benjamin Clarke Sr., c.1919.
Fogo Marconi Station, View from South, c.1920.
Fogo Marconi Station, View from West, c.1920.

Scott, Doreen (Troake).
Captain Peter Troake.

Shand, Brenda.
Change Islands, Early 1900s.

Sibley, Donna (Old Photographs of Fogo Island Facebook Group).
Allan K. Collins.
Dr. Solan and Nurse Coles.
Fogo Courthouse, Early 1950s.
Fogo Hospital, 1950s.

Troke, James.
James Oakley's Boot Store, Twillingate.

Town of Fogo.
Lemuel "Lem" Anthony.

Royal Canadian Legion, Twillingate Branch. Memorial Wall. Notre Dame Bay
Memorial Health Centre.
Alfred Jenkins.
Chesley Pelley.
Eric G. Woodford.
George Hawkins.
Harry James Vineham.
Harvey Earle.

Herbert G. Osmond.
Herbert Stuckey.
Isaac Keefe.
Jim Anstey.
Neil W. Harnett.
Ralph White.
Raymond White.
Reginald John Holwell.
Stanley Stockley.
Stephen Lambert.
Sydney Donald Wheeler.
Wilfred Gillard.
William Stephen Lloyd Linfield.

All other images are author's photographs, from the author's family collection, or of unknown provenance. All images used herein are believed to be in the public domain and free of copyright, or else used with permission.

Bibliography

MANUSCRIPT SOURCES

Government of Newfoundland and Labrador. Registry of Deeds.
Volume 03. Northern District.
Volume 11. Northern District.
Volume 18. Northern District.
Volume 20. Northern District.
Volume 21. Northern District.
Volume 57.

Memorial University of Newfoundland. Centre for Newfoundland Studies.
Community files. Fogo Island.

_____. Maritime History Archive.
Royal Naval Reserve Drill Register.
Slade Papers. 1791-1852.

Provincial Archives of Newfoundland and Labrador. The Rooms, St. John's
GN 1/3. Newfoundland Naval Reserve.
GN 1/3/A. Governor's Office. Local and Miscellaneous Correspondence.
GN 2/2. Colonial Secretary. Incoming Correspondence 1832.
GN 2/5. Colonial Secretary's Office – Special Files.
GN 2/15/A. Colonial Secretary's Office – Non-Series Records – Misc.
GN 5/3/B/19. Magistrate's Court Northern Circuit.
GN 13/1/B. Justice Department. General Administration.
GN 19. Royal Newfoundland Regiment.
GN 19/2. Newfoundland Forestry Companies. Service Records, 1914-1918.
GN 38. Commission of Government Public Health and Welfare. General Administration.
MG 40. The Rice Collection.
MG 200. John Guy.
MG 257. Rev. John Leigh.
MG 323. Thomas Peyton.
MG 411. Helen Mackay.
MG 438. Nicholson, G. W. L. Colonel.
MG 439. Captain Leo Murphy.
MG 460. John Slade & Co.

MG 464. Earle Sons & Co.
MG 458. Cox & Company.
MG 619. Newfoundland Medical Board.
MG 621. Newfoundland Ranger Force Association.
MG 922. J & W Fryer.
MG 940. McNeily Collection.

Royal Newfoundland Constabulary Archives. Fort Townsend, St. John's.
Applications for Employment.
Ludlow, John. 1872.
Shave, William. 1883.

Twillingate Museum & Craft Shop.
Peyton Papers.

Twillingate Public Library.
Letter Books of the Twillingate Telephone & Electric Company. 1915-20, 1924-8.

NEWSPAPERS AND OTHER PERIODICALS

The Cadet.
The Daily News (St. John's).
Decks Awash.
Downhome (formerly the *Downhomer*).
The Fogo Island Flame.
Health Matters. Twillingate/New World Island Primary Health Care Project.
Lewisporte Pilot.
Lest We Forget.
The Main Tickle, Change Islands News.
The Montreal Star.
The Newfoundland Ancestor.
Newfoundland Quarterly.
The Telegram (St. John's).
Twillingate Sun.
Twillingate Sun. New series.
The Veteran Magazine.

Bibliography

BOOKS, ARTICLES, THESES

Anauta. *Wild Like the Foxes. The True Story of an Eskimo Girl*. New York: John Day Company, 1956.

Andrieux, J.P. *Marine Disasters and Shipwrecks of Newfoundland and Labrador*. Vol. 1. St. John's: Flanker Press, 2004.

Anon. "Twillingate by a Native." *Newfoundland Quarterly*. July, 1906, 15-16.

Balsom, Maralyn. "Twillingate." *EPA Horizons*. August/September, 1974.

Blunt, Edmund M. *The American Coast Pilot; Containing Directions for the Principal Harbors, Capes and Headlands, on the Coasts of North and South America*. New York: Edmund and George W. Blunt, 1847.

Brett, Reverend Raymond. *From the Punt to the Pulpit. A Walk Through My Life*. St. John's: HUB Printers, n.d.

_______ "Way Back When. A Journey from Twillingate to St. John's in Winter." *The Downhomer*. July, 1998, 62-3.

Broders, Sean. "The Legend of Michael Turpin." *The Downhomer*. April, 2000, 59.

Brown, Cassie, with Harold A. Horwood. *Death on the Ice*. Toronto: Doubleday Canada, 1972.

Brown, G. A. and R. D. Newman. "Brief History of Joe Batt's Arm." Academic paper, 1968.

Bulgin, Harvey. *Adventures and Inventions: Sparkling Vignettes of One Man's Experience in Outport Newfoundland*. Grand Falls: Robinson-Blackmore, 1991.

_____. *From Out of the Past. The Newfoundland Community of Summerford, New World Island...its Past, its Present, its People*. Grand-Falls-Windsor: Robinson-Blackmore, 1992.

Butler, Paul and Maura Hanrahan. *Rogues and Heroes of the Island of Newfoundland*. St. John's: Flanker Press, 2005.

Butt, Howard. "Celebrating a Century. Arm Lads Brigade." *Lewisporte Pilot*. 13 August, 2008, 4B.

_______. "Crow Head Gets to Blow its Own Horn – Fog Horn, That is!" *Lewisporte Pilot*. 9 March, 2005, 1B and 3B.

_____. "A Dream in the Making. 100-Year-Old Pipe Organ Being Restored." *Lewisporte Pilot*. 7 June, 2006, 1 and 4.

________. "Facelift Started on Former Twillingate General Retail Store." *Lewisporte Pilot*. 12 November, 2008, 1B and 3B.

____. "Former American Coast Guards Reunited at Twillingate." *Lewisporte Pilot*. 31 August, 1994, 8.

_____. "Happy 100th. Twillingate Masons Temple Anniversary." *Lewisporte Pilot*. 14 November, 2007, 1B and 4B.

______. "An Historic Site Worth the Price of Admission." *Twillingate Sun*. New series, 28 July, 1995, 5 and 16.

_____. "Headline: Veteran Recalls Overseas Experiences." *Lewisporte Pilot*. 11 November, 2009, 1B.

_____. "The Music Teacher." *The Downhomer*. November, 2001, 63-65.

_____. "The MV 'Bessie Marie' of Twillingate and Her Legacy." *Twillingate Sun*. New series. 20 July, 2000, 8.

____. "Newfoundland's Longest Serving Wharfinger." *Twillingate Sun*. New series. 22 July, 1993, 16.

______. "Old Sunday School Building Comes Down." *Lewisporte Pilot*. 13 August, 2008, 5B.

_____. "Remember When?" *Lewisporte Pilot*. 30 January, 2008, 2B.

_____. "St. Andrew's Anglican Closes. Bishop David Torraville Declares Building Deconsecrated." *Twillingate Sun*. New series. 16 July, 2008, 3.

____. "Twillingate's Counterfeiter Makes Pact with the Devil." *Twillingate Sun*. New series. 24 July, 2002, 11 and 15.

____. "Uncle Gus: 96 Years Young." *Twillingate Sun*. New series. 22 July, 1993, 14-15.

_______. "Veteran Recalls 166th Regiment Action." *Lewisporte Pilot*. 11 November, 1998, 1A and 3A.

____. "Victoria Hall: A Brief History." *Twillingate Sun*. New series. 29 July, 1994, 18-19.

Byrne, Cyril J. (ed.). *Gentlemen-Bishops and Faction Fighters: The Letters of Bishops O Donel, Lambert, Scallan and Other Irish Missionaries*. St. John's: Jesperson Press, 1984.

Campbell, Gerald. *Edward and Pamela Fitzgerald. Being an Account of Their Lives Compiled From the Letters of Those Who Knew Them*. London: Edward Arnold, 1904.

Cardoulis, John N. *A Friendly Invasion. The American Military in Newfoundland: 1940-1990*. St. John's: Breakwater Books, 1990.

Cartwright, F. D. (ed.). *The Life and Correspondence of Major Cartwright*. 2 vols., London, 1826.

Chaulk, Cyril R. *Snippets in Time*. St. John's: DRC Publishing, 2009.

____. "Growth and Development of Fogo, Twillingate & Dependencies." A paper presented to the History Department of Memorial University of Newfoundland as partial requirements for History 429. Prof. Dr. K. Matthews. 10 April, 1969.

Connor, J. T. H. "Twillingate." *Newfoundland Quarterly*. Summer, 2007, 12-15 and 30-35.

Conners, William. *By the Next Boat. A Photo History of Newfoundland Coastal Boats*. St. John's: Johnson Family Foundation, 2002.

Coish, Calvin. *Distant Shores. Pages from Newfoundland's Past.* Grand Falls-Windsor: Lifestyle Books, 1994.

_____ . "Princess Pamela." *Atlantic Advocate*. July, 1985, 22-24.

Coish, Della (ed.). *Tales of Fogo Island.* Gander: Economy Printing, 1999.

Cole, Doug. *Rhodes Scholars of Newfoundland.* Forward by John C. Crosbie. Portugal Cove, NL: ESP Press, 2000.

Cooper, Dave. "Statue Creator Speaks at Interpretation Centre." *Lewisporte Pilot*. 17 October, 2007, 3A and 7A.

Cramm, Richard. *The First Five Hundred. Being a Historical Sketch of the Military Operations of the Royal Newfoundland Regiment in Gallipoli and On the Western Front During the Great War 1914-1918.* Albany, NY: C. F. Williams & Son, n.d.

Cranford, Gary. *Not Too Long Ago...Seniors Tell Their Stories*. St. John's: Seniors' Resource Centre, 1999.

Crellin, J. K. (comp. and ed.). *No One is a Stranger. The Wit and Wisdom of Captain Peter Troake...Former Captain of the Christmas Seal and the Pied Piper of Newfoundland.* St. John's: Downhome Publishing, 1999.

Cuff, Robert and Derek Wilton (eds). *Jukes' Excursions. Being a revised Edition of Joseph Beete Jukes' "Excursions in and About Newfoundland During the Years 1839 and 1840."* St. John's: Harry Cuff Publications, 1993.

Curran, Tom. *They Also Served. The Newfoundland Overseas Forestry Unit 1939-1946*. St. John's: Jesperson Press, 1987.

Currey, Rev. John E. "Down to the Sea in Ships. Remembering Captain Peter Troake." *The Downhomer*. December, 1998, 27-28.

Dahl, Richard S. "The Indian Scrape." *The Newfoundland Quarterly*. October, 1914, 32.

Dalley, Carl. "A Small Island with a Big Past." *Twillingate Sun*. New series. 22 July, 1993, 8-9.

Davis, George. "Davis Letter. 1764, to Capt. J. Cook, Re First Settler in Twillingate." *Newfoundland Ancestor*. Summer, 1989, 89.

DeWitt, Robert L. *Newfoundland Social and Economic Studies No.8. Public Policy and Community Protest: The Fogo Case*. St. John's: ISER, Memorial University of Newfoundland, 1969.

Downer, Don. *Uprooted People: The Indian Islands*. St. John's: Harry Cuff Publications, 1991.

Dwyer, Allen. "An Economic Profile of Fogo Island Planters and the Slade Merchant Company, 1785-1805."MA Thesis. McGill University, 1989.

Dwyer, Mark. "Healing Fogo. Can the Island Come Together After Nasty Debate?" *The Newfoundland Herald*. 18 May, 2001, 26-27

Dwyer, Roy. *Old Harbours: A Strange Twilight – Tilting Harbour et al. Essays & Short Stories*. St. John's: Transcontinental Printing, 2007.

Earle, George H. *Old Foolishness...or Folklore*. St. John's: Harry Cuff Publications, 1987.

Ecke, Robert Skidmore. *Snowshoe and Lancet: Memoirs of a Frontier Newfoundland Doctor 1937-1948*. Portsmouth New Hampshire: P. E. Randall, 2000.

English, L. E. F. *Historic Newfoundland and Labrador*. St. John's: Newfoundland Department of Tourism, 1988.

Evans, Calvin D., with Philip Evans. *Master Shipbuilders of Newfoundland and Labrador. Volume One: Cape Spear to Boyd's Cove*. St. John's: Breakwater Books, 2013.

Farrington, Karen. *World War II Ground, Sea & Air Battles.* Wigston, Leicestershire, UK: 1995.

Fitzgerald, Jack. *The Hangman is Never Late. Three Centuries of Newfoundland Justice.* St. John's: Creative Book Publishers, 1999.

_____. *Newfoundland Disasters.* St. John's: Jesperson Publishers, 1984.

_____. *Untold Stories. Mysteries of Newfoundland and Labrador.* St. John's: Creative Book Publishers, 2004.

Gillespie, Bill. *A Class Act: An Illustrated History of the Labour Movement in Newfoundland and Labrador.* St. John's: Newfoundland and Labrador Federation of Labour, 1986.

Gogos, Frank. *The Royal Newfoundland Regiment in the Great War. A Guide to the Battlefields and Memorials of France, Belgium and Gallipoli.* St. John's: Flanker Press, 2015.

__________, and Morgan MacDonald. *Known Unto God. In Honour of Newfoundland's Missing During the Great War.* St. John's: Breakwater Books, 2009.

Greene, John P. *Between Damnation and Starvation. Priest and Merchants in Newfoundland Politics, 1745-1855.* Montreal: McGill-Queen's University Press, 1999.

Greenham, Erica. *Fighting for Freedom. Our Twillingate, New World Island and Change Islands Men Overseas.* Twillingate: Twillingate Public Library, 1998.

Guttridge, Roger. "The Old World Connection. Old Harry, the Great White Widower." *The Downhomer.* April, 1998, 31.

_______. "The Old World Connection. The Twillingate Connection." *The Downhomer.* September, 1997, 26-28.

Guy, Wilson. *Historic St. Peter's: Twillingate Newfoundland 1845-1995.* Publishing information not given, 1995.

Bibliography

Hamlyn, Norma E. *Borrowing From the Past, Lending to the Future. A History of the Twillingate Public Library 1944-2009*. Twillingate: Twillingate Public Library, 2009.

Hammond, John W. "The Rice Family." *The Newfoundland Ancestor*. Spring, 2009, 40-44.

Hanrahan, Maura. *The Alphabet Fleet. The Pride of the Newfoundland Coastal Service*. St. John's: Flanker Press, 2007.

Harrington, Michael. *Goin' to the Ice. Offbeat History of the Newfoundland Sealfishery*. St. John's: Harry Cuff Publications, 1986.

____. *Prime Ministers of Newfoundland*. St. John's: Harry Cuff Publications, 1991.

Harris, Elayne. "Fogo Island: Birthplace of a Communication Process." *University Affairs*. March, 1972, 6-7.

Head, C. Grant. *Eighteenth Century Newfoundland*. Toronto: McClelland and Stewart, 1976.

Hewitt, Benson. "Conflicts with our Native People on Fogo Island." *Lewisporte Pilot*. 29 August, 2007, 4B.

_____. "How Joe Batt's Arm May Have got its Name." *Lewisporte Pilot*. 19 September, 2007, 3B.

_______. "The Kerosene Lamp, Yesterday's Light." *Lewisporte Pilot*. 14 November, 2007, 2B.

_____. "The Last Great Auk Eaten in Fogo." *Lewisporte Pilot*. 18 June, 2008, 2B.

_____. "Remembrance Day 2009." *Lewisporte Pilot*. 4 November, 2009, 2B.

____. "Seldom-Come-By and All That." *Lewisporte Pilot*. 5 December,2007, 2B.

______. "The Story of a Mailbag, and a Remarkable Teacher." *Lewisporte Pilot.* 12 March, 2008, 3B.

_____. "War Memorial, Fogo." *Lewisporte Pilot.* 9 November, 2011, 4B.

________. "William Cull, Explorer, Barr'd Islands." *Lewisporte Pilot.* 17 October, 2007, 5B.

Hibbs, Richard. *Who's Who In and From Newfoundland.* St. John's: R. Hibbs, 1927.

Hicks, Ada et. al. *Twillingate Times: A Collection of Oldtime Recipes and Folklore Twillingate, Newfoundland.* St. John's: Jesperson Press, 1981.

Horwood, Andrew. *Newfoundland Ships and Men. Schooner, Square Rigger, Captains and Crews.* St. John's: Marine Researchers, 1971.

Horwood, Harold. *A History of the Newfoundland Ranger Force.* St. John's: Breakwater Books, 1986.

Howley, James P. *The Beothucks or Red Indians: The Aboriginal Inhabitants of Newfoundland.* Cambridge: Cambridge University Press, 1915.

Howley, Rt. Rev. Bishop. "The Late Archbishop Howley's Newfoundland Name-Lore." *Newfoundland Quarterly.* December, 1933, 29-30.

____. ""Newfoundland Name-Lore." *Newfoundland Quarterly.* March, 1904, 9.

_____. _____. _____. June, 1904, 3.

_____. _____. _____. March, 1908, 1.

Hunter, Mark. *To Employ and Uplift Them. The Newfoundland Naval Reserve, 1899-1926.* St. John's: ISER Books, 2009.

Hoxie, Frederick E. (ed.). *Encyclopedia of North American Indians.* New York: Houghton Mifflin Company, 1996.

Inglis, Gordon. *More Than Just a Union: The Story of the NFFAWU*. St. John's: Jesperson Press, 1985.

Jackson, *Doug. "On the Country." The Micmac of Newfoundland*. ed. Gerald Penny. St. John's: Harry Cuff Publications, 1993.

Janes, Christy. "New Name, New Ferry," *Lewisporte Pilot*. 18 March, 2015, A1.

Jarvis, Dale Gilbert. *Haunted Shores. True Ghost Stories of Newfoundland and Labrador*. St. John's: Flanker Press, 2004.

_____. "The Ghost of Long Point Lighthouse." *The Downhomer*. November, 2001, 67-69.

_______ (ed.). *Heritage Inventory of the Twillingate Islands: Preliminary Inventory Report of Selected Pre-1920 Structures in the Twillingate Islands*. First Edition. St. John's: Heritage Foundation of Newfoundland and Labrador, 1998.

Johnson, D. W. *Methodism in Eastern British America*. Sackville, NS: Tribune Printing Company, 1926.

Jones, Edward A. et al (eds.). *Land, Sea & Time*. Book Three. St. John's: Breakwater Books, 2002.

Jukes, J. B. *Excursions in and About Newfoundland During the Years 1839 and 1840*. Toronto: Canadiana House, 1969.

King, Arlène. "Beaumont Hamel, Our Place in the Sun." *Newfoundland Quarterly*. Summer, 2003, 9-15.

Lind, Francis T. *The Letters of Mayo Lind. Newfoundland's Unofficial War Correspondent 1914-1916*. St. John's: Creative Publishers, 2001.

Loveridge, John C. *1875-1975. 100th Anniversary St. Peter's Lodge No. 12, Society of United Fishermen*. Twillingate, 1975.

_____. *A Brief History of Twillingate. Marking 40th Year of Medical Service by John McKee Olds, S.M., M.D.* Grand-Falls: Robinson-Blackmore, 1970.

_______. "Newspapers of Newfoundland – The Twillingate Sun." *Atlantic Guardian.* June, 1948, 24-35.

Macdonald, Louise. "Royal Blood Difficult to Trace." *Twillingate Sun.* New series. 22 July, 1993, 3 and 19.

Macleod, Donald. "A Red Paint Burial Site in Northeastern Newfoundland." Paper presented to the Society for American Archaeology, thirty-second annual meeting, Ann Arbour, Michigan, USA. 5 May, 1967.

Macleod, Malcolm. "Migrant, Intern, Doctor — Spy? Dr. Eric Wermuth in Second World War Newfoundland." *Newfoundland Studies.* 1997, 79-89.

McBurney, Margaret, Byers, Mary and John DeVisser. *True Newfoundlanders: Early Homes and Families of Newfoundland and Labrador.* Toronto: Boston Mills Press, 1997.

McCarthy, Mike. *The Irish in Newfoundland 1600-1900. Their Trials, Tribulations & Triumphs.* St. John's: Creative Book Publishing, 1999.

McDonald, Ian D. H. *To Each His Own: William Coaker and the Fisherman's Protective Union in Newfoundland Politics, 1908-1925.* ed. J. K. Hiller. St. John's: ISER Books, 1987.

McGrath, Carmelita, Halfyard, Sharon and Marion Cheeks. *To Be My Father's Daughter.* St. John's: Educational Resource Development Co-operative, 2008.

McGrath, Darrin. *Last Dance. The Knights of Columbus Fire.* St. John's: Flanker Press, 2002.

_____. (ed). *From Red Ochre to Black Gold.* St. John's: Flanker Press, 2001.

_____, Smith, Robert, Parsons, Ches and Norman Crane, *The Newfoundland Rangers*. St. John's: DRC Publishers, 2005.

Magnusson, Magnus (ed.). *Chambers Biographical Dictionary*. Edinburgh: Chambers Harrap Publishers, 1993.

Major, Kevin. *As Near to Heaven by Sea. A History of Newfoundland and Labrador*. Toronto: Penguin Books, 2001.

Manuel, Edith M. *St. Peter's Anglican Church, Twillingate. One Hundred and Twenty-Five Year History, 1845-1970*. St. John's: The Morgan Printing Company, 1970.

Marin, Clive. *Fogo Island*. Philadelphia: Dorrance & Company, 1974.

Marshall, Ingeborg. *A History and Ethnography of the Beothuk*. Montreal & Kingston: McGill-Queen's University Press, 1996.

______. *Reports and Letters by George Christopher Pulling Relating to the Beothuk Indians of Newfoundland*. St. John's: Breakwater Books, 1989.

Marston, Daniel. *Essential Histories. The French-Indian War 1754-1760*. Oxford: Osprey Publishing, 2002.

Martin, Mike. "Discovery on Twillingate Island. Excavate Burial Site of Beothuck Ancestors." *The Daily News*. 29 July, 1968, 4-5.

Mellin, Robert. *Tilting. House Launching, Slide Hauling, Potato Trenching, and Other Tales From a Newfoundland Fishing Village*. New York: Princeton Architectural Press, 2003.

Mercer, Muriel (Roberts). "Memories of the Twillingate Sun." *Twillingate Sun*. New series. 24 July, 2002, 7 and 13.

Mercer, W. Edgar. *A Century of Methodism in Twillingate and Notre Dame Bay*. Twillingate: Twillingate Sun Printers, 1932.

Mitchell, Beverley. "His Glue still Sticky, Old Salt Fled to Sea at 66." *The Montreal Star*. 13 August, 1976, A1 and A.

Mooney, Conleth. "Why One Doctor Left Fogo Island." *Telegram*. 21 May, 2003, 21.

Morris, Don. "Early Twillingate Residents Petition Government: No Sunday Work." *Twillingate Sun*. New series. 25 July, 1991, 38.

____. "Twillingate's Unusual Sealing Season – 1862." *Twillingate Sun*. New series. 25 July, 1991, 13.

_____. "The Voice of Don." *Western Star*, c.1963.

Morris, Edward. "The Wreck of the "Queen." A Christmas Memory of Forty Years Ago." *Newfoundland Quarterly*. December, 1906, 7-9.

Mosdell, H. M. *When Was That? A Chronological Dictionary of Important Events in Newfoundland Down to and Including the year 1922*. St. John's: Trade Printers and Publishers Ltd., 1923.

Mott, Henry Youmans (ed). *Newfoundland Men. A Collection of Biographical Sketches With Portraits, of Sons and Residents of the Island Who Have Become Known in Commercial, Professional and Political Life*. Concord, NH, USA: T. W. & J. F. Cragg, 1894.

Murphy, Dee. "The Women's Institute...The Best Kept Secret." *The Downhomer*. February, 1998, 3-4.

Murrin, Florence. *Newfoundland: Now and Then. A Collection of Photographs of Recent Times and Days Gone by Arranged for Easy Comparison*. St. John's: Harry Cuff Publications, 1985.

Neimi, John (ed). *Mass Media and Adult Education*. Englewood Cliffs, NJ: Educational Technology Publications, 1971.

Newfoundland Historical Society. *A Short History of Newfoundland and Labrador*. Portugal Cove-St. Philip's, NL: Boulder Publications, 2008.

Newfoundland Historic Trust. *Ten Historic Towns: Heritage Architecture in Newfoundland*. St. John's: Valhalla Press, by arrangement with the Newfoundland Historic Trust, 1978.

Nicholson, G. W. L. *The Fighting Newfoundlander. A History of the Royal Newfoundland Regiment*. Montreal: McGill-Queens, 2006.

________. *More Fighting Newfoundlanders. A History of Newfoundland's Fighting Forces in the Second World War*. Aylesbury, UK: Hazell Watson & Viney, 1969.

Nolan, Stephen M. *A History of Health Care in Newfoundland & Labrador*. St. John's: Newfoundland and Labrador Health and Community Services Archive and Museum, 2004.

Notre Dame Bay Memorial Hospital, Twillingate, Newfoundland: 50 Years in the Life of Our Hospital 1924-1974. Grand Falls: Robinson-Blackmore, 1974.

O'Flaherty, Patrick. *Lost Country: The Rise and Fall of Newfoundland 1843-1933*. St. John's: Long Beach Press, 2005.

_____. *Old Newfoundland: A History to 1843*. St. John's: Long Beach Press, 1999.

O'Halloran, Lorie. "Lifelong Commitment to Nursing. Makkovik Nurse Awarded the Nurses Association Centennial Award." *Lewisporte pilot*. 3 September, 2008, 1B.

O'Neill, Paul. *Breakers. Stories from Newfoundland and Labrador*. St. John's: Breakwater Books, 1982.

Parsons, Robert. *Salt Water Tales. The Strange and Tragic, Illustrated*. Vol. II. St. John's: Creative Book Publishing, 2005.

Parsons, W. David. *Pilgrimage. A Guide to the Royal Newfoundland Regiment in World War One*. Revised edition. St. John's: DRC Publishing, 2009.

_________. and Ean Parsons. *The Best Small-Boat Seamen in the Navy. Newfoundland Royal Naval Reserve 1900-1922*. St. John's: DRC Publishing, 2009.

Pastore, Ralph T. *Shanawdithit's People. The Archaeology of the Beothuks*. St. John's: Atlantic Archaeology Ltd., 1992.

Parents' Committee, R.C.S.C.C. Briton. *Come Cook with Us. R.C.S.C.C. 83 Briton Twillingate, Newfoundland, 1952-2005*. Winnipeg: Rasmussen Company, 2005.

Parsons, A. A. "First Settlers at Twillingate and Their Conflicts with the Red Indians." *Newfoundland Quarterly*. December, 1905, 16.

Pedley, Rev. Charles. *The History of Newfoundland From the Earliest Times to the year 1860*. London: Longman, Green, Longman, Roberts and Green, 1863.

Peyton, Amy Louise. *Nightingale of the North: Georgina Stirling, Marie Toulinguet*. St. John's: Jesperson Publishing, 1983.

_____. *River Lords: Father and Son*. St. John's: Flanker Press, 2005.

Pickering, David. *Cassell Dictionary of Superstitions*. London: Cassell, 1995.

Pickett, Patrick. *A History. Town of Fogo, Newfoundland*. Upper Sackville, NS: Historical Views, 1997.

Pilot, William. "This Newfoundland Girl Might Have Become Queen of France." In Joseph R. Smallwood (ed.). *The Book of Newfoundland*. St. John's: Newfoundland Book Publishers, 1967, 137-142.

Poole, Cyril F. *George Halden Earle. A Concert Unto Himself*. St. Johns: Creative Book Publishing, 2001.

Prowse, D. W. *A History of Newfoundland. From the English, Colonial and Foreign Records*. London: Macmillan & Co., 1895.

_____. (ed.). *A History of the Churches in Newfoundland by Various Writers*. London: Macmillan & Co., 1895.

Pumphrey, Marilyn. "The Twillingate Sun Rises Again." *Twillingate Sun*. New series. 25 July, 1991, 7.

Redmond, Kevin. *Landscapes & Legacies. Parks, Natural Areas and Historic Sites of Newfoundland and Labrador*. St. John's: Creative Publishers, 2004.

Richard, Agnes. "Threads of Gold: A History of Women's Institutes in Newfoundland." *Newfoundland Quarterly*. Fall, 1989, 14-15.

Riggs, Bert. "Archival Notes. Tilt Cove: Newfoundland's First Mining Town." *Newfoundland Quarterly*. Fall, 2003, 8.

Roberts, Edward. *How Newfoundlanders Got the Baby Bonus*. St. John's: Flanker Press, 2013.

Roberts, Harry D. with Michael O. Nowlan. *Sailing Ships of Newfoundland. The Newfoundland "Fish Boxes."* St. John's: Breakwater Books, 1986.

Robinson, Cyril. *Men Against the Sea. High Drama in the Atlantic*. Hantsport, NS: Lancelot Press, 1971.

Rogers, J. D. *A Historical Geography of the British Colonies, Vol. V, Part 5, Newfoundland*. Oxford: The Clarendon Press, 1911.

Rompkey, Bill and Bert Riggs (eds.). *Your Daughter Fanny. The War Letters of Francis Cluett, VAD*. St. John's: Flanker Press, 2006.

Rowe, Frederick W. *Extinction: The Beothuks of Newfoundland*. Toronto: McGraw-Hill Ryerson, 1977.

Rusted, Nigel. *Medicine in Newfoundland c.1497 to the Early 20th Century. The Physicians and Surgeons. Biographical Gleanings*. St. John's: Memorial University of Newfoundland Faculty of Medicine, 1994.

Ryan, Shannon. *Fish Out of Water. The Newfoundland Saltfish Trade 1814-1914*. St. John's: Breakwater Books, 1986.

Sheldon, John. "Medical Services on New World Island." In *Notre Dame Bay Memorial Hospital. 50 years in the Life of Our Hospital 1924-1974*. Grand Falls: Robinson-Blackmore, 1974, 68.

Smallwood, Joseph R. *Newfoundland Miscellany*. Vol. 1. St. John's: Newfoundland Book Publishers, 1978.

_____. *Newfoundland 1941 Handbook Gazetteer and Almanac*. St. John's: Long Brothers, 1941.

_____ (ed.). *The Book of Newfoundland*. 6 Vols. St. John's: Newfoundland Book Publishers, 1975.

_____ ."Stories out of our History." Provenance Unknown.

Smith, Eileen (ed.). *From Me...to You. A Collection of Stories by Adult Learners*. Gander: Newfoundland and Labrador Rural Development Council, 1996.

Speck, Frank G. *Beothuk and Micmac*. New York: Museum of the American Indian, Heye Foundation, 1922.

Stacey, Jean Edwards. *Historic Homes of Newfoundland*. St. John's: DRC Publishing, 1998.

Story, G. M., Kirwin, W. J. and J. D. A. Widdowson. *Dictionary of Newfoundland English*. Toronto: University of Toronto Press, 1982.

Stuckless, Yvonne and Norma Jennings. "The Twillingate Sun." *Twillingate Sun*. New series. 26 July, 1991, 35 and 39.

Such, Peter. *Vanished Peoples. The Archaic, Dorset & Beothuk People of Newfoundland*. Toronto: NC Press, 1978.

Sydenham, John. *The History of the Town and County of Poole*. Poole: Sydenham, 1839.

Tizzard, Aubrey M. *On Sloping Ground: Reminiscences of Outport Life in Notre Dame Bay Newfoundland*. St. John's: Breakwater Books, 1984.

Townsend, Charles Wendell (ed.). *Captain Cartwright and His Labrador Journal*. Boston: Dana Estes & Co., 1911.

Tucker, Rev. H. W. *Memoir of the Life and Episcopate of Edward Feild, D. D. Bishop of Newfoundland 1844-1876*. London: W. Wells Gardner, 1877.

Way Back When...Remembering Twillingate and New World Island. Youth Services Canada, 2000.

Washburne, Heluiz Chandler and Anauta Ford Blackmore. *Land of the Good Shadows; The Life Story of Anauta, an Eskimo Woman* . New York: John Day Co., 1940.

Wells, Herb. *Comrades in Arms. A History of Newfoundlanders in Action, Second World War*. Vol. 1. St. John's: Robinson-Blackmore, 1986.

_____. *Under the White Ensign. A History of Newfoundland Naval Seamen Second World War*. Vol. 1. St. John's: Robinson-Blackmore, 1986.

_____. *Under the White Ensign. A History of Newfoundland Naval Seamen Second World War and Korean War*. Vol. 2. St. John's: Robinson-Blackmore, 1995.

Wells, Martha (ed.). *Newfoundland and Labrador Book of Everything*. Lunenburg, NS: MacIntyre Purcell Publishing, 2006.

Wetzel, Gerry Michael. "Decolonizing Ktaqmkuk History." MLA thesis. Dalhousie University, 1996.

Wheeler, Annie Violet. *Cherished Memories*. St. John's: Commercial Printing, 1994.

White, Harry. "Twillingate Schooner Turned Movie Star." *The Downhomer*. April, 2000, 85-86.

Williams, Andrew. *The Battle of the Atlantic. Hitler's Gray Wolves of the Sea and the Allies' Desperate Struggle to Defeat them*. USA: Basic Books, 2003.

Winsor, Naboth. *Building on a Firm Foundation: A History of Methodism in Newfoundland 1825-1855*. Vol.2. Printing information not given.

Witcher, Eric R. *Historic Barr'd Islands. From English Roots.* St. John's: Flanker Press, 2011.

A Year Book & Almanac of Newfoundland. St. John's: J. W. Withers, King's Printer, Various years.

Young, Lila Mercer and Ron Young. *Tonic for the Woman's Soul. Downhomer Household Almanac and Cookbook 3.* St. John's: Downhome Publishing, 2004.

Young, Ron. *Dictionary of Newfoundland and Labrador. A Unique Collection of Language and Lore.* St. John's: Downhome Publishing, 2006.

_____ . "A Legend Passes." *The Downhomer.* February, 1998, 14-15.

UNPUBLISHED

Anon. "[Twillingate] Diary 1907."

_______. "History of Moreton's Harbour." Handwritten work. Moreton's Harbour Museum collection.

Buckner, Mary B. "Descendants of John Ford, Kingsbridge, Devon." n.d.

Clarke, David J. "The Capital of the North: An Introduction to the Community of Twillingate." 1993.

_______. "Marconi, Merchants & Mariners. Tour Guide Manual – Fogo Wireless Relay Station & Interpretation Centre." Prepared for the Town of Fogo, 2006.

_____. "Stories from the Sun: Twillingate and Notre Dame Bay's Old Local Newspaper." Manuscript.

"Interview with Mrs. Lorna Stuckless, Women's Institute." Transcript. Date unknown.

Jennings, Joseph. "Register of Fishing Rooms Peyton Collection, PANL 1806-1829 Twillingate and Adjacent Rooms." n.d.

"Letter. "Bishop Edward Feild to Rev. E. Coleridge." 2 September 1846. Exact provenance unknown.

"List of [Durrell] Council Members Past & Present." Twillingate Town Council file.

Loveridge, Stephen. "Diaries." Transcribed by Donald Loveridge. Various years.

Manuel, Edith M. "Women's Institute Building." From notes. Transcribed by Irene E. Pardy.

May, George Hamilton. "Development of Moreton's Harbour Notre Dame Bay, Newfoundland." 1991.

Olds, John M. "A Brief Account of Medical Services in Notre Dame Bay." 1966.

Pardy, Irene E. "Around Twillingate in 30 Minutes +." Paper presented to Twillingate Island Tourist Association. 13 May, 2000.

Templeton, John. "The Rice Family of Twillingate: A Family History of Devonshire and Newfoundland." Manuscript, Winnipeg, 1993.

AUDIO-VISUAL

Barrett, Heather (producer/narrator). "My Own Private Twillingate." CBC Sunday Edition, 2009.

Bott, Gavin (producer). *Stalemate in Italy. Assault on the Gustav Line.* Cromwell Productions, 2000.

Cook, Linda A. "Twillingate: A Community History 1700 to 1978." CBC Radio Newfoundland School Broadcasts, 1978.

Smallwood, Joseph R. and Cyril F. Poole (editors-in-chief). *The Encyclopedia of Newfoundland and Labrador*. 5 volumes. CD-ROM Edition. Version 1.8. St. John's: Harry Cuff Publications, 1997.

Starowicz, Mark (executive producer). *Canada: A Peoples' History*. Vol. I. Canada: CBC/Radio Canada, 2000.

Wadden, Marie (producer/narrator). "Voyage to the Happy Island." From *East of Canada: The Story of Newfoundland*. St. John's: Fortis, 1997.

Wolochatiuk, Tim (director). *Stealing Mary: Last of the Red Indians*. Windup Filmworks & Firecrown Productions, 2005.

INTERNET

166th Home Page. www.infonet.st-johns.nf.ca/providers/166th_nfr/Home.html

"All Saints' Anglican Church, Ambrose Street, Hunters Hill. Henry Bevington & Sons 1887 (3/25 mechanical)." *The Organ Music Society of Sydney*. http://www.sydneyorgan.com/HH.html

Baker, Melvin and Janet Miller Pitt. "A History of Health Services in Newfoundland and Labrador to 1982." www.ucs.mun.ca/~melbaker/PublicHealthNL.pdf

"Battle of Cassino." *Answers.com*. http://www.answers.com/topic/battle-of-cassino

"Bevington & Sons – Organ Builders." *The Church of Saint Andrew*. http://www.st-andrewschurch.org.uk/organ/bevington.htm

British Banjo Makers Part 1. www.whitetreeaz.com/vintage/brit1.htm

Canada. Library and Archives Canada. "1770; Déclarations des capitaines à leur retour." Série C11F. Correspondance générale; Terre-Neuve et les pêcheries. Microform. Microfilm reel F-522. Finding aid no. MSS0447. On-line at *Library and Archives Canada website.* www.collectionscanada.gc.ca

__________. __________. *Dictionary of Canadian Biography Online.* www.biographi.ca/EN

_____. Statistics Canada. *2011Census.* http://www12.statcan.ca/census-recensement/index-eng.cfm

The Canadian Encyclopedia. www.thecanadianencyclopedia.com

Canadian Nurses Association. "Goldie White." http://www.cna-nurses.ca/centennial/documents/White_e.pdf

Community Profiles. www.k12.nf.ca/interisland/communities.htm

"Edith Manuel." *St. John's Women's Walk.* www.heritage.nf.ca/society/womenswalk

EyeWitness to History.com. www.eyewitnesstohistory.com

Genealogy. Rowsell-Anstey Field-Taylor-Pike Elliott McDemid, website, http://norma.fritzy.ca/Genealogy/ClippingQueenofSwansea.html

Google Books. http://books.google.com

Handcock, W. Gordon. *Coles Tips*, http://ca.geocities.com/colestips/Slade.htm

Hewitt, Benson. "The View From Fogo Island. Francis P Duke." *The Pilot.* http://www.lportepilot.ca/Columnists/Benson-Hewitt/2012-01-18/article-2867291/----The-View-From-Fogo-Island/1

________. ________. "James Rolls, Sr., of Barr'd Islands." *The Pilot.* www.lportepilot.ca/Columnists/Benson-Hewitt/2011-11-23/article-2812562/The-View-From-Fogo-Island/1

"HMS Bayano." *Great War Forum.* http://1914-1918.invisionzone.com/forums/index.php?showtopic=30516

"HMS Pembroke Royal Naval Barracks, Chatham." *Kent History Forum.* www.kenthistoryforum.co.uk/index.php?topic=358.0

Holly, Donald. "An Archaeological Survey of Fogo Island, Newfoundland. 1997." www.nfmuseum.com/977Ho.htm

Holmes, Michael I. "Banjo Wrenches." www.mugwumps.com/wrenches.html

The Internet Archive. www.archive.org

Juno Beach Centre. www.junobeach.org

The Kittiwake Coast. www.kittiwakecoast.ca

McLeod, James. "What About That Fish Plant, B'y?" *The Telegram.* http://www.thetelegram.com/News/Local/2011-09-24/article-2759146/%26lsquo%3BWhat-about-that-fish-plant,-b%26rsquo%3B%3F%26rsquo%3B/1

McMullen, Cliff. "Royal Navy Armed Merchant Cruisers." *World War I. The War at Sea.* www.gwpda.org/naval/rnamc.htm

Marcher. "A Look at Bugler and Musician Losses in Home Waters During the First World War." *The Blue Band Magazine Online.* www.royalmarinebands.co.uk/history/TimeForRemembrance.html

Memorial University of Newfoundland. Alumni and Friends. *Alumni Spotlight – Dr. Otto Tucker.* http://my.munalum.ca/news/spotlight/ottotucker.php

_____. Digital Archives Initiative (DAI). http://collections.mun.ca/index.php

_____. Maritime History Archive (MHA). *Map of Notre Dame Bay Locals.* www.mun.ca/mha/fpu/notre_dame_bay.php

Bibliography

Mersereau, Virginia. McGill University. *Canadian Biodiversity. The Great Auk.* http://biology.mcgill.ca/undergra/c465a/biodiver/2000/great-auk/great-auk.htm

Naval-History.net. www.naval-history.net/index.htm

Newfoundland and Labrador. Finance. Newfoundland & Labrador Statistics Agency. *2001 Census Data and Information.* www.stats.gov.nl.ca/Statistics/Census2001/

________. ________. ________. *2006 Census Data and Information.* www.stats.gov.nl.ca/Statistics/Census2006/

__________. __________. __________. *Road Distance Database.* www.stats.gov.nl.ca/DataTools/RoadDB/Distance/

_____. Tourism, Culture and Recreation. News Releases. *NLIS 2 August 8, 2001.* www.releases.gov.nl.ca/releases/2001/tcr/0808n02.htm

Newfoundland & Labrador GenWeb. Notre Dame Bay Region. www.rootsweb.com/~cannf/nd_index.htm

Newfoundland and Labrador Heritage. www.heritage.nf.ca

Newfoundland & Labrador's Registered Heritage Structures. www.heritage.nf.ca/society/rhs

Newfoundland Historic Trust. Southcott Awards. www.historictrust.com/southcott.shtml

Newfoundland's Grand Banks. http://ngb.chebucto.org

Parsons, David. "Loss of HMS *Viknor*, 13 January 1915." *World War I. The War at Sea.* www.gwpda.org/naval/viknor.htm

Parsons, W. David (MD). "The Spanish Lady and the Newfoundland Regiment." *WWI. The Medical Front.* www.vlib.us/medical/parsons.htm#f20

Pocock, Michael W. "Daily Event for January 13, 2006." *Maritime Quest.* www.maritimequest.com/daily_event_archive/2006/jan/13_hms_viknor.htm

Riggs, Bert. "Georgina Stirling." *Memorial University of Newfoundland's Archival Treasures.* www.heritage.nf.ca/cns_archives

Royal Navy Research Archive. www.royalnavyresearcharchive.org.uk

Ryan, Shannon. "The Newfoundland Cod Fishery in the Nineteenth Century: Is There Anything to be Learned?" From *History of the Newfoundland Cod Fishery.* www.cdli.ca/cod/history5.htm

Stacey, C. P. *Official History of the Canadian Army in the Second World War. Six Years of War. The Army in Canada, Britain and the Pacific.* Vol. 1. *HyperWar.* Originally published by Department of National Defence. www.ibiblio.org/hyperwar/UN/Canada/CA/SixYears/index.html#contents

"Telegraph and Telephone Companies." *Unofficial Clarenville Website.* http://clarenville.newfoundland.ws/Clar_Telegraph.asp

"Tilting Registered Heritage District." *Canada's Historic Places.* www.historicplaces.ca/rep-reg/affichage-display_e.aspx?/Id=2731

Town of Cottlesville. www.cottlesville.com

Town of Fogo. www.town-fogo.ca

Town of Joe Batt's Arm. www.joebattsarm.ca

Travel Central Newfoundland. www.centralnewfoundland.com

uboat.net. www.uboat.net

ubootwaffe.net. www.ubootwaffe.net

"World War I - Naval Casualties 1915-1918." *Northbourne Sources.* Http://freespace.virgin.net/andrew.parkinson4/wwi_bac.html

PERSONAL COMMUNICATION[2]

Mr. Kevin Anstey.
Mr. Milt Anstey.
Ms. Elaine Anton.
Ms. Audrey Ashbourne.
Mr. Donald Best.*
Ms. D. Gloria Black.
Rev. Raymond Brett.
Ms. Barbara Burton.
Mr. David Burton.
Mr. Stewart Burton.
Ms. Kathleen Boyd.
Ms. Christine Caskey.
Ms. Carolyn R. Parsons Chaffey.
Mr. John Clarke Jr.
Mr. Leonard Clarke
Mr. Howard Coish.*
Mr. Chet Caruthers.
Ms. Madeline Donahue.
Mr. Austin Earle.*
Mr. Brian Earle.*
Ms. Gaye Ann Flyer.
Mr. Randell Earle, QC.*
Mr. Frank Gogos.
Mr. Norman Gosse Jr.*
Mr. Herbert Hardy Jr.*
Ms. Mary Healy.*
Mr. Burton Janes.
Ms. Elizabeth Jenkins, RN, NP.
Mr. William Keats.
Ms. Elsie King.*
Mr. Hayward King.*
Ms. Sylvia Ewer Koenig.
Ms. Peggy Linfield.

2

Names marked with an asterisk (*) represent communication – interviews, correspondence, etc. – carried out as part of the Fogo Wireless Interpretation Centre project, March-August, 2006.

Mr. Donald Loveridge.
Mr. Arthur Ludlow.
Mr. Keith Ludlow.
Dr. Wayne Ludlow.
Mr. Clarence Lukeman.*
Ms. Elsie McCarthy.*
Mr. Christopher Osmond.
Ms. Irene Pardy.
Ms. Jean Pearcey.*
Ms. Carol Penton.*
Ms. Rebecca Rogers.
Hon. William Rompkey.
Ms. Mary Sharpe.
Mr. Andrew Shea.
Mr. Jim Smith.
Mr. Austin (Bill) Thistle.
Ms. Lucie Thistle.
Mr. James Troke.
Mr. Harry White.
Mr. Augustine Walsh.*